WISCONSIN

A Story of Progress

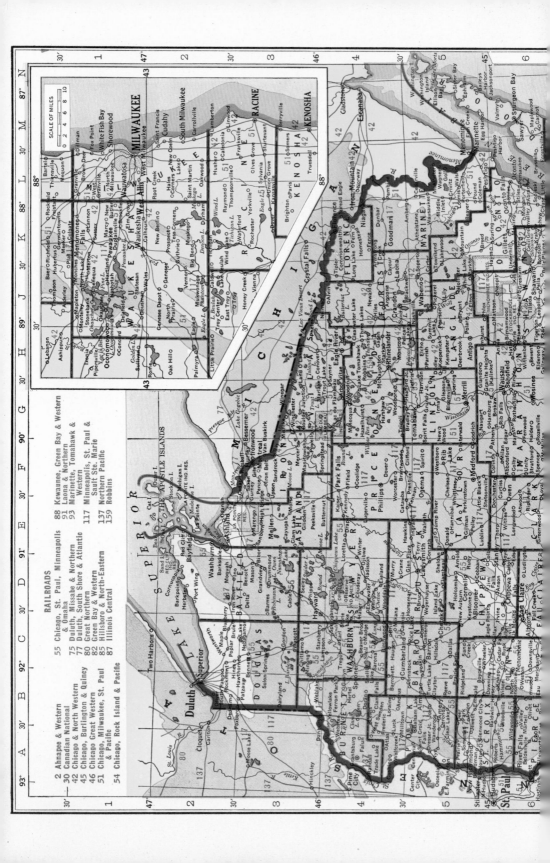

RAILROADS

2	Ahnapee & Western
30	Canadian National
42	Chicago & North Western
45	Chicago, Burlington & Quincy
46	Chicago Great Western
51	Chicago, Milwaukee, St. Paul & Pacific
54	Chicago, Rock Island & Pacific
55	Chicago, St. Paul, Minneapolis & Omaha
75	Duluth, Missabe & Northern
77	Duluth, South Shore & Atlantic
80	Great Northern
82	Green Bay & Western
85	Hillsboro & North-Eastern
87	Illinois Central
88	Kewaunee, Green Bay & Western
91	Laona & Northern
93	Marinette, Tomahawk & Western
117	Minneapolis, St. Paul & Sault Ste. Marie
137	Northern Pacific
159	Robbins

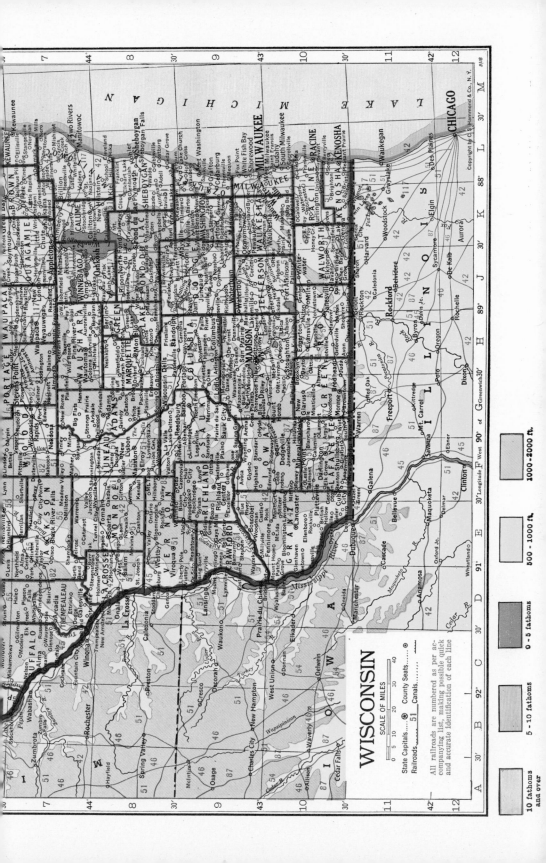

WISCONSIN

SCALE OF MILES

0 5 10   20   30   40

State Capitals...... ✪
County Seats...... ◉
Railroads...... 51 Canals...... 51

All railroads are numbered as per accompanying list, making possible quick and accurate identification of each line

Copyright by C. S. Hammond & Co., N.Y.

0 - 5 fathoms   5 - 10 fathoms   10 fathoms and over   500 - 1000 ft.   1000 - 2000 ft.

WISCONSIN

A Story of Progress

BY

WILLIAM FRANCIS RANEY, Ph.D.

Professor of History, Lawrence College

New York : 1940

PRENTICE-HALL, INC.

TO

C. P. R.

PREFACE

THIS book is designed to provide a readable and up-to-date summary of the growth of Wisconsin from the arrival of the first European visitor in 1634 down to the present. It is chiefly concerned, however, with the creation of the present way of living, of which the simplest distinguishing marks are the use of the English language and the enjoyment of Anglo-Saxon political institutions. Americans began moving into the lead-mining region in significant numbers about 1824, and the federal government first offered farm lands for sale in Wisconsin ten years later. From these beginnings, the building of the modern commonwealth has continued without interruption.

Through four generations since that time, the inhabitants of the state have lived and worked together, thinking, doubtless, that their chief task was to make their living. But all the while, and unconsciously for the most part, they were abandoning old ideas, inventing and initiating new equipment and new forms of social coöperation, and forging the society of the future. This book is not primarily a description or analysis of present social arrangements and relationships. It is offered as a narrative, however, in the belief that there can be no clear grasp of the present without a thorough understanding of the past; that to know "what we are," we must also know "how we got that way."

Furthermore, the evolution of old institutions and the creation of new ones have proceeded more rapidly since about 1900 than at any other period since Wisconsin became a state. The number and importance of recent developments explain and justify the allotment of more than a third of the book to the twentieth century.

In writing a history that spans more than three centuries, I am inevitably under great obligations to those who have preceded me in the field. No one can write of the French regime, for example, without leaning heavily upon the editorial work of Reuben Gold Thwaites and others, and upon modern work covering the period such as that of Louise Phelps Kellogg. In dealing with later periods, I am likewise indebted to forerunners whose work is indispensable, although material on the immediate past is widely dispersed and its discussion lacks finality. The Selected Bibliographies accompanying the various chapters are intended to encourage and facilitate further reading; but they will serve, in part at least, to indicate my numerous debts to other writers.

The president and trustees of Lawrence College, a number of years ago, granted me leave of absence for a semester with full salary. I was thereby enabled to do much of the preliminary work that has issued in this book. I hope the trustees will feel that their generosity in this instance was not ill-advised. Many of my colleagues on the staff of the same institution have answered questions or have made fruitful suggestions. I can identify contributions in these pages from so many of my fellow teachers—sixteen or seventeen, at least—that I must thank them as a group and count myself fortunate in having their friendship and access to their learning.

My debts to libraries and librarians are many. In this city I have been greatly aided by the Appleton Public Library and the Samuel Appleton Library of Lawrence College. At Madison I gathered material in the libraries of the State Historical Society and of the University of Wisconsin, and at the Legislative Reference Library in the State Capitol, everywhere receiving the most friendly assistance and courtesy. I am under special obligation to Dr. Joseph Schafer, Superintendent of the State Historical Society. Chapters X and XI of this book appeared in the *Wisconsin Magazine of History*. Dr. Schafer has kindly given permission to use them here. I am glad to thank him and Miss Kellogg, also, for their generosity in allowing me to use maps from works by them published by the society. To all others who furnished, or allowed me to use, maps, charts, or pictures, I offer my thanks. Detailed acknowledgment is made with each item.

Dr. Carl Wittke, Dean of Oberlin College and editor of the series in which this book appears, read two successive versions of it in manuscript and made many helpful suggestions. The editorial staff of Prentice-Hall greatly improved what I had written. Finally, I wish to thank my wife for her invaluable assistance in the making of this book. For the faults that still remain, I alone am responsible.

WILLIAM F. RANEY

Lawrence College
Appleton, Wisconsin
February 11, 1940

TABLE OF CONTENTS

MAPS AND ILLUSTRATIONS

CHAPTER I

THE LAND AND ITS FIRST INHABITANTS

THE history of Wisconsin does not stand by itself; it is part of a larger history. Many tendencies and events in Europe helped to make this Middle Western state, and its history is so deeply embedded in that of America as a whole that the two are inseparable. Yet Wisconsin had beginnings peculiar to itself and inevitably developed in its own way. The millions of persons whose lives, added together, have made Wisconsin's history were not the same individuals as those of other states. Nor did they act their parts upon the same stage. There is a constant interplay between human effort and economic resources; man's life is mightily affected by such things as fertility of soil, abundance of rainfall, facility of travel, and distance from the commercial centers of a nation and of the world. These economic factors influence the course of political struggles, and the latter in turn are often transmuted into moral issues. Furthermore, it makes a great difference whether a constitution was written in 1802 or 1848, whether the principal farming settlement was made with or without the steamboat and the railroad. Industrialization does not appear everywhere at the same time nor develop at the same pace. The story of each state, while always a part of the great American drama, is nevertheless set apart by its own dramatis personae, its physical environment, and the time of its unfolding. We turn first to a description of the scene.

THE PHYSICAL BASIS

Wisconsin's boundaries are partly natural features and partly man-made. On the one side are Lake Michigan and Green Bay; on the other, the Mississippi River and its tributary, the St. Croix. From the St. Croix River a surveyor's line dividing Wisconsin from Minnesota runs north some forty miles to the St. Louis River, which flows into Lake Superior from the west and is the state boundary for about twenty-seven miles. Wisconsin has a frontage on Lake Superior of 150 miles. The line between Wisconsin and upper Michigan is made up of the Montreal River at the western end and the Menominee River and its tributary, the Brule, at the east, with 65 miles of land boundary between them. The line that separates Wisconsin from Illinois is about 145 miles in length. Neither Lake Michigan nor the Mississippi can be counted a barrier, since both were used as highways by traders and travelers in the French period, and, especially before the railway age, by incoming Anglo-Saxon settlers, and both have borne Wisconsin products to distant markets.

The state extends from 42° 30′ north latitude to just beyond 47 degrees. Its maximum length is about 320 miles, and its width, 295 miles. Excluding the waters of Lake Michigan and Lake Superior that are part of it, its area is 56,066 square miles.

The geologist tells us how the state was made. Beneath the loose and tillable soil that nearly everywhere in the Middle West makes up the visible surface of the earth, there is always solid rock. From the northern border of Wisconsin down to about Waupaca and Stevens Point, this foundation is made up of igneous rocks formed by the cooling of molten material. Included are many kinds of rock—granite, quartzite, and iron and copper ore, all very ancient. Millions of years ago this core of northern Wisconsin rose in lofty summits, but the processes of nature, working through countless ages, wore away the greater part of these mountains, leaving only their foundations, which are older than the Appalachians or the Rocky Mountains.

During the ages that followed, Wisconsin was more than once submerged, and each time it was covered with water new layers of rock were formed of materials deposited on the ocean floor. Of these sedimentary rocks the oldest is sandstone. One layer, called the upper Cambrian or Potsdam sandstone, is the immediate foundation of the soil of Wisconsin over a large crescent-shaped area surrounding the igneous rock on east, south, and southwest; at the center of the state this sandstone reaches as far south as Dane County. Newer than the sandstones are the various types of limestone and shale, also sedimentary, which underlie the rest of the state. Wherever any rocks were elevated above the sea, heat and cold, wind and rain, flood and stream, and, in course of time, vegetation and animal life, worked to decompose them, to break them down into various clays, and mingle them. These processes, observable today, have operated through the ages, and thus, on the earth's surface, solid rock has given way to soil.

Perhaps a million years ago—not a long period as geologists reckon time—glaciers first descended from Labrador and the regions about Hudson Bay and covered all of Canada and the northern part of the United States. In the Mississippi Valley they reached as far south as Topeka, St. Louis, and Louisville. The glaciers advanced and receded several times, the last recession being as recent as about seventeen thousand years ago; and they modified the landscape considerably, leveling off the high places, filling in the depressions, carrying away much soil and leaving instead other materials brought from the north. This "glacial drift" included clays, sand, and boulders, and was a valuable addition to the soil of Wisconsin.

The glaciers failed, however, to cover an area some 15,000 square miles in extent, most of it in southwestern Wisconsin, and the rest in adjacent parts of Illinois, Iowa, and Minnesota. This "driftless area" of Wisconsin is about 180 miles north and south and 120 miles east and west, and from the Mississippi River south of Alma extends eastward and a little northeastward to Stevens Point, Kilbourn (now Wisconsin Dells), and Monroe. This area differs from the rest of Wisconsin in many ways. Curious weathered rocks, many ridges and precipitous slopes, and deep-gullied streams give the region great scenic beauty. These features probably indicate, too, what all of Wisconsin would have been like if the glaciers had not come. But the driftless area lacks the gently rolling hills and the lakes so characteristic of glaciated Wisconsin, and there can be no doubt that, generally speaking, farms in the driftless area are less productive than those on the glaciated land to the east of it.

Wisconsin may be described as a swell of land sloping gently toward three depressions, Lake Superior, Lake Michigan, and the Mississippi River. At the north, adjoining upper Michigan, is an area varying from 1,400 to more than 1,800 feet above sea level, which the geographers call the "height of land." It includes all of Vilas and Oneida counties, and large parts of Forest, Langlade, Price, and Iron counties. The higher parts of the state form a T-shaped watershed with the height of land as its cross-bar, and with a general pitch from north to south. This watershed has its foot in Lafayette County on the Illinois border, at an elevation of about 1,100 feet, and though deeply cleft by the Wisconsin River, and reduced in height in its vicinity, it continues northward through Richland and Monroe counties, has the form of a low plateau as it climbs through Jackson, Clark, and Taylor counties, and eventually joins the east and west height of land in Price County. The highest point in the state is the isolated Rib Mountain in Marathon County, which rises to an elevation of 1,940 feet. The Penokee-Gogebic iron range of Wisconsin and Michigan is about equally divided between the two states. Wisconsin's part lies in Ashland and Iron counties, and occasionally reaches a height of 1,800 feet. The hills in the Bayfield peninsula rise 400 to 600 feet above Lake Superior. There are a few isolated elevations somewhat like Rib Mountain, though considerably less in height, scattered about the northern part of the state. The lowest land in Wisconsin is the Lake Michigan shore line, which is 581 feet above sea level. Lake Superior has an elevation of 602 feet, and the

Mississippi River, as it borders Wisconsin, descends from 670 feet above sea level at Prescott to 600 feet on the Illinois border.

About one-fourth of the area of Wisconsin is drained by tributaries of the St. Lawrence River; the rest belongs to the basin of the Mississippi. The Fox and the Wolf rivers, which unite just west of Oshkosh, and the Menominee River are the chief affluents of Lake Michigan. The Mississippi receives the waters of the St. Croix, the Chippewa, the Black, and the Wisconsin, and of many smaller streams. Of all these tributaries, the greatest is the Wisconsin River, which gave its name to the state. It rises in Lac Vieux Desert, on the edge of upper Michigan, flows south through the heart of the state, and then westward to join the Mississippi at Prairie du Chien. The part of Wisconsin adjoining Illinois is drained by several small streams which eventually reach the Mississippi; of these the largest is the Rock River. The glaciers that once covered three-fourths of Wisconsin dug out the basins of many small lakes, which today number nearly four thousand. These and the many woodland streams attract increasing numbers of vacationists; in fact, to cater to them has become one of the state's chief industries.

For nearly two hundred years the greatest streams of Wisconsin were main highways, used by Indian, French fur trader, and missionary alike. The Fox and Wisconsin rivers, which come very close to each other where the city of Portage now stands, were the usual route for travel between Canada and the Mississippi Valley. Again, in the nineteenth century, when the pine forests were being harvested, these streams had great economic importance. Now, when water has yielded to railway and motor transport, the rivers have a different function: they are used, especially in their upper courses, as sources of electric power.

Wisconsin's climate combines with its varied soil to favor agriculture, while making the state very desirable for residence. The average mean temperature is about 43 degrees. There is a variation from 48 degrees in Rock County and in the two southernmost counties along the Mississippi River, to 39 degrees in Vilas

and neighboring counties on the height of land. Equally important with temperature to agriculture is the length of the growing
season between killing frosts. The moderating influence of Lake
Michigan gives to its shores from Manitowoc southward an average of 170 days, and the southeastern counties where tobacco is
raised have almost as long a season. Farmers can count on 130
to 140 days as far north as Marathon County, and also along the
shore of Lake Superior. The height of land, however, has a very
short season; in some places there the average season is less than
one hundred days.

The mean annual precipitation is about thirty-one inches. The
greatest amount of rain, thirty-three or thirty-four inches, falls
along the line of higher land from Lafayette County north to
Price County, and small areas about half way between this and
Lake Michigan are equally favored. The driest part of the state
is along Lake Superior. Everywhere, however, the rainfall in
normal years is sufficient for agriculture and fruit growing. The
distribution throughout the year is exceptionally good, for half
the precipitation occurs in the four months from May through
August.

Thanks to excellent soil and propitious climate, Wisconsin is a
fair and fertile land. Until the nineteenth century it was covered
with magnificent forests. Now that most of these are gone, the
soil supports a great variety of crops. The growing period in the
northern part of the state is so short that only special varieties of
corn will mature, but corn for silage has been grown everywhere
in the state for many years, while the southern counties really belong to the nation's corn and hog belt. Conditions are favorable
to the growth of small grains and hay throughout the state, and
the farmer's choice of crops is determined not so much by climate
and soil as by the demands of the markets and the chance for
profit in commercial farming. There are some crops, to be sure,
which are successful because of local conditions, such as the tobacco
of Dane and adjoining counties, the fruits of the Door County

peninsula, and the potatoes of certain sandy-soiled midland counties. There are also cut-over areas where the cost of clearing the land is prohibitive, but in general, Wisconsin is well fitted for agriculture.

Wisconsin's mineral resources were relatively more important in the past than they are at present. The lead mines of the southern part of the driftless area were known to the Indians and attracted white settlers thither more than one hundred years ago. Some lead and more zinc are still extracted there. Iron ore was once mined profitably in the Penokee range and in Florence County, but these enterprises have declined in the face of competition from the cheaper Minnesota ores. Clay for brick is found in many localities and building stone is easily accessible as are also materials for road building. Wisconsin, unfortunately, has no deposits of coal.

PREHISTORY

The Indians who peopled Wisconsin before the coming of the white men had no written records, and the history of their past is largely lost to us. Those best qualified to have an opinion believe that the ancestors of all the American Indians crossed over from Asia to Alaska, perhaps ten thousand years ago. They probably came in several successive waves or migrations. Most of the Wisconsin tribes had traditions of having moved into the state from one direction or another, but their traditions really tell us very little. The best approach to prehistory is by way of the mounds and buried artifacts to be found in Wisconsin and neighboring states. The upper Mississippi Valley and the region of the Great Lakes have a great store of this material which is being patiently uncovered and interpreted by the archaeologists.

Prehistoric man-made mounds are scattered through many states from the Alleghenies westward to the great plains beyond the Missouri River. Erosion and the work of man have obliterated many of them, but the number known to have existed within the past century in Wisconsin alone runs to about twelve thousand. They occur in all parts of the state except the upper Wisconsin Valley, although they are most frequent in the southern part of the state. In some areas they are surprisingly numerous; around Lake Wingra in Madison, for instance, there were once 148 mounds, of which 69 still remain. They vary greatly in shape and size. They may be round or oval or in the form of straight, curved, or broken lines. Others again—and in this Wisconsin is distinguished above all her neighbors—are effigy mounds: that is, they have the shape of some bird or other animal. The only effigy having a human form is in Man-Mound Park near Baraboo. It "represents a man in the attitude of walking toward the west. On its head are two protuberances, probably intended to represent a buffalo horn or other headdress." It was 210 feet long before road-grading destroyed the feet and a portion of the legs, and 47 feet across the shoulders.

Opinions about the purposes of these mounds are largely guesswork. A few were graves, but many have no contents. Those with animal shapes may have been totem signs and may have had religious or ceremonial uses. The arrowheads, shards, and other artifacts found in or near them usually show that the culture of the mound-builders was the northern woodland type and did not differ from that of the historic tribes of the same region; in other words, the mound builders were not a separate race. The Nicholls Mound in Trempealeau County has yielded broken pottery that has the marks of the Hopewell culture, best represented in Ross County, Ohio, but this culture was, so far as is now known, limited in Wisconsin to a few small areas. Besides the mounds, there are of course hundreds of campsites and burial grounds that yield objects illustrating the same period and the same culture as the majority of the mounds.

The most famous prehistoric site in Wisconsin is at Aztalan, about two and one-half miles east of Lake Mills in Jefferson County. It was discovered in 1836, and the newspapers made it known throughout the eastern states. The name was taken from Alexander von Humboldt's writings on Mexico. The Aztecs, according to the legends which he recounts, had come from a place in the north called Aztalan. Fortunately the site was carefully surveyed and described by Dr. Increase A. Lapham in 1850, when most of the area was still uncultivated. He found an earthen wall or ridge which even today rises in places four or five feet above the surrounding fields. This enclosed, on the north, west, and south, an imperfect rectangle which had on its eastern side the Crawfish River, formerly known as the West Branch of the Rock River. The enclosure is roughly seven hundred by fifteen hundred feet and has an area of about twenty-one acres. Inside the enclosure were a large rectangular platform from two to five feet high, and, in the corners farthest from the river, two flat-topped mounds of considerable height. There were many other mounds outside the enclosure.

After the World War the site was surveyed and excavated by Dr. Stephen A. Barrett of the Milwaukee Public Museum. The outer ridge was the line of a stockade which had been made by setting logs upright in the ground. It had been made firmer by heaping earth against the logs both inside and outside the enclosure. The logs were buried to a depth of seven or eight feet, and probably protruded ten or twelve feet above the surface. The logs rotted into black mold long ago, but their bases, being black, were easily located in the yellow sand and clay of the site. It was possible to trace the line of the outer stockade, not only along the previously known three sides, but along the river bank as well. Remains of other lines of defense inside the outer one were also found. Dr. Barrett and his helpers also collected from the mounds and refuse pits many objects that illustrate the culture of the builders. The stockade, the evidences of cannibalism, the types of implements, and particularly the pottery were all completely foreign to the usual Wisconsin types. They composed a tiny island of "Middle Mississippi culture," the northernmost outpost thus far discovered of the people who built the Cahokia Mounds in southern Illinois opposite St. Louis and the Angel works in Vanderburg County, Indiana.

INDIANS IN THE SEVENTEENTH CENTURY

Indian tribes of historic times may be classified according to their languages, and usually when a group of tribes spoke related languages they also had in common methods of house building, ways of gaining food, weaving, the making of pottery, and other handicrafts. We need to distinguish three such linguistic and cultural groups: the Algonquian, the Siouan, and the Iroquoian.

The Algonquian group included most of the tribes in the United States and Canada north of the Ohio River and east of the Mississippi. When first the white man came, the upper Great Lakes were, with the exception of the Winnebago and the Hurons soon to be noted, encircled by Algonquian tribes. Along the northern and part of the eastern shore of Lake Huron were the Ottawa. In the east-central part of the lower peninsula of Michigan were the Chippewa (Ojibway) and the Potawatomi, and along the St. Clair River the Mascouten and the Kickapoo, related tribes, and the Sauk and the Foxes, also closely related. In upper Michigan and the adjacent parts of Wisconsin were the Menominee. Later the Menominee were to move southward along the Wisconsin shore of Lake Michigan as far as Milwaukee. South of Wisconsin were other Algonquian tribes, the Miami in the valley of the Wabash and the Illinois along the river of that name. These tribes had permanent village sites, grain fields, and burial grounds, but were semi-nomadic and at certain seasons of the year hunted far from home.

From the preceding enumeration it will be seen that the great central part of Wisconsin had no Algonquian Indians. The land between the Menominee and the Illinois was peopled by the Winnebago, and they belonged to the Siouan group, most of whose members lived between the Mississippi and the Rocky Mountains. Representative tribes were the Dakota, the Iowa, the Kansa, and the Omaha. Of these peoples the Winnebago were an eastern offshoot, and they seemed utterly foreign to all the Algonquians who had any knowledge of them. No wonder the French first heard of them as men of another race!

The Iroquoian tribes were an island in a sea of Algonquians that surrounded them on all sides. The Five Nations of New York and northern Pennsylvania formed the nucleus of this group. To it belonged also the Erie or Cat nation of northern Ohio, and the Hurons, who lived in the angle of present Ontario between Lake Erie and Lake Huron. All these tribes, besides speaking related dialects, were distinguished by their peculiar pottery and other utensils, and by their domestic and military architecture. Women were held in especially high esteem among them, and descent was reckoned from the mother. The economic life of the Iroquoian group was more advanced than that of their Algonquian neighbors, since they had come to depend almost entirely upon a settled agriculture. The Five Nations—Mohawk, Oneida, Onondaga, Cayuga, and Seneca—at some time before contact with the white men, probably about 1560, entered into a sort of federal union that was destined to great permanence. In fact, for certain ceremonial purposes, it is still in existence.

The Indian geography as just detailed was greatly changed by the warlike activities of the Iroquois in the middle of the seventeenth century. They secured firearms from the Dutch on the Hudson, and, thus equipped, began a rapid conquest of their neighbors. Their period of greatest violence was from about 1640 to 1667. They threatened for a time to exterminate the French in the St. Lawrence Valley, and they caused migrations that greatly altered the distribution of the Indian tribes. The Chippewa and the Potawatomi left the lower for the upper peninsula of Michigan and halted temporarily near the outlet of Lake Superior, which the French had christened Sault Ste. Marie. When the French found the Chippewa in that vicinity, they called them the Saulteurs, a name used to the end of the French period. In the course of the next hundred years or more, the Chippewa came to occupy the whole southern shore of Lake Superior and to possess large parts of upper Michigan and northern Wisconsin. Their further expansion westward was limited by the Sioux tribesmen. The Potawatomi in time moved southward along the Wisconsin shore of Lake Michigan. All these changes were made, appar-

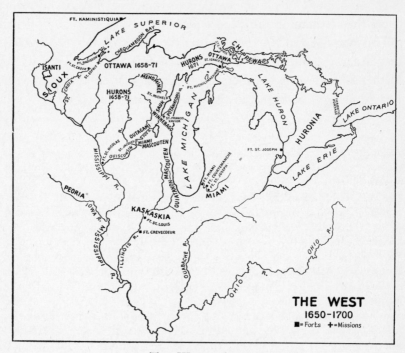

THE WEST, 1650-1700*

ently, with no resistance on the part of the Menominee, who continued to occupy these regions as their ancestors had done. The Foxes moved first from the eastern to the western side of lower Michigan, and then appeared with their kindred, the Sauk, in east-central Wisconsin. Their chief villages were first near New London and then on the shore of Little Lake Butte des Morts, on or near the site of Menasha. The Mascouten and the Kickapoo left lower Michigan and settled on the upper Fox near Berlin,

---

* From Louise P. Kellogg, *The French Régime in Wisconsin and the Northwest* (1925). By courtesy of the State Historical Society of Wisconsin.

Wisconsin. When, about 1655, the Iroquois began to raid the valleys of the Wabash and the Illinois, many Miami and Illinois settled in the valley of the upper Fox, not far from the Mascouten and the Kickapoo. Meanwhile, in this same period, obscure causes greatly reduced the numbers and importance of the Winnebago, and apparently they were unable to resist the Algonquian tribes then swarming into Wisconsin.

This was the situation which met the French when about 1660 they began to come into Wisconsin in considerable numbers. The further history of these tribes and especially their dealings with Europeans will be found in the chapters that follow.

SELECTED BIBLIOGRAPHY

Physiography: The geography of the North American continent in its relation to human history is treated in Livingston Farrand, *Basis of American History,* American Nation Series, Vol. II (New York, 1904), Chapters 1-3; and in Ellen G. Semple, *American History and Its Geographic Conditions* (Boston, 1903). B. A. Hinsdale, *The Old Northwest* (New York, revised edition, 1899), opens with a study of geography.

The geography of Wisconsin is best studied in Lawrence Martin, *The Physical Geography of Wisconsin,* Wisconsin Geological and Natural History Survey, Bulletin No. XXXVI (Madison, 1916). A second edition prepared by Ernest F. Bean, State Geologist, was issued in 1932. The bibliographies are extensive and excellent. Shorter descriptions of the state are found in Joseph Schafer, *A History of Agriculture in Wisconsin* (Madison, 1922), pp. 1-22; and in Milo M. Quaife, *Wisconsin, Its History and Its People* (4 vols., Chicago, 1924), Vol. I, pp. 11-22. A. R. Whitson and O. E. Baker prepared a very interesting pamphlet, *The Climate of Wisconsin and Its Relation to Agriculture,* Agricultural Experiment Station Bulletin No. 223 (Madison, second revision, 1928). *A Study of Wisconsin: Its Resources, Its Physical, Social and Economic Background* (Madison, 1935), is the First Annual Report of the Wisconsin Regional Planning Committee. It is a comprehensive survey of the state; on geography, see especially pp. 1-14, 190-196. *Home Regions of Wisconsin,* by Loyal Durand, Jr., and Leavelva M. Bradbury (New York, 1933), though designed for school use, will interest many adults.

Prehistory: The best introduction to this field is Henry C. Shetrone, *The Mound-Builders* (New York, 1930). Though Ohio furnished more data than any other state, pp. 291-308 are devoted to Wisconsin. The files of the *Wisconsin Archaeologist* enable one to keep abreast of archaeological work. W. C. McKern in "Wisconsin Hopewell Culture," *Bulletin of the Public Museum of the City of Milwaukee,* Vol. X, pp. 185-328, tells of his findings in Trempealeau County. Dr. Stephen A. Barrett reported on the excavations at Aztalan, *ibid.,* Vol. XIII, pp. 1-602, and summarized the same material very briefly in the *Wisconsin Archaeologist,* Vol. XII, pp. 74-81.

Indians in Wisconsin: A comprehensive and scholarly introduction to the study of the American Indians is provided by Clark Wissler, *The American Indian* (New York, 1922). Louise Phelps Kellogg in *The French Régime in Wisconsin and the Northwest* (Madison, 1925) has no separate chapters devoted to the Indians, but in telling the history of the French she writes more clearly than anyone else about the Indians in the Northwest down to 1763. See also Milo M. Quaife, *Wisconsin, Its History and Its People* (4 vols., Chicago, 1924), Vol. I, pp. 23-52. Emma Helen Blair edited a memoir of Perrot (see next chapter) and in her commentary added much about the Indians in the seventeenth and later centuries. The work was published with the title, *Indian Tribes of the Upper Mississippi Valley* (2 vols., Cleveland, 1912). *The Handbook of American Indians North of Mexico,* edited by Frederick W. Hodge (2 vols., Washington, 1907-1910), is a standard work of reference about the separate tribes.

CHAPTER II

THE FRENCH PERIOD, 1634–1763

The Coming of Jean Nicolet

THE French period of Wisconsin history began with the voyage of Jean Nicolet to the shores of Green Bay in 1634 and closed with the Treaty of Paris in 1763, when sovereignty over all lands east of the Mississippi River passed to the British. Throughout this span of 129 years Wisconsin was but a distant fringe of that French-Canadian life which had its heart along the St. Lawrence River. The founder of New France was Samuel de Champlain, who guided its destinies from the first settlement at Quebec in 1608 until his own death twenty-seven years later. Champlain had a notable part in laying down the lines along which New France was to develop, and in so doing placed his stamp upon the French regime in Wisconsin. He encouraged missionary work and promoted the fur trade. He realized the necessity of dominating the Indians, and besides making many treaties with native tribes he sent young Frenchmen out to live among them and learn their languages and customs.

Jean Nicolet came from France and spent fourteen years in apprenticeship among the Indians, living first on the upper reaches of the Ottawa River and then farther west on the eastern shore of Lake Huron. Champlain sent Nicolet on his memorable voyage with two ends in view. Hostilities had arisen between the Ottawa and the Winnebago beyond the limits of French influence, and the French fur trade was suffering therefrom. Nicolet was to pacify the Indians in the interests of the fur trade. He was also to visit the Winnebago to inquire about a possible route to the

Pacific. "Winnebago," so the French had been told, meant "People of the Sea." Perhaps they lived by the salt sea, or perhaps they knew the way thither!

Nicolet took the usual route westward by way of the Ottawa River and reached Georgian Bay. Thence he traveled on—a solitary Frenchman with seven Indians in one canoe. He skirted the northern shore of Lake Huron, and, it is supposed, stopped at the outlet of Lake Superior. Then on he went westward along the southern side of the upper peninsula of Michigan, through the Straits of Mackinac, and thus became the discoverer of Lake Michigan. He followed the shore of the lake and entered Green Bay. His coming, which had been announced before, was something of an event.

They [the men of the Winnebago village] dispatched several young men to meet the Manitourinion—that is to say, "the wonderful man." They meet him; they escort him, and carry all his baggage. He wore a grand robe of China damask, all strewn with flowers and birds of many colors. No sooner did they meet him than the women and children fled at the sight of a man who carried thunder in both hands— for thus they called the two pistols that he held.[1]

Where Nicolet made his dramatic landing is quite uncertain. There are monuments to mark the site at Menasha and at Red Banks, eight miles northeast of Green Bay. He duly performed his functions as a diplomat, eating many huge feasts in the process. He also attempted without much success to find out about the western sea. He heard of a route out of Lake Michigan, a great river upon which he might travel to "the great water." Perhaps the Indians were trying to tell him of the Chicago-Desplaines route to the Mississippi. It seems unlikely, in view of the short time that he had for the whole trip, that he went far into the interior of Wisconsin. The remaining eight years of his life he spent as an Indian agent and fur trader at Three Rivers. His great voyage was a fitting close to the explorations directed by Champlain.

[1] *Jesuit Relations and Allied Documents,* edited by Reuben Gold Thwaites (Cleveland, 1896-1901, 73 vols.) Vol. XXIII, pp. 277, 279.

The Great Missionaries and the Discovery
of the Mississippi River

There were strong economic reasons for communication and trade between the West, represented by Wisconsin, and the French-Canadian community on the St. Lawrence River. The French wanted furs to send to Europe, and the Indians wanted goods of European origin, but for some time the western Indians brought the furs to Montreal. Only gradually did it come to be a trade practice for Frenchmen to go west. In 1658 two of them whom we know by name, Radisson and Groseilliers, went out to the southern shore of Lake Superior, and on Chequamegon Bay near Ashland they built the first white man's habitation in Wisconsin. They spent two winters there, ranging far afield in the meantime, and eventually piloted sixty canoes of western Indians and western furs from Sault Ste. Marie to Montreal. Their example was followed by other Frenchmen, until by 1665 a new era with new methods was fairly inaugurated. The intermediaries of the trade were to be French and not Indian.

While laymen were establishing the fur trade, devoted priests sought to convert the natives. Missionary work began almost with the beginning of New France. Before the Iroquois fury broke, there was successful work among the Hurons in Ontario, and as early as 1645 the Jesuits had a mission to the Ottawa with headquarters on Manitoulin Island. When the Iroquois came to burn and murder, the missions perforce came to an end in these localities, and pastors followed the surviving members of their flocks into the west. An elderly Jesuit, René Ménard, has the distinction of being the first missionary in Wisconsin. He came out to care for some remnants of the fugitive Ottawa tribe, and in April, 1661, at Chequamegon Bay, he established a mission which he named St. Esprit. The place came to be called La Pointe du St. Esprit, and a village on Madeline Island in the Bay is still called La Pointe.[2] During the course of that summer, Ménard

---

[2] Ménard's mission was on the mainland, on the west shore of the Bay.

lost his way and his life in the forests while trying to take the consolations of religion to some dying Hurons in the interior.

The second missionary in Wisconsin was Claude Jean Allouez, who worked in the western missions from 1665 until his death in 1689. His first assignment was to reopen, after an interval of four years, the mission of St. Esprit. While the mission was maintained at La Pointe (from 1665 to 1671), no less than seven tribes were ministered to, including some Illinois. In 1669 Allouez went to the Fox River region, and the mission of St. Esprit was continued by Father Jacques Marquette. The Ottawa, for whom the mission had been established, eventually moved eastward again, and in the spring of 1671 work on the shore of Chequamegon Bay was ended, and the Ottawa mission was continued at St. Ignace, on the northern side of the Straits of Mackinac.

In the Fox River region Allouez founded four missions, of which the most important was that of St. Francis Xavier at De Pere. It was begun in 1669, and permanent buildings were erected in the winter of 1671-1672. It was established primarily to minister to the Potawatomi and the Sauk, but after separate missions to the Menominee and the Foxes were ended, it cared for them also. The Foxes left the Wolf River about 1680, and brought their villages and their name to the Fox, and at the same time came within reach of the De Pere mission. In one sense, the missionary work in seventeenth-century Wisconsin was not very successful. Some hundreds of Indians were baptized, but most of them were small children or aged persons about to die. None of the Indian tribes accepted Christianity as a way of life which they would gladly pass on to their children. There were many reasons for this failure. French support grew less vigorous and missionary recruits were not forthcoming to carry on the work. The most docile tribes left Wisconsin, while those that chanced to remain were not receptive. Traders often debauched the Indians and robbed them by sharp practices, and this caused the Indians to react against missionary effort. Yet these missionaries have given examples for all later time of men willing to sacrifice the material and the temporal for the spiritual and the eternal.

Missionary work sometimes dovetailed with what might be called official exploration. There was a memorable ceremony of "taking possession" at Sault Ste. Marie in June, 1671. The French king was represented by a nobleman, St. Lusson, the royal arms of Louis XIV were attached to a tree, and French and Indians exchanged presents. At least fourteen tribes were represented, and missionaries, traders, and officers signed the document drawn up to attest the great event. The missionaries sanctified the pageant with Latin hymns, and the proclamations which were made claimed for France the whole of North America, as bounded by the Arctic, Atlantic, and Pacific oceans.

The expedition under Jolliet and Marquette, which resulted in the discovery of the Mississippi, likewise had the approval of the highest officials of both church and state in New France. Jolliet, born in Canada, was an experienced traveler, especially proficient in surveying and map making. Jacques Marquette was born in France, and from boyhood was bent on becoming a missionary. He came out to Canada in 1666, and at once showed great ability in learning native tongues. In succession he had charge of mission stations at the Sault, at St. Esprit on Chequamegon Bay, and at St. Ignace, whither he had removed with the Ottawa. Jolliet came on to St. Ignace in December, 1672. The two leaders and five men left the mission station on May 17, 1673. The journey was a pleasant one. They ascended the Fox, doubtless pausing at the mission of St. Francis Xavier. They were well received by the Miami and the Mascouten on the upper Fox, and the Miami furnished them with guides who saw them safely over the portage to the Wisconsin River. Marquette was the first to write down the name of the river which became the name of the state. He spelled it "Meskousing" and "Meskous" within a few lines. It was June 17, 1673, when they issued from the Wisconsin

River and first beheld the Mississippi, "with a joy," Marquette wrote, "that I cannot express." The party continued down the Mississippi. After a month's travel southward they were certain that it flowed into the Gulf of Mexico, and they feared that if they continued they might fall into the hands of the Spaniards. On July 17, being then at the mouth of the Arkansas River, they turned about and began their homeward voyage. Marquette spent the ensuing winter at the mission house at De Pere. Jolliet paused at the Sault long enough to leave a copy of his records there, and went on. When he was nearing Montreal, his canoe was overturned, all the occupants except Jolliet lost their lives, and his maps and journals were lost. In the meantime the records left at Sault Ste. Marie were destroyed by fire. When Marquette heard of these losses, he prepared his own journals for publication, and his is thus the only account of the great voyage.

After a year spent in recuperating at St. Francis Xavier, Marquette set out late in 1674 for further missionary work in the Illinois country. Winter overtook him and he passed some months in a hut near the mouth of the Chicago River. Just before Easter he reached his goal, a great village on the Illinois River near the present city of Peoria. He preached on the Thursday before Easter to an audience that was estimated at fifteen hundred men, women, and children. After another service on Easter morning he departed, promising that others would continue his work. He was a dying man, and as his canoe sped northward along the eastern shore of Lake Michigan he grew ever weaker. At the mouth of the Marquette River, not far from where Ludington, Michigan, now stands, he died as he had desired, almost alone in the forests of the West, a martyr as much as if he had died in the arena. Wisconsin has chosen to place Marquette's statue in the Capitol at Washington as one of her immortals. Other Europeans may have seen the Mississippi before Jolliet and Marquette did, but the latter were the first to travel most of its majestic length and they are rightfully its discoverers.

TRADE AND EMPIRE BUILDING

New France grew more slowly than the English colonies on the Atlantic seaboard, but by 1681 the French population in the St. Lawrence Valley was about nine thousand. The community raised much of its own food, but its great economic interest lay in the gathering of furs. All ambitious young men looked to the trade for their careers. How many engaged in it we do not know, but it is recorded that in 1680 six hundred *unlicensed* traders were temporarily outlawed in the western woods. There was a steadily growing fund of geographical knowledge about the western country, and the permanent methods of the trade were being hammered out by experience. Many of those who engaged in it were illiterate, and others preferred that their activities, often illicit, be not recorded, so that many of the forward steps were taken by men who are nameless to us. To some the trade offered a livelihood, to others the hope of a fuller competence, and to still others the vision of a great French empire that should reach the western or southern sea.

The man who dreamed the grandest dreams of all was Robert-René Cavalier, best known as the Sieur de La Salle. He came to Canada in 1666, and there has been much speculation about his travels during the next decade. He probably reached the Ohio River; he may have visited Lake Michigan. In 1678 La Salle returned from a visit to France with a charter authorizing great business activities and exploration in the Mississippi Valley. Since the Iroquois were still hostile to the French, it seems to have been La Salle's idea to organize the Algonquian tribes in the Illinois country into a confederation, build forts among them, and teach them to withstand the Iroquois. The Mississippi River would become the highway to France, and the profits of the fur trade would pay the expenses of empire building.

La Salle began by constructing at the eastern end of Lake Erie the *Griffon,* the first sailing vessel on the Great Lakes. Men were sent ahead to gather its cargo around Detroit and in eastern Wisconsin. In the autumn of 1679, La Salle loaded it with furs at the entrance to Green Bay and sent it eastward, but it disappeared without reaching its destination. Whether it was lost in a gale or destroyed by unfriendly Indians is unknown. La Salle then went southward along the western shore of Lake Michigan, the first to travel that route, and on into the Illinois country. In the spring of 1682, he reached the mouth of the Mississippi, and there on April 9 was held the usual elaborate ceremony of taking possession in the name of Louis XIV. Toward the end of that year, the strongest fort in the Illinois country was built at Starved Rock on the Illinois River and was christened Fort St. Louis. Partly because of La Salle's activities and diplomacy, and partly no doubt because the food supply in Wisconsin was not adequate to the population since the great migration of a generation before, several tribes in whole or in part at this time moved southward and eastward out of Wisconsin, among them the Miami, the Mascouten, and the Kickapoo. Because of a change of policy determined upon at the royal court of France, La Salle was rather suddenly relieved of his command at Fort St. Louis, and in August, 1683, he left the Illinois country, never to return. The last episode of his life scarcely belongs to the history of Wisconsin. He went back to France and organized a large party to found a colony at the mouth of the Mississippi River. The landing was made on the shore of Texas, far to the west of the Mississippi. The enterprise gradually dissolved in bitter tragedy, and in March, 1687, La Salle was murdered by one of his own men. La Salle did more than any other man of his generation to make the Mississippi Valley known to Europe and to gain it for France.

An able contemporary of La Salle was Daniel Greysolon, Sieur Duluth, whose activity in the West falls within eleven years, 1678 to 1689. On his first expedition to Lake Superior he arranged one peace between the Sioux and the Chippewa, and another between the Sioux and the Assiniboin, thereby opening to French traders extensive territories to the west and north of Lake Superior. On July 2, 1679, at Lake Mille Lacs in central Minnesota, he took possession of all the Sioux country in the name of Louis XIV of France. There is a river once called the Boise Brûlé, and now known as the Brule, which flows into Lake Superior from the south about twenty-five miles east of the present city of Superior. Duluth ascended this, portaged to the headlake of the St. Croix River, and by it reached the Mississippi. Duluth used this route a number of times, traversing it in both directions, and, probably in 1683, built a small fort at this portage, the first in interior Wisconsin. It was Duluth's hope to explore far to the north and west, and possibly reach the Pacific Ocean, but because the French community in the St. Lawrence Valley was fighting the Iroquois and, after 1689, the English also, Duluth was commanded to turn from his plans for distant exploration and lead Indian allies from the western Great Lakes to help defend the St. Lawrence Valley. After 1689, he never traveled west of Lake Ontario.

The third great Frenchman of the West in this generation was Nicolas Perrot. He was of humbler origin than La Salle and Duluth, had less formal education, his plans were not so grandiose, but no one approached him in understanding and managing the Indians. He was born in Canada in 1644, and before he was of age he was in business as a fur trader on his own account. In 1667 he was at Chequamegon Bay, where Allouez was carrying on the mission of St. Esprit. The next year he was with the Potawatomi around Green Bay and composed a quarrel between them and the Menominee, and also made a close alliance between the latter and the French. He was the first European to visit the Fox Indians on the Wolf River, then living in a very primitive way. He visited the Miami and the Mascouten on the Upper Fox. Thus he laid the foundation for his unrivaled influence among the tribes of the Fox River area. It was Perrot who went ahead of St. Lusson in the spring of 1671 to arrange for the great ceremony of taking possession at Sault Ste. Marie. He persuaded many tribes to attend, acted as interpreter, along with Allouez, and was one of the orators of the day. Perrot continued to trade in the West, exploiting the connections he had made.

After new Iroquois outbreaks began in 1680, Indian loyalty to the French began to waver, and many tribes were attracted by Iroquois strength and the advantages of trade with the English. Perrot had no small part in keeping the tribes he knew faithful to the French interest. At the summons of the governor at Quebec he, like Duluth, led western tribes eastward—the Winnebago, Sauk, Foxes, and Menominee.

In 1685 Perrot began to open new fields to French trade. He followed the Fox-Wisconsin route to the Mississippi, turned northward, and spent the winter at Trempealeau. In the spring he founded Fort St. Antoine on the east shore of Lake Pepin, and carried on a profitable business with the Sioux in that vicinity. A little later he built Fort Nicolas at the mouth of the Wisconsin. In 1687 he was summoned to lead the western Indians eastward again, but in 1689 he was back again at Fort St. Antoine on Lake Pepin. There he went through a ceremony of taking possession, the only one on Wisconsin soil. In 1690 we find him inspecting lead mines about Dubuque and Galena. By this time war had begun between the English and the French, and the English are supposed to have encouraged the Iroquois. At any rate these old enemies of the French, in August, 1689, fell upon the village of La Chine just west of Montreal and massacred two hundred men, women, and children. Disaffection against the French flared up all through the West. The forts on the Mississippi were abandoned, and Perrot had to leave a thriving trade. During the years that followed he traveled about among the tribes in the Fox River Valley, holding them true to the French. No one else could have done it and it was not easy for him. His life in the West was ended when it was decided in Paris—they knew better in Quebec —to abandon all posts west of Mackinac, to summon all traders home to the colony, and to ask the Indians to bring their peltries to Montreal.   So in 1698 Perrot left forever the forests of the West, where he had labored for nearly thirty-five years.

THE ERA OF THE FOX WARS

The decision to abandon the West seemed wise in Paris.   The prices of furs were low, and it was desired to restrict the supply at its source.   Jesuit influence was for the moment uppermost at

THE WEST, 1700-1760*

court, and the Jesuits wanted as little contact between the traders and the natives as possible.   Yet the Indians must be kept friendly or they would endanger the whole French frontier.   Trade must go on in some form.   Almost at once there was evolved a plan for concentrating the trade: It would not require such a wide scatter-

---

*From Louise P. Kellogg, *The French Régime in Wisconsin and the Northwest* (1925).   By courtesy of the State Historical Society of Wisconsin.

ing of French posts as hitherto, but instead, a few military centers around which French communities would grow; about them in turn would gather Indian tribes to become acquainted with French civilization while their hunters came and went, gathering furs to sell to the French. Soon there were French posts at New Orleans and at points in Illinois, including Chicago. Cadillac founded Detroit in 1701, but there was no French post in Wisconsin. In this region the first third of the eighteenth century was marked by recurring warfare with the Fox Indians.

After the evacuation of the West in 1698, the Foxes were left in control of all eastern and central Wisconsin. In order to keep French goods away from their enemies, the Sioux, the Foxes closed the Fox-Wisconsin waterway to the French, except for an occasional party that would pay them toll in goods. What is known as the first Fox War began indirectly as a result of the policy of concentration. When Cadillac founded his post on the Detroit River, he sent invitations to the Indians far and wide to come and live nearby. A part of the Fox tribe, some two hundred warriors in all, left Wisconsin in 1710 and traveled back to the region whence their ancestors had fled two generations earlier. Many tribes were living in a small area about Detroit, and, as was almost inevitable, a quarrel arose in which the Foxes had a part. The commandant, Cadillac's successor, saw an opportunity to pay off the old score with this tribe, and took the side of their enemies. The cannon and mortars of the French fort were used against the stockade of the Foxes. The latter made a defense that aroused the wonder of the other Indians, but the French were relentless, and most of the Foxes that had come to Detroit at the invitation of the French were killed.

After this episode of 1712, the Foxes gave no quarter, and far and wide through the western country no Frenchman was safe. In the spring of 1715 young men of two noble families of Canada were killed between Kaskaskia and Detroit. The French wrongly attributed this deed to the Foxes, and decided upon punishment. In 1716 Louvigny left Montreal with two hundred

French and Canadians, and by the time he reached Mackinac he had nearly one thousand Indians. This force, the first army to invade Wisconsin, found the Foxes prepared for defense in a stockaded village, probably west of Little Lake Butte des Morts, which had not yet received its name. Louvigny besieged in the best European fashion for three days without result, and then arranged an unexpected and rather ignominious peace. All the French officers expected to get beaver skins, and one of the terms of this remarkable peace was that the Foxes would pay the expenses of the expedition by sending in peltries yet to be gathered. The tribe yielded sullenly, cowed but by no means conquered. Thus ended the first Fox War.

The death of Louis XIV in 1715 was followed by changes in western policy. The plan of concentration was given up, and traders, controlled by a system of licenses, were allowed to go out among the Indians. This made necessary the building of forts and the sending of garrisons. In 1717 a fort was erected at Green Bay, known as Fort La Baye, and the next year Fort La Pointe was built on Chequamegon Bay.

In the years after Louvigny's fiasco, the Foxes angered the French by continuing to wage war against the Illinois Indians, and from time to time Frenchmen were scalped there. The Fox leader of the time, Kiala, like Pontiac and Tecumseh of later times, had in view a pan-Indian league which should drive all white men from the land. He had bound together in an alliance not only most of the Wisconsin tribes, but also, west of the Mississippi, the Sioux, the Iowa, and even the distant Missouri. A new governor, Beauharnois, arrived in Canada in 1727 and determined to act vigorously and promptly. To control the Sioux a new fort was built on the Minnesota bank of Lake Pepin and received the governor's name. This was maintained for ten years.

In 1728 another military expedition invaded the Fox territory and began the second Fox War. The army was led by the Sieur de Lignery, and consisted of four hundred white soldiers and militiamen and eleven or twelve hundred Indians. The invaders

marched from one Fox village to another, only to find them deserted.   The white soldiers found the going very hard and finally
refused to go farther; some of the Indian allies doubtless sympa-
thized with the Foxes; and not far from the present city of Oshkosh, Lignery abandoned the enterprise and turned back.   As he
left Wisconsin, he burned the post at La Baye, which was rebuilt
three years later.   This surprising and disgraceful manner of ending the campaign is not to be explained by any opposition offered
by the Foxes.

Yet in spite of Lignery's fiasco, which should have encouraged
the enemies of the French, Kiala's great confederacy began to fall
apart.   Within the next two years, small groups of Fox warriors
were overpowered by superior numbers of Indians who had turned
again to the French.   Thus surrounded by enemies in the western
country, the Foxes determined to move eastward and join the
Iroquois.   Their plans became known, and three hundred Fox
warriors and their families were caught in central Illinois, in
1730; after a brave stand in a fort they had built on the prairies,
they and their women and children were massacred.   The
strength of the Foxes was now almost spent.   Kiala and some of
the other leaders, hoping to gain a respite for the remnant of their
people, offered to give themselves up to the French.   Villiers, the
commandant of the new post at La Baye, treacherously carried
them to Montreal, and Kiala ended his days soon after as a slave
in the French West Indies.

Still the French were not satisfied.   When Villiers returned to
Fort La Baye, he appeared before a village of the Sauk close by,
and ordered them to give up the Foxes sheltered there.   The Sauk
hesitated, Villiers imprudently insisted, and in the skirmish he
and one of his sons were killed.   The Sauk and Foxes retreated
up the river with the French in pursuit, and a battle followed, in
September, 1733, that resulted in the naming of Butte des Morts,
the Hill of the Dead, on the outskirts of Menasha.   In the winter
of 1734-1735, a last expedition of white men and mission Indians
from Canada pursued a miserable remnant of Foxes into Iowa,

but their quarry escaped. Finally some years later, a new commandant at La Baye began to conciliate rather than to murder, and only then were the Fox Wars at an end. The scattered Foxes, now closely bound to the Sauk tribe, slowly gathered into villages, not in their former homes, but in southern Wisconsin and northern Illinois.

ECONOMIC AND SOCIAL LIFE OF THE FRENCH PERIOD

The fur trade was the basis of the economic life of all New France. The beaver furnished the most desirable and the greatest number of the furs. It is estimated that, before the coming of the white men, there were ten million beaver in North America. When Duluth ascended the Brule River for the first time, he had to cut more than one hundred beaver dams. As the supply of beaver diminished, the hunters had to go farther and farther afield. It was the constant aim of the French explorers and traders to reach Indian tribes which had not yet traded with Europeans—that is, which had not begun to exhaust their wild life. Always the Indians demanded more and more bulky articles, especially kettles and woolen blankets. During most of the period after 1715, the Canadian government regulated the trade by selling licenses. A license permitted the purchaser to go into the Indian country with four canoe loads of goods. A license might be divided and the fractional parts bought and sold. For a short time (1741-1749), a different method was used. A monopoly of all trade at one post was auctioned off. A group of Montreal merchants bought the rights at La Baye, and then sublet their monopoly to men who actually went out to trade. In the latter part of the French period, after a return to the license system, the trade was very profitable. Governor Vaudreuil in Canada, and the Marins, father and son, formed a ring that had charge of the trade at Green Bay, at La Pointe on Chequamegon Bay, and at a post on the Upper Mississippi, and their profits rose to 150,000 francs a year.

Whatever the system of government regulation and higher

finance, the lower strata engaged in the trade showed little change. The unit of work was a canoe carrying from five to eight men and a cargo of trading goods. One of the men might be the owner of the goods and of a license; if so, he was the *bourgeois,* a word generally used for employer. His hired men were *engagés.* If they were hired especially to propel a canoe and work on a long trip, they were *voyageurs,* but some *engagés,* such as the blacksmiths, canoe builders, and warehousemen might have more stationary work. The more experienced *voyageurs* spent the winter dealing with the Indians. They could judge, buy, and care for furs. It was a life full of hard labor and often beset with danger. There were other Frenchmen trafficking with the Indians, unlicensed men called *coureurs de bois* (rangers of the woods). They secured trade goods, often indirectly and sometimes directly, from Montreal merchants, at other times from the English colonies. Corrupt officials at the posts connived at their business, or sometimes were partners in it. Some of the *coureurs de bois* were desperate or debased men and brought the French into disrepute with the Indians. When advancing years or infirmities made it impossible for a *voyageur* or *coureur de bois* to travel any longer, he might marry and "settle down." Some of them took up little farms near the posts; others "went native" and lived out their days with the Indians. A French-Canadian historian has estimated that no less than fifteen thousand French-speaking men went west as traders or *voyageurs* between 1670 and 1760.

When France gave up her dominion in North America in 1763, the French population in Wisconsin was very small indeed. There had been perhaps fifty families, or between two and three hundred persons, in the region of La Baye. After the departure of the garrison at the end of 1760, the population declined considerably. At Portage and Prairie du Chien there may have been a few families. The latter place was a great trade mart by 1766. Some French settlers were found at these places in the British period. The posts on Chequamegon Bay and on the Upper Mississippi were abandoned at the end of the French regime.   There is no "French life" to describe, except at La Baye.

In the period before 1698 the center of the group on the Lower Fox was at De Pere.   After the fort was built at La Baye in 1717, this became the heart of the community.   Even the Jesuit priest moved into the shelter of the fort.   The people in the little community were of two classes.   The military commandant was highest in the social scale, and with him might be grouped the other officers and some educated businessmen connected with the fur trade.   This group often contained men from the Canadian nobility, seigneurs who were landowners and born to a military career.   The other class was made up of typical French-Canadian peasants or *habitants,* drawn a few generations earlier chiefly from Normandy.   Its stock furnished most of the settlers in the Illinois country, as well as the hired men (*engagés*) needed in the fur trade.   On the whole this group, which made up the majority of the population, was disinclined to change.   Its members preserved their loyalty to the Roman Catholic church, and observed its festivals with proper feasting.   At La Baye after 1728 there was no priest, the nearest one being at Mackinac, 240 miles away; to Mackinac they went for marriages and christenings.   In some cases a man brought a family, and the ecclesiastical marriage and the christening of several children occurred on the same day. These people were also loyal to those above them, and apparently the frontier did not work in them the change it did in the Anglo-Saxon people and make them believe in equality and self-government.   At La Baye the commandant was the judge, and he ruled as an autocrat alike over residents, visiting traders, and Indians. In a community where there was no priest, and where most of the adults were illiterate, education was difficult to obtain.   Children might be sent to Canada to school, or a tutor might be brought in by those who could afford one.

Agriculture began and slowly grew as an adjunct to the fur trade.   Food was produced for local use and not for export, as it was in the Illinois country.   The garden and the orchard were relatively more important than they frequently are with farmers today. Plowing was done with a rather heavy home-made wooden plow shod with iron by the local blacksmith. It was often drawn by six bulls. As late as 1831, the land under cultivation was only about twenty-five hundred acres. Following a Canadian custom the farms were long and narrow, with the end on the river, the common highway. The cattle were small but hardy, and had come either from Canada or Detroit. Horses were numerous, and so were hogs, which ran wild.

The building materials, whether for dwellings, storehouses, or forts, were drawn from the neighboring forests. As a result, the danger from fires was constant; fires ravaged La Baye in 1746 and again in 1756. When an *habitant* built a log cabin, he usually set the logs upright in the ground. Some of the better houses, however, erected towards the end of the century, were built of squared logs laid horizontally. For clothing the lower classes used deerskin a good deal, though they used trade cloth too. There was no weaving in the French community. The well-to-do could import fancy cloths from Europe by way of Montreal.

These French-speaking people were but a tiny oasis in a desert of savagery, and their relations with the surrounding Indians were constantly present in their minds. To begin with, they had certain responsibilities towards the Indians. The Indians had given up the arts and crafts by which they had made their livelihood in the stone age in which the white men found them, and were absolutely dependent on the white men for a continuous supply of knives, kettles, and, above all, guns. The Indians did not learn to make gunpowder or to repair their guns. When something was in need of repair or adjustment, the Indians took it to the blacksmith at the post. For the most part the French at La Baye got on peaceably with the Indians. The tribe of which they saw most was the Menominee, who had a village close at hand. But Indians came from a wide area to get supplies and the services of the blacksmith. After the posts on the Mississippi were discontinued, even the Sioux came to Green Bay. On one occasion, in 1758, the Menominee, angered by dishonesty to which the commandant was a party, fell upon the French and murdered eleven men before they could be calmed; but this was the only outbreak of the sort in the history of the post.

The French Yield to the English

On battlefields far from Wisconsin and by treaty-makers in Europe it was decided that Wisconsin was not to continue as a part of French Canada. The period from 1689 to 1763 was marked in Europe by a series of four conflicts between England and France, and each had its counterpart on the North American continent. We have seen how Duluth and Perrot took Indians eastward to participate in the first of these struggles. All the while and with growing intensity there was an accompanying commercial and diplomatic struggle in which the prize was the control of the fur trade of the West. The French built a number of forts in the latter part of this period. Some of them, like La Baye (1717) and La Pointe on Chequamegon Bay (1718) were merely to keep the Indian tribes and the traders in order; others, like Ouiatanon on the upper Wabash (1720), Niagara (1726), and Vincennes (1731), faced toward the English invasion. Throughout this period, also, there was a movement of Indian tribes eastward and southward, of which we saw the beginning in the time of La Salle. The Miami were moving into western Ohio, giving their name first to the Maumee and then to the Miami rivers. The Mascouten were now on the Upper Wabash. Most of the Kickapoo were in northern and eastern Illinois, and the greater part of the Potawatomi were along the southern shore of Lake Michigan from about Chicago to the St. Joseph River. The southward movement of the Sauk and Fox has already been mentioned. Thus many tribes that had been in Wisconsin in the days of the great missionaries were there no longer.

Englishmen from Virginia had reached waters flowing into the Ohio by 1670, but it was only after 1740 that traders and land speculators from Pennsylvania and Virginia began a westward advance that alarmed the French. In 1744 the Iroquois acknowledged the English as the overlords of all land north of the Ohio, and four years later the Miami made an alliance with the British. The Miami were then founding a new village called Pickawillany, near the present town of Piqua, Ohio, and sometimes fifty British traders were to be found there. In 1749 the governor of Canada sent an able officer named Céloron de Blainville down the Ohio River to persuade the Indians to return to their allegiance, but he accomplished little beyond burying some lead plates stating the French claims. French prestige was clearly waning.

Then, in 1752, the French hold on the deserting tribes was restored by an act as bold as it was unexpected. A French-Canadian merchant at Mackinac named Augustin de Langlade had married a half-breed Ottawa woman; their son, Charles de Langlade, now 23, led a party of Ottawa Indians by way of Detroit into the Miami village of Pickawillany and completely destroyed it. Booty worth three thousand pounds was taken, and the Miami chieftain who had led the desertion to the British was killed and eaten. At one stroke, French control of the west was restored—to last until French forts fell during the latter part of the French and Indian War.

Shortly after this, the Seven Years' War in Europe (1756-1763) took place in which England was allied with Prussia while Prussia was beset by Russia, France, and Austria. In North America the rivalry between France and England led on to war two years before the declaration of hostilities in Europe. The steps that each side took were characteristic. The English were bent on securing good farm lands. The French built forts the better to secure control of the fur trade country. A number of gentlemen, mostly Virginians, with some English financial supporters, organized the Ohio Land Company, and secured a grant from the English Government. After proper spying out of the land, a fort was begun by Captain William Trent at the forks of the Ohio in January, 1754. Meanwhile, in 1753, the

French had built two forts, Presqu'isle where Erie, Pennsylvania, now is, and Fort Le Boeuf, on a tributary of the Allegheny River. Then, in April, 1754, they took possession of the forks of the Ohio, sent Captain Trent home to Virginia, completed the fort he had begun, and renamed it Fort Duquesne. The issue was now fairly joined.

The details of the war belong rather to the general history of the United States than to Wisconsin history. The year 1755 is best known for the defeat and death of the English general, Edward Braddock, who was ambushed eight miles from Fort Duquesne. During this and the two succeeding years the French successfully resisted the English and the English colonials. In 1758, however, the tide turned. In July the English took Louisburg, the great fortress on Cape Breton Island. General Wolfe, ably assisted by Admiral Saunders, took Quebec in September, 1759, and both Montcalm and Wolfe were killed. General Amherst took Ticonderoga and Crown Point that summer, and held French troops at Montreal that might otherwise have been used at Quebec. At Niagara Sir William Johnson defeated a force of savages and Frenchmen from the West, capturing Fort Niagara. Fort Pitt was built on the site of Fort Duquesne. In 1760 English armies closed in on Montreal. The inevitable surrender took place September 8, 1760.

Many Frenchmen who had served their king at the western posts had leading parts in the decisive struggle in the east. It was the elder Marin who was called from La Baye to build Forts Presqu'isle and Le Boeuf in 1753. Marin died at Fort Le Boeuf in October of that year. The most active of the westerners was Charles de Langlade, the victor of Pickawillany. Year after year he brought his contingent of western Indians to aid the French. He prepared the ambush that led to the famous defeat of Braddock. Langlade and his Indians were present at Quebec from July to September, 1759. Again, for the last time, Langlade brought his Indians to Montreal in 1760. A few days before the end the Governor of Canada sent them home. After the surrender of Montreal in September, 1760, the British proceeded to occupy the French posts in the West. On November 29, the French commander at Detroit surrendered to the English under Major Robert Rogers.

It was Charles de Langlade who brought to Mackinac in the autumn of 1760 the news that the English would soon be masters in the West. The French commandant, rather than surrender, set out with all his soldiers for the Illinois country, crossing to the Mississippi by the Fox and Wisconsin Rivers. En route he was joined by Robert Couterot, French commander at La Baye. Thus at the close of the year, the last French officers and soldiers left Wisconsin. During the next summer, that of 1761, British soldiers were sent from Detroit to Mackinac, and from there to La Baye. Fort Chartres in the Illinois country, "regarded as the most commodious and best-built fortification in America," still remained in French hands. Pontiac's rising caused delay; but finally, on October 10, 1765, the British took possession of Fort Chartres and became masters of the Illinois country. This marked the end of the French regime in the whole of continental North America.

SELECTED BIBLIOGRAPHY

Louise Phelps Kellogg has written the master work on the French period in *The French Régime in Wisconsin and the Northwest* (Madison, 1925). Its footnotes provide the best guide to the sources and to much modern literature. Reuben G. Thwaites in *Wisconsin* (American Commonwealth Series, Boston, 1908), pp. 1-124, gives an attractive account of the same period. Other narratives of the French period are: *Wisconsin in Three Centuries,* Henry Colin Campbell, secretary of the board of editors and writers (4 vols., New York, 1906), Vol. I; and Milo M. Quaife, *Wisconsin, Its History and Its People* (4 vols., Chicago, 1924), Vol. I, pp. 53-223. An excellent survey of the French occupation of the upper Mississippi Valley is Clarence W. Alvord, *The Illinois Country, 1673-1818* (Springfield, 1920, Centennial History of Illinois, Vol. I). Francis Parkman (1823-1891) wrote the history of the struggle between the French and the English in North America in eleven volumes that still delight by their style. Those that touch the upper Mississippi Valley and Wisconsin are: *The Jesuits in North America* (Boston, 1892), and *LaSalle and the Discovery of the Great West* (Boston, 1892).

To understand the French period of Wisconsin one should be familiar with the history of the French in the St. Lawrence Valley. This may be read in George M. Wrong, *The Rise and Fall of New France* (2 vols., New York, 1928); or in the first two volumes of *Canada and Its Provinces,* Adam Shortt and Arthur G. Doughty, general editors (23 vols., Toronto, 1913). Reuben G. Thwaites provides a briefer summary in *France in America* (New York, 1905, American Nation Series, Vol. VII).

There is a vast assemblage of source material on the French in North America in *Jesuit Relations and Allied Documents,* edited by Reuben G. Thwaites (73 vols., Cleveland, 1896-1901). The original language, usually French, and the English translation are on facing pages. From this collection Edna Kenton has edited two overlapping works, all in English: *Jesuit Relations and Allied Documents* (New York, 1925), and *The Indians of North America* (2 vols., New York, 1927). Louise P. Kellogg has translated and edited accounts of voyages, most of them touching Wisconsin, *Early Narratives of the Northwest, 1634-1699* (Boston, 1917, Original Narratives of Early American History, Vol. XVIII). In the *Collections of the State Historical Society of Wisconsin* are documents from the French period in translation, particularly Vol. XVI for the years 1634-1727, Vol. XVII for 1727-1748, and Vol. XVIII, pp. 1-222, for 1743-1760. This material was edited, 1902-1908, by Reuben G. Thwaites. Other source material, all translated, is found in the following: *Journeys of René Robert Cavalier, sieur de La Salle,* edited by Isaac J. Cox (2 vols., New York, 1922); Louis Armand de Lom d'Arce, Baron de Lahontan, *New Voyages in North America,* edited by Reuben G. Thwaites (2 vols., Chicago, 1905); *Hennepin's New Discovery,* edited by Reuben G. Thwaites (Chicago, 1903); and *The Indian Tribes of the Upper Mississippi Valley and the Region of the Great Lakes as Described by Nicolas Perrot . . . *[and others], edited by Emma Helen Blair (2 vols., Cleveland, 1912). There is a biographical sketch of Perrot in Vol. II, pp. 249-256.

Narrative accounts of the last phase of the struggle between the French and the English, besides those found in books already mentioned, are the later volumes by Francis Parkman, *A Half Century of Conflict* (2 vols., Boston, 1892) and *Montcalm and Wolfe* (2 vols., Boston, 1892); and George M. Wrong, *The Conquest of New France* (New Haven, 1918, Chronicles of America Series, Vol. X).

CHAPTER III

THE BRITISH PERIOD

THE CONSPIRACY OF PONTIAC AND THE ESTABLISHMENT OF BRITISH POWER IN THE WEST

THE French and Indian War was ended by the preliminary articles of peace of November 3, 1762, and the final Peace of Paris of February 10, 1763. All lands on the mainland of North America east of the Mississippi River now belonged to the British Empire, while west of the Mississippi sovereignty rested with the Spanish. Before peace had been concluded, British soldiers were in the Northwest. Lieutenant William Leslye with twenty-eight men took charge at Mackinac, while at La Baye was stationed Ensign James Gorrell, with one sergeant, one corporal, fifteen privates, and a French interpreter. He was there from October 12, 1761, to June 21, 1763. During that period he was promoted Lieutenant. The old fort was rebuilt and called Fort Edward Augustus, in honor of a brother of George III. Gorrell's principal duty was to gain and hold the good will of the Indians. They came and went in considerable numbers, and Gorrell gave them what presents he could from his scanty stores, made speeches, and was generous with promises. He estimated that thirty-nine thousand Indians were dependent for supplies on the traders going out from that post.

The British had almost immediately to deal with the conspiracy of Pontiac, one of the most striking episodes in the history of the American Indians. Pontiac was a member of the Ottawa tribe which lived around the Straits of Mackinac and along the northern

38

shore of Lake Huron. He had conceived the idea of making an end of all white men on the continent, and his message met with favor from most of the tribes between the Alleghenies and the Mississippi, and between the Great Lakes and the Ohio River. One notable group that did not follow him was, as we shall see, the tribes of eastern and central Wisconsin. At an appointed time in May, 1763, the Indians were to fall upon the white men everywhere. Several of the less important posts fell at once and the garrisons were massacred. Detroit was besieged from May to November, a thousand braves took part in the operations, and Pontiac was there to direct, but in spite of great superiority in numbers, the Indians could not take Detroit. Fort Pitt and Fort Niagara also successfully withstood Indian attacks, and failure at these three points practically decided the war.

At Mackinac the blow fell on June 2. There were both Chippewa and Ottawa about the fort, but curiously enough, in spite of the fact that the great Pontiac was an Ottawa, on this occasion the Ottawa stood by and did nothing while the Chippewa attacked the post and killed more than half the garrison. Then the Ottawa seized the two officers, Major Etherington and Leslye, now a captain, and eleven privates, and paddled off with them to L'Arbre Croche, a point on the northern shore of Little Traverse Bay some fifty miles southwest. From this point, Etherington summoned Gorrell to join him with all his soldiers and the traders then at La Baye. Gorrell laid the situation before the Indians in the vicinity, and as he traveled eastward, he was escorted by ninety men of the "Four Nations," as he put it, Menominee, Sauk, Fox, and Winnebago. All were ready to fight for the British. Gorrell and his men rescued Etherington and his fellow prisoners, and the Europeans reached Montreal in safety. Thus ended the British military occupation of Wisconsin.

When the attacks on the greater forts failed in 1763, the rising of Pontiac lost most of its vigor. In 1764 two British military expeditions were sent over the Alleghenies, one into Ohio and the other along the lower Lakes and on to Detroit. In 1765 a

Pennsylvania trader named George Crogan, who was very success-ful in dealing with the Indians, held a council at Ouiatanon on the Wabash at which Pontiac made his submission to the British power. Later on in that summer Crogan held another council at Detroit and cemented peace with all the western tribes. In June, 1769, Pontiac was killed at Cahokia by an Illinois Indian.

It was now the duty of the British government to formulate and put into execution a policy for the control and development of the West. Should that West be administered for the benefit of the Indians, or of the Englishmen and colonials wishing to perpetuate the Indian trade, or of the white men who wanted farm lands? During the summer of 1763, the Board of Trade was maturing a plan according to which it intended, among other things, to survey a line between settlers' land and Indians' land, and temporarily to hold back the settlers. News of Pontiac's rising emphasized the grievances of the Indians. Some-what hastily and with several changes, the partially prepared plan was published as the Proclamation of October 7, 1763. Quebec, East Florida, and West Florida were named as new colonies, their boundaries were defined, and in them some features of English government were ultimately to be established. At the west of the Atlantic colonies, to keep the settlers out of the Indian lands, the most obvious physical feature was indicated as a boundary—the watershed between rivers flowing into the Atlantic and those flowing into the interior. Lands west of that line and not included in the new colonies were reserved for the use of the Indians, and all purchases of land there were forbidden. Squatters were "forthwith to remove themselves." Trading with the Indians was permitted to those who secured licenses from colonial governments. The boundaries of Quebec province nowhere fell within the present United States, and thus the French settlements in Wisconsin and Illinois were severed from the mother colony on the St. Lawrence. They were in the area reserved for the Indians. No civil government was provided for the French communities in the West, no provision made for the punishment of crime. Wisconsin was left, therefore, by the first British ordinance relating to it, a land without governance, except such as the military officers at Mackinac might exercise.

The Proclamation of 1763 remained the law of the West for eleven years, until it was superseded by the Quebec Act on the very eve of the Revolution. There were still, as there had been since 1756, two superintendents of Indian affairs appointed by imperial authority; but the making of regulations and all supervision of traders were in 1768 given over to the several colonies; this meant discordant regulations and virtually no control. In the eastern end of the Ohio Valley farm makers continued to encroach on Indian lands, contrary to the proclamation. There were also many projects for the development of definite regions of the West promoted by capitalists and speculators. Three or four of these projects, which never advanced beyond paper sketches, included parts of what is now Wisconsin, but none led to settlement there. A certain William Murray, in the West as the agent of a well-known Philadelphia trading firm, in 1773 bought two tracts of land from the Illinois Indians in open disregard of the proclamation.

The prime purpose of the Quebec Act, which was the next measure for the control of the West, was to remedy certain wrongs suffered by the French population in Canada; particularly, it guaranteed to them French law in civil cases and gave legal standing to the Roman Catholic church in Canada. The opportunity was seized to put at least a part of the West under definite government. The boundary of Quebec was extended southward and westward to the Ohio and the Mississippi, and the governor of Canada was to have power throughout this area. Frontiersmen and fur traders, who had rather a bad reputation in England, would be controlled. Such open flouting of the law as Murray's Illinois purchase would be impossible. Settlement was still prohibited between the Ohio River and the Great Lakes. The act was a "last effort of the mother country to throw the protection of imperial power over at least a part of the Mississippi Valley." Thus was Wisconsin again brought within the orbit of a government seated at Quebec. Pursuant to the act, plans were laid for dividing up the Indian country within the new boundaries of the province into four areas and establishing civil officers and courts in each one. The outbreak of the Revolutionary War, however, made it impossible to do more than begin the execution of these designs.

JONATHAN CARVER

In 1766 and 1767 a New Englander named Jonathan Carver made a voyage which resulted in the first description of Wisconsin in the English language, and the book which he wrote came to be "the best known book by an American author in the eighteenth century." From August, 1766, for about a year and a half, the commander of the British forces at Mackinac was Major Robert Rogers. During the French and Indian War he had attained considerable renown as a commander of irregular troops known as Rogers' Rangers. It was he who had received the surrender of Detroit and other posts in the West in the winter of 1760-1761, and two years later he was again at Detroit helping to quell Pontiac's rising. In 1765 he was in London, where he was quite a social lion. For some time he had been interested in finding a water route to the Pacific. He laid before the Board of Trade a detailed project for finding a northwest passage in the interior of North America. Responsible men in the colonies like Sir William Johnson and General Gage doubted both his ability and his integrity, but influential friends in England got him the appointment to Mackinac, and he returned to America apparently believing that his great project had the approval of the English government. If it was impossible for Rogers to explore the far Northwest, he could at least send others.

Early in September, 1766, Captain Jonathan Carver appeared at Mackinac. He had a record of service in the French and Indian War, and he had some experience and skill as a map-

maker. On his way out from England, Rogers had arranged for
Carver to come west. Now at Rogers' behest Carver went out
to the Mississippi by the Fox-Wisconsin route and then turned
northward. That winter he lived among the Sioux of Minnesota. In the spring of 1767 he went down to Prairie du Chien
and there met Captain James Tute, another New Englander,
also in the employ of Rogers, who brought orders that revealed
in full what Rogers planned for them. They were to cross the
continent, and if possible reach the Pacific by the river "Ouragan,"
or some other waterway. Tute was in charge, and a trader named
Goddard was second; Carver found himself but third in command. The guides secured at Prairie du Chien were afraid of
the Sioux about the upper Mississippi and so the party went up
the Chippewa River and finally reached Lake Superior. It had
been arranged that they should receive food and the necessary
presents for the Indians on Pigeon River near the western end
of Lake Superior, but instead Rogers sent word that he was
unable to send supplies. They therefore gave up any attempt
to go further northwest and returned eastward along the northern
shore of Lake Superior, eventually to Mackinac. It was too late
in the year to go on to New England, and so Carver stayed at
Mackinac until the spring of 1768. During that winter a quarrel
arose between Major Rogers and others at the fort, and Rogers
was accused of treason and arrested. He was taken to Montreal
in irons, was tried there, and was ultimately cleared of all
charges. But his reputation, which was not unblemished before
this, was sadly damaged. Carver in 1778 published the account
of his experiences in the West; perhaps because of Rogers' waning
prestige he left him out of the story altogether, and appeared
himself merely as a gentleman who traveled for pleasure, and
for the advancement of knowledge. He took to himself a good
deal of credit that rightly belonged to Rogers.

Descriptions of the Northwest had been written by the French
authors, Hennepin, Lahontan, and Charlevoix. These had
appeared in English translation, but by Carver's time they were

out-of-date and largely unknown. Carver's book, *Travels in the Interior Parts of North America,* appeared in London in 1778 just in time to satisfy a great and general curiosity. It ran through many editions and was translated into several continental languages. As we read the book today, we find a vivid picture of Wisconsin in 1766. From all the Indian tribes he received "the most hospitable and courteous treatment." The name "La Bay," as he spells it, was just giving way to Green Bay, because in the spring of the year travelers were wont to come down from Mackinac, from a region still in winter gray, and find the landscape robed in green. Within the old fort on the west side of the river a few families were living. On the opposite side were some French settlers "who cultivate the land and appear to live very comfortably." Where Neenah and Menasha now stand was a "Great Town of the Winnebagoes." Their ruler was a queen, "a very ancient woman, small in stature," who was very much pleased at Carver's attentions. Her name, Glory of the Morning, Carver does not give. The portage between the Fox and the Wisconsin was partly a morass and partly a "plane with some few oaks and pine trees growing thereon." On the lower Wisconsin he visited the well-built town of the Saukies (Sauk), where Sauk City is today, and two villages of the "Ottigaumies" (Foxes). At Prairie du Chien there was an Indian community of three hundred families, a neutral trading mart to which furs were brought by many tribes from far and near. Carver traveled with two traders bound for the Mississippi, and some of his pseudo-history may be derived from them; but he gives much keen first-hand observation. The second part of his book is devoted to the manner of life of the Indians, and is largely plagiarized from Hennepin and others. Besides the published *Travels,* there are still extant, in the British Museum, diaries written by Carver on his journey and a narrative composed almost immediately thereafter. The *Travels* were apparently composed some years later without access to the diaries and the earlier narrative.

Historians may therefore check the *Travels,* which are not always accurate in detail, by the diaries, and glean from them further particulars of what Carver actually saw in Wisconsin.

One of the most curious bits of history connected with Carver developed after his death in London in 1780. In his *Travels* he mentioned a council of the Sioux Indians held in a cave within the present limits of St. Paul, Minnesota. In 1781 a third edition of the book was arranged by a distinguished physician of London, Dr. Lettsom, to help Carver's English widow, who was almost penniless. To this edition Dr. Lettsom prefixed a sketch of Carver's life, and in the course of it printed a deed purporting to have been signed by two Sioux chiefs at the council in the cave near the Mississippi. This document transferred to Carver about ten thousand square miles of land, almost all of it in Wisconsin, though it included also the site of St. Paul. Dr. Lettsom stated that the original was then in his possession, but a few years later it had disappeared. If the deed was actually drawn up and signed, the conveyance could not be upheld by any British court. Yet the claims based upon it had a long history. Carver's heirs—he left a wife and seven children in New England, and a wife and two children in London—sold their rights to various persons. Appeals were made to the British and American governments, but all efforts to get the "grant" validated came to naught. Yet often during the nineteenth century, gullible persons parted with their money to secure a share in the Carver claims.

THE REVOLUTIONARY WAR AND THE WEST

The Revolutionary War and the establishment of American independence were events full of moment, not only for the original thirteen states but for all those created later. Wisconsin's status today results not alone from what men have done within her borders, but also from what they wrought and endured everywhere to establish the new nation. To write the history of one state is to tear a seamless web and to select arbitrarily such parts of the nation's history as seem to have the most interest for the inhabitants of that state.

At the time of the War of American Independence the population of Wisconsin consisted almost entirely of Indian tribes, and the region was connected with the East only by traders who came out with their supplies and returned eastward, mostly to Mackinac and Montreal, with their peltries. British power and the majesty of the law were represented by the ranking officer or official at Mackinac. From 1774 to 1779 this was Captain De Peyster, and after that one who was technically a civil official, Lieutenant-Governor Patrick Sinclair. At Detroit also there was a succession of two during the war years, Lieutenant-Governor Henry Hamilton to 1779, and Captain De Peyster thereafter. From 1772 to 1776 there were a captain and a few British soldiers at Kaskaskia in Illinois. There were no British soldiers stationed in Wisconsin after Gorrell's departure in 1763.

As the Revolutionary War began, the line of contact between Indians and English-speaking farmers lay through western Pennsylvania and along the Ohio River in what is now West Virginia and Kentucky. Cornstalk, the great Shawnee chieftain, had been convinced of the strength of the whites by his defeat at the hands of the frontiersmen at Point Pleasant in October, 1774. The following year, at a great concourse of Indians at Fort Pitt, many tribes made treaties of friendship with the revolting colonists. For the next two years the Indians in the Ohio Valley remained in uneasy neutrality.

In the Wisconsin area the fur trade continued at first much as in peace time. De Peyster at Mackinac raised Charles de Langlade to the rank of Captain in the British Indian service and invited him to lead Indians eastward as he had done in the French and Indian War. He took one band eastward in 1776, chiefly Chippewa and Ottawa, but they did not actually engage in fighting that year. In the following summer he led another band to Quebec and they were sent on to Lake Champlain to aid General Burgoyne. The worthy general urged them to fight humanely. An American woman was murdered and scalped, Burgoyne tried to tighten up discipline over the Indians, and most of them went home. By the spring of 1778 it was becoming more difficult to persuade Wisconsin Indians to undertake these long journeys, partly because those who had gone in previous years were poorer thereby, and partly because they were listening to American and Spanish agents. One of the British agents most active in this work was Charles Gautier de Verville, a nephew of Langlade. By dint of months of travel among the Indians of Wisconsin and eastern Minnesota, he gathered at Green Bay for the eastern expedition of 1778 some 210 warriors, half of them Winnebago, who made part of the 550 that Langlade led east that summer.

The quiet that marked the upper Ohio in the early years of the Revolution gave way to active warfare in 1777. In the spring of that year Cornstalk and his son were murdered in cold blood at the American Fort Randolph, where he had gone with a friendly warning. After that the Shawnee and most tribes of the vicinity were implacable enemies of the Americans. Furthermore, Henry Hamilton at Detroit had asked and received permission from Canada to organize parties of Indians to attack the American frontier. The warfare thus begun continued until almost the end of 1782. The aim of the British and their Indian allies was to destroy the new settlements in Kentucky and West Virginia and to push back the frontier everywhere, while the Americans sought to capture Detroit. For lack of adequate resources neither side was successful. The Americans struck into the Indian country from Pittsburgh and from Kentucky, and on the whole the efforts originating in Kentucky were more effective.

Throughout the period of the war, the population in Kentucky continued to increase, and in 1776 the Virginia legislature established Kentucky County. Its militia was under the command of Major George Rogers Clark, who did more than any other one man for the American cause in the West. In the autumn of 1777 he went to Virginia and obtained authorization, supplies, and some men. On his return to Louisville he was joined by a few men from eastern Tennessee and some Kentuckians. He went down the Ohio beyond the mouth of the Tennessee River, and then, with his 175 soldiers, he struck across southern Illinois. On July 4, 1778, he took Kaskaskia. The other French-speaking villages in the vicinity soon fell into his hands. The *habitants* sent a delegation headed by their priest, Father Gibault, to Vincennes on the Wabash which persuaded the French there to go over to the side of the Americans. Lieutenant-Governor Hamilton came down from Detroit with a force of five hundred men, most of them Indians, and recaptured Vincennes. It was now December, and Hamilton sent away the Indians and all but ninety of the white soldiers and sat down to pass the rest of the winter at Vincennes, intending to move on to the Illinois country in the spring. Clark did not wait for the British attack. With 172 men he crossed the flooded plains of southern Illinois in February weather, and retook Vincennes. Clark's biographer writes: "Courage born of desperation was manifested by men and leaders alike, for all were fully conscious that failure would mean the loss, not alone of the Illinois country, but also of Kentucky." [1] The rest of the war in the West showed a stalemate. Clark, who from 1780 made his headquarters at Louisville, kept hoping that he would be able to take Detroit, but with the resources at his command that was impossible. On the other hand the British could not recover Vincennes and the Illinois country.

During the latter part of the war, the Indians of Wisconsin were frequently incited to participate in it, but the resulting action was not important. When George Rogers Clark had captured the French villages in Illinois, he summoned a great assembly of Indians to meet at Cahokia in August, 1778, and there he explained the American cause and offered an alliance. Many tribes from Wisconsin and the region of the upper Mississippi

---

[1] James A. James, *George Rogers Clark* (Chicago, 1928), p. 145.

were present and accepted the proffered alliance. At Milwaukee in those years there was a mixed village of Chippewa, Ottawa, and Potawatomi. The chief of this village, Blackbird, or in Indian, Siggenauk, had a private conference with Clark, and adhered to the American side. Apparently from this time forward, the Indians of southern Wisconsin were at heart pro-American.

For the spring of 1779 the British had planned that three forces should converge on the American headquarters established by George Rogers Clark at Kaskaskia. Hamilton would cross from Vincennes, Langlade would come from Green Bay by way of Lake Michigan and the Illinois River, and Gautier would lead southward the Indians of the upper Mississippi. The capture of Hamilton, February 25, 1779, made it impossible to carry out these plans. Langlade got as far south as Milwaukee, but he found the tribes there neutral or anti-British, and his own followers would go no further. Gautier led about two hundred warriors down the Mississippi to the mouth of the Rock River. He found the Sauk Indians there intractable, pro-American, and consequently insolent to him; he could only retire.

Louisiana had been a Spanish possession since 1763, and from the beginning of the Revolutionary War the Spanish officials at New Orleans and St. Louis had helped the Americans in every way that neutrals could. In June, 1779, Spain declared war on Great Britain. The English decided to strike at once, and for the year 1780 they planned a concerted effort to gain the Mississippi Valley. From the Americans they would take the French villages in Illinois; from the Spanish, St. Louis and other near-by posts. Indians were gathered at Prairie du Chien for the descent of the Mississippi. From the upper Mississippi and from almost all Wisconsin they came, until they numbered twelve hundred men and represented a dozen tribes. Economic distress even compelled some, like the Sauks and the Foxes, whose real preference was for the American cause, to join halfheartedly in their traders' enterprise. The Spanish commander in upper

Louisiana prepared to defend St. Louis, erecting a blockhouse with cannon. George Rogers Clark arrived to aid in the defense. On May 26, 1780, the assault was made. The cannon were not to the liking of the Indians, and the attacking army speedily lost heart and became a retreating mob. Clark sent 350 men in pursuit, but they soon had to desist for want of provisions.

Blackbird of Milwaukee, true to the alliance made with Clark two years before, mobilized to aid the Americans, but seems not to have accomplished much. During the ensuing winter, however, Blackbird urged upon the Spanish governor at St. Louis an expedition against the British post at St. Joseph (Niles, Michigan). The governor accepted the plan, and the attacking force was made up of Spaniards, Illinois Frenchmen, and Indians from Milwaukee. As a consequence British stores were seized and the Spanish flag flew over a corner of Michigan for twenty-four hours.

The last years of the Revolution were marked by many raids against the frontier and forays into the Indian country, but these were almost all in Ohio and Kentucky. In and near Wisconsin, both sides confined themselves to diplomacy with the Indian tribes. In these activities the Americans and the Spaniards seemed to be gaining at the expense of the British.

The fate of Wisconsin was determined not on its own soil but in military campaigns fought chiefly east of the Alleghenies. When John Jay and John Adams went to Paris, there to join with Benjamin Franklin in making peace, the fate of the West was again in the balance. If France and Spain had had their wish, the new nation would have been limited by the Alleghenies. But the American commissioners broke with their French friends and insisted that the United States should extend westward to the Mississippi. Commercial interests in England were looking forward to trade with the United States, and wished to conciliate the new nation, and so England conceded the western country. To the north, the most natural physical feature, the line of the Great Lakes, was chosen as the boundary. Thus, by the treaty

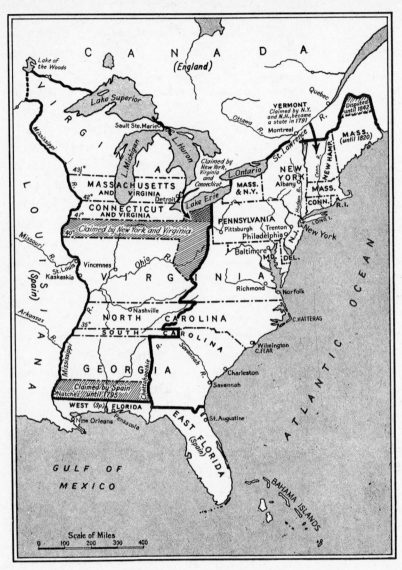

THE UNITED STATES BY THE TREATIES OF 1783*

* From Wilson P. Shortridge, *The Development of the United States*. By permission of The Macmillan Company, publishers.

signed September 2, 1783, Wisconsin was included within the United States.

The Fur Trade from 1763 to 1812

Wisconsin's only important export throughout the British period and for a long time afterwards was furs. As the outcome of the French and Indian War became apparent, three groups of traders were ready to compete for the western trade, the French and Spanish from beyond the Mississippi, the English from the Atlantic seaboard, and the Canadians.

During and after the war which ended in 1763, many French from Canada, from the Illinois country, and from New Orleans took up their abode on Spanish soil on the west bank of the Mississippi, and from that vantage ground traded not only up the Missouri, which was now in Spanish territory, but throughout northern Illinois and in most of what is now Wisconsin, even coming into the valley of the Fox River. St. Louis was founded in 1764 mainly for this trade. All the furs bought by this French-Spanish group of traders were sent down the Mississippi to New Orleans. It was estimated in 1771 that peltries worth between seventy-five and one hundred thousand pounds sterling were exported annually from that port, chiefly to France. Even Englishmen engaged in the fur trade in the West found better prices in New Orleans than at Montreal. Louisiana was delivered to the United States in 1804, and after that, American capital came to be invested in the St. Louis enterprises. By that time, however, we hear less of this group in the upper Mississippi Valley and in Wisconsin.

English from the Atlantic seaboard did not have much success in the West unless they came westward by way of Mackinac and combined with the traders and *voyageurs* of the French regime. Some Philadelphia merchants made a great effort to establish trade with the French settlements in the Illinois country along the Mississippi River, and hoped to make this region the base for a large Indian trade. They used land transport to Pittsburgh, built new boats for each trip down the Ohio, and could scarcely compete with the traders whose goods came largely by water. Trade by this Ohio River route survived to supply not the Indians directly, but the French. The traders across the Mississippi used Philadelphia goods in their trade with the Indians.

Throughout the British period as before, however, Montreal continued to attract the largest part of the furs gathered in Wisconsin and in the regions beyond it to the west and north. The Montreal capitalists had a great advantage in the quality of their servants in the field. There were hundreds of hardy men, many of them half-breeds, all speaking French and most of them Indian languages as well, who had grown up in the trade and possessed an intimate knowledge of the West. When financial assistance and executive direction still came to them from Montreal, they continued to ply the trade with the Indians with skill and vigor. The chief new feature in the situation was the entrance of many British, mostly Scotch, into its management. The new connection with England was a great help to the trade in one way, for the quality and cheapness of English goods were well known, even to the Indians. As we have seen, the Proclamation of 1763 required traders to secure licenses and to obey regulations. The first rules, issued in 1765, attempted to keep the traders near the garrisoned forts and forbade the granting of credit to Indians, but these features proved to be impracticable, and within a few years the trade was allowed to return to its familiar methods.

At the beginning of this period Wisconsin was the best territory in the West, and the English-speaking traders made haste to seize their opportunity. When James Gorrell came to his post at Green Bay in 1761, two traders came with him. Alexander Henry arrived at Sault Ste. Marie in 1762. Mackinac suffered massacre in 1763, but two years later it was swarming with traders. This early trade was in the hands of men of small means, most of them with one or very few canoes. Alexander Henry took four canoes of goods to La Pointe in 1765. Peter Pond and a partner in 1773 had their trade goods sent out from New York to Mackinac. There they loaded twelve canoes for different parts of the Mississippi River, each in charge of a clerk. The

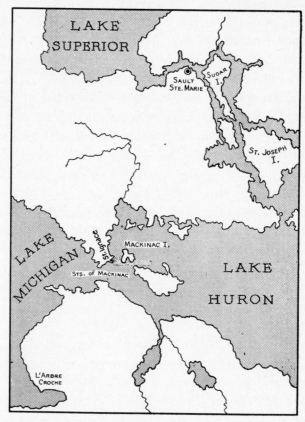

MACKINAC AND VICINITY

Revolutionary War made surprisingly little impress upon the trade.

As time passed, the beaver became less plentiful in Wisconsin and there was better trade north and west of Lake Superior. As the distances to be traversed increased, traders and their financial backers in Montreal tended to draw together in large groups, thus to avoid ruinous competition. Beyond Lake

Superior, after 1775, there was coöperation in enterprise, such as scouting out new territory, and by 1787 this group had become the Northwest Company, the "Nor'westers," as they were called. This company had a great history and grew until its enterprises touched the Pacific Ocean. It was the chief rival of the Hudson's Bay Company until the two united in 1821. The Northwest Company did much trading in northern Wisconsin for about twenty years, sometimes becoming involved in bitter rivalry with local individuals or firms to the south of it. These small concerns often tried to combine, but none of the combinations was large or permanent. There was, for example, an organization built up by an able red-headed Scot named Robert Dickson. He first went out to the upper Mississippi in 1786 from Mackinac, distributing the king's presents to the Indians at many points on the way, including Green Bay and Prairie du Chien. A few years later he was organizing a small partnership to eliminate competition. Among the partners were the leading traders of the Green Bay region, Jacques Porlier, John Lawe, Jacob Franks, and the Grignons, as well as Joseph Rolette and Thomas G. Anderson of Prairie du Chien. These men and others like them competed with the Northwest Company in many parts of Wisconsin, and competition ate up profits.

In 1806 the Michilimackinac Company was formed; its leaders were Montreal capitalists, but an attempt was made to include all responsible traders south of Lake Superior. A friendly division of territory was made with the Northwest Company, and all of Wisconsin except a small bit in the extreme northwest was allotted to the new concern. For various reasons—the increasing scarcity of beaver in these southern regions, the necessity of paying duty on trade goods, and the unfriendliness and even the competition of the United States government—this new concern did not prosper, and by 1810 it went out of existence.

Changes in the methods of the trade were few and were mostly due to the increasing distances that had to be traveled. Transportation between Mackinac and Montreal deserted the

Ottawa River route, favored for a hundred years, to go by way of Lake Erie and Huron. Here great sloops and schooners up to seventy tons could be used. The *voyageurs* were then used out of Mackinac only. By 1790 the Northwest Company was using large ships on Lake Superior. Foodstuffs, as far as possible, were grown in the West, at Detroit and at L'Arbre Croche south-west of the Straits of Mackinac, and space in the canoes could be used for trade goods.

It thus appears that the manner of life of the French in Wisconsin was not greatly altered during the British period. Green Bay received a few new residents. Augustin de Langlade, long a trader at Mackinac, built a warehouse and opened a branch business at Green Bay about 1748. In 1764 he and his famous son, Charles, began to reside at Green Bay. Augustin died about 1771, leaving Charles the leading figure in the community. In 1773 a French Canadian named Pierre Grignon settled in Green Bay and married a daughter of Charles de Langlade; by this marriage he became the father of six sons, leading figures in the fur trade and in the Fox River Valley until far into the nineteenth century.

These arrivals, however, reinforced the former customs of Green Bay; they did not change its essentially Canadian character. In 1766, when Jonathan Carver passed the portage where the city of Portage now is, he found one French Canadian living there. About this time, too, we begin to hear of permanent settlers at Prairie du Chien who were not Indians. Hundreds of *voyageurs* must have visited every part of the present state, but, as in the previous period, their activities were rarely recorded.

The War of 1812 and the End of British Influence

The Treaty of Paris of 1783 left within the United States several posts counted essential in the control of the western fur trade, among them Niagara, Detroit, and Michilimackinac, the post on Mackinac Island. The treaty had stipulated that the posts should be delivered over to the Americans "with all convenient speed," but the British continued to hold them and to send out from them agents with medals, certificates, and gifts. Indeed, the Indians were encouraged to visit the posts, where they were feted and loaded with presents. Thus British dominance over the natives was perpetuated in the interests of the fur trade. During the years after 1790, the Indians were resisting the advance of the American frontier in Ohio, and the Americans were convinced that these Indians had advice and aid from the British at Detroit. Another treaty, commonly called the Jay Treaty, was concluded in November, 1794, and finally brought about the transfer of these posts. The little fort on Mackinac Island, the last to be given up, was evacuated in August and occupied by American soldiers in October, 1796. But the British had no intention of giving up the fur trade, now in its heyday. They continued to operate in much the same way from new posts on the British side of the boundary. The Indians who had been reached from Detroit now received presents and counsel at Malden, a few miles to the southeast. Mackinac was refounded, in a sense, forty miles northeast on St. Joseph Island. Jay's treaty provided that British subjects might travel freely over waterways and portages within the United States. Thus, there was really no impediment to the continued control of the fur trade or essential change in conditions in the Northwest until the War of 1812.

The second war against Great Britain used to be explained as arising from the impressment of American sailors for the British navy and the interference with American neutral rights; but there were causes of at least equal weight to be found west of the Alleghenies. The vociferous elements in the newer states were clamoring for war, and even for the annexation of Canada, in order to satisfy the frontier desire for territorial expansion and to end the danger of Indian attack which was again imminent. The leader of the Indians in this generation, who may well be compared with Pontiac, was Tecumseh, a Shawnee orator and warrior. He was aided by his brother, the Prophet, a medicine man who knew well how to play on the superstitions and emotions of his people. The two leaders advocated the complete repudiation of the customs of the white men, especially the use of firewater, and their teaching was accepted far and wide as a sort of new religion. On the political side Tecumseh insisted on the union of all Indians and the end of land cessions to the whites. In 1808 or 1809 the brothers removed from Ohio to central Indiana near the junction of the Tippecanoe with the Wabash, and established a great village, Prophetstown, which was intended to be the capital of the Indian race.

All this was very alarming to the English-speaking farming frontier. George Rogers Clark and many of his generation were still alive, and for the third time within their memory the frontier was about to suffer attack. Rightly or wrongly much of the responsibility was placed at the door of the British. Henry Clay said in urging the invasion of Canada: "Is it nothing for us to extinguish the torch that lights up savage warfare?" As Clay spoke for the West in Congress, so William Henry Harrison was its favorite leader on the battlefield. Harrison had been territorial governor of Indiana since 1800. He had been active and successful, if somewhat unscrupulous, in negotiating treaties of cession with the Indians. In the autumn of 1811 he led some nine hundred men, partly regulars and partly volunteer frontiersmen, from Vincennes up to Prophetstown and a little beyond. On November 7, the Indians tried to storm his camp. Later historians consider Harrison fortunate in getting back to Vincennes after his rash incursion into the Indian country, but to the frontier he was a hero. This Battle of Tippecanoe was the real beginning of the War of 1812 in the West.

In the thirty years that had passed since the Revolutionary War, the ascendency of the British over the Indians in Wisconsin had become almost absolute. The traders were all British subjects and loyal to the British cause. The most active in leading the Indians, recalling Charles de Langlade of an earlier generation, was Robert Dickson, who had been trading along the Mississippi, chiefly with the Sioux, since 1786.

The declaration of war passed Congress, June 18, 1812. General Hull, governor of Michigan territory since 1805, was in command of the American forces in the West for the first months of the war. He crossed into Canada, but did not take Malden, his objective, and on August 16, 1812, he surrendered to the British at Detroit. Harrison was in command in this area thereafter.

The British at St. Joseph Island were waiting for the declaration of war in 1812 in order to pounce upon Mackinac. The number of regular troops at the two posts was not greatly different, but the British were stronger in number of fur traders and Indians. The *engagés* of the fur traders at St. Joseph Island were organized, and the men at Sault Ste. Marie came to St. Joseph to help. Robert Dickson had brought sixty Sioux from the Mississippi; Michael Cadotte, Jr., came from La Pointe on Chequamegon Bay, and Charles Langlade, Jr., led Indians from the Mackinac region. Winnebago and Menominee were there from Wisconsin. Among the latter were Chief Tomah and Oshkosh, a young man later to be a chief. This motley throng, numbering in all some five or six hundred men, white and red, descended upon Mackinac Island before dawn on July 17, 1812. Resistance was worse than useless, and it is greatly to the credit of all concerned, and especially of those responsible for the control of the Indians, that the transfer was made without shedding a drop of blood.

A month after the capture of Mackinac, Fort Dearborn suffered a worse fate. This fort had been founded a half mile up the Chicago River in 1803. In the summer of 1812 there were fifty-five in the garrison under Captain Heald, and some twelve to fifteen civilians who could bear arms. On August 9 Heald received orders from Hull at Detroit to evacuate Fort Dearborn and retire to Fort Wayne. The little column of men, women, and children that left the fort on August 15 was almost immediately attacked by hundreds of savages, and only a few escaped after long privations as prisoners among the Indians. Among the attacking Indians were Winnebago, Menominee, and Potawatomi from Wisconsin. After the fall of Mackinac, Detroit, and Fort Dearborn, the line of military contact was in the forts of Ohio, Indiana, and Illinois.

The year 1813 showed progress towards American victory, though there was as yet no sign of this in Wisconsin, which was still entirely enemy territory. A part of Harrison's troops met with disaster in the "Massacre of the River Raisin," southwest of Detroit, in January, 1813. In August, George Crogan of Kentucky repulsed an attack by British and Indians on Fort Stephenson at Lower Sandusky in Ohio. In September, Perry gained control of Lake Erie, and Harrison was able to advance into Canada. The British burned Detroit and Malden as Harrison approached, and retreated eastward. He overtook the British and Indians at the River Thames and there, October 5, 1813, made the Northwest secure again. Tecumseh was killed, and with him passed the strength of his Indian confederacy.

On January 1, 1813, Robert Dickson received a Canadian commission as Superintendent of Indian Affairs west of Lake Michigan. In the summer he led six hundred warriors to Mackinac, more than half of them from Wisconsin, and sent eight hundred more by the land route to Detroit. Dickson and Tomah, the Menominee chief, were present at the attack on Fort Stephenson. The Menominee were then sent home, but there were Wisconsin Winnebago with Tecumseh in his final defeat. In the late fall Dickson went west again by way of Mackinac. He took with him twenty-eight soldiers to garrison the Green Bay district, and they wintered in that vicinity. Dickson himself took up quarters on Garlic Island in Lake Winnebago, remaining there until April, 1814. In May he made a hurried trip to Prairie du Chien and departed eastward again with Indian followers, reaching Mackinac in June.

The Americans were not unaware of the value of Prairie du Chien as a point from which to control the Indians. William

Clark, who had crossed the continent with Meriwether Lewis, was Superintendent of Indian Affairs for the upper Mississippi, with headquarters at St. Louis. From there he led a force of fifty regular troops and 150 volunteers to Prairie du Chien, where, in June, 1814, he built Fort Shelby, named after the governor of Kentucky. This was the first building in what is now Wisconsin to fly an American flag. Clark soon went back to St. Louis, leaving the new fort in charge of Lieutenant Perkins with about sixty men.

A few days after Dickson reached Mackinac, word was brought there that the Americans were in Prairie du Chien. It was at once determined, for the sake of British prestige with the Indians, to drive back the Americans. The leaders of the expedition were Dickson and Major William McKay. The main reliance was a body of ninety-five men, mostly fur traders enlisted near Mackinac, and called the "Michigan Fencibles." About thirty more white men were added at Green Bay. The number of Indians, which grew as the party progressed, was about five hundred. Against such a force Perkins was powerless, and after a short attempt at resistance, he surrendered July 19, 1814. The fort was renamed Fort McKay, and under successive officers was held for George III until May, 1815, when the British got away to Canada.

The War of 1812 ended with the Treaty of Ghent, negotiated in the closing months of 1814, and again the future of Wisconsin was decided by treaty-makers in Europe. The British tried to secure a change of boundary which would leave the western posts and most of the fur trade outside the United States, either under British sovereignty or in a neutral Indian state west of the Great Lakes. The American commissioners refused any such terms, and eventually a settlement was reached on the basis of pre-war boundaries. In the interests of their native allies, the British stipulated that the United States should immediately make peace with all the Indian tribes, and to this the Americans gladly assented. Along with the news of the treaty came orders to the

British soldiers to evacuate all American territory. In obedience to these orders, Fort McKay at Prairie du Chien and the post on Mackinac Island were surrendered. This time British control in the Northwest was finally at an end, and the responsibility for the Indian population of Wisconsin rested with the government and people of the United States.

SELECTED BIBLIOGRAPHY

Louise Phelps Kellogg has provided the best summary of the whole period in *The British Régime in Wisconsin and the Northwest* (Madison, 1935). Its footnotes are a convenient guide to the sources and to the modern literature. Older narratives that continue to be of value are: Thwaites, *Wisconsin* (Boston, 1908), pp. 125-178; *Wisconsin in Three Centuries* (New York, 1906), Vol. II, pp. 43-178; and Quaife, *Wisconsin, Its History and Its People* (Chicago, 1924), Vol. I, pp. 225-359. Quaife has much of interest for the student of early Wisconsin in his *Chicago and the Old Northwest* (Chicago, 1913).

The European influences shaping the destiny of the Mississippi Valley are set forth in Clarence W. Alvord, *The Mississippi Valley in British Politics* (2 vols., Cleveland, 1917) and also in his *The Illinois Country, 1673-1818* (Springfield, 1920); and in Clarence E. Carter, *Great Britain and the Illinois Country, 1763-1774* (Washington, American Historical Association, 1910).

The interesting journal of Lieutenant James Gorrell may be read in *Collections of the State Historical Society of Wisconsin,* Vol. I, pp. 24-48. Francis Parkman, *The Conspiracy of Pontiac* (2 vols., Boston, 1883) is the most famous work on its subject. In *Collections,* Vol. XI, pp. 46-60, will be found the Proclamation of October 7, 1763, and the Quebec Act of 1774 (14 Geo. III., Cap. 83).

The most satisfactory discussion of the designs of Robert Rogers and Jonathan Carver is by Louise P. Kellogg, *British Régime,* pp. 49-92. Allan Nevins prefaced an edition of a literary effort by Rogers with a sketch of his life, in *Ponteach or the Savages of America* (Chicago, Caxton Club, 1914). William W. Folwell discussed Carver in his *History of Minnesota* (4 vols., Minneapolis, 1921-1930), Vol. I, pp. 53-66. There is also an article on Carver in the *Dictionary of National Biography.*

James A. James, *George Rogers Clark* (Chicago, 1928), gives an admirable account of the Revolutionary War in the West. In the *Collections of the State Historical Society of Wisconsin,* Vol. VII, pp. 123-187, is a "Memoir of Charles de Langlade," with illustrative documents, prepared by Joseph Tassé.

The best picture of the daily life of the fur trader, charmingly written, is *The Voyageur* (New York, 1931), by Grace Lee Nute. Business and political aspects of the trade are dealt with in Wayne E. Stevens, *The Northwest Fur Trade, 1763-1800* (Urbana, University of Illinois, 1926), and H. A. Innes, *The Fur Trade in Canada* (New Haven, 1930). Marjorie G. Reid (Mrs. K. B. Jackson) makes a valuable contribution in "The Quebec Fur Traders and Western Policy, 1763-1774," *Canadian Historical Review,* Vol. VI, pp. 15-32 (March, 1925). An earlier study by Frederick Jackson Turner is, "The Character and Influence of the Indian Trade in Wisconsin," *Johns Hopkins University Studies,* 9th series, Nos. 11-12 (Baltimore, 1891). Milo M. Quaife edited *Alexander Henry's Travels and Adventures in the Years 1760-1776* (Chicago, 1921), and *John Long's Voyages and Travels in the Years 1768-1788* (Chicago, 1922). Both are excellent pictures of the time. *Collections of the State Historical Society of Wisconsin,* Vol. XVIII, pp. 223-468, and Vols. XIX and XX are devoted to the fur trade and to the British period. Vol. XVIII, pp. 314-354, gives the "Journal of Peter Pond," a vivid and homely narrative.

The standard work on the treaty of 1794 is by Samuel Flagg Bemis, *Jay's Treaty: A Study in Commerce and Diplomacy* (New York, 1924). A good idea of the Indian unrest may be obtained from Ethel T. Raymond, *Tecumseh, a Chronicle of the Last Great Leader of His People* (Toronto, 1918, Chronicles of Canada, Vol. XVII). The *Collections* contain a group of papers and documents relating to Prairie du Chien in the War of 1812, Vol. IX, pp. 137-302. *Ibid.,* Vol. XII, pp. 133-153, is a study by Ernest A. Cruikshank, "Robert Dickson, the Indian Trader." Julius W. Pratt, *Expansionists of 1812* (New York, 1925), presents the western attitude which helped to bring on the War of 1812.

CHAPTER IV

THE INDIANS AND THE FUR TRADERS LEAVE THE STAGE

GOVERNMENT AND THE INDIAN FRONTIER

WHEN the British soldiers left for Canada in 1815, Wisconsin contained only Indians and a few small settlements of French-speaking *habitants*. It had been legally a part of the United States since 1783, but the Wisconsin population and the American government had paid very little attention to each other. For a century or more after 1776, the English-speaking population was on the march westward from the Alleghenies. As it moved forward, it conquered the Indians in its path, ended the fur trade, and set up a new way of living. The federal government was the servant of this movement. When a territorial government for Wisconsin was set up in 1836, it meant that the advance guard of the new civilization had arrived. The process of depriving the Indian of his land was by that time well under way, and the long-established economic order based on hunting by the Indians and the fur trade with them was soon to disappear.

The United States government dealt only with those Indian tribes near enough to the settlements to cause trouble or impede the advance of the white frontier. During the generation between the War of 1812 and the Mexican War, Wisconsin was in the zone of contact between the two races. The federal government exercised control partly military and partly civil.

An irregular line of garrisoned forts, established at various times, swept across Wisconsin and Iowa to the Missouri River and back across Arkansas and Louisiana. Along this frontier of some fifteen hundred miles a part of the regular army maintained peace and respect for the United States. Fort Howard at Green Bay and Fort Crawford at Prairie du Chien were established in 1816, and Fort Winnebago was added at Portage in 1828. Each of these forts usually had between one and two hundred soldiers. While the forts were maintained, their garrisons, and especially their officers, were of great influence. They sometimes clashed with the civilians of the adjacent villages, but on the other hand they represented the majesty of the law in an almost lawless period. Many distinguished soldiers served their country in these Wisconsin posts, among them Zachary Taylor and Jefferson Davis. At Green Bay, Portage, and also at Prairie du Chien the officers and their families were the centers of the society of the time.

The highest civil power was vested in the territorial governor. From 1813 to 1831 Lewis Cass was governor of Michigan Territory, which, after 1818, included Wisconsin. A territorial governor was also usually commissioned as Superintendent of Indian Affairs, and Governor Cass had authority over the Indian agents at Green Bay and Chicago. At St. Louis the superintendent from 1807 to 1838 was the very able William Clark, whose authority extended northward to the sources of the Mississippi and included the agency at Prairie du Chien. The duties of the local agent were varied. He had to work for peace among the Indians, and justice between the two races. If the tribes received payments or annuities under treaties with the United States, the agent distributed them. One of his hardest tasks was to keep white squatters off the lands of the Indians in his charge.

As long as the population of Wisconsin was mostly Indian, the fur trade continued. One of the great figures in the trade in the latter days was John Jacob Astor of New York, called "the Old Tiger" by his employees. After several earlier ventures in financing the fur business, he promoted from 1809 to 1814 the Pacific Fur Company, which built Astoria at the mouth of the Columbia River. This enterprise would doubtless have turned out well but for the War of 1812. Meanwhile the Montreal magnates who had founded the Michilimackinac company were not satisfied with returns, and in 1811 they transformed their enterprise into the South West Company, with Astor as the dominant partner. In 1816 Congress, at Astor's instigation, passed a law that forbade foreigners to engage in the fur trade within the United States without special license. At the same time he founded the American Fur Company. The actual field work of the new company was organized and directed by Ramsay Crooks, a native of Scotland, who had been in fur trading since 1806 and who had worked for Astor in the Pacific Fur Company. Crooks spent his winters in New York and the rest of the year traveling through the West. His western headquarters were Mackinac, and Green Bay and Prairie du Chien saw him almost every year. The company was an early instance of a "big business" trying to gain a nationwide monopoly. Its monopoly was not complete over the whole United States, but it had little competition within the bounds of present Wisconsin. Every stream in the state seems to have been traveled by its representatives, and the history of a great many Wisconsin towns begins with the French Canadian who traded there for the American Fur Company. Crooks chose as his agents able and experienced men, many of them with local connections already established. He selected John Lawe at Green Bay and, after 1818, Solomon Juneau at Milwaukee. Joseph Rolette and Hercules Dousman worked for the company at Prairie du Chien. In its earlier years the company was constantly reaching further west into Minnesota and the Dakotas and far up the Missouri River. An amicable arrangement was made with the fur magnates of St. Louis.

From 1795 to 1822 the United States government engaged in the Indian trade. Posts or factories were established and it was hoped to save the Indian from sharp practices and the corrupting influences of the lowest type of trader.   At the same time Indian opinion would be brought to favor the Americans.   Before the War of 1812 there were such factories at Mackinac, Chicago, and Sandusky in the Northwest, and at Fort Madison in Iowa.   During the war these were all captured by the British or British-allied Indians.   After the war new government factories were set up at Green Bay, Prairie du Chien, Chicago, and Fort Edwards in Illinois.   Major Matthew Irwin, a conscientious man, was in charge at Green Bay but it was told there later that in the seven years during which he was factor he did not succeed in buying more than $50 worth of furs.   This statement may be exaggerated but the system never worked well.   The factors were often inexperienced in Indian trade, and, since salaries were not dependent on results, they did not put forth their best efforts.   In fairness we must admit that trade with the Indians could not succeed unless credit was advanced, and the government gave no credit.   Those regularly engaged in the trade resented government competition and the efforts of the American Fur Company had a large part in inducing Congress to end the experiment.

Encroachments and First Cessions

The lands possessed by the various tribes had no well-defined boundaries.   In their pursuit of furs the hunters ranged far from home, and several tribes often hunted over the same area.   The most definite map we can get is that of their cessions to the United States.   A part of the Sauk and Foxes had crossed to the west side of the Mississippi.   The rest of them had come to have their chief village at the mouth of the Rock River in Illinois.   In 1804 five representatives of these tribes, who had gone to St. Louis on other business, were persuaded to sign away their possessions east of the Mississippi, defined as running from the Illinois River to the Wisconsin, and to definite boundaries on the east.   They might hunt over this ground for the present, but when the land was needed they would retire west of the Mississippi. By this same treaty, a tract two miles square was reserved for a fort at the junction of the Wisconsin with the Mississippi "on the upper side of the Wisconsing or on the right bank of the Mississippi." No immediate use was made of this tract. In 1816, also at St. Louis, the Sauk and Foxes repeated this relinquishment. At the same time the United States ceded as much of this land just yielded by the Sauk and Foxes as lay north of the latitude of the southern tip of Lake Michigan to the "Ottawa, Chippewa and Potawatomi residing on the Illinois and Milwaukee rivers and their waters."

In 1825 an important conference was held at Prairie du Chien by Lewis Cass and William Clark. The purpose was to establish peace among the tribes and definitely to set the limits of their respective holdings. The southeastern and southwestern corners of present Wisconsin with adjacent parts of Illinois were assigned to certain Chippewa, Ottawa and Potawatomi. The rest of southern Wisconsin was recognized as belonging to the Winnebago, whose irregularly shaped holdings touched the Mississippi north of Prairie du Chien and stretched northeast to Lake Winnebago and north to the Black River. The Menominee had the northeastern part of the state from the Milwaukee River to the mouth of the Escanaba, and their triangular holding had its western point beyond the Wisconsin River. In 1825 the Chippewa had all northern Wisconsin west of the Menominee tribe and most of upper Michigan; in the course of 150 years the Chippewa had wrested all the northwestern part of the state from the Sioux, who in 1825 held the left bank of the Mississippi from the St. Croix River almost to the mouth of the Wisconsin. This apportionment of the state was largely done at Prairie du Chien, though some details had to be worked out by other treaties within the next few years.

In the pockets of rock in southwestern Wisconsin and in the adjoining parts of Illinois and Iowa were great stores of lead. This fact was known to the French from the earliest days of their exploration. Nicolas Perrot did some mining in this region, and ever after, by crude methods probably learned from Perrot, the Indians continued to get out lead. The American settlers gradually became aware of the richness of the deposits, and from 1822 onward were crossing the Indian country from central Illinois or going up the Mississippi to reach the "Fever River" district, whose center soon came to be called Galena. Henry Dodge was not the first to begin lead mining in Wisconsin, but when he arrived there in 1827, he took his place as the natural leader of the mining community. He had mined lead with his father in Missouri; he had been a sheriff; and he had commanded militia against the Indians in the unrest of 1812 to 1814. The advance of miners into their country made the Indians very uneasy, the Winnebago most of all. Dodge came in the midst of alarms caused by the Indians, and since the miners were beginning to organize a company of mounted volunteers, they chose Dodge their captain. This was his first office in Wisconsin where he was later to be twice territorial governor and after that United States Senator.[1]

The situation in 1827 was critical, and out of it might have come a serious outbreak. In October, 1826, the garrison of Prairie du Chien, the natural defense of southwestern Wisconsin, was sent to Fort Snelling two hundred miles up the Mississippi. The Indians were demanding toll and other payments from the miners. The young warriors, whose reputation for courage was at stake, were more savage. In the autumn of 1826 a French-Canadian settler named Methode, his wife, and five children were killed on the Iowa side of the Mississippi River about twelve miles north of Prairie du Chien. In June, 1827, a young Winnebago chieftain named Red Bird and two others killed Registre Gagnier and an old soldier who lived with him, and scalped a baby who, marvelous to tell, survived. On the same day two keelboats descending the Mississippi from Fort Snelling were attacked by Winnebago and

---

[1] The settlement of the lead mining district is discussed more fully in Chapter V, pp. 89-91.

Sauk about forty miles above Prairie du Chien, and four deaths resulted.

It happened that in June, 1827, Governor Lewis Cass had come to Wisconsin to make treaties with the Chippewa and Winnebago at Butte des Morts about matters left unfinished in 1825. There he learned of what had taken place along the Mississippi. He hastened westward by the Fox-Wisconsin route through the heart of the Winnebago country. Stopping but a short time at Prairie du Chien and again at Galena to advise about measures of defense, he sped on to Jefferson Barracks near St. Louis to ask for troops. He returned by way of the Illinois River, Chicago and Lake Michigan to Green Bay and Butte des Morts, having made the circuit of sixteen hundred miles in four weeks. Mostly as a result of his efforts soldiers rapidly poured into the endangered area. Four companies returned from Fort Snelling. General Henry Atkinson came up from Jefferson Barracks with more than five hundred soldiers of the regular army, arriving at Fort Crawford July 29. He waited to learn the result of the negotiations which Cass was resuming at Butte des Morts. Red Bird and his Winnebago braves fled from the neighborhood of Prairie du Chien up the Wisconsin River. After hearing from Cass, Atkinson started up the Wisconsin on August 29, assisted by Dodge and his mounted volunteers from the lead mines. Meanwhile Major William Whistler was marching up the Fox from Fort Howard. On September 1, he reached the portage and began to fortify himself. Red Bird and his men were between two forces. On September 3, a body of unarmed Indians with a white flag approached Whistler's camp. Rather than subject his people to a hopeless war with the white men, Red Bird had come to give himself up. He was such a magnificent physical figure, and he sacrificed himself with such dignity and courage that he impressed American officers as a prince "born to command and worthy to be obeyed." On the fifth two other murderers were delivered to Atkinson, and still later two who had had a part in the attack on the keelboats; on

September 22, Atkinson issued a proclamation of peace. Thanks to the decision of Cass and the promptness of other leaders, there had really been no war, but only some movements of troops and the surrender of some guilty Indians. Red Bird died in prison at Prairie du Chien. Two of the prisoners were condemned to death and then pardoned by President Adams. Against the others there was not sufficient evidence to connect them with the crimes charged against them and they were released. Meanwhile, the white men were to use the lead mines until a new treaty should be arranged.

Apart from small bits of land used as the sites of Forts Howard and Crawford, and what had been occupied by French-Canadian settlers long before and secured to them by European treaties, Wisconsin was in 1827 still legally the property of the Indians. In 1825 Secretary of War John C. Calhoun outlined an Indian policy, not, of course, entirely new, that was followed faithfully for nearly twenty years. The Indians in the eastern part of the United States were to sell their lands and go west into the great plains that would never be needed for white settlement. Once they had taken up their new locations, the Indians were to be cared for and civilized. One president after another approved of this course, while Congress voted the money to buy lands and pay the expenses of removal. This policy governed relations with the Wisconsin tribes in this period, though removal westward proved difficult.

A settlement was first made with regard to the lead-mining region. In 1826, as a preliminary, the Winnebago were promised goods to the value of twenty thousand dollars to compensate for trespasses already made on their lands. The great council was held at Prairie du Chien during the latter part of July, 1829. The Chippewa, Ottawa, and Potawatomi of the Illinois River gave up their claims to land along the Mississippi between the Illinois and the Wisconsin. The Winnebago parted with the western half of what they had south of the Wisconsin River. The crooked line

dividing what they gave up from what they retained ran southward from a point a little northeast of Portage, passed just west
of where Madison was soon to be, and entered Illinois about the
middle of the interstate boundary.   Both the Winnebago and
the other group were to receive immediate payments and annuities.   For the present they might hunt on this land.   The lead-
mining area east of the Mississippi was now the property of the
United States.

Many men interested in the welfare of the Indians in the eastern
states had long felt that their Indian charges would be better off,
at least morally, in the West.   Beginning with a few Oneida leaders in 1821, several groups of Indians left western New York state
for eastern Wisconsin.   Treaties were made with the Menominee
to get land for these settlements, the principal cession being one
of 500,000 acres made in 1831.   The process of removal was a long
and tedious one, continuing through many years.   Oneida and
Munsee established themselves on Duck Creek southwest of Green
Bay.   Here a church was begun in 1823.   The Stockbridges and
Brothertown Indians, remnants of New England tribes that had
moved to New York, settled on the eastern shore of Lake Winnebago in 1834 and afterwards.

One of the leading figures in this westward movement was the
Rev. Eleazer Williams, an Oneida Indian with a little white blood.
He had been educated in mission schools, and was ordained in the
Episcopal church.   In the divided councils of his tribe, he was the
most enthusiastic for going west.   Apparently he hoped to be the
leading figure in the new community.   He took part in the negotiations with the Menominee, which became so bitter and complicated that the United States had several times to intervene.
Williams married the daughter of a French Canadian who had
settled at Green Bay with his Menominee wife.   The Menominee
tribe granted several thousand acres of land to Williams, and in
1840 the United States government confirmed his title to this
property.   In 1849 this curious individual, who by that time had

lost the respect of most who knew him, gained a nationwide notoriety by claiming to be the "Lost Dauphin" of France, the little son of Louis XVI who died in a Paris prison in 1795.

The first of three large cessions by the Menominee Indians was made February 8, 1831, by a number of chiefs taken to Washington, D. C., for that purpose. The half million acres for the New York Indians were secured from the Menominee at that time. The lands then surrendered to the United States lay east of the waters of Green Bay, Lake Winnebago and the Milwaukee River. In the ample area still retained by the Menominee, the United States would instruct them in the arts of civilization. A model farm, with five farmers to teach agriculture and their wives to teach household arts to the Indians, was begun on the island now a part of Neenah and Menasha. A mill was built, and log houses for the farmer-teachers. When the Menominee gave up more land in 1836 and this island was no longer near them, the enterprise was abandoned.

THE BLACK HAWK WAR, 1832

From about 1823 white squatters began to encroach on the lands near the Fox and Sauk villages at the mouth of the Rock River in northwestern Illinois. In 1830 Chief Keokuk yielded to the inevitable and led most of these Indians across the Mississippi. Black Sparrowhawk, or Black Hawk, who had fought with the British in the War of 1812, wished to remain by the graves and cornfields of his ancestors, and only the gathering of several hundred soldiers and militiamen in June, 1831, compelled him also to go over into Iowa. Nine months later, on April 6, 1832, he recrossed the Mississippi at the mouth of the Rock River with about four hundred warriors and some six hundred women and children. His immediate object was not to make war, but to "make corn." If he had a good crop, and if help from the British and from certain Indian tribes was forthcoming, he would perhaps fight in the autumn or later, but for the present his intentions were

peaceable.   Black Hawk's return into Illinois was regarded by the
white settlers of Illinois as an act of war, and they enlisted in considerable numbers.   Abraham Lincoln was the captain of one of
the companies.

Black Hawk moved slowly up the valley of the Rock River, dis-
regarding an order from Fort Armstrong (Rock Island, Illinois)
to turn back.   By the middle of May he knew that all hopes of
help in warfare from the British and from the Indians he had
counted on were vain, and he desired only to go back to Iowa.
He tried to enter into negotiations with a force under Major Stillman.   He sent three of his men with a white flag, and had others
watch from a distance.   Militiamen shot two of the watchers, the
sound was heard in Stillman's camp, and the white men promptly
shot one of the flag-bearers.   Black Hawk had come to negotiate,
not to fight, and he had only about forty warriors with him.   In
the gathering darkness little groups of Stillman's undisciplined
militiamen rode on to find other Indians.   Black Hawk waited
until the foremost white men were almost upon him and then
fired.   The result was a panic that grew as it traveled southward
to the settlements.   Black Hawk had ambushed them with two
thousand warriors!   No one was more surprised than the Indians,
and further fighting was now inevitable.

Black Hawk placed his women and children at Lake Koshkonong in southern Wisconsin, and then proceeded to harry the
frontier in northern Illinois.   In all, about two hundred white persons were killed between May 14 and July 31, 1832.   General
Henry Atkinson was in command of the Americans, and gradually the Indians were pushed northward.   To this period belong
a number of small episodes celebrated in border story as battles.
Major Henry Dodge, who again commanded his neighbors, was
the hero of one such encounter on the Pecatonica River, in which
eighteen white men killed thirteen Indians.   Black Hawk was
compelled to retire into Wisconsin where he hoped the Americans
would not follow.   He left Lake Koshkonong and moved north-

west through the region of the Four Lakes. His whole band had been underfed for a year and was weak from starvation. Major Henry Dodge and General James D. Henry, an Illinois blacksmith, were bringing supplies from Fort Winnebago and came upon Black Hawk's fresh trail. Following it, they overtook the Indians just as they were about to cross the Wisconsin River. With a few chosen warriors Black Hawk held the Americans at bay until his band was safely across the river. This was the battle of Wisconsin Heights, July 21. At dawn the next day the startled Americans were awakened by a long harangue in an Indian language. Unfortunately there was no interpreter in the camp, and it was not learned until later that this was a speech of surrender.

After they had crossed the Wisconsin River the Indians begged canoes and rafts of the Winnebago and as many as could do so floated down the Wisconsin, hoping to cross the Mississippi to Iowa. The garrison at Prairie du Chien saw the Indians and captured or shot most of them. Some were drowned and others who got to land were hunted down in the woods by Menominee Indians under white officers. Meanwhile Major Dodge and General Henry fell back and joined forces with Atkinson, and the whole body made all possible speed in pursuit of Black Hawk, who was leading toward the Mississippi those who had been unable to find places in the craft going down the Wisconsin. Some twenty-five warriors wounded at Wisconsin Heights dropped behind to die and marked the trail; old men and children died of hunger. As the desperate remnant came out on the banks of the Mississippi the steamboat *Warrior,* U.S.N., appeared. Black Hawk for the last time tried to surrender, but the captain of the steamboat professed to believe that the flag of truce was a ruse, and opened fire with a six-pounder and with musketry. He ceased only when his supply of fuel gave out. The infantry now came up, pushing the Indians from behind. Men, women, and children were driven into the river at the point of bayonets, to be drowned or picked off by sharpshooters. This massacre of the Bad Axe lasted three hours, and at least 150 were killed and an equal number were drowned. Of some three hundred of Black Hawk's followers who in one way or another reached the west bank of the Mississippi half were killed by Sioux unleashed by General Atkinson.

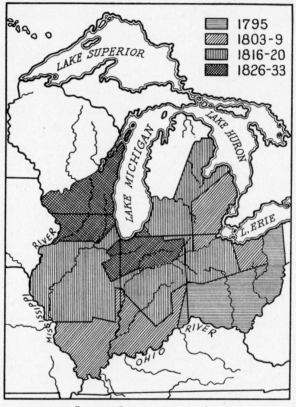

INDIAN CESSIONS, 1795-1833

Of the band of about a thousand that had crossed the Mississippi in April, only about 150 were alive four months later. Black Hawk was captured and after being taken through the eastern states was released in June, 1833.

THE FINAL CESSIONS

Within a little more than a year after the Black Hawk War, two important treaties were made which together completed the holdings of the United States south and east of the old waterway of the Fox and Wisconsin rivers.   In September, 1832, the Winnebago signed away the rest of what they possessed south of that line.   A year later a great meeting was held with the southern Chippewa, the Ottawa, and the Potawatomi at Chicago.   From five to seven thousand Indians were present, and the United States there paid or promised to the Indians and their creditors no less than a million dollars.   The Indians gave up southern Wisconsin east of the Rock River and the adjoining part of Illinois.   Pursuant to the treaty these Indians gathered at Chicago two years later for a final payment, held a last frenzied war-dance, and, barbaric to the end, departed toward the setting sun.   Thus far had the elimination of the Indians proceeded when in 1836 Wisconsin was separated from Michigan.

During the twelve years in which Wisconsin was a territory the extinguishment of Indian title was all but completed.   In 1836 by a treaty made at the Cedars, between Appleton and Kaukauna, the Menominee gave up nearly four million acres at a cost to the United States of about seven hundred thousand dollars.   The cession lay between the Wolf River and Green Bay and ran northward into upper Michigan.   On the map of cessions by Indian tribes to the United States government, this area is cut into three pieces by the cession previously made by the Menominee to the Oneida, but in 1838 the Oneida gave most of this to the United States.   Another parcel of land along the middle of the Wisconsin River was also yielded by the treaty of 1836.   Three treaties of 1837 with Chippewa, Sioux, and Winnebago, respectively, covered the western half of the state from the Wisconsin River almost to Lake Superior.   In 1842 the Chippewa gave up the rest of what they had within the limits of Wisconsin.   When Wisconsin became a state in the spring of 1848, only a wedge-shaped piece in the east-central part of the state remained in the hands of the Indians, and this was ceded by the Menominee in October of that year. In the nineteen years from 1829 to 1848, the Indians had given up the whole of the state.

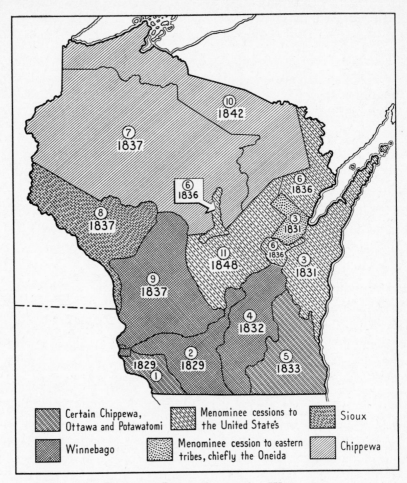

PRINCIPAL INDIAN CESSIONS IN WISCONSIN

The area comprised in the state of Wisconsin was acquired from various Indian tribes by eleven treaties of cession. The exact dates of the treaties, together wtih the places where they were negotiated and the Indian tribes concerned, are given in the following list. The numbers of the treaties correspond to the numbered areas on the map.

Five of these treaties were negotiated while Wisconsin was a part of Michigan Territory, and covered all the area south and east of the Fox and Wisconsin rivers.

    1. July 29, 1829—Prairie du Chien—Chippewa, Ottawa, and Potawatomi nations of the waters of the Illinois, Milwaukee, and Manitowoc rivers.

    2. August 1, 1829—Prairie du Chien—Winnebago.

    3. February 8, 1831—Washington, D. C.—Menominee. In addition to the cession to the United States, the Menominee ceded land to eastern Indians. The many changes in the holdings of these eastern Indians are not further noticed here.

    4. September 15, 1832—Fort Armstrong, Rock Island, Illinois—Winnebago.

78

Most of these later treaties stipulated that the tribes concerned should have new homes farther west, and western lands were assigned to several of them. A good many Winnebago were removed by the United States Army, and their descendants are found in eastern Nebraska today, but many made their way back to their old homes. The Sioux, who were not numerous in Wisconsin in the nineteenth century, withdrew to Minnesota. The Menominee and the Chippewa were gathered or "condensed" into reservations. In 1854 a tract twenty-four miles by eighteen was set apart for the Menominee on the upper Wolf River. Not long afterwards they sold two of their twelve townships to the Stockbridge Indians who came up from Calumet County. Also in 1854 three good-sized reservations and some smallers ones were assigned to the Chippewa. The larger ones were the Bad River, the Lac de Flambeau, and the Lac Court Oreilles reservations in Ashland, Vilas, and Sawyer counties. The census of 1930 showed somewhat more than ten thousand Indians residing in Wisconsin. In round numbers there were four thousand Chippewa, two thousand Menominee, three thousand Oneida, twelve hundred Winnebago, six hundred Stockbridge, and four hundred Potawatomi.

THE END OF THE FUR TRADE

When the Indians were gathered into reservations or removed beyond the Mississippi River, and when farm making drove away

---

5. September 26, 1833—Chicago, Illinois—Chippewa, Ottawa, and Potawatomi nations.

Five treaties were made while Wisconsin was a territory.

6. September 3, 1836—Cedar Point, on the Fox River below Appleton—Menominee.

7. July 29, 1837—St. Peter's, at the confluence of the St. Peter's and Mississippi rivers—Chippewa.

8. September 29, 1837—Washington, D. C.—Sioux.

9. November 1, 1837—Washington, D. C.—Winnebago.

10. October 4, 1842—La Pointe of Lake Superior—Chippewa of the Mississippi and Lake Superior.

When Wisconsin became a state, the Indian title had been extinguished to all land except what the Menominee retained in the east-central part of the state. The cession of this soon followed.

11. October 18, 1848—Lake Pow-aw-hay-Kou-nay (Lake Poygan)—Menominee.

the wild life of forest and stream, the day of the fur trader was over. The end was gradual, of course. John Jacob Astor saw the decline in business; in 1834, he sold his interests to a new company in which Ramsay Crooks was the largest shareholder. The first two annual dividends after the change amounted together to 25 per cent, but the panic of 1837 gave the company a severe blow. In the early forties its business declined partly from causes over which it had no control, such as changing fashions in Europe and England's war with China. Crooks directed affairs almost single-handed. Under the new company western headquarters were moved to La Pointe on one of the Apostle Islands in Chequamegon Bay. From 1834 to 1841 the company engaged extensively in fishing in Lake Superior, preparing for market several thousand barrels of salted fish a year; but it proved impossible to build up a sufficient demand to make this a success. Crooks did not want his agents in the Indian trade to use whiskey, but the company's competitors used it. "Solomon Juneau solved the difficulty by purchasing his competitor's stock of whiskey, but this method was neither sanctioned nor advised by officials of the company." [2] The incoming of settlers and the plans for the removal of Indians west of the Mississippi doomed the fur trade to extinction. Some of the agents, among them Solomon Juneau, thought that trade with white settlers might replace trade with the Indians but Crooks advised against this, except incidentally. The Indians from about 1835 onward were discouraged by the coming of white farmers and lumbermen, and demoralized by annuities, and so made little effort to hunt. Returns from Wisconsin ceased to show a profit. In 1845 Ramsay Crooks sold all his western interests to the St. Louis firm of Pierre Chouteau, Jr., and Company, and in the same year the agency at Green Bay was closed. The St. Louis firm continued to operate in Minnesota and in northwestern Wisconsin until about 1860 and was often locally referred to still as the

---

[2] J. Ward Ruckman, "Ramsay Crooks and the Fur Trade of the Northwest," *Minnesota History*, Vol. VII (1926), p. 26.

American Fur Company. But by the time Wisconsin became a state, fur trading was a thing of the past in its eastern and southern counties.

The garrisoned forts passed into history about the same time. They were part of the Indian frontier, and it was useless to maintain them when the Indians were gone. The end actually came when the garrisons were needed elsewhere. The soldiers left Fort Howard in 1841 to fight the Seminoles in Florida. The other two forts were abandoned when the Mexican War was impending. Fort Howard and Fort Crawford were reoccupied after that war, the former till 1851 and the other till 1856, but soon the very ground on which the forts had stood was sold and another feature of the Indian frontier had become a memory.

Selected Bibliography

The older narratives that parallel this chapter are: Reuben G. Thwaites, *Wisconsin* (Boston, 1908), pp. 169-231; Milo M. Quaife, *Wisconsin, Its History and Its People* (4 vols., Chicago, 1924), Vol. I, pp. 361-439; and *Wisconsin in Three Centuries* (4 vols., New York, 1906), Vol. II, pp. 181-207.

For the Indian policy of this period see Frederic L. Paxson, *History of the American Frontier* (Boston, 1924), pp. 275-285. Ruth A. Gallaher wrote two valuable articles, "The Indian Agent in the United States Before 1850," *Iowa Journal of History and Politics,* Vol. XIV, pp. 3-55 (January, 1916); and "The Military Indian Frontier, 1830-35," *ibid.,* Vol. XV, pp. 393-428 (July, 1917). There is a study of "William Clark, the Indian Agent," by Harlow Lindlay, in the Mississippi Valley Historical Association *Proceedings,* 1908-1909, pp. 63-73. See also, "William Clark," in the *Dictionary of American Biography.* Annie Heloise Abel made a detailed study entitled, "Indian Consolidation West of the Mississippi," American Historical Association *Report,* 1906, Vol. I, pp. 233-438. Pages 388-396 deal especially with Wisconsin. There are papers on the "Advent of the New York Indians into Wisconsin," in the *Collections* of the State Historical Society of Wisconsin, Vol. II, pp. 415-449. The entry of the federal government into the fur trade business is discussed in "Fur Trade and Factory System at Green Bay, 1816-1821," *ibid.,* Vol. VII, pp. 269-288. Milo M. Quaife treated the same subject in "An Experiment of the Fathers in State Socialism," *Wisconsin Magazine of History,* Vol. III, pp. 277-290 (March, 1920).

The posts of the federal army in Wisconsin have occasioned considerable writing. "The Arrival of American Troops at Green Bay in 1816," a contemporary account, is in *Collections,* Vol. XIII, pp. 441-447. The report of the officer in command of the arriving troops is in *Mississippi Valley Historical Review,* Vol. XIII, pp. 549-553 (March, 1927). An attractive account of garrison life at Fort Howard is found in Deborah N. Martin, *History of Brown County* (2 vols., Chicago, 1913). To this may be added Louise P. Kellogg, "Old Fort Howard," *Wisconsin Magazine of History,* Vol. XVIII, pp. 125-140 (December, 1934). Bruce E. Mahan, *Old Fort Crawford and the Frontier* (Iowa City, 1926), is excellent. "The History of Fort Winnebago," by Andrew J. Turner, and the "Fort Winnebago Orderly Book, 1834-36," are to be found in *Collections,* Vol. XIV, pp. 65-117. *Wau-Bun, the Early Day in the Northwest,* by Mrs. John H. Kinzie, is in large part an account of life at Fort Winnebago from 1830 to 1833. First issued in New York in 1856 and often reprinted, it has recently been re-edited by Louise P. Kellogg (Menasha, 1930). Another charming book of reminiscences, partly of Wisconsin army posts, is *Three Score Years and Ten* (Minneapolis, 1888), by Charlotte Ouisconsin Van Cleve. Marcus L. Hansen, *Old Fort Snelling, 1819-1858* (Iowa City, 1918), has much about western Wisconsin.

For details of Indian cessions, one relies on the compilation by Charles C. Royce, *Indian Land Cessions in the United States,* Eighteenth Annual Report of the Bureau of American Ethnology, 1896-1897 (2 vols., Washington, 1899, 56th Cong., 1st Sess., House Doc. No. 736, serial numbers, 4014, 4015). The map of cessions in Wisconsin is in Vol. II, No. 64. The manner of making a treaty is vividly described in Louise P. Kellogg, "The Menominee Treaty at the Cedars, 1836," *Transactions of the Wisconsin Academy of Sciences, Arts, and Letters,* Vol. XXVI (1931), pp. 127-135.

Reuben G. Thwaites wrote "The Story of the Black Hawk War," for the *Collections,* Vol. XII, pp. 217-265. Other accounts are Frank E. Stevens, *The Black Hawk War, Including a Review of Black Hawk's Life* (Chicago, 1903); and Theodore C. Pease, *The Frontier State, 1818-1848* (Chicago, 1922, Centennial History of Illinois, Vol. II), pp. 151-172. Black Hawk's autobiography was edited by Milo M. Quaife, *Life of Black Hawk* (Chicago, 1916). The latest study of him is Cyrenus Cole, *I Am a Man—The Indian Black Hawk* (Iowa City, 1938). Dodge's part may be seen in Louis Pelzer, *Henry Dodge* (Iowa City, 1911).

One gets a clear idea of the ending of the fur trade from Grace L. Nute, "Papers of the American Fur Company," *American Historical Review,* Vol. XXXII, pp. 519-538 (April, 1927). One may also read J. Ward Ruckman, "Ramsay Crooks and the Fur Trade of the Northwest," *Minnesota History,* Vol. VII, pp. 18-31 (March, 1926); and the articles on Ramsay Crooks and John Jacob Astor in the *Dictionary of American Biography.* Scattered through the twenty volumes of the *Collections* are the reminiscences of many persons, too numerous to be listed here, who participated in the fur trade in its latter days.   Typical is "Seventy-two Years Recollections of Wisconsin," by Augustin Grignon, *Collections,* Vol. III, pp. 197-296.

CHAPTER V

THE TERRITORIAL PERIOD:
I. SETTLEMENT AND EARLY POLITICS

American Methods of Establishing New Communities

IN THE great struggle between the Indians and the fur traders on the one hand and the Americans on the other, we have told in the preceding chapter of those who were compelled to yield. We turn now to the victorious Anglo-Saxons, the founders of present-day Wisconsin. But before narrating their arrival, we must again give attention to events in the East where a procedure had been developed for opening up the West. We are wont to think of government under the Articles of Confederation as rather ineffective, but in their time three steps were taken that were destined to be vastly important for the West. They were: the surrender by several states of their claims to lands in the West and the resultant creation of a national domain; the beginning of a system of surveying and land description; and the passing of the Northwest Ordinance, a basic law for the Old Northwest.

Not all the states had western lands nor were the origins of their claims in all cases the same. Some went back to royal charters. New York's rights arose from treaties with the Indians, principally with the Iroquois tribes. Virginia, besides having a royal charter, possessed by right of conquest, the achievement of George Rogers Clark. The Virginia claim covered the whole of what is now Wisconsin. That of Massachusetts stretched in a band about eighty miles wide across the southern end of the state. Maryland, one of the states without western lands, led in the demand that these areas should become the property of the thirteen states as a whole. New York gave up her claim in 1780, and one by one others fell into line. Virginia's final deed of cession was dated May 1, 1784, and Massachusetts' strip was given up late in the same year. The transfer of these lands to the central government made possible uniform administration in the western country.

In Wisconsin, as in all the Northwest, there is a standard system of surveying land and describing it for record of ownership. The unit is the surveyor's township, sometimes called the congressional township, a rectangle six miles square, and within the township the sections or square miles are always numbered in the same order. This system originated with the committee on western lands in the Congress under the Articles of Confederation, of which Thomas Jefferson was chairman. Its report became the Land Ordinance of May, 1785. It proposed the rectangular unit containing thirty-six square miles, and it made the rule that the survey of any region should be completed before it was opened to sale and settlement. Under Thomas Hutchins, geographer of the United States, the survey was begun in southeastern Ohio in 1785. It was nearly half a century later, in 1833, that the federal surveys reached Wisconsin.

In the year in which Virginia gave up her lands and made the public domain a certainty, the Congress passed an ordinance for the future partition of the Old Northwest and laid down certain general principles to be applied to it. There were to be ten states with rather odd-sounding names: present Wisconsin fell within Sylvania, Michigania, and Assenisipia. More important than these details was the decision that in due course there would be equality of status between the new states and the original thirteen.

The Northwest Ordinance of July 13, 1787, was more mature and adequate in every way than the one of 1784, and repeated all that was of value in it. While names were not given, there were to be three or five states. If five, the southern three were to have north and south boundaries as do Ohio, Indiana, and Illinois today. Wisconsin and Michigan, however, were to be bounded on the south by an east and west line drawn through the southern tip of Lake Michigan. It was assumed also that the northwestern-most of the five states would extend to the international boundaries, on the north Lake Superior and Pigeon River to the Lake of the Woods, and on the west the Mississippi River. For the states to be made out of the Northwest the ordinance prescribed three stages of progress: a period of simple autocracy, presumably short; when there were five thousand voters, a territorial stage with practical self-government, but with tutelage to rather than membership in the national government; and lastly, when there should be sixty thousand free inhabitants, full statehood. Religious freedom was guaranteed. There was to be jury trial, no *ex post facto* laws were to be passed, and the writ of habeas corpus was not to be suspended. Jefferson's hand is seen in the provision that an intestate estate was to be divided equally among brothers and sisters; if there was a widow, however, she should have one-third of the estate. Schools and the means of education were to be encouraged. Slavery and involuntary servitude, except in punishment of crime, were forbidden. In 1787 there were perhaps four hundred Negroes as well as some Indians, called *panis,* held in slavery by the French and Canadians in their various settlements in the Northwest. It was not the intent of the ordinance to free these slaves. This was repeatedly stated by General Arthur St. Clair, who could speak not only as Governor of the Northwest but also as the presiding officer of the Congress that passed the ordinance. On the other hand, St. Clair also said while he was governor that owners might not bring in slaves from other parts of the United States.

It is sometimes forgotten that the Ordinance of 1787 was binding only until the people of the states set up in the Northwest should make their own constitutions. The ordinance was valid in Ohio only until 1802, throughout Wisconsin only until 1848. Of course the people of a state might put into their constitutions such parts of the ordinance as they chose to adopt, or their legislature might repeat clauses from it in their laws; but when a state entered the union it was no longer under the ordinance.

Thus, by the various enactments of 1784, 1785, and 1787, the lines were laid down which were to guide the development of the Northwest. Nearly fifty years passed before the farming frontier reached Wisconsin. During that time Ohio, Indiana, and Illinois became full-fledged states, and Michigan was ready to become one. All the while the people and the federal government were gaining experience and forming habits. Since most of those who came to Wisconsin in the van of settlement expected to purchase land, the laws and regulations about public lands are part of the social and economic history of Wisconsin.

From 1800 to 1820 the minimum price of government land was two dollars an acre, one-fourth to be paid at the beginning and the rest in installments spread over several years. The smallest amount purchasable (after 1804) was 160 acres. In 1820 buying on the installment plan was ended, the price was reduced to a dollar and a quarter an acre, and as few as eighty acres might be purchased. The next milestone in public land legislation was the general pre-emption law of 1841. All through the years bold spirits had anticipated the government's program by going onto the land before it was ready for sale and occupancy. There had been laws from time to time in aid of this class, turning them into owners or giving them precedence in buying. Finally, in 1841, the general pre-emption law was passed, and, from that time on, settlers usually occupied the choicest lands before the government had offered them for sale. These pre-emptioners were permitted to buy at the minimum price before the sale was opened to the general public. Thus they obtained their lands ahead of the speculators so much feared and hated on the frontier. There was a growing opinion in the West that it was wrong of the government to ask money for land of those who under conditions of hardship were advancing the bounds of civilization. The fruit of this reasoning was the Homestead Act of 1862, by which one who lived for five years on a piece of land received it free or for the payment of a small fee. This law was much used in northern Wisconsin; but through the years when southern and eastern Wisconsin were settled, the price remained a dollar and a quarter an acre, with no credit extended by the government.

The process of preparing land and inviting settlement was entirely in the hands of the federal government, and by the 1830's the routine to be followed was familiar. The steps were: extinction of the Indian title, survey, establishment of land offices, advertisement, sale at auction, and, after the auction, sale of the remaining land at minimum prices. As we have already seen, the Indian cessions of 1829 and 1833 transferred to the federal government all of Wisconsin south of the Fox and Wisconsin rivers. Immediately the federal surveyors began their important part in the conquest of the wilderness. It was usual to run the township lines first and cover the map with squares six miles each way. Other surveyors, sometimes a year or two later, marked the sections within the townships. Work was under the direction of the surveyor-general at Dubuque, Iowa, who had charge of three or four states or territories. The survey south and east of the two rivers was done before the panic of 1837, and then there was a pause. By the end of 1849, a little less than fifteen million acres, or about three-sevenths of the state, had been surveyed, and nearly all of this had been offered for sale. At this time something more than four million acres had been sold, and the federal government had also parted with a million acres to the state of Wisconsin to be sold for the benefit of schools and the state university. There were also over eight hundred thousand acres set aside in aid of internal improvements. Much of the land under these two heads was put on the market in competition with the federal lands. The survey of Wisconsin kept on in its steady course until the completion of field work in 1865 and of office work in the following year. The services of the surveyors in laying squarely the foundations of the state have been too little appreciated. Besides marking the ground or "establishing the monuments," they brought back descriptions of the country that were of great help to farmers in choosing lands and that now, when the face of the earth has been so altered by the hand of man, are of great historic interest.

Sales of federal land were conducted through land offices established on the lands to be sold. Each office cared for a definite area or "district," and notices and proclamations informed the public in advance what was to be offered for sale. The first two offices in Wisconsin were set up at Green Bay and Mineral Point in the autumn of 1834. A third was opened at Milwaukee in 1838, and a fourth at St. Croix Falls in 1848. By 1865, when the work of surveying was completed, the three first offices had been closed or moved elsewhere, and the whole state was divided into six districts and the offices were at Menasha, Stevens Point, La Crosse, Eau Claire, Bayfield, and St. Croix Falls. One by one these offices were discontinued as the work in their respective districts was finished. The office of the Wisconsin River District was moved to Wausau in 1873, and this, the last federal land office in Wisconsin, closed its books in 1928.

THE LEAD MINERS

The occupation of Wisconsin by English-speaking Americans began in two widely separated parts of the state. More in accord with the usual pattern and eventually much greater in numbers was the settlement along the Lake Michigan shore. Earlier in point of time was the occupation of the southwest, where the attraction was at first not farm land, but deposits of lead.

The Wisconsin lead mining region extended, in terms of a modern map, over the counties of Grant, Iowa, and La Fayette and included the western edge of Dane and Green counties. This community had a different origin and at first a different development from the rest of Wisconsin. The Indians had known something of the lead deposits for more than a century, and the first Europeans to mine lead were Indian traders. Julian Dubuque lived from 1788 to 1810 on the site of the city in Iowa that bears his name, and there he bought furs and mined lead. He probably obtained some of his mineral from east of the Mississippi. Mining in Wisconsin by English-speaking Americans was an extension of beginnings in Illinois at Fever River, or Galena, as it was called after 1825. A trader named Davenport took lead from this vicinity to St. Louis in 1816, and six years later Colonel James A. Johnson, a Kentuckian, began large-scale operations using both white miners and Negro slaves. From the middle of 1825 to the end of August fourteen months later, the number of miners grew from 100 to more than 450, and in 1827 there was a considerable mining boom. In that year lead production in Wisconsin and the adjacent part of Illinois was over 5,000,000 pounds; in 1828 it was 11,000,000, and the next year, 12,000,000 pounds. By this time most of the good "diggings" in the whole area north to the Wisconsin River had been discovered. The majority of the inrushing population was southern, coming from southern Illinois, Kentucky, and Tennessee, with smaller numbers from other southern states. It was in 1827 that Henry Dodge, William S. Hamilton, son of the great Alexander Hamilton, and many other well-known leaders came in. In time there came to be an increasing part of the population from other sources. Many professional men were from the eastern states, and from about 1835 onward there were many Englishmen from Cornwall, who brought valuable technical skill acquired in the Cornish mines.

The usual methods of disposing of government lands were not followed in the case of mineral lands. Here was supposed to be a great source of income for the nation, and so the mineral-bearing lands were reserved from sale and leased for one-tenth of their product. The Indian agents tried to keep the white settlers out of the region, for the Indian title was not extinguished until 1829. There was also a superintendent of the lead mines, an officer of the Ordnance Department, but he could not control the movements of the miners nor collect the rent due to the government. In October, 1834, a land office was opened at Mineral Point, the "metropolis" of the lead region, for the sale of agricultural land, and some mineral land was bought as farmland; but it was not until 1847 that the reserved lands were sold. By that time agriculture was coming to be more important than mining, even in this region; most of the miners had become farmers. Some of them who wanted to continue mining went to California in the gold rush of 1849, and a few went north to the copper country in Upper Michigan.

Connected with the rise and decline of lead mining is the story of the shot tower at Helena. This place, probably the earliest village in Iowa County, was begun in 1827 or 1828 on the south bank of the Wisconsin River and served for many years as a shipping point for the lead mines. Daniel Whitney of Green Bay began building a shot tower there in 1831, and while the Black Hawk War delayed his enterprise somewhat, he commenced pouring shot before the end of 1832. The manufacture was continued there until 1861. The site is now included within the Tower Hill Park, the property of the state.

THE GREAT IMMIGRATION AND ITS ORIGIN

The occupation of the southeastern part of Wisconsin was slightly later than the settlement of the lead-mining southwest; it was also different in character. The stream of migration that had once flowed from New England and New York down the Ohio River was now following the Erie Canal westward. In 1825 a military road from Detroit to Chicago was begun, and this, with the daily steamboat service from Buffalo to Detroit, became an extension of the Erie Canal. This road was an axis of settlement for all southern Michigan, and soon became a much-traveled route to the regions west and north of Chicago. The great initial growth that turned a territory into a state came in Michigan before the panic of 1837, while in Wisconsin it came largely after the panic and the succeeding depression. This growth is recorded both in the sales of public lands and in census figures. Regarding the first, after a negligible beginning in the fall of 1834, sales for the year 1835 were 217,000 acres and for the next year, 646,000 acres. It is said, however, that three-fourths of the sales of the first two years were made to speculators. Then the panic caused light sales for two years, after which regular progress was resumed. A high point of 700,000 acres was reached in 1846, and almost as much was sold the next year. Emphatically, Wisconsin was the area most favored by homeseekers from the East in the late 1840's. Between 1842 and 1846, the population increased from 46,000 to 155,000, while during the next four years it almost doubled, reaching 305,000 in 1850. Ten years earlier it had been 30,747. Nine-tenths of the mature citizens had come to the state within the decade, and half of them within the last four years. The institutions and customs that make up civilization had been brought in by these recent immigrants, and hence their origins have great significance.

The incoming people of the decade 1840-1850 may be divided into two groups—immigrants and those born within the United States. Of the first group, which comprised a third of the population of the state, a little more than half were born under British sovereignty. There were 21,000 Irish, 19,000 English, and Wales, Scotland, and Canada each furnished a few thousands. This element, except possibly a few Welsh, had no language barrier to overcome, and found it easy to adjust itself to a new community and to contribute to it. Among the alien-born who did not speak English, the two most important groups were some 40,000 Germans and German-speaking Swiss, and about 8,600 Norwegians. The Germans tended to gather most closely in the counties along Lake Michigan, although there were some Germans in every county. The Norwegians took up their abode in a band of farming country across the southern end of the state east of the lead region, being most numerous in the counties of Dane, Rock, Walworth, and Racine. Two-thirds of all the Norwegians in the United States at that time were in Wisconsin. It was only after these Germans and Norwegians had, at least in the persons of their leaders, mastered the English language, that they could exert an influence commensurate with their numbers in the community and political life of the state, though from the beginning they were taking their part in economic upbuilding and progress.

It is when we observe the origins of the American-born migrants

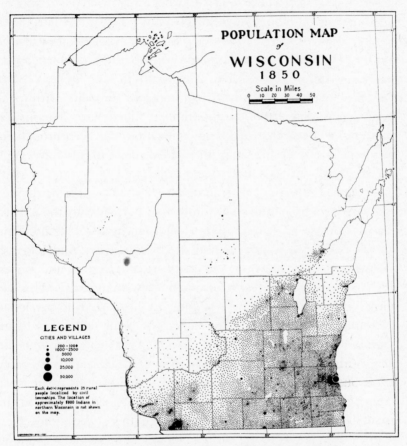

POPULATION DISTRIBUTION IN WISCONSIN, 1850*

of the 1840's that we get the reason for much that is most characteristic in the foundations of Wisconsin. There were 198,000 born in the United States, and if we subtract those born in Wisconsin, most of whom would be children, we have left about 135,-

* By courtesy of Guy-Harold Smith and the American Geographical Society of New York.

ooo. Of these, 68,000 were born in New York state. About 10,-
ooo may be credited to each of the following: Vermont, other New
England States, Ohio, and Pennsylvania. Much of Ohio and
northern and western New York, whence came the migrants to
Wisconsin, had been strongly influenced in their formative periods
by migration from New England. Yet New England, New York,
and Ohio accounted for 100,000, or two-thirds, of the adult native-
born population of Wisconsin. The southern states and southern
Illinois, which was of the same complexion, furnished the dominant element in the lead-mining counties, but elsewhere had a very
slight representation. When we come in a later chapter to see
what sort of a government was provided for Wisconsin, we shall
not be surprised to find that it was a New York adaptation of New
England institutions.

When a garrison was established at Fort Howard in 1816, the
old fur-trading settlement had about fifty families, or perhaps
250 persons. The various federal activities put new life into the
community. About twenty thousand dollars were spent in putting up the buildings of the fort. As enlistments expired, many
soldiers remained to make a livelihood in the town or in the country round about. Several men later prominent in the state had
come to Green Bay by 1827: James D. Doty, to be a judge; his
cousin, Morgan L. Martin, a young lawyer; Daniel Whitney, an
active businessman. The list might be extended. In 1820 Isaac
Lee as government land commissioner mapped the lands of the
French-Canadian settlers with their long strips of land stretching
away at right angles to the river. Not one of them had a frontage
of more than five hundred feet on the river and none, apparently,
made farming more than a side-line; they were still fur traders.
About Green Bay the Indian title east of the river was extinguished
in 1831, and west of it in 1836, except for what the Oneida and
other eastern Indians held. The land office was opened in 1834,
and about that time the first town plat was made and recorded.
During the next fifteen years some of the French Canadians actu-

ally became farmers. They were joined by other farmers of American origin. Villages were founded on the lower Fox, most of them with high hopes of water power development.

Settlement in the southeastern part of the territory was much more rapid than around Green Bay. At the end of 1833 Milwaukee was merely a fur-trading post where Solomon Juneau and his brother and occasionally one or two other French Canadians were to be found with their families. In the fall of that year Morgan L. Martin decided that the spot had promise, and bought a half interest in what Solomon Juneau owned, and, as soon as possible, entered it at the Green Bay land office. Their holdings were in the point east of the river. The west side was developed by Byron Kilbourn, while south of the Menominee George H. Walker laid out a village. Similar beginnings were made at Racine and Kenosha.

More typical, because far more people were concerned, was the making of farms in the southeastern part of the state. Men from the East came to the Wisconsin lake ports by sailing ship or steamer, or else came up from Chicago by the road opened in 1835. They spied out the land and chose farms to their liking. What they sought, if they could find it, was a piece of land having some open prairie for immediate plowing, some woodland to provide shelter from the winds and to furnish building material, and some lowland or marsh where the pasture or hay supply would never give out. The great influx began in 1835; by July of 1836 there were 2,893 people in the southeastern part of the state; in 1840 there were more than nine thousand. The new land district of Milwaukee was set up, but sales were repeatedly postponed. A few sales were made in November, 1838, but the great land sale began on February 17, 1839, and continued for four weeks. During that time lands to the value of $600,000 were sold, all but a negligible part of it at a dollar and a quarter an acre. Up to that time all these farmers on the land had had merely the status of squatters or would-be pre-emptioners. They had organized a great claims society, and thanks to this they got the lands of their choice. With this sale southeastern Wisconsin began to develop as an American community.

THE BEGINNINGS OF GOVERNMENT AND POLITICS

The Ohio Land Company began a town at Marietta, Ohio, in May, 1788, and in July the appointed governor, General St. Clair, with a secretary and three judges, took up his residence there. With the arrival of these officials, the Northwest Territory began its governmental evolution. In February, 1799, the first representative assembly in the Northwest met at Cincinnati. In the following year Indiana Territory was erected, and William Henry Harrison ruled it from Vincennes. It included, at first, all of Illinois and Wisconsin. Harrison issued to several residents of Wisconsin commissions to be justices of the peace, some directed to traders at Prairie du Chien, and one, dated 1803, to Charles Reaume of "La Bay, St. Clair County, Indiana." Curiously enough, those who received these commissions were at that time British subjects. Wisconsin was part of Illinois Territory from 1809 to 1818, and of Michigan Territory from 1818 to 1836.

Lewis Cass was governor of Michigan Territory from 1813 to 1831. While he held sway, government was extended west of Lake Michigan in several ways. Two forts were established in 1816 and another in 1828. The first steps were taken to secure land from the Indians. In 1818 Cass set up the three counties of Brown, Crawford, and Michilimackinac. Before 1836 three more counties were added, Chippewa, Iowa, and Milwaukee. Four of these, though afterwards greatly reduced in size, have had a continuous existence since their establishment, and hence are considerably older than the state of Wisconsin.

In accordance with an Act of Congress of 1823, a judge was to be provided for the part of Michigan Territory west of Lake Michigan, and James Duane Doty was appointed to the office. He was born in New York state in 1799, and in 1819 he began the practice of law in Detroit, where he won the favor and friendship of Governor Cass. Doty began his work in 1824, and until 1832, he held court, now in Green Bay where he made his home, now in Prairie du Chien or in Mineral Point. His travels about the future state, sometimes by canoe and sometimes on horseback, gave him a great familiarity with its resources. David Irwin held the same office from 1832 to 1836. The people of

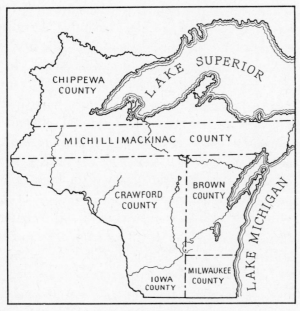

COUNTIES IN 1836*

Michigan gradually advanced in the degree of self-government that they enjoyed. For a time all officials were appointed; then there was a legislative council of nine men chosen from eighteen elected by the people; and finally, in 1827, the people had the privilege of choosing councillors. The people west of the lake took part in this rather meager political life. Brown County sent Robert Irwin, Jr., to the council in 1827, and from 1832 to 1835 the West was represented at Detroit by Morgan L. Martin of Green

* From Joseph Schafer, *Agriculture in Wisconsin* (1922). By courtesy of the State Historical Society of Wisconsin.

Bay. One year he was accompanied by James Duane Doty. The Michigan legislative council chartered the first bank of Wisconsin as well as some other business corporations. While Lewis Cass was governor he often visited the western part of his territory, and the published accounts of his journeys awakened considerable interest throughout the eastern part of the United States.

The people of Michigan set up a state government in the spring of 1835. Their boundary disputes delayed their admission to the union until January, 1837, and in the meantime the region west of Lake Michigan was not to be left without government. The acting governor at Detroit directed the holding of an election in Wisconsin in October, 1835, and the western "remnant" chose a territorial delegate and a council. Their choice for delegate was George Wallace Jones, for some years past one of the leaders in the lead mining community. Born in Indiana, he had spent his boyhood in Missouri, save for four years in college at Lexington, Kentucky. He was a genial Southerner and a skilful politician. He took his seat in the lower house of Congress in December, 1835, and though still called the delegate from Michigan Territory, he was really a spokesman at Washington for the people of Wisconsin and Iowa.   In the autumn of 1836 he was again elected territorial delegate, this time from "Wisconsin Territory." Of the council elected in October, 1835, nine men met at Green Bay on January 1, but in the absence of the acting governor they could do nothing but pass resolutions. It was known as the "Rump Council"; its president was William S. Hamilton.

The act of 1836 which set up the Territory of Wisconsin took effect on July 3. Wisconsin was the fifth state to grow up under the Ordinance of 1787. For the four older states there had been a first stage of autocratic rule, a second grade of territorial life, and then statehood. Wisconsin was permitted to begin life at once in the second grade, perhaps because as a part of Michigan Territory she had already tasted it. The governor received fifteen hundred dollars as governor and an additional thousand dollars as superintendent of Indian affairs. Members of the legislature

were paid three dollars for each day of the session. The first
territorial governor of Wisconsin was Henry Dodge, a Democrat,
who was well and favorably known to President Jackson. While
still engaged in the Black Hawk War he had been given command
of a regiment of mounted men in the United States Army, and
for the next four years he had served his country on the Indian
frontier. He was governor from July, 1836, to October, 1841. In
1840 the Whig victory made certain that a supporter of Harrison
and Tyler would rule in Wisconsin, and Tyler chose James Duane
Doty. Doty held office for almost three years (to September,
1844), and then the Whig regime was continued nine months
longer under Nathaniel P. Tallmadge, who had been a United
States Senator from New York. When the Democrats came into
power again at Washington, President Polk restored Henry
Dodge, and he was governor for the last three years of the territorial period.

The most important expression of political opinion lay in the
election of a delegate to Congress. George Wallace Jones, the first
delegate, fell from favor by acting as a second in a duel at Washington that had a fatal issue. He soon removed to Iowa and there
had a long and distinguished political career. After him as delegates came James Duane Doty for three years (1838-1841), Henry
Dodge for four (1841-1845), and Morgan L. Martin for two (1845-
1847). Party lines were not closely drawn until 1841 when both
Whigs and Democrats perfected local organizations. Before that
time the territorial delegate was supposed to be nonpartisan, but
undoubtedly up to at least 1841, the majority in the territory were
Democrats, and in harmony with Andrew Jackson and Martin
Van Buren. It was later held up as a reproach against Doty that
while he was delegate he made friends with the Whigs and so
gained the appointment as territorial governor. All the while
the New England element was becoming more numerous, especially in the southeastern part of the state, and in 1847 the Whigs
elected the last territorial delegate, John H. Tweedy, a lawyer of
Milwaukee. The factors in this election were complicated, but

the majority in the territory was probably still Democratic. Moses M. Strong, the Democratic candidate, had a reputation for drinking that is said to have lost him the votes of the stricter New England elements, and there was also a third-party movement that may have thrown the election to the Whigs.

Wisconsin's territorial legislature was made up of a council of thirteen, who served four years, and a house of representatives of twenty-six members serving two years. Six times all or part of this assembly was chosen by the people of Wisconsin Territory. For two years a great area west of the Mississippi was temporarily attached to Wisconsin, and during that time nearly half the legislators came from what is now Iowa. There were twelve regular annual sessions and four short special sessions.

The first assembly met at Belmont, now called Old Belmont, October 25, 1836. Four counties in what is now Wisconsin were represented. The assembly at once created fifteen new counties, dividing up the land south and east of the Fox and Wisconsin rivers almost as it is at present. All this area had been surveyed between 1833 and 1836, and the surveyors' lines were used as boundaries of counties. By the time Wisconsin become a state in 1848 there were twenty-nine counties.

One of the most important acts of this assembly was to locate the capital at Madison. The population east of the Mississippi lay in three widely separated districts, the southwest, the southeast, and the old Green Bay area, and each sought to have the capital. In a sense the choice of Madison was a compromise, but there is more to the story. James Duane Doty had been familiar with the site for years. Federal surveyors had done their work there in 1834, and in October, 1835, Doty entered a hundred acres in what is now the eastern part of Madison at the land office in Green Bay. A few months later he and a company of associates entered twelve hundred acres more. In June, 1836, we find Doty writing to George Wallace Jones, the delegate at Washington, offering him a share in the real estate enterprise: "I think it is obvious we can make something handsome out of this." Doty had the site surveyed and platted, and the surveyor testifies that the unique plan of Madison is Doty's own. Doty also won the necessary votes in the Assembly; some who hesitated were given choice lots in the new town. Thus was the compromise effected. But all who love the beauty of Madison may be glad that Doty chose and planned as he did. At the time when it was chosen to be the seat of government, in December, 1836, it had no inhabitants. In April, 1837, an innkeeper's wife came on to superintend some laborers in the erection of a hotel, and in May workmen arrived from Milwaukee to begin work on the capitol building.

The construction of this building was the cause of much contention. The federal government gave $40,000 for this purpose, and the legislature that chose Madison as the capital also appointed a commission of three to supervise the construction. Of this first body, the treasurer was James Duane Doty. The commissioners at first tried to carry on the work themselves; then they entered into an agreement with a contractor. Then the legislature of 1839 investigated the commission, found that it had misappropriated funds, and appointed a second commission. Before the capitol was finished there were two sets of commissioners and two successive contractors who wrangled with each legislature and among themselves.

During the territorial period the lead mining region furnished political leaders and office holders out of all proportion to its population. Henry Dodge was the natural leader of that part of the territory, and in twelve years he was governor eight years and delegate to Congress for four. While Doty was territorial governor the Dodge partisans persecuted him in every possible way. Dodge, then delegate at Washington, tried to get Doty removed from office because he had misapplied the funds put into his hands to build the capitol. Doty on his part rather abused his position, refusing to do business with a legislature which had assembled without a call from himself as governor, and apparently making more of small points of procedure than of public desires and public welfare. He even insisted on an odd spelling of the word Wisconsin until a joint resolution of the legislature dictated the spelling that we use today. The older states of the Northwest went through their territorial periods under governors who had an absolute veto power. In 1839 Congress changed the executive veto in Wisconsin from an absolute to a suspensive one, and Governor Doty in 1843 had to see six laws passed over his veto by the required two-thirds of each branch of his legislature. This practice was later written into the constitution of Wisconsin.

A sad incident in the history of the territory happened February 11, 1842, when John Vinyard of Grant County shot Charles C. P. Arndt of Green Bay. Both were members of the council, and in a council session Vinyard had called a statement by Arndt a falsehood. After adjournment for the day, but while the councillors were still in their place of meeting, Arndt pressed the quarrel and either struck Vinyard with his fist or was about to do so. Vinyard drew a pistol and shot Arndt, who died within a few minutes. Vinyard was within his rights in defending himself, but not in doing so with a deadly weapon. The Grant County jury before whom Vinyard was tried for manslaughter returned a verdict of not guilty. The episode gave the territory an unpleasant notoriety. Charles Dickens was traveling in the United States at that time, and in his *American Notes* comments on the occurrence as something typical of frontier society in the United States.

When the Mexican War came, the federal government did not care to use the proffered militia of Wisconsin Territory or the German riflemen of Milwaukee. Many who wanted to enlist went back to the older states to do so. Then a company of volunteers was enrolled at Milwaukee, and the command was given to an able young lawyer of Southport (Kenosha) named Augustus Quarles. In all 146 men joined this company. Most of them left Milwaukee by steamer early in May, 1847. After reaching Lake Erie they crossed Ohio by river and canal to Covington, Kentucky, and, after some camp experience there, went on to New Orleans. August 27, 1847, the company took part in the storming of Charubusco, and Captain Quarles was killed. Altogether some forty of the company never returned. In June, 1848, the burial of Captain Quarles was made the occasion of a public ceremony at Milwaukee with appropriate orations. About seven hundred men in all enlisted in Wisconsin for this war, but it ended before most of them left American soil.

Selected Bibliography

The older narratives that cover the matter of this and the following chapter are: Reuben G. Thwaites, *Wisconsin* (Boston, 1908), pp. 229-287; Milo M. Quaife, *Wisconsin, Its History and Its People* (Chicago, 1924), Vol. I, pp. 441-472, 497-526; *Wisconsin in Three Centuries* (New York, 1906), Vol. II, pp. 293-311; Vol. III, pp. 107-136; and Alexander M. Thomson, *A Political History of Wisconsin* (Milwaukee, 1902), pp. 17-72. To these may be added the work of a contemporary, Moses M. Strong, *History of the Territory of Wisconsin from 1836-1848* (Madison, 1885, published by the state). Repellent on account of its annalistic method, but of great usefulness, is Charles R. Tuttle, *An Illustrated History of Wisconsin* (Boston, 1875), pp. 176-252.

The public land system before 1862 may be studied in Frederic L. Paxson, *History of the American Frontier* (Boston, 1924), pp. 220-225, 381-391; or in George M. Stephenson, *Political History of the Public Lands, 1840-1862* (Boston, 1917). Roy M. Robbins, "Preëmption, A Frontier Triumph," *Mississippi Valley History Review,* Vol. XVIII, pp. 331-349 (December, 1931), is also helpful. Archer B. Hulbert, *Ohio in the Time of Confederation* (Marietta, Ohio, 1918) has an excellent account of the beginning of rectangular surveys.

Joseph Schafer has written for the State Historical Society of which he is superintendent a series of volumes known as the Wisconsin Domesday Book. In addition to usual sources he has utilized descriptions of land by surveyors and geologists, land office records, and the manuscript census sheets, state and federal. *Town Studies,* Vol. I (Madison, 1924), describes twenty-three towns (townships) in the older part of the state. The valuable introduction tells, among other things, how farmers and speculators chose land a century ago. Then came *Four Wisconsin Counties* (Madison, 1927), dealing with farm making in the counties of Kenosha, Racine, Milwaukee, and Ozaukee. *The Wisconsin Lead Region* (Madison, 1932) covered three counties in the southwest. Both these volumes add, to economic and social accounts, a good deal of political history, especially for the period before 1860. The most recent in the series, *The Winnebago-Horicon Basin* (Madison, 1937), deals with four counties surrounding and to the south of Lake Winnebago.

Guy-Harold Smith, "The Settlement and Distribution of the Population in Wisconsin," *Transactions of the Wisconsin Academy of Sciences, Arts, and Letters,* Vol. XXIV (1929), pp. 53-108, besides the text, has a series of eight maps based on federal census reports from 1850 to 1920. These maps have been frequently reproduced in other books.

Reuben G. Thwaites wrote "Notes on Early Lead Mining in the Fever (or Galena) River Region," *Collections of the State Historical Society of Wisconsin,* Vol. XIII, pp. 271-291. This is followed by Orin G. Libby, "Significance of the Lead and Shot Trade in Early Wisconsin History," *ibid.,* pp. 293-334; and "Chronicle of the Helena Shot Tower," *ibid.,* 354-374. John A. Wilgus contributed "The Century Old Lead Region in Early Wisconsin History," *Wisconsin Magazine of History,* Vol. X, pp. 401-410 (June, 1927). Louis Pelzer, *Henry Dodge* (Iowa City, 1911), is the standard biography of the lead region's greatest leader. Another prominent man of that region found his biographer in Sylvan Joseph Muldoon, *Alexander Hamilton's Pioneer Son; the Life and Times of Colonel William Stephen Hamilton, 1797-1850* (Harrisburg, 1930). John C. Parish wrote an interesting biography, *George Wallace Jones* (Iowa City, 1912).

A modern estimate of political leaders of the territorial period is by Joseph Schafer, "Sectional and Personal Politics in Early Wisconsin," *Wisconsin Magazine of History,* Vol. XVIII, pp. 442-465 (June, 1935). Joseph Schafer also edited the record of the Rump Council at Green Bay in January, 1836, for the *Proceedings, 1920.* "The Papers of James Duane Doty," dated 1820-1827, are given in *Collections,* Vol. XIII, pp. 163-246. The "Narrative of Morgan L. Martin," *ibid.,* Vol. XI, pp. 385-415, derives from one who was the leading citizen of Green Bay for nearly sixty years. It was his daughter, Deborah N. Martin, who wrote the *History of Brown County* (2 vols., Chicago, 1913), which is of great value for the early history of the Green Bay region. James S. Buck, *Pioneer History of Milwaukee* (Milwaukee, 1876), preserves many documents not elsewhere available. At page 17, there is a letter of reminiscences by Morgan L. Martin.

The shooting of Charles C. P. Arndt is the subject of Milo M. Quaife, "Wisconsin's Saddest Tragedy," *Wisconsin Magazine of History,* Vol. V, pp. 264-283 (March, 1922).

A paper by H. W. Bleyer, "Wisconsin in the Mexican War," appeared in the *Milwaukee Sentinel,* August 13, 1899.

CHAPTER VI

THE TERRITORIAL PERIOD:
II. ELEMENTS OF COMMUNITY LIFE

TRANSPORTATION

BY THE middle of the nineteenth century large numbers of people had entered Wisconsin, and the Yankee origin of the majority had largely determined the form of local and state government. But life comprised more than the presence of people and a framework of government. The pioneer settlers needed roads and other means of communication, and in those days government did little in that direction; they wanted schools and churches and lodges; to carry on their business they needed money and banks. With reference to most of these things they had brought ideas with them, although at first there had to be makeshifts such as log houses for dwelling places and canoes as means of travel. They might for a time, too, do without parts of what constituted an older society, but not for long. From the moment of their arrival they began to build what seemed to them the essentials of civilized life.

During the French and British period the canoe had been the chief means of travel and transport in Wisconsin. Through the 1820's Americans on official business, like Lewis Cass and James Duane Doty, traveled by canoe or on horseback. The fur traders had also developed the *bateau*. This was propelled with oars or small poles by a crew of ten or twelve men, could carry up to twelve tons of freight, and drew about two feet of water. The first innovation that marked the arrival of the Americans was the

Durham boat, named for a Pennsylvanian who invented it about 1750. This craft ranged from forty to sixty feet in length, was ten or twelve feet wide, carried twenty to thirty tons, and yet drew only eighteen or twenty inches of water. A crew of seven or eight men could thus transport some two and a half times as much as ten or twelve men in a *bateau*. Along the straight sides of the Durham boat was a platform about fourteen inches wide along which walked the men who were propelling the boat. Each man, starting at the bow, set his pole in the river bottom, walked the length of the board, disengaged his pole and carried it to the bow to repeat the process. The Durham boat was introduced to Wisconsin by John P. Arndt, who built one at Green Bay in 1825, and continued to manufacture them for many years. Within five years they had monopolized the heavy traffic on the Fox and Wisconsin, and they kept it until the advent of the steamboats.

The Indians had many trails by which they went from place to place on foot, and sometimes the first white settlers used them; they were, however, quite impassable for vehicles. The first roads in the territory probably led from some of the lead mines in the southwest down to the river ports on the Mississippi and the Wisconsin. Of much more general importance were the military roads. The earliest of these to be laid down began at Fort Howard, ran east of the Fox River and Lake Winnebago, turned west at Fond du Lac, and continued to Fort Winnebago and then to Fort Crawford at Prairie du Chien. In the southwest it followed the divide between tributaries to the Wisconsin and those running south into Illinois. In the first part of its course it ran through forests, and considerable labor was expended in felling trees and removing stumps. Southwest of Fond du Lac it usually ran through openings or along prairie, and nothing was done beyond marking out the route with parallel furrows. Low spots were occasionally corduroyed with logs but there were no bridges and of course no surfacing of any kind. This road was cleared— one could hardly say constructed—in 1835. A second military road, ready a year and a half or two years later, connected Fort

Howard with Chicago. The federal government made one small appropriation of $10,000 in 1845 to keep the first military road in better condition and to make roads out to Sheboygan and Racine, but, aside from this, Wisconsin had to do her own roadmaking. From about 1846 until past the Civil War the principal improvement was the building of plank roads. They were constructed by private companies chartered by the legislature, and users paid toll. The wooden plank laid on the ground soon rotted, but in most cases these roads served until the railroads came. The chief public conveyances were the stage coaches, usually drawn by four horses. They, too, largely disappeared at the advent of the railways. While the stages continued they were served by many country hostelries.

Three great transportation projects were much discussed in the territorial period of Wisconsin: a canal which would link Milwaukee with the Mississippi River by way of the Rock River; the canalization of the old Fox-Wisconsin River route; and the building of railways. The first has its history almost entirely in the territorial period. The "first public meeting in Milwaukee" in December, 1835, passed resolutions asking Congress for land to help with a canal or a railway. Byron Kilbourn had worked as an engineer at canal building in Ohio, and he led many in Milwaukee and elsewhere to favor the canal project. The Milwaukee and Rock River Canal Company was chartered on January 5, 1838, and Kilbourn became its president. He went to Washington and, through an act of June 18, 1838, secured, to help finance the canal, a grant of the odd-numbered sections of a strip along its course ten miles wide. This grant amounted to nearly 140,000 acres. The act transferred the lands to Wisconsin Territory in trust, and also provided that they should be sold at $2.50 an acre. The route having been determined upon, the first sale of land embracing about 43,000 acres took place in July, 1839. The territorial legislature made generous terms for settlers; they need pay only 10 per cent of the purchase price to begin with. The first sale produced about $12,000 in initial cash payments.

This canal project had many competitors and enemies. Some favored railways; some, the Fox-Wisconsin canal, and some hated the enterprise merely because it was Kilbourn's. It was difficult to borrow money after the panic of 1837 and most of the time the legislature was either lukewarm or hostile. When Doty became governor in October, 1841, he withdrew all Kilbourn's powers and ended the activities of the company. The legislature, on February 18, 1842, stopped payments due to the company from purchasers of canal lands and closed all other avenues of income. The canal had not even been begun, and this act made clear that it never would be constructed; but the company had issued bonds backed by the credit of the territory, and it was many years before the financial involvements were cleared away. For a time it looked as if the territory had in effect repudiated its obligations, but the second constitutional convention in resolutions later approved by Congress assumed responsibility. This canal enterprise accounts for most of the small debt which the territory handed on to the state.

The Milwaukee and Rock River Canal never advanced far enough to float anything, and was scarcely begun before it was given up, but in the old river route from Green Bay to Prairie du Chien nature seemed to indicate a waterway which needed only a little improvement to make it fit for steamboats. In 1828, a year of exceptionally high water when the portage was flooded, barges had brought soldiers and their equipment from St. Louis to Fort Howard at Green Bay without unloading. The waters of Green Bay are about 170 feet below the level of Lake Winnebago, and the problem on the lower Fox was one of building locks around the numerous rapids. In the upper Fox and in the Wisconsin west of Portage the difficulty was rather one of wide shallow streams with sandbanks and shifting channels.

The man most closely associated with this project was Morgan L. Martin. Martin was born in New York state in 1805 and must have heard much about canals all through his youth. After a few months in Detroit, he came on to Green Bay in May, 1827, and there he lived for the next sixty years. He made an excellent beginning in law and politics. For four years he served in the legislative council of Michigan Territory, and for two, as the territorial delegate at Washington. He presided over Wisconsin's second constitutional convention. He also engaged in town development and other real estate transactions in many parts of the state, his most successful venture being his partnership with Solomon Juneau in laying out part of Milwaukee. He would doubtless have risen still higher in politics or as a lawyer had he not given his best energies and much of his wealth to the improvement of the Fox and Wisconsin rivers.

Agitation for the improvement of the route began with a public meeting at Green Bay in 1829, at which Martin presided. In 1838 the War Department lent its support to the project; it would facilitate the transport of soldiers along what was then the Indian frontier. Throughout the whole territorial period the plan had enthusiastic support in all the communities along the way. After repeated appeals, Congress in 1846 granted for this enterprise half the land in a strip six miles wide running from Green Bay to Portage, a distance of 216 miles. The gift was accepted by the state in August, 1848, and the project was put in charge of a board of public works, with C. R. Alton as chief engineer. In 1851 the state made a contract with Martin, who undertook to carry on the work with his own resources. He looked, of course, to the sale of the land granted for the purpose to reimburse him. He began at once with five hundred men in his employ. In 1853 the Fox and Wisconsin Improvement Company was formed, in which Martin as president associated with himself a number of Wisconsin capitalists. The work went on vigorously. In October, 1855, a boat could pass by means of locks from Green Bay to Appleton, and in June, 1856, there was a great celebration upon the arrival of the steamer *Aquila,* which had come from Pittsburgh down the Ohio, up the Mississippi, and along the Wisconsin and Fox rivers to Green Bay.

In 1855 Congress added two sections a mile to the land grant,

making more than a thousand sections in all. Land sales were
too slow to keep pace with construction costs, and the Wisconsin
men, having expended $400,000, were at the end of their means.
In their extremity they had recourse to eastern capitalists, chief
among whom was Horatio Seymour, twice governor of New York
state and after the Civil War a democratic candidate for President
of the United States. For some years after 1856 the lower Fox
and Lake Winnebago were alive with traffic, but in 1863 the
Chicago and North Western Railway reached Green Bay and
the use of the river rapidly declined. Morgan L. Martin in later
years said that the eastern men interfered sadly with his plans;
but whoever had control, it may be doubted whether the waterway could have maintained a successful competition with the
railway. In 1866 the company went into the hands of a receiver,
and in 1872 the United States government purchased the improvements while the eastern capitalists took the unsold parts of the
land grants. The federal government still keeps up the locks
and the other aids to navigation, and coal comes to the towns of
the lower Fox and Lake Winnebago on barges from Pennsylvania,
but the chief effect of Morgan L. Martin's great enterprise was
temporary. For a few years it attracted immigration to the Fox
River Valley and aided settlement there.

The first steamboat in the West went down the Ohio River in
1811. On the Great Lakes there was a good deal of travel by
sailing vessels before the steamboat appeared. The garrisons that
were to build and occupy Fort Howard and Fort Crawford came
to Green Bay in August, 1816, on three schooners and a sloop.
The first steamboat on the Great Lakes was the *Walk-in-the-
Water,* built near Buffalo in 1819. She visited Green Bay in 1820
and again in 1821, but was lost in a storm on Lake Erie in the
autumn of that year. By 1833 there were eleven steamers on the
Great Lakes. The first regular steamboat line on Lake Michigan
was established in 1834, and connected Buffalo with Chicago.
Through the early years of settlement in the southeastern part of
the state, both sailing vessels and steamboats brought people from

the east to the ports of Milwaukee, Kenosha, and Racine. Owners of steamboats calling at Milwaukee asked Congress as early as 1834 to improve the harbor there, and Governor Dodge in his first message to the territorial legislature in October, 1836, urged them to petition Congress for a survey of all possible harbors along the Lake. The federal government put a lighthouse at Milwaukee in 1838, and a few years later voted small sums to improve the harbors of Milwaukee, Racine, and Kenosha. Until after the Civil War, however, these cities and the counties in which they lay did more in the way of harbor building than did the federal government.

Meanwhile, steamboats had begun to ply along the western side of the state. In 1823 the *Virginia* went up the uncharted Mississippi to the falls of St. Anthony. For many years steamers came and went when and where they could find cargoes. Regular service began between St. Louis and St. Paul in 1848, the year when Minnesota Territory was organized and when the land office was opened at St. Croix Falls. Through the 1850's the river steamers on the Mississippi and its tributaries did a wonderful business. After the railways reached Prairie du Chien (1857) and La Crosse (1858), settlers and lumbermen on their way to Minnesota and northwestern Wisconsin crossed Wisconsin by rail and made the rest of their journey by steamboat. The Civil War closed the lower Mississippi to commerce and destroyed the southern markets, and after the war commerce went eastward by rail rather than southward along the Mississippi. But steam power had a second great period on the river, as we shall see, in the service of lumber.

The inventor of the telegraph was Samuel F. B. Morse. The historic message "What hath God wrought?" was sent from Washington to Baltimore in May, 1844, but when Morse offered his invention to the government for $100,000 the offer was declined and commercial companies began to exploit the invention. In 1847 the Erie and Michigan Telegraph Company was launched, linking Buffalo, Cleveland, Detroit, Chicago, and Milwaukee.

The construction contract in Michigan and Wisconsin was given to John J. Speed, and so the lines were often in those days called the Speed lines. The first message was received in Milwaukee from Chicago January 15, 1848. By the end of 1849 Milwaukee had connections with Madison and Mineral Point in one direction, and with Sheboygan and Green Bay in another, and thereafter progress was rapid. In 1855, seven major telegraph companies, including the Erie and Michigan, united to form the Western Union, in which Ezra Cornell was one of the financial leaders. For many years the chief local competitor of the Western Union was the Wisconsin State Telegraph Company, of which Charles C. Sholes was president. In southern Wisconsin the telegraph almost everywhere preceded the railroads.

Early Churches

The first chapter in the history of Christianity in Wisconsin was the work of the Roman Catholic missionaries to the Indians in the French period, but this had come to an end in 1728, and there was no resident priest in Wisconsin again until 1823. In the interval the French of Green Bay sometimes traveled 240 miles to Mackinac for weddings and christenings. In the 1820's and early 1830's several denominations sent out men to do "home missionary work." This was intended at first chiefly for the Indians, though early white settlers were glad to avail themselves of the church services thus brought to their vicinity.

The Roman Catholic record begins anew in 1823 with an extended visit at Green Bay of the Rev. Gabriel Richard. A church was built which was destroyed by fire in 1825. Other French-speaking priests followed Richard. A gifted Italian, Samuel Mazzuchelli, began work at Mackinac in 1830. He spent six months at Green Bay in 1831 where a church building was in process of construction. In 1833 he removed his headquarters to Green Bay, and for several years gave his energies mainly to work among the Indians. The first bit of job printing in Wisconsin that has survived is a little almanac in the Menominee

language prepared by Mazzuchelli in 1834.   In 1835 he started a
parish at Prairie du Chien where four years later a stone church
was erected.   He was chaplain of the first legislature that met at
Belmont.   As an architect he planned many buildings, both sacred
and secular, including the first state capitol of Iowa.   He continued his work in several states along the upper Mississippi, and
before he died in 1864 he had established over thirty parishes, most
of them with schools.

Frederic Baraga, best known as a missionary to the Chippewa,
was of Slovenian origin.   After seven years as a priest in Austria,
he came to the United States in 1828, and began missionary work
with the Ottawa at Arbre Croche, Michigan.   In 1835 he removed
to La Pointe on Madeline Island to work among the Chippewa
and there in 1837 a church was built.   Constantly traveling among
many mission stations, he was, after 1843, more in upper Michigan
than in Wisconsin.   His grammar and dictionary of the Chippewa (Ojibway) language gave him distinguished rank as a philologist.   Bishop of Upper Michigan and then Bishop of Marquette, he worked on until his death in 1868.   Father F. J. Bonduel was a Belgian priest who came to Wisconsin in 1837.   He
spent twenty-four years in Wisconsin, most of it at Green Bay or
as a missionary among the Menominee.   Meanwhile immigration, chiefly from Europe, was bringing thousands of Catholics
into Wisconsin.   Father Bonduel had celebrated mass in Juneau's
house in Milwaukee in 1837, and two years later a Roman Catholic
church was erected there.   Wisconsin became a diocese in 1843,
and John Martin Henni, a German Swiss, came to Milwaukee
the following year to serve as the first bishop.   In 1875 Milwaukee
became an archdiocese, with Henni as the first archbishop.

The Episcopal church had done missionary work among the
Oneida while that tribe was still in New York state.   Their first
band reached Wisconsin in 1822, and the church soon designated
Eleazer Williams as teacher and pastor in the new community
near Green Bay.   The notorious Williams, however, was quite
ineffective as a clergyman.   The Rev. Richard Fish Cadle visited

and preached in Green Bay in 1827, and two years later was permanently stationed there, both to care for the Oneida and to organize the church of Americans at Green Bay. The man who had the greatest part in shaping the Episcopal church in Wisconsin was Jackson Kemper. After a first tour of the west in 1834, he was the next year appointed missionary bishop for a district of seven states, and over this he traveled for nearly a quarter of a century. In 1841 a number of young men who had just completed their course in the General Theological Seminary in New York came to Wisconsin and founded Nashotah in Waukesha County. Their leader, James Lloyd Breck, wished to found a brotherhood of celibate clergy. This feature has not been followed out, but Nashotah has since its founding been very successful in training Episcopal clergymen. Bishop Kemper had this enterprise close to his heart, and after he gave up his missionary bishopric for the diocese of Wisconsin, he lived nearby, and Nashotah was for a time virtually the seat of the bishop.

Among the Protestant denominations the Methodist Episcopal church came nearest to keeping pace with the frontier. Usually several places were visited periodically by a minister called a circuit rider. In the absence of the traveling preacher, zealous laymen exhorted. Methodist records indicate that there was a preacher at Galena, Illinois, from 1824 onward, and, as he rode his circuit, he was probably the first of his denomination to preach with any regularity in Wisconsin. There was, however, a Methodist church near Green Bay before there was any in the lead region. John Clark, a Methodist preacher, reached Green Bay in 1832 to supervise several widely scattered missionary efforts, most of them undertaken for the Indians. He it was who, in September, 1832, dedicated the first Methodist house of worship in Wisconsin, a log structure which stood in what is now the village of Kimberly, four miles from Appleton. In 1833 a Methodist society was organized at Platteville and the next year one was begun at Mineral Point. A class of Methodist laymen was begun in Milwaukee in 1836 and became an organized church within a few months. Progress in the last years of the thirties was rapid, while by 1850 there were 110 Methodist churches in Wisconsin, which was about thirty per cent of all the churches in the state.

The Presbyterians and Congregationalists coöperated in supporting the American Board of Commissioners for Foreign Missions, which had to do both with missions to the Indians and with organizing churches among the incoming Americans. In 1827 one of its preachers, the Rev. Jesse Miner, visited the Stockbridge Indians at Statesburg (South Kaukauna), and remained as their pastor until he died in 1829. He was followed by the Rev. Cutting Marsh, a Congregationalist, who served the Stockbridges, first at Statesburg and then in Calumet County, until 1845. In response to the plea of devout men in the employ of the American Fur Company, an American Board mission was begun at La Pointe on Madeline Island. The first teacher was Frederick Ayer, and he was joined the next year by the Rev. Sherman Hall and his wife, who labored there and at Odanah on the adjoining mainland until 1854. For a few years there was a related mission at Yellow Lake in Burnett County. The church at La Pointe is often called the first Congregational church in Wisconsin. Cutting Marsh organized a small group at Green Bay to whom he preached from time to time, but there was no permanent church until the fall of 1836, when under the Rev. Moses Ordway, the group was organized there that is counted the first Presbyterian church of the state. The first presbytery was formed at Milwaukee in 1839.

In 1840 there were eight churches of each denomination and they formed the "Presbyterian and Congregational Convention of Wisconsin." Any church in the convention might choose which name and which system of church organization it preferred. The greatest organizer of churches for the convention was the Rev. Stephen Peet, himself a Presbyterian. He reported in 1845 that there were sixty churches in the Territory, forty Congregational and twenty Presbyterian, twenty-two of which he had organized. From 1851 onward many Presbyterian churches were organized that were not in the convention, and they gathered into presbyteries; in time there were few besides Congregational churches left in the convention.

The Baptists count as their first church one founded in 1834 at Brotherton, among the Indians on the east shore of Lake Winnebago, but this did not prove permanent. Their first church in Milwaukee was organized in 1842, though the Baptists had held meetings there as early as 1836. By 1850 this denomination had more than three thousand members in its sixty churches. The coming of German and Norwegian immigrants meant also the organization of Lutheran communities. One of the German groups founded the village of Freistadt, sixteen miles northwest of Milwaukee, in 1839. The census of 1850 showed twenty Lutheran churches in Wisconsin. The principal growth of the Lutheran organizations came after the middle of the century.

As we have seen, the coming of a few of the earliest church leaders, both Catholic and Protestant, was occasioned by the desire to teach or convert the Indians, but, viewed in general, this motive did not play a very important part in providing Wisconsin with churches. By 1850 the Indians made up not much more than three per cent of the population. As the settlers poured into southern and eastern Wisconsin, whether they came from New England, or from the British Isles or from continental Europe, a church was to them a normal part of personal and community life. The missionary urge in the East joined with the desires of a majority, perhaps of almost all, of the immigrants. The pioneers, though they wanted churches, were in the beginning too few and often too poor to maintain them. At Southport (Kenosha), for instance, the village was two years old before it had a church. But to church leaders both in Europe and in the eastern part of the United States the frontier was a challenge and a great opportunity. Probably most churches founded in Wisconsin before 1850 began as mission churches; they had to have money from outside to meet expenses. But in this matter the East did not fail the West. By 1850 the churches in Wisconsin numbered 365, and 401 persons told the census-takers that they were clergymen.

CERESCO AND VOREE

In the earlier part of the nineteenth century there were stirrings of a new heaven and a new earth both in Europe and in America. The means of transforming life were, according to some, a different economic ordering of society. According to others a new religion was called for; and many were the purveyors of new religion. We shall discuss briefly two communities in Wisconsin, utterly different in conception and aims, and here taken together only as enterprises both of which sought to reorder society.

During the 1830's the ideas of Robert Fourier, a Frenchman, were much discussed in New England and helped on, though they did not originate, the famous Brookfield Farm experiment. During the winter of 1843-1844, the communal life advocated by Fourier was much discussed in a club or lyceum at Southport, and a number of idealistic Yankees decided to put the community life to the test of experience. Led by Warren Chase, they organized a company in which they took stock at $25 per share. An expert land agent chose a beautiful location for them where Ripon now stands, and in May of 1844 the first twenty of their company went up from Southport to their promised land. They named the new home Ceresco after Ceres, the goddess of the grain fields. Besides ordinary houses they built the famous "Long House," 32 by 208 feet, which contained quarters for twenty families and some single rooms. In it also were the common dining hall and kitchen, the use of which was optional. By the end of 1845 they had a sawmill, a grist mill, a school house, a great barn, and other buildings. The company numbered 80 at the close of 1845, and 180 a year later when they reached their maximum. At first most of them took their meals together in the common dining-hall, but after a year or two practically every family was eating by itself. There was a strong religious tone pervading the com-

munity, and no alcoholic liquors were sold. Crops were boun-
tiful while the community lasted, and on the economic side the
enterprise was a success. In 1849, however, the company agreed
to disband and got permission from the legislature to sell their
property. They were able to retire their stock at a small pre-
mium. Some of the members simply did not want to share the
fruits of their industry with the less able and industrious. Some
of them wished to take the profits that had accrued from the rise
in value of their real property. Apparently nearly all of them
wanted to go back to a regime of individual enterprise.

The story of Voree is a remarkable chapter in the tangled history of Mormonism. In 1843, James J. Strang, a young lawyer
from New York, settled in Burlington, Wisconsin, then a strong
center of the Mormon faith. He was not a Mormon at the time
of his coming, but in February, 1844, he paid a visit to Nauvoo,
Illinois, and there he was baptized by Joseph Smith himself, and
a week later was ordained an elder. On June 27, 1844, Joseph
Smith and his brother were slain by a hostile mob at Carthage,
Illinois. Brigham Young captured the leadership of the larger
part of the Mormons in Illinois, and ultimately led them to Utah.
Upon receiving the news of the death of Joseph Smith, Strang
at once claimed to have had advance knowledge of that event,
and attempted to persuade the community at Burlington, and
eventually the whole of Mormondom, that he was the heaven-
appointed successor to Joseph Smith. He tried to build up a great
new Mormon center at a town of his founding called Voree, about
two miles west of Burlington. A man of great ability and charm
of manner, Strang made numerous missionary journeys, but his
community did not grow rapidly. In 1850 he led his faithful
followers to Beaver Island in Lake Michigan, and from that time
on he professed to be not only a religious leader but a reigning
king, who required of his subjects an oath utterly incompatible
with loyalty to the United States. He adopted polygamy at this
time, and by this and other measures he made himself unpopular,
not only with the fisher folk who had lived on Beaver Island

before his settlement there, but among his own followers as well. In 1856 he was murdered and the faithful were immediately scattered. So ended one of the most amazing careers ever founded upon human credulity.

Early Banking

Those who established the first banks in Wisconsin had to petition the territorial legislature for a charter, and after July, 1836, a charter granted by a territorial legislature had to have also the approval of the Congress of the United States. The first to open, the Bank of Wisconsin, had its charter from the Legislative Council of Michigan Territory. It opened in Green Bay, in November, 1835, with Morgan L. Martin as chairman of the board of directors, and James Duane Doty and other leading men on the board. It was soon overtaken by the depression of 1837, and suspended specie payment in June of that year. The territorial legislature of Wisconsin, in March, 1839, ordered the attorney general to start suit to obtain possession of its assets and close up its affairs. The suit dragged on until 1842 and the last of its property was not sold until 1846. Its assets were sufficient to pay about fifty cents on the dollar.

At the first session of the legislature of Wisconsin Territory in 1836, charters were granted to two banking corporations desiring to do business east of the Mississippi, the Bank of Milwaukee and the Bank of Mineral Point. The first never really got under way, and three years later the legislature repealed its charter. The Bank of Mineral Point passed into receivership in 1841 and had its charter annulled the following year. Its failure was said to have caused a loss of over $200,000 to the community.

In 1839 an act creating a territorial bank, to be called the State Bank of Wisconsin, passed the legislature, but it was not approved by Congress. Its chief promoter was a resident of the lead-mining region already mentioned, William S. Hamilton, son of Alexander Hamilton. The projected territorial bank was obviously modeled after a national bank. Had the project not been throttled by Congress, the territory would have issued bonds to finance this bank.

While Wisconsin had some unfortunate experiences with its early banking enterprises, other western states had even more painful ones, and throughout the West there was widespread distrust of banks, which in Wisconsin was at its height about the time the territory set about making a state constitution. An act of 1845 incorporating the "First Congregational Society in Milwaukee" says: "Nothing herein contained shall be so construed as to give to the said society banking powers."

The institutions chartered specifically to carry on banking had all disappeared insolvent, but certain corporations created ostensibly for other purposes served in part the needs of the public. In 1836 the Fox River Hydraulic Company, located at De Pere, was authorized to build a dam across the Fox River, and two years later, by an amendment to its charter, to "issue evidences of debt." On the basis of this permission it issued notes which served as currency. Much more important was the Wisconsin Marine and Fire Insurance Company which was incorporated by legislative act in 1839. The two men most concerned in its organization were George Smith, president, and Alexander Mitchell, secretary, both natives of Scotland. Almost from the beginning it did a general banking business, issuing certificates of deposit payable on demand, which, in denominations of one, two, three, five, and ten dollars, circulated as currency. The company had offices in a number of cities, outside the state as well as within it, where its notes were redeemable in specie, and it never defaulted. By 1843 it had notes in circulation to the value of more than $70,000, and ten years later the amount was $1,470,-000. The company was of great assistance to those purchasing land. According to the famous circular of July, 1836, land bought from the federal government must be paid for in specie. When the land in southeastern Wisconsin was being sold, the company was able to aid many honest settlers. It usually bought and paid for the land and then resold it on a land contract. Because of the strong antipathy to banks in general, the company was repeatedly attacked in the territorial legislature, and this hostility culminated, in 1846, in an act repealing its charter; but the company denied the right of the legislature to revoke the charter and continued business as usual. George Smith early withdrew, leaving Alexander Mitchell as the controlling figure. His stature grew with the growth of Wisconsin until he stood out, long before his death in 1887, as one of the great financiers of the nation. Often spoken of still as "Mitchell's bank," the institution he built still continues as the Marine National Exchange Bank. In 1939 it stood third among the banks of the state in the amount of its assets.

Another of Wisconsin's famous banks was also founded in the territorial period. Samuel Marshall began a private banking business in Milwaukee on April 21, 1847, and in 1849 he was joined by Charles F. Ilsley. Ninety years later, the Marshall and Ilsley Bank ranked second among Wisconsin banks. The First Wisconsin National Bank, in 1939 much the largest in the state, traces its history back to the opening of the Farmers' and Millers' Bank in Milwaukee in 1853. No other city in Wisconsin has produced financial institutions that rival in resources those of the metropolis.

Selected Bibliography

Grace L. Nute in *The Voyageur* (New York, 1931), pp. 23-34, tells how canoes were made and handled. John W. Arndt discussed "Pioneers and Durham Boats on the Fox River," in Wisconsin Historical Society *Proceedings, 1912*, pp. 180-220. H. E. Cole, "The Old Military Road," *Wisconsin Magazine of History*, Vol. IX, pp. 47-62 (September, 1925), is concise and useful. The same author's *Stagecoach and Tavern Tales of the Old Northwest*, edited by Louise P. Kellogg (Cleveland, 1930), is interesting. Joseph Schafer discusses "Ferries and Ferryboats," in *Wisconsin Magazine of History*, Vol. XXI, pp. 432-456 (June, 1938).

There is much about the Milwaukee-Rock River canal project in William Rudolph Smith, *History of Wisconsin* (Vols. I and III, Vol. II never issued, Madison, 1854), Vol. III, pp. 354-443. It is discussed also in the political narratives mentioned in the bibliography of Chapter V. The Fox-Wisconsin improvement is dealt with in Joseph Schafer, *The Winnebago-Horicon*

Basin (Madison, 1937), pp. 90-131. His footnotes refer to the essential documents. An older account is that of John B. Sanborn, "The Story of the Fox-Wisconsin Improvement," *Proceedings, 1899* (Madison, 1900), pp. 186-194. Stewart Mitchell, *Horatio Seymour of New York* (Cambridge, 1938), pp. 189-201, *et passim,* tells of Seymour's connection with the Fox-Wisconsin canal project.

An interesting phase of internal improvements is discussed by Ralph G. Plumb, "Early Harbor History of Wisconsin," Mississippi Valley Historical Association *Proceedings,* Vol. IV (1910-11), pp. 189-198. Steamboating on the Mississippi has two historians: George B. Merrick, a river pilot, wrote *Old Times on the Upper Mississippi* (Cleveland, 1909); William J. Peterson is the author of *Steamboating on the Upper Mississippi: The Water Way to Iowa* (Iowa City, 1937). James B. Butler contributed "Early Shipping on Lake Superior," *Proceedings, 1895,* pp. 83-96.

Ellis B. Usher gives a good account of "The Telegraph in Wisconsin," in *Proceedings, 1913,* pp. 91-109.

Early Churches: Important documents and the titles of books may be found in Peter G. Mode, *Sourcebook and Bibliographical Guide for American Church History* (Menasha, 1921). Material on Protestantism in the Middle West is found on pp. 409-441. The bibliography for Wisconsin is at pp. 415-416. There is material on missionary work and early churches in *Collections of the State Historical Society of Wisconsin.* Vol. XIV, pp. 155-205, is devoted to the Roman Catholics; *ibid.,* pp. 394-515, to the Episcopalians; and Vol. XV, pp. 25-264, to the Presbyterian-Congregational work. J. N. Davidson, *In Unnamed Wisconsin* (Milwaukee, 1895), pp. 45-172, recounts the history of Protestant missions to the Oneida, Stockbridge, and Brothertons.

There are articles in the *Dictionary of National Biography* on Baraga, Mazzuchelli, John Henni, and Henni's assistant and successor, Michael Heiss. Attention may also be called to two biographies of Baraga, one by Chrysostom A. Verwyst (Milwaukee, 1900) and the other by Joseph Gregorish, *The Apostle of the Chippewas* (Chicago, 1932). Samuel Mazzuchelli is the author of *Memoirs Historical and Edifying of a Missionary Apostolic of the Order of St. Dominic* (Chicago, 1915), a translation of an Italian original which covers his activities only to 1844. For the story of his whole life we have recourse to Soeur Rosemary Crepeau, *Le Père Samuel-Charles Gaétan Mazzuchelli* (Paris, 1932). *The Catholic Church in Wisconsin* (Milwaukee, 1895-1898), after narrating Roman Catholic history of the seventeenth and eighteenth centuries, gives details, parish by parish, for much of the state.

There is a short biography of *Richard Fish Cadle* by Howard Greene (Waukesha, 1938). The *Dictionary of National Biography* includes Bishop Jackson Kemper and James Lloyd Breck, where further references will be found. J. H. A. Lacher, "Nashotah House, Wisconsin's Oldest School of Higher Learning," *Wisconsin Magazine of History,* Vol. XVI, pp. 123-162 (December, 1932), pictures the pioneering of the Episcopal church.

William W. Folwell, *History of Minnesota* (4 vols., Minneapolis, 1924-31), Vol. I, pp. 170-212, has an excellent review of missions to the Chippewa, both in Wisconsin and in Minnesota. A series of "La Pointe Letters," dating from 1838 to 1842, *Wisconsin Magazine of History,* Vol. XVI (1932), pp. 85-95, and 199-210, mirrors daily life in a Protestant mission station.

P. S. Bennett and James Lawson, *History of Methodism in Wisconsin* (Cincinnati, 1890), a standard work for nearly half a century, is now being superseded by a coöperative work of which the first part has appeared: Elizabeth Wilson, *Methodism in Eastern Wisconsin,* Section I, 1832-1850 (Milwaukee, 1938). Ella C. Brunson wrote of her father, "Alfred Brunson, Pioneer of Wisconsin Methodism," *Wisconsin Magazine of History,* Vol. II, pp. 129-140 (December, 1918). Frank N. Dexter, *A Hundred Years of Congregational History in Wisconsin* (Wisconsin Congregational Conference, 1933), is a clear and well-balanced summary. A part of the story of the Lutheran migration to Wisconsin is told by Philip von Rohr Sauer, "Heinrich von Rohr and the Lutheran Immigration to New York and Wisconsin," *Wisconsin Magazine of History,* Vol. XVIII, pp. 247-268 (March, 1935).

Samuel M. Pedrick, "The Wisconsin Phalanx at Ceresco," Wisconsin Historical Society *Proceedings, 1902,* pp. 190-226, records the history of the Ceresco experiment. Joseph Schafer retells the story in "The Wisconsin Phalanx," *Wisconsin Magazine of History,* Vol. XIX, pp. 454-474 (June, 1936). The life of James J. Strang has twice been written in recent times: Milo M. Quaife, *The Kingdom of St James; A Narrative of the Mormons* (New Haven, 1930); and O. W. Riegel, *Crown of Glory: The Life of James J. Strang, Moses of the Mormons* (New Haven, 1935).

Matthew B. Hammond wrote "The Financial History of Wisconsin Territory," *Proceedings, 1893,* pp. 131-167; and William W. Wight followed with "Early Legislation Concerning Wisconsin Banks," *Proceedings, 1895,* pp. 145-161. An early account of its subject is "Alexander Mitchell, The Financier," *Collections,* Vol. XI, pp. 435-450. Mitchell also appears in the *Dictionary of National Biography.* Banking before 1852 is well discussed in Leonard B. Krueger, *History of Commercial Banking in Wisconsin,* University of Wisconsin Studies in the Social Sciences and History, No. 18 (Madison, 1933), pp. 7-58. This book is an expanded Ph. D. thesis.

CHAPTER VII

WISCONSIN BECOMES A STATE

BOUNDARIES

TERRITORIAL status was avowedly but a transitory stage. Governor Dodge urged the legislature to order a popular vote for or against statehood as early as 1839, and four times in the period from September, 1841, to September, 1844, the people had the opportunity to vote, as they did vote, against statehood. Many factors contributed to this repeated negative. These referendums were all taken in the time of the Whig governor, James D. Doty. The majority in the state was Democratic, and Doty dealt with the Democratic legislature in such a way as to make himself very unpopular. Doty not only insisted that Wisconsin become a state, but that it extend as far south as the southern tip of Lake Michigan in accordance with the Ordinance of 1787. If northern Illinois joined Wisconsin, and many who lived there wanted this to happen, it would bring its share of the notoriously large public debt of Illinois. As long as Wisconsin remained a territory, the expenses of its government, the salaries of its officials and legislators, came from the federal treasury. On the other hand admission to statehood would make Wisconsin more attractive to immigrants and investors. The federal law of 1841 about the public lands, besides legalizing pre-emption, promised five hundred thousand acres for internal improvements as soon as Wisconsin became a state. The gift of the highest offices of the state would be transferred from the President and Senate at Washington to the voters in Wisconsin and this spurred on the politicians. Thus, when the second inauguration of Henry Dodge as governor in May, 1845, restored harmony between the legislative and executive branches of government, the Democrats as well as the Whigs were ready to take steps leading to statehood. In April, 1846, another referendum resulted in a vote of nearly six to one in favor of becoming a state.

In the meantime, in the spring of 1846, an enabling act began its course through Congress, and was signed by President Polk, August 6, 1846. It was the last legislation setting the boundaries of Wisconsin, though several questions of interpretation were later to come before the Supreme Court of the United States. Certain statements about future boundaries, as we have seen, had been made in the Ordinance of 1787, but in practice these were repeatedly disregarded. When Illinois became a state in 1818, her northern boundary was put at 42° 30' north latitude, or about sixty-one miles north of the southern extremity of Lake Michigan. Thus an area of about 8,500 square miles was subtracted from Wisconsin, as it might have been, so that Illinois could have commerce on the Great Lakes. In the middle of the territorial period under the leadership of Governor Doty, Wisconsin made some spirited demands for the "return" of this area, but to no avail.

In 1835 Michigan was just assuming statehood. Basing her claim on the Ordinance of 1787, she insisted with some vehemence that she ought to possess a strip of Ohio territory including the city of Toledo. But Congress declined to reopen a matter that had been settled when Ohio became a state, and, in lieu of the contested strip, gave to Michigan what we today call her Upper Peninsula. This was accepted by Michigan only because it was a condition of her admission to the Union.

According to the act which established Wisconsin Territory in 1836, the line between Wisconsin and Michigan ran through the middle of Lake Michigan and along the main channel of Green Bay to the mouth of the Menominee River, "thence through the middle of the main channel of said river to that head of said river nearest to the Lake of the Desert (Lake Vieux Desert); thence in a direct line to the middle of said lake; thence through the middle of the main channel of the Montreal River to its mouth." All this is said to go back to the use by a congressional committee of a faulty map which pictured the Montreal and Menominee Rivers as issuing from Lake Vieux Desert, and Upper Michigan, therefore, as an island. Some doubt must have arisen about the Menominee River, to judge from the wording of the Act.

Captain Thomas Jefferson Cram spent the summers of 1841 and 1843 surveying this boundary. He found that Lake Vieux Desert was the headlake of the Wisconsin River and that neither the Montreal River nor the Menominee was connected with it. He produced a map that has since been counted official and indicated what is the present interstate boundary. The dividing line goes up the Menominee to its tributary, the Brule,[1] then up the Brule to Lake Brule, then fourteen miles straight through the forest to a point between two islands in Lake Vieux Desert, then by another straight line to a point about fifty miles away on the east fork of the Montreal River. The enabling act for Wisconsin of August 6, 1846, described this boundary again and referred to the survey by Captain Cram as authority. In the summer of 1847 another government surveyor finally established and marked the line laid down by Captain Cram.

From 1836 to 1838 Wisconsin was bounded on the west by the Missouri River and a tributary to it on the north, the White Earth River in North Dakota. When Iowa Territory was set up in 1838, the Mississippi River from the northwestern corner of Illinois to its source in Lake Itasca came to bound Wisconsin on the west. Thence the line ran to the Lake of the Woods on the Canadian border. When the Webster-Ashburton Treaty of 1842 made more definite the international boundary, especially the part between Lake Superior and Rainy Lake, it delimited the northern border of Wisconsin as it then was. For two years all of the present state of Minnesota was a part of Wisconsin Territory, and then

---

[1] The name appears as "Brulé" in the Enabling Act of 1846 and as "Brule" in the Constitution of 1848. Usage long varied, even in official publications; but the United States Geographic Board has declared for the form without the accent mark.

for ten years more Wisconsin included about a third of it, the part that had belonged to the Old Northwest.

In this northwestern part of Wisconsin Territory, two counties were set up, St. Croix in 1840 and La Pointe in 1845. The county seat of St. Croix County was at a village called Dakotah that had no existence for many years except on paper, and now is part of Stillwater, Minnesota. One of the territorial judges went up from Madison to this place in 1840 to hold court, but found no cases to try. A fort, after 1825 called Fort Snelling, had been founded in 1819 on the west side of the Mississippi where Minneapolis now stands. Except from 1836 to 1838 this was not in Wisconsin Territory, but a few civilians, driven out of the military reserve about the fort, founded a village east of the Mississippi that in 1841 received the name of St. Paul. Lumbering began on the St. Croix River in 1837, and the first sawmill in that valley began work the next year; Stillwater and St. Anthony were begun about 1840. St. Paul was the head of navigation on the Mississippi, and steamboats to that place had a regular schedule from 1848 onward. A community was forming that was too far from Madison for convenience and satisfaction in government, and it made its feeling known at Washington. Consequently the Wisconsin enabling act of 1846 separated this region from Wisconsin by a line which from Lake Superior went up the St. Louis River to its first rapids, a distance, if one follows the river, of some twenty-seven miles, then due south forty-one miles to the St. Croix River, and then down this stream to the Mississippi. Thus the St. Croix valley was divided between Wisconsin and Minnesota, and St. Paul now stands about fifteen miles from the Wisconsin border.

By the admission of Wisconsin to the Union most of La Pointe and St. Croix counties were left without government, as the western part of Michigan had been left in 1835. By a fiction similar to that of thirteen years before, it was assumed that what was left outside of the state of Wisconsin continued to exist as Wisconsin Territory. On October 30, 1848, an election was held by the "remnant," and Henry H. Sibley was chosen delegate from Wisconsin Territory. Contrary to his own expectations, he was admitted to Congress in December. After Congress established Minnesota Territory in 1849, its citizens sent Sibley to Washington again.

THE TWO CONSTITUTIONAL CONVENTIONS

After the passage of the enabling act of August, 1846, the first constitutional convention of 125 members was chosen. It sat for ten weeks and two days, and adjourned December 16, having produced the constitution of 1846. For reasons that will presently appear, this was rejected in April, 1847, by a vote of about 20,000 to 14,000. A second convention of sixty-nine members was in session from December 15, 1847, to February 2, 1848, a period of seven weeks. Its work was approved in March, by about two and one-half to one (16,799 for—6,384 against), and on May 29, 1848, Wisconsin was admitted to the Union. A canvass of the "fathers" shows that in both conventions the great majority of the members came from New York and New England.

Though the two constitutions differed in their wording, they were in substantial agreement in describing the framework of government. The majority in the first convention belonged to the Democratic party, and had the Democrats been united in favor of the constitution of 1846, it would have been accepted, but the Democrats were divided into a radical group and a more conservative one. There were some points in the first constitution that were too radical for the conservative Democrats, and they joined with the Whigs in opposition and brought about the rejection of the document.

By 1846 the appointment of judges was gradually but widely giving way to popular election. The constitution of 1846 provided for election, and this provision was repeated in the accepted constitution. Another advance that the conservative mind of that day could not approve was that a married woman might have property, either real or personal, separate from her husband. This was provided in 1846, omitted in the second constitution, and then accomplished by the legislature soon after admission to statehood.

The frontier was always peculiarly sensitive to the afflictions of the debtor. Wisconsin Territory borrowed the Michigan code of laws almost entire, but in 1837 was careful to abolish imprisonment for debt, which that code authorized. When making a constitution in 1846, the "fathers" went a step further. A homestead, not to exceed forty acres in the country, or property worth $1,000 in a town, was exempt from seizure and forced sale to satisfy a debt. This, too, was omitted from the constitution that was adopted, but was enacted by the legislature soon after.

The Jacksonian distrust of banks and the experience of the people of Wisconsin in the territorial period account for the provision of 1846: "There shall be no banks of issue in this state." The chairman of the committee on banking in the first convention drafted this article; he was Edward G. Ryan, then of Racine. During the debates in the convention Ryan became known as one of the ablest speakers and lawyers of the Territory. The second constitution provided that if a general law permitting banks were desired at any time, the legislature should submit to the people the question of "banks" or "no banks." If a banking law were thus demanded, the legislature might then pass a general banking law and submit it to the people for approval. This procedure was followed in 1851 and 1852, and both votes were overwhelmingly in favor of banks. Of the four points in the first constitution to which exception had been taken, one was left unchanged in the second constitution, and two were omitted or rather transferred to the competence of the legislature. During the six months of public debate in 1847, the matter of banks was discussed in the press and on the platform much more than any of the others, and the second convention referred this most contentious matter to the people.

Another question which had divided opinion in Wisconsin Territory and in the first constitutional convention was solved in a different way. In 1840 there were in the territory 165 free colored persons and eleven slaves, and ten years later there were more than six hundred Negroes, all of them free. No colored person might vote while Wisconsin was a territory, but in the southeastern counties there were many members of the Liberty party who were demanding equal rights for all men. As a concession to this group, the first convention provided for a referendum on this matter. In April, 1847, Negro suffrage was defeated along with the first constitution.

THE CONSTITUTION OF 1848

The constitution of Wisconsin opens with a preamble that echoes the greater part of the preamble of the Constitution of the United States. Article I, a "Declaration of Rights," had been called a "Bill of Rights" in 1846. It sums up centuries of struggle against tyranny and abuses in government. Three-fourths of its sentences copy Article I of the constitution of Michigan of 1835, while some other parts come from the New York instrument of 1846. Beyond these immediate models lie centuries of English and American experience; the various ideas can be referred back one by one to struggles and grievances along the route of English political growth and American colonial development. The last section of the article runs in part: "The blessings of a free government can only be maintained by . . . frequent recurrence to fundamental principles." The Ordinance of 1787 had mentioned "the fundamental principles of civil and religious liberty" on which the republics then in the Union, their laws and constitutions, were founded. Apparently the fathers of Wisconsin were likewise looking back into history, and the "Declaration of Rights" at the head of the constitution was intended to state the most important lessons of the past.

Voters must, according to Article III, be males aged twenty-one years, white citizens of the United States or white foreign-born men who have declared their intention of becoming citizens. Certain Indians might vote, but, in accordance with the referendum of 1847, Negroes were omitted from the list of those qualified. It was left to the legislature to extend the right of suffrage to "persons not herein enumerated," subject to approval by a popular vote. A law allowing Negroes to vote was enacted and approved in 1849, but its validity was subsequently assailed, only to be upheld by the Wisconsin Supreme Court in 1866.[2] It was not, however, until 1882 that an amendment brought the constitution of Wisconsin, in the matter of Negro suffrage, formally into agreement with the Fifteenth Amendment of the federal constitution.

The legislature was to consist of a senate and an assembly. The constitution fixed the maximum number of the assembly at a hundred, and of the senate at thirty-three. The state began with nineteen senators and sixty-six assemblymen, but in 1856 the senate was enlarged to thirty and the assembly to ninety-seven, and still later both were raised to their constitutional maximum. At first there were annual elections with one-year terms for assemblymen and two-year terms for senators. In 1881 the sessions were made biennial, and the respective terms for assemblymen and senators were made twice as long.

The governor had the usual executive powers, was commander-in-chief of the military and naval forces of the state, and had power to reprieve and pardon. Legislation required the approval of the governor. He might veto laws, but the legislature by a two-thirds vote in both houses could override his veto. This practice had been in effect during the territorial period. The constitution named several elective officers besides the governor, among them the secretary of state, the treasurer and the attorney general. This did not prevent the legislature from providing that other state officers should be elected. Some specified county

---

[2] Gillespie *v*. Palmer, 20 *Wisconsin Reports*, 544.

officials were also to be elected, but while the people might elect these county officers, the governor for cause might remove any of them.

The act of Congress establishing Wisconsin Territory in 1836 provided for a judiciary consisting of a chief justice and two associate justices, to be appointed by the President. Each of the three acted as a district judge in a definite area; when the three met together, they composed the supreme court. This system prevailed in the early years of statehood, except that the number of districts and of judges was raised by the constitution to five. The legislature was empowered after five years to establish a separate supreme court, and in 1853 created one of three members. In 1877 the number of justices was raised to five, and later still to seven. Below the supreme courts are the circuit courts, probate courts, courts of the justices of the peace, and municipal courts.

The constitution provided that taxes should be uniformly levied on such property as the legislature should prescribe. The territory's experience with the Milwaukee and Rock River Canal Company and the grief of neighboring states account sufficiently for the provision that "The credit of the State shall never be given or loaned in aid of any individual association or corporation." Debts might be contracted for a limited amount, but at the same time taxes should be imposed which would extinguish the debt, interest and principal, within five years. "Pay as you go" was definitely imposed as a requirement on the future Wisconsin. The last clause on finance attempted to make assurance doubly sure by saying: "The State shall never contract any debt for works of Internal Improvement, or be a party to carrying on such works," but went on to permit the administration of federal gifts for such purposes. The grant for the improvement of the Fox and Wisconsin rivers had been made in 1846. The legislature was directed to restrict the powers of cities and incorporated villages to borrow money, contract debts, and loan their credit, but unfortunately, in the years that followed, these bodies as well as the counties and towns were under no real restraint.

Local Government

Wisconsin had to choose between two types of local government, but the choice was practically made before she became a state. The lead miners were largely of southern extraction, and they preferred to have local government carried on by a few county officers whom they called commissioners. The settlers from New England and New York desired a county board made up of township representatives known as supervisors. While Wisconsin was a territory, this matter was twice the subject of fundamental legislation. In 1837, when the politics of the territory was still dominated by the lead miners, a general law provided for commissioners in each county. Townships existed, also, but there was no county board. This was not satisfactory to the Yankees, who were rapidly increasing in numbers. In 1841 it was enacted that each county might, by popular vote, choose which form of government it preferred. With the exception of three counties, Green, Crawford and Iowa, they all indicated their preference for the county board type. By 1848 there were twenty-nine counties in Wisconsin, and with the exception of five in the southwest, they all had a government of the supervisor or county board type. By the constitution of 1848, the legislature was required to establish a uniform system, and of course it followed the preference of the majority.

After considerable wavering the smallest political unit of the state was called a town rather than a township. Today this is usually, though by no means always, coterminous with the surveyor's township. The residents of the town choose three supervisors and at the same time indicate one of them as chairman, who is thus designated to represent the town on the county board. Besides the supervisors from the purely rural areas, other supervisors are chosen, one from each ward of the incorporated villages and cities. In many counties the board numbers more than forty people and in a few cases exceeds seventy. At times since 1848 attempts have been made to get a smaller body, but every town is represented on the board at present, and thus far democracy has triumphed over alleged economy and efficiency, and the large board continues.

Free Schools and the School Fund

The first schools within the present Wisconsin were private schools, of which there were several before 1836. Parents usually paid fees directly to the teacher. In the fall of 1836 the first school district in the territory was organized in Milwaukee, and that winter Edward West taught district school there. The use of the words, "district school," however, did not at that time mean, as it does today, that instruction was free. The second territorial legislature, in 1837, enacted legislation providing that as soon as twenty electors should reside in a surveyed township in which there was a school section, they should elect three commissioners of common schools and apply the proceeds of the leases of school lands to pay the wages of teachers.

A hundred years ago the free and almost universal education at the expense of the public treasury which we now enjoy was unknown, even in most parts of the United States. Some New England towns in the early nineteenth century and even earlier had free common schools, but this practice was not by any means universal. Pennsylvania adopted local option in this matter in 1849, and a little more than half of its districts took advantage of the permission to set up tax-supported schools. Until about the same time New York state had schools in which the expenses were apportioned among the parents according to the number of children they had in school. Michigan also dealt with expenses in this way until after the Civil War, and the district established in Milwaukee in the fall of 1836 followed the old Michigan law, though Wisconsin Territory had by that time been set up. In spite of the fact, however, that free schools were still largely wanting, they had many strong advocates and the whole subject was under lively discussion in the states from which most settlers were coming to Wisconsin. It was by no means a novel problem.

In the territorial period the only way for a district to have a free public school was to request a special act of the legislature permitting the district to levy a tax to meet the school expenses. Several districts before 1848 got authority to raise money for school buildings in this way, but the only one to ask leave to tax itself for the maintenance of a school was District Number One of Southport (Kenosha). The local leader of this movement was a native of New York named Michael Frank, at that time a newspaper editor. As a member of the legislative council he introduced a bill in 1844 pointing toward a general free school system for the state, but the bill was not passed. Early in 1845 he secured a permissive act for Southport, which provided for a referendum in the district. The result was favorable; yet progress was slow. In 1847 and 1848 a brick school building was erected at public cost, and finally, on June 30, 1849, the first tax-supported and entirely free school in Wisconsin began its work.

Meanwhile, the principle of free schools had made a wider conquest. One of the great proponents of free and universal education was Henry Barnard, superintendent of education in Rhode Island. He spoke to a convention of educators in Chicago in October, 1846, and then came on to speak in Milwaukee and Madison. At the latter place he made two addresses before Wisconsin's first constitutional convention, then in session. Apparently his audience agreed with him; for according to the constitution of 1846, "the common schools shall be equally free to all children." In the second constitution, the schools were to be "free and without charge for tuition to all children between the ages of four and twenty years."

The constitution vests the supervision of education in an elected state superintendent. Several sections in the article on education are concerned with the "School Fund," its sources and the distribution of the income from it. The enabling act of 1846 set aside for education section sixteen of every township, or its equivalent if it had been sold. This vast endowment, amounting to nearly a million acres, was to be sold and the proceeds put into the school fund. The second constitution resolved, subject to approval by Congress, to divert to the school fund the five hundred thousand acres granted for internal improvements by the federal law of 1841. Besides these two great federal gifts the constitution added to the school fund forfeitures, escheats, fines, and unassigned gifts to the state. The federal government had also given two townships or seventy-two sections of land for a state university, and this was set aside for a "University Fund."

The income from the school fund was assigned chiefly to the partial support of district schools. A district might share in its benefits only if it raised a certain amount of taxes for school purposes and maintained a school "free and without charge for tuition." In 1850 there were 1,425 public schools in the state employing 1,529 teachers and caring for over 58,000 pupils. One-fifth of their expenses was derived from public funds and four-fifths from local taxes; income from other sources, including fees, was negligible, being only about one twenty-fifth of the whole. The principle of free schools, thanks to the constitution, had won a rapid victory. Universal attendance had not been attained. There were then 105,000 inhabitants of the state over five and under twenty years of age, and only 58,000 were in the public schools and less than 3,000 in private schools and academies.

SELECTED BIBLIOGRAPHY

The enabling act of 1846 and the Constitution of 1848 are to be found in *Federal and State Constitutions,* Francis N. Thorpe, compiler and editor, 7 vols., 59th Cong., 2d Sess., House Doc. No. 357 (serial numbers 5190-5194), pp. 4065-4104. The constitution, as altered by amendments, is regularly printed in the biennial *Blue Books* and biennial *Statutes.* Copies of the constitution in this form, in which amendments cannot be distinguished from the text of 1848, may always be obtained from the Secretary of State for a few cents. The *Memorial Record of the Fathers of the Constitution,* prepared by H. A. Tenney and David Atwood (Madison, 1880), contains both constitutions. Milo M. Quaife edited for the *Collections of the State Historical Society of Wisconsin* four volumes known as the Constitutional Series, issued at Madison, as follows: Vol I, *The Movement for Statehood* (1918); Vol. II, *The Convention of 1846* (1919); Vol. III, *The Struggle over Ratification* (1920) and Vol. IV, *The Attainment of Statehood* (1928). These contain some modern essays, all official records, and a vast amount of contemporary newspaper comment. The rejected constitution of 1846 is in Vol. II, pp. 732-755. Louise Phelps Kellogg wrote "The Admission of Wisconsin to Statehood," Vol. I, pp. 18-29; and Frederic L. Paxson, "Wisconsin—A Constitution of Democracy," Vol. I, pp. 30-53. This also appeared in *Mississippi Valley Historical Review*, Vol. II, pp. 3-24. A valuable study is *State Constitutional Development in the United States, 1829-51* (MS, Ph. D. thesis, University of Wisconsin, 1933), by Bayrd Still, whose "State-Making in Wisconsin, 1846-48, An Illustration of the Statehood Process," *Wisconsin Magazine of History*, Vol. XX, pp. 34-59 (Sept., 1936), shows the tendencies of the time at work in Wisconsin. Kate Everest Levi, "The Press and the Constitution," *Wisconsin Magazine of History*, Vol. XVI, 383-403 (June, 1933), summarizes contemporary opinion on most of the controverted points.

The study by Reuben G. Thwaites, "The Boundaries of Wisconsin," *Collections of the State Historical Society of Wisconsin*, Vol. XI, pp. 451-501, with its series of maps has been very useful. The maps reappear in the *Blue Book* of 1937, pp. 187-192. Attention should also be called to Louise Phelps Kellogg, "The Disputed Michigan-Wisconsin Boundary," *Wisconsin Magazine of History*, Vol. I, pp. 304-307; and the Appendix entitled "Boundaries of Wisconsin," in Lawrence Martin, *The Physical Geography of Wisconsin* (Madison, 1932), pp. 481-487.

David E. Spencer studied "Local Government in Wisconsin," in the Johns Hopkins University *Studies in Historical and Political Science*, Vol. VIII, pp. 89-103 (1890). The same material, in simpler form, appears in *Collections of the State Historical Society of Wisconsin*, Vol. XI (1888), pp. 502-511. Louise P. Kellogg performed a most useful service in writing "Organization, Boundaries and Names of Wisconsin Counties," State Historical Society *Proceedings, 1909*, pp. 184-223.

Joseph Schafer set forth the "Origin of Wisconsin's Free School System," in *Wisconsin Magazine of History*, Vol. IX, pp. 27-46 (Sept., 1925). Further material on the history of education in Wisconsin, with references, will be found in Chapter XXI.

Other narratives that parallel this chapter are: Milo M. Quaife, *Wisconsin, Its History and Its People* (4 vols., Chicago, 1924), Vol. I, pp. 473-495; and *Wisconsin in Three Centuries* (4 vols., New York, 1906), Vol. II, pp. 279-289, and Vol. III, pp. 29-34.

CHAPTER VIII

THE YEARS 1848 TO 1860

GROWTH IN POPULATION

IN THE political history of the United States the years just before the Civil War were dominated by the impending conflict, or so it appears to the historian of today. While the great struggle was not without premonitory symptoms and episodes even in Wisconsin, there is much else in the history of the period to make it a significant one for the state. Immigration, both American and European, continued to increase the actual economic and potential military strength of the state. The census of 1860 showed 775,881 people in Wisconsin. The increase of about 470,000 since 1850 was larger than in any other decade in the history of the state. In population Wisconsin now stood fifteenth among the thirty-three states in the Union, and ranked above four of the New England states, three others on the Atlantic seaboard, and Michigan. The inhabitants fell into three roughly equal groups: those born in Wisconsin, in round numbers, 247,000; those born in other parts of the United States, 251,000; and those born in foreign countries, 277,000. The various states to the east and southeast of Wisconsin had continued to contribute to Wisconsin's population in much the same way as before 1850. New York had given 120,000, the six New England states had given 54,000, Pennsylvania had sent 21,000, and the four older states of the Old Northwest, 42,000. If the 3,300 natives of New Jersey are added, there remain to be accounted for only some ten or twelve thousand people who had come from

all the southern states and the area west of the Mississippi. The
dominant elements in Wisconsin's population were still Yankees
of New England, Ohio, and the rest of the Northwest.

Each migration to Wisconsin proceeded from the migrant's dis-

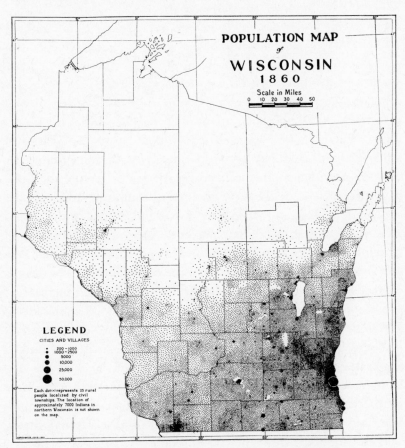

POPULATION DISTRIBUTION IN WISCONSIN, 1860*

satisfaction with conditions in his old home. To analyze the
causes of the movement which peopled Wisconsin would lead us
far afield into the political, religious, and, most of all, the economic history of many parts of Europe, as well as of the eastern

* By courtesy of Guy-Harold Smith and the American Geographical Society of New
York.

part of the United States. Once settlement had begun in Wisconsin, efforts were made by those who had arrived to persuade others to follow them. Private persons, individually or in groups, wrote to friends or to the newspapers in the communities they had left, setting forth the advantages of Wisconsin. Many of these letters are being published in our time, a hundred years later, in the *Wisconsin Magazine of History* and elsewhere, and are valuable sources on the beginnings of Wisconsin. There were, for example, fourteen German-born citizens of Manitowoc who composed a letter of which many thousands of copies were distributed in northern Germany. Speculators and land agents, aware that a rapidly increasing population would enhance the value of their holdings, zealously advertised the new state. Increase A. Lapham, often called Wisconsin's first scientist, wrote a *Geographical and Topographical Description of Wisconsin* of 256 pages in 1844, and *Wisconsin, Its Geography and Topography* two years later; these little volumes were widely circulated throughout the eastern part of the United States. Roman Catholic priests and Lutheran leaders alike, after living for a time in Wisconsin, toured Germany and other foreign countries, spreading the good news about opportunities in Wisconsin among their fellow religionists.

The Wisconsin legislature provided for a "commissioner of emigration" in 1852, and he was appointed and opened an office in New York in the same year. He gave notice of his existence in the newspapers of Germany and other countries, indicated what services he could render, distributed printed matter at home and abroad, and sought the coöperation of American consuls and of foreign officials. In New York he tried to protect immigrants from sharpers, gave them information about Wisconsin, and helped them with arrangements for their journey westward. Three men held the post in succession, and all of them apparently did most of their work with Germans. In 1855 the office was abolished by the legislature. This action was said to be due to nativist or antiforeign sentiment. There was no office of the sort again until after the Civil War. Between 1867 and 1887 there was first a board of immigration headed by the governor, then an elected commissioner, and then, after an interval, another board. In the eighties the Wisconsin Central Railroad maintained an agent in Switzerland and Germany, who induced many Germans to settle on land which the railroad had for sale.

The numerical importance of Wisconsin's foreign-born, and especially its German element, is sometimes overstated. The foreign-born numbered 106,000 in 1850, or 36.2 per cent of the whole population, the highest percentage in the history of the state. In 1860 they had risen in number to 277,000, but constituted only 35.7 per cent of the total; and although the number of foreign-born was larger at each decennial census until after 1890, their percentage in the whole population became slowly but steadily less. The 38,000 Germans in 1850 were 36 per cent of the foreign-born, and about one-eighth of the whole population. In 1860 they numbered about 124,000, which was about one-sixth of the population of the state (15.4 per cent); and although there were more German-born at each census until 1900, their percentage of the population was never again as high as it was in 1860.

That which gave the German element its importance in Wisconsin was not so much its numbers as its concentration. For some decades most of the Germans settled in an area east of Lake Winnebago and the upper Rock River and north of the southernmost tier of counties. Their steady increase in numbers and the location of most of them in a fairly compact area established there the German language and civilization. In some of their differences from their American neighbors, they made permanent and valuable contributions to the common experience and tradition of the state. In choosing farms the Germans were much more concerned than the Americans about proximity to a market, and this explains in part their concentration near Lake Michigan. As farmers they used a greater variety of crops from the beginning, not depending on wheat alone, but paying more attention to the vegetable garden and the orchard. In the towns, and especially in Milwaukee, the Germans were often possessed of skill in the various crafts superior to that of the Americans. The population of Milwaukee in 1860 was about 20,000 and of these almost 6,000 were born in Germany. With their children they made up the largest homogeneous group in the city, and many of American origin found it expedient to master the German language. The building trades, tanning, blacksmithing, and other metal work fell almost entirely into German hands. In 1860 not all the breweries, but the most successful ones, were managed and staffed by Germans.

Next to the Germans the most numerous foreign element in 1860 came from the British Isles. Of nearly 94,000 from this source almost 50,000 were Irish. Some of them found their first work helping to build early Wisconsin railroads. The first Norwegian colony in Wisconsin was in southeastern Rock County in 1838, and in the following year a settlement began on the shores of Lake Muskego in Waukesha County which became a famous stopping place for newly arrived immigrants. The region about Lake Koshkonong, too, soon received many of the same nationality. Wisconsin's 8,600 Norwegians of 1850 had become 21,400 in 1860. The first Swedish settlement in the United States, after that in Delaware in 1638, was made at Pine Lake in Waukesha County in 1841, but Swedish settlers in Wisconsin were very few until after the Civil War.

The outstanding fact about the economic life of Wisconsin in this period was the unchallenged leadership of agriculture. According to the federal census of 1850, there were 40,865 farmers in the state, and to farming should be credited some of the 11,000 counted as laborers. No other occupation had a tenth as many following it. Miners numbered 3,000, and lumbermen, sawyers, and shingle-makers together accounted for only a little more than 1,300. Ten years later the supremacy of agriculture was just as unquestioned. Farmers and farm laborers accounted for 125,000 out of a total of 233,000 whose occupations were tabulated. Miners had declined almost to 2,400 and the group of lumbermen and allied workers now amounted to 2,100. The main product of the farm was wheat. The predominance of farmers in the population and the fact that they wanted their wheat transported to eastern markets were to prove important not only as a phase in economic history, but, as we shall see in later chapters, in the political evolution of Wisconsin.

THE TEMPERANCE MOVEMENT

The generation of New Englanders that was in its prime as the Civil War drew near was given to crusades and "isms" of many sorts. They were engaged with James Russell Lowell in a march to the last New Jerusalem, and some of them were too serious to smile about it with Lowell. Of course, not all New Englanders were Puritans and crusaders. Yet we are dealing with something very characteristic of New England and its westward dispersion. Not least of the matters resting on the New England conscience was the use of alcoholic beverages. In the 1830's a great temperance movement was in full swing in the eastern part of the United States, and no sooner did the settlement of Wisconsin begin than anti-alcoholic agitation began. All over southeastern Wisconsin there were total abstinence societies. Missionaries of the Protestant denominations who were starting churches were frequently zealous temperance crusaders besides. Walworth County was named in 1836 after a great temperance leader of New York state. The movement was a natural part of the life of the Yankee element in the state and issued eventually in legislative action. This outcome was not at all relished by the recent immigrants from Europe, and their revolt against this legislation was the earliest definite impact of the Germans upon the political life of the state.

In the autumn of 1849 it became the law of Wisconsin, in spite of protests from German leaders, that every vendor of liquor should furnish a bond of $1,000 on which he could be sued for damages either to the community or to an individual resulting from his sale of liquor. This law seems to have been a Wisconsin invention. There were almost no prosecutions under the act, although it was strengthened the next year. In 1851 the laws of the two previous years were repealed, and the liquor seller was required to pay a license of $100 and give a bond of $500. "In principle though not in detail this was the law which continued to govern liquor traffic down to very recent times."[1] The state of Maine enacted complete prohibition in 1851, and a similar law became the goal of temperance leaders in other states. In 1852 the Whigs and Free Soilers of Wisconsin, according to their platforms, desired temperance legislation, while the Democrats took the opposite stand. In November, 1853, the election results were curiously contradictory. The temperance candidates for state offices were defeated, as was believed, by the German vote, but at the same time a referendum was taken in which 27,000 voted for prohibition and 24,000 against it. The next legislature, in spite of this mandate, did not pass a temperance law. In the following year, 1855, a new legislature did pass such a law, but Barstow, the Democratic governor, vetoed it. Gradually after 1855 political interest turned from temperance toward the interrelated problems of slavery and states' rights.

National Issues and Wisconsin Politics

During the generation before the Civil War serious differences between the North and South arose again and again, but by arrangement or compromise the two sections were able to continue their partnership in the Union. The Missouri Compromise of 1820 helped the nation through one crisis, but in the course of time became obsolete. The matter of the extension of slavery was reopened, California applied for admission to the Union, the South came to complain of the underground railway—a host of things appeared that had been below the horizon in 1820. The Wilmot Proviso marshaled the strength of the North to keep slavery out of the lands about to be taken from Mexico.

---

[1] Joseph Schafer, "Prohibition in Wisconsin," *Wisconsin Magazine of History,* Vol. VIII (1925), p. 289.

In the turmoil that followed arose the famous Compromise of 1850.

During the first settlement of Wisconsin by Americans and for some time after its admission into the Union, the Jacksonian Democrats and the Whigs were alternately in charge of the national government, and with one or the other of these parties most of the newcomers in Wisconsin were naturally aligned. Recent arrivals from Europe, the Irish and the Germans, tended to be Democrats rather than Whigs. The Whigs to them were the party of the rich, and they were almost all poor. Besides, for many of them, the label "Democrat," the idea of rule by the people, summed up what had led them to leave the land of their birth. New England and New York had given Wisconsin its many Whigs.

The Puritan conscience that had found one outlet in the temperance crusade also expressed itself in anti-slavery groups of various sorts. The first abolition society in Wisconsin was formed in Racine County in 1840, and soon there were many in the territory. The group had a newspaper, the *American Freeman*, edited at first by C. C. Sholes. Their most prominent leader came to be Sherman M. Booth. For six years he was a leader in the Liberty party and a professional abolitionist in Connecticut. Then in 1847 he migrated to Wisconsin, and in May of the following year became editor of the *American Freeman*. He soon moved it from Prairieville (Waukesha) to Milwaukee and renamed it the *Free Democrat*. The abolitionists were counted extremists and were often criticized very harshly by the more moderate and more numerous men who desired merely to see slavery restricted to the states where it already existed.

If we follow the chronicle of Wisconsin politics from the middle of the territorial period to 1854, the most important tendency as we look at it now was not the frequent victories of the Democrats or the rarer ones of the Whigs, but the persistent interest of an important minority in third-party efforts connected with the slavery issue. Out of this and similar movements in other states issued the Republican party. The Liberty party existed on the national scene to combat slavery from 1840 to 1848. In Wisconsin the Liberty men in 1845 supported Charles Durkee unsuccessfully for the office of territorial delegate, and in 1847 secured from the first constitutional convention the referendum on the question of Negro suffrage. Later in the same year they put up Durkee again as a candidate for the office of delegate. While he secured only 973 votes, this number was sufficient, if subtracted from what the Democratic candidate might have had, to give the victory to the Whig, John H. Tweedy. In the autumn of 1848 the Liberty party was merged throughout the North in the larger Free Soil party. The presidential election of this year was the first in which Wisconsin took part, and while Lewis Cass, the Democratic candidate and the former governor of Michigan Territory, carried Wisconsin along with the other states of the Old Northwest, it is noteworthy that the third party movement, that of the Free Soilers and Van Buren, attracted a little over a fourth of the votes in the state. At the same time Durkee was sent to Congress from the southeastern counties. In the spring of 1849 the state legislature instructed the Wisconsin senators and representatives in Congress to oppose the passage of any act for the government of New Mexico and California that did not specifically forbid slavery there. The old politician, Henry Dodge, one of the two senators, obeyed instructions, but Isaac P. Walker, the other, voted for a bill without the desired prohibition. The legislature promptly asked him to vacate his seat, a request to which he paid no attention.

The Compromise of 1850 was intended to end controversy about slavery. The leaders of the old parties, Whig and Democrats alike, had much to say about "finality" and a permanent peace, though many in the North found it hard to stomach the new fugitive slave law. Still, something must be endured as the price of finality.

The lessening of tension on the slavery issue was clear in Wisconsin politics between 1850 and 1854. In 1851 both Whigs and

Free Soilers supported Leonard J. Farwell, a Whig, who was chosen governor, though the Democrats continued to have a majority in both houses of the legislature. In the national election of 1852, many who had been Free Soilers in 1848 re-entered the regular Democrat party, and in Wisconsin 52 per cent of the voters favored Franklin Pierce. The third party, however, calling itself the Free Democrat party, received about 13 per cent of the popular vote. The state election of 1853 was dominated not by the slavery or free soil issue, but by that of temperance. The candidates for governor were a Democrat, an old-line Whig, and one supported by Free Soilers and many discontented or reforming Whigs. All the Free Soil candidates were avowed temperance men, while Barstow, the Democrat, was not. As a result the Germans turned out in large numbers to vote for Barstow, who won 30,400 votes and was elected. The Free Soilers and discontented Whigs stood second with 21,800 votes, while the old-line Whigs mustered less than 3,400. This election marked the end of the old Whig party in Wisconsin.

In 1854 the political peace secured by the Compromise of 1850 came to an end. In January the Kansas-Nebraska bill was introduced into the United States Senate, and in a short time the whole North was aflame with opposition to it. Innumerable public meetings were held to protest against the measure, which was called a breach of a solemn contract between the states. At many of these meetings it was proposed to found a new party based on the principles of the Free Soil party of 1848, and at some of them the name Republican was urged for the new organization. At that time a friend of Horace Greeley, named Alan E. Bovay, was living at Ripon, Wisconsin. He called a meeting of protest for March 1, 1854, in the Congregational Church. A few days later, on March 20, he arranged a second meeting in a little frame schoolhouse. There is reasonable ground for claiming that here was born the Republican party, although there were some meetings of earlier date in other parts of the country to protest against what Congress was about to do. The first state organization of the new party was effected July 6, at Jackson, Michigan. The Republican party of Wisconsin was organized a week later, and in November it elected the lieutenant governor and two of the three congressmen, and gained control of the assembly by a narrow margin.

Besides their lively interest in national politics, the people of Wisconsin were stirred deeply by an incident in their midst in 1854. In 1852, Joshua Glover, a Negro slave, escaped from his master in Missouri and came up to Racine where for two years he worked in a mill. His owner discovered his whereabouts and came on to Milwaukee where he secured from the United States court commissioner an order for Glover's arrest. On the night of March 10, 1854, the master and some United States officials seized Glover in his cabin near Racine, brought him to Milwaukee, and lodged him in the county jail. A public meeting at Racine the next morning declared in its resolutions that the Fugitive Slave Act was "disgraceful and also repealed," and having thus disposed of a federal law, they sent a hundred men to Milwaukee by the afternoon boat to release Glover. In the meantime Sherman M. Booth was rousing the citizens of Milwaukee. Booth afterwards maintained that he counseled only legal and peaceable protest, but a mob battered in the door of the jail and Glover was soon on shipboard on his way to Canada. So ended the memorable Saturday, March 11, 1854. Glover was never recaptured.

For the next six years Sherman M. Booth was the center of legal proceedings initiated by the federal authorities under the Fugitive Slave Act. He was arrested, and while in the custody of the United States marshal was released on a writ of habeas corpus issued by a judge of the Wisconsin Supreme Court. The whole court reviewed the case and on July 19, 1854 upheld the habeas corpus. Arrested again and tried by a federal court, Booth was sentenced to a month's imprisonment and a fine of $1,000 in January, 1855. He was again set at liberty by a writ of habeas corpus issuing from the state supreme court. At this time the full court declared the Fugitive Slave Act unconstitutional and void. When the Supreme Court of the United States asked for a copy of the record in order to review the case, the Supreme Court of Wisconsin took no notice of the request. In March, 1857, the United States assumed jurisdiction, procured a copy of the record, and on March 7, 1859, gave judgment reversing that of the Wisconsin Supreme Court. In March, 1860, Booth was again arrested by federal authorities and released by friends and rearrested, and the case was finally ended when President Buchanan pardoned him in March, 1861.

The Wisconsin Supreme Court in its opposition to federal officers and federal courts in the Booth case had the support of public opinion in the state. Within the years 1855 to 1859, three judges were chosen for the state supreme court, and in each election the people favored the most determined supporter of the state against the claims of the national government. In Wisconsin, as in several other states, the legislature in 1857 passed what was known as a Personal Liberty Bill, which assured to those claimed as fugitive slaves the benefit of habeas corpus and the right of trial by jury, and prevented kidnaping. The act rendered null and void the federal statute of 1850 which was part of the famous Compromise. A Republican caucus in 1857 resolved that it was a "duty to stand by the Supreme Court of Wisconsin in asserting the right of the state tribunals to pronounce final judgment in all cases involving the reserved rights of the states, in declaring the Fugitive Slave Law unconstitutional and in shielding the inhabitants of the state from the operation of the unconstitutional enactments without right of review by any federal tribunal." Republican candidates for the office of United States Senator at the time subscribed to these opinions and referred approvingly to the Virginia and Kentucky Resolutions of 1798, the classic expression of the principles of states' rights. When the Civil War came, and it was seen that states' rights menaced the Union, the Republican party became a strong advocate of enlarged federal powers; but there is no doubt that Wisconsin

Republicans of the late 1850's generally held the contrary opinion.

POLITICAL LEADERS

The Act of Congress admitting Wisconsin to the Union was approved May 29, 1848, and on June 7, the officers of the new state entered upon their duties. Nelson Dewey of Lancaster, a Democrat, was the first governor. He was twice elected and served altogether three years and seven months. With his exit passed the political supremacy of the lead mining region, which had been so marked in the territorial years. While Farwell, his successor and Wisconsin's only Whig governor, was in office, the Democrats held all other elective state offices and controlled the legislature.

The years 1854 to 1858 may claim to be the most unsavory in Wisconsin's political history. Barstow, the third governor, had been secretary of state for one term under Nelson Dewey, and as such had been a member of the state printing board. Political opponents were fond of reproaching him with the phrase "Barstow and the balance," because a Madison editor had said he was determined to get the contract for the state printing even if he had to buy up Barstow and the balance of the printing board. Barstow's first term as governor, in the words of a modern historian, "was characterized by scandalous irregularities in the handling of the funds of the state." [2] Yet he was the choice of his party for a second term, his opponent being Coles Bashford, a Republican. Barstow was at first declared elected, but the Republicans were convinced that there had been fraud. On January 7, 1856, Barstow was inaugurated a second time, but on the same day Bashford also took the oath of office. Barstow was left *de facto* governor pending an examination of the evidence by the supreme court. Barstow's lawyers denied the right of the court to take jurisdiction over a coördinate branch of the government, but the court assumed jurisdiction. Evidence showed that

[2] M. M. Quaife, *Wisconsin, Its History and Its People* (4 vols., Chicago, 1924), Vol. I, p. 539.

votes from nonexistent precincts had been counted. Barstow immediately resigned, and Arthur MacArthur, the lieutenant-governor, became chief of the state, holding the office from March 21 to 26, 1856. When the supreme court announced its decision in favor of Bashford, MacArthur retired, and the crisis was over. Armed men had been gathering in support of each side, and some professed to believe that Barstow and MacArthur in yielding had averted civil war. In this manner was the first Republican governor ushered into office. The Bashford administration, in its turn, was disgraced by the bribery of the governor, the legislature, and other officials in the interests of the LaCrosse and Milwaukee railroad, as will be related in detail in connection with the history of the railroads.

With statehood came the right to send men to the federal Congress. The first two United States Senators, Henry Dodge and Isaac P. Walker, both Democrats, have been mentioned. To succeed them the Legislature chose Charles Durkee in 1855 and James R. Doolittle two years later, both Republicans. Durkee had been a leader of the Liberty party in the territorial period and spent four years in the lower house before he went to the Senate. Doolittle had been a favorite orator of the Free Soil or Barnburner faction in New York state before he came to Wisconsin. He was destined to stay twelve years in the Senate and to attain national prominence as a friend of Andrew Johnson. For part of one Congress Wisconsin was represented in the lower house by two men appointed by the governor, and then for the next twelve years Wisconsin had three representatives. Among them were Durkee and James Duane Doty, who sat for two terms. He was appointed territorial governor of Utah in 1863 and died in that office two years later. One of Wisconsin's representatives, John F. Potter of East Troy in Walworth County, achieved nation-wide prominence in an unusual way. In 1860, at the close of a stormy debate about the abolition movement, Roger A. Pryor of Virginia challenged Potter to a duel. As a recipient of the challenge, Potter had the right to choose the weapons and indi-

EDWARD G. RYAN*

* By courtesy of the Bureau of Visual Instruction, University of Wisconsin. From a photograph in the possession of the State Historical Society.

cated his preference for bowie knives. As Potter had anticipated, Pryor declined to use such barbarous weapons and the duel never took place. It is said that the mirth of the nation over this incident helped to end the practice of dueling.

One of the most prominent Democratic leaders of the period was Edward G. Ryan, a very able lawyer. He had become known throughout the state by the vigor with which he opposed banks in the first constitutional convention. In 1853 the assembly impeached Levi Hubbell, a circuit judge of the Second Wisconsin Circuit, which included Milwaukee, on several charges of which eventually he was acquitted. The list included bribery, embezzlement, and tyrannical usurpation of authority. Ryan was employed to aid in the prosecution, and the feature of the trial was Ryan's closing argument, which was long considered the greatest speech ever delivered in Wisconsin. It occupied four half-days in delivery and fills 152 rather large printed pages. To the men then living it seemed a marvelous performance; today it seems much too elaborate and marred by "over-wrought tempests of passion," but it could have been made only by a man of superlative ability, and it placed Ryan at the head of his profession for a generation. In politics Ryan was an unswerving Democrat and hence was in the minority during and after the Civil War.

Carl Schurz for a short time played a great part in the Republican party in Wisconsin. After services to the popular cause in the German revolutionary movement of 1848, he came to the United States in 1852, and to Watertown, Wisconsin, in 1855. In 1856 he was an unsuccessful Republican candidate for the state legislature, and in the autumn of that year he made, in German, his first political speeches. The leaders of the Republican party were anxious to capture the German vote, and in 1857 nominated Schurz for the office of lieutenant-governor. Only as the campaign proceeded did the Republicans discover that in Schurz they had their most effective campaign orator, whether in English or in German. Randall, who headed the

Republican ticket, was elected, but Schurz was defeated by the narrow margin of 107 votes. Many who favored Randall must have voted against Schurz because he was foreign-born. Undoubtedly Schurz had turned enough votes to Randall to elect him.

Schurz never ran for office again in Wisconsin, and his activity came to be more and more concerned with the national scene. He took a prominent part in the senatorial campaign in Illinois in 1858, in which Lincoln secured the majority of the popular vote, but not choice by the legislature. In the federal campaign of 1860 he was probably the most effective speaker in the whole country. As already noted, the Germans in the United States were usually Democrats. The austerities of certain of the New England Whigs clashed with the German's love of the simple pleasures of life. Moreover, the Whig party was also distinctly anti-foreign, shot through with nativism or Know-nothingism. Many Americans came into the Republican party from the Whig camp by way of Know-nothing lodges, and hence the new party was suspect to Germans and other recent immigrants. It was the peculiar contribution of Schurz at this stage of his career on the one hand to convince the German voters that the new Republican party was without the taint of nativism, and on the other to teach native-born Republicans to value and be generous to foreign-born voters. Beyond and greater than this was Schurz' genuine abhorrence of slavery, which he held to be incompatible with the principles of the founders of the American government. His arguments against the peculiar institution compare favorably with those of Abraham Lincoln, and his speeches were widely read throughout the North. He thus contributed in no small measure to the Republican victory in the Northwest, and consequently in the nation, in 1860. Thereafter Schurz lived but little in Wisconsin, and in 1867 he sold his property near Watertown. The most distinguished of the Forty-eighters, he had come to belong to the nation of his adoption. It was, however, as a citizen of Wisconsin that he was transformed into an American.

SELECTED BIBLIOGRAPHY

Several of the narratives listed for previous chapters continue to be of use: Reuben G. Thwaites, *Wisconsin* (Boston, 1908), pp. 305-325; Milo M. Quaife, *Wisconsin, Its History and Its People* (4 vols., Chicago, 1924), Vol. I, pp. 527-553; *Wisconsin in Three Centuries* (4 vols., New York, 1906), Vol. III, pp. 37-103. Alexander M. Thomson, *A Political History of Wisconsin* (Milwaukee, 1900), pp. 63-153, is an entertaining chronicle. Charles R. Tuttle, *An Illustrated History of Wisconsin* (Boston, 1875), pp. 254-367, is full of information.

The successive reports of the federal census will still yield much to the zealous student. An excellent discussion of the German contribution to Wisconsin is by Joseph Schafer, "The Yankee and the Teuton in Wisconsin," in five installments in the *Wisconsin Magazine of History*, Vols. VI and VII (1922, 1923). Somewhat related to the foregoing is the same author's "Prohibition in Wisconsin," *ibid.*, Vol. VIII, pp. 281-299 (March, 1925). Ellis B. Usher discussed "Puritan Influence in Wisconsin," in Wisconsin Historical Society *Proceedings, 1899*, pp. 117-128. Guy-Harold Smith has two brief studies of foreign settlement, each accompanied by a map: "Notes on the Distribution of the German-born in Wisconsin in 1905," *Wisconsin Magazine of History*, Vol. XIII, pp. 107-120 (December, 1929); and "Notes on the Distribution of the Foreign-born Scandinavians in 1905," *ibid.*, Vol. XIV, pp. 419-436 (June, 1931). Albert O. Barton recounts some Norwegian beginnings in Wisconsin in "Muskego: The Most Historic Norwegian Colony," *ibid.*, Vol. XXI, pp. 129-138 (December, 1937). Filip A. Forsbeck contributed "New Upsala: The First Swedish Settlement in Wisconsin," *ibid.*, Vol. XIX, pp. 3-31, 161-181 (1935), and 294-318 (1936).

The third party tendency at this time may be studied in detail in two works by Theodore C. Smith, "The Free Soil Party in Wisconsin," *Proceedings, 1894*, pp. 97-161; and *The Liberty and Free Soil Parties in the Northwest* (Harvard University Press, 1897). Helpful also is Andrew W. Crandall, *The Early History of the Republican Party* (Boston, 1930).

Various aspects of the slavery issue in Wisconsin are detailed in the following articles: Vroman Mason, "The Fugitive Slave Law in Wisconsin," *Proceedings, 1895*, pp. 117-144; George W. Carter, "The Booth War in Ripon," *Proceedings, 1902*, pp. 161-172; Kate Everest Levi, "The Wisconsin Press and Slavery," *Wisconsin Magazine of History*, Vol. IX, pp. 423-434 (June, 1926); James L. Sellers, "Republicans and State Rights in Wisconsin," *Mississippi Valley Historical Review*, Vol. XVII, pp. 213-229 (September, 1930).

Lawyers' statements of the controversy between the Wisconsin and the federal courts may be found in John B. Winslow, *The Story of a Great Court* (Chicago, 1912), pp. 67-121; and in *Selected Opinions of Luther S. Dixon and Edward G. Ryan* edited by Gilbert S. Roe (Chicago, 1907), case of Ableman *v.* Booth, pp. 69-101. The editor's note, pp. 69-101, is a con-cise summary of the whole episode that began with the rescue of Glover.

Schurz' first ten years in America, substantially the years spent in Wis-consin, are the subject of Chester V. Easum, *The Americanization of Carl Schurz* (Chicago, 1929). Joseph Schafer covered Schurz' whole life in *Carl Schurz: Militant Liberal* (Madison, 1930).

CHAPTER IX

THE PERIOD OF THE CIVIL WAR

The Issues and Wisconsin's Leaders

WHEN the Civil War began, Wisconsin had been a state for less than thirteen years, and the great struggle could not fail to affect the young commonwealth in many ways. In these antecedent years the state, as we have seen, had grown rapidly in population and wealth. The issues that were leading the nation toward the irrepressible conflict had been in the forefront of political thinking in Wisconsin, and when the storm broke, Wisconsin, along with the rest of the North, was ready, not perhaps in a military sense, but mentally and emotionally, to exert herself to the utmost. The idea that the war was a crusade to free the slaves was entertained by very few anywhere in the North. The main point at issue was whether the southern states might withdraw from the Union. Among constitutional lawyers this was subject to debate down to 1861. To be sure, great national leaders like Jackson, Clay, and Webster had stated that the Union must be preserved, that it was indissoluble; but there was high authority on the other side as well. When the southern states actually seceded, however, and put theory to the test of practice, the North sprang to the defense of the Union as of something held most dear. Alexander W. Randall, entering on the fourth year of his governorship, spoke the mind of Wisconsin in his message to the legislature in January, 1861: "A state cannot come into the Union when it pleases and go out when it pleases. Once in it must stay in until the Union is destroyed. Secession is revolution:

revolution is war: war against the Government of the United States is treason."

In Wisconsin, as in all the Northwest, the election campaign of 1860 was a spirited one. At the Republican national convention in Chicago, the Wisconsin delegation had favored Seward for president until the final vote that made the nomination of Lincoln unanimous. In the months that followed, however, there was no lack of enthusiasm for Lincoln. Almost every community had its marching club of younger Republicans, called "Wide-Awakes," whose torchlight parades ushered in and concluded every evening of political oratory. Two young men of Hartford, to protect their clothes from dripping torches—candles fastened on rails—put pieces of black cambric over their shoulders; from this developed, with the substitution of oil-cloth for cambric, the uniform of the Wide-Awakes. At the polls Lincoln received 86,000 votes to 67,000 for Douglas, and of fifty-one counties Douglas carried only nine. The most important Democratic counties were Milwaukee, where the vote stood about 4,800 for Lincoln to 6,700 for Douglas, Ozaukee, and Washington; and further north, the counties of Outagamie, Brown, and Kewaunee. In these three taken together about 2,000 voted for Lincoln, and 3,000 for Douglas. Lincoln carried every state in the Old Northwest, and the Republican victory precipitated the long-threatened secessions. South Carolina determined to secede in December, 1860, and by February, 1861, before Lincoln's inauguration, five more states had made the same decision and a provisional government had been organized in the South. Fort Sumter was fired upon in April, and thus the Civil War began.

Randall's position as the first war governor was in some respects more and in others less difficult than that of his successors; the initial enthusiasm was less universal in later years. The governor showed his own intensity of feeling in speaking before the governors of several states in May: "Rebellion and treason are abroad in our land. . . . We know where this commenced and we know where it must end. . . . Charleston should be razed till not one stone is left upon another, till there is no place for the owl to hoot nor the bittern to mourn. Had I the power of the thunderbolts of Jove, I would wipe out not only traitors but the seed of traitors." With such sentiments animating loyal citizens, it was the task of the first governor to guide and organize rather than to urge. He sought arms and equipment for the gathering regiments, from the federal authorities and in the open market. He took a deep interest in safeguarding the health and assuring the comfort of the Wisconsin men in the field. He appointed Dr. E. B. Wolcott of Milwaukee, formerly a surgeon in the United States Army, as head of the state medical service. Every regiment was provided with at least three months' supply of medicine, instruments, and hospital stores. Aid commissions were organized, generally composed of physicians, and these commissions, helped by local relief societies, gathered large amounts of supplies, such as clothing, fruits, and tobacco, besides additional medical supplies, and took them to Wisconsin regiments in the field. The Governor personally aided in much of this organization. All classes of people wrote to him, setting forth their needs, or offering their services. Like all the governors of the war period, he was a real father to his people.

At the close of his second term as governor (January, 1862) Randall desired to enter military service, but President Lincoln sent him to Rome as minister to the Papal States. After a few months there he returned to the United States and again sought service in the army, but again Lincoln had other use for him and named him assistant postmaster general. In the cabinet of Andrew Johnson he was postmaster general. As an adherent of Johnson he was out of harmony with the radical Republicans dominant in Wisconsin after the war. He later entered upon the practice of law at Elmira, New York, and died there in 1872 at the age of fifty-three.

Louis P. Harvey, Wisconsin's second war governor, was a native of Connecticut, possessed of a very active New England conscience. After experience as a teacher and editor in Kenosha, he settled in

Rock County, where he conducted a general store. He bought a distillery in order to demolish it, and erected in its stead a grist and sawmill. In 1847 he married Cordelia A. Perrine, a very able woman. Having served as secretary of state during Randall's second term, he was well able to continue what Randall had begun. He was especially concerned, as was Mrs. Harvey, also, in caring for Wisconsin's soldiers at the front. When the news came of the battle of Shiloh, in which many Wisconsin men were killed or wounded, Governor Harvey assembled ninety boxes of supplies for the soldiers and went down to Tennessee. There he visited and encouraged hundreds of the victims of the recent battle. His errand of mercy was practically complete when, on April 19, 1862, in attempting to step from one steamboat to another in the darkness of night, he fell into the Tennessee River and was drowned. He had been governor for seventy-three days. The state was deeply shocked, and the month following his death was the gloomiest of the whole war in Wisconsin. Mrs. Harvey devoted herself henceforth to the care of wounded and needy soldiers. The field of her work extended over many states, and she arranged to bring the sick and wounded to hospitals in the North, cutting much official red tape in the process. As the war was closing she established at Madison an orphanage for the children of Union soldiers killed in the war. These activities caused her to be held in general esteem; to many she became one of the saints of Wisconsin history.

Harvey's death elevated the lieutenant governor, Edward Salomon, then only 33 years old, to the chief magistracy of the state. He was born in Prussia, and was Wisconsin's only German-born governor until 1939. A brother preceded him to the United States as a refugee Forty-eighter, and Edward became a close friend of Carl Schurz. He read law in the office of Edward G. Ryan, but parted company politically with the Democratic leader and joined the Republican party. During the twenty-two months of his governorship (April, 1862—January, 1864) he had to meet the greatest difficulties. In August, 1862, Sioux Indians in Minnesota began an uprising, and before the end of the tragic affair, 350 white people were massacred on their farms and ninety were killed in military operations. There were few Sioux left in Wisconsin, but there were many Chippewa, and the northwestern part of the state was in a condition of panic. In the same year conscription began, and Salomon by his firmness incurred criticism from those who disapproved of the draft. In the difficult times in which he governed, Salomon gave a good account of himself, and it seems unfortunate that the Republican politicians declined to give him renomination. He practiced law in New York City for many years after the War, and finally returned to Germany because of his wife's health and died there.

Governor James T. Lewis (January, 1864—January, 1866) was a native of New York who had practiced law in Columbus, Wisconsin, for nearly twenty years. He sat in the second constitutional convention, and subsequently held a great variety of local and state offices, including those of secretary of state and lieutenant governor. For the most part it fell to him to carry on what others had begun. As the successive calls for men came from the federal government in the later years of the war, he dealt with the provost marshal general in Washington to get the quotas of Wisconsin adjusted downward to their proper numbers. He assisted Mrs. Harvey in her work of bringing wounded soldiers back to the North, and coöperated also in establishing the orphanage for soldiers' children at Madison.

THE SUPPLY OF SOLDIERS

When the first call to arms came, Wisconsin responded with great zeal. The existing militia companies at Milwaukee, Madison, and other cities were at once mustered into federal service. Three graduates of West Point leading civilian lives in Wisconsin re-entered the army, of whom the best-known was Rufus King, editor of the Milwaukee *Sentinel*. At every opportunity during the first year of the war, Wisconsin offered more volunteers than the federal government could accept. Even those in authority at Washington did not realize in the beginning what huge armies would be required. In the spring of 1862, as the Peninsular Campaign was opening in Virginia, there were over 637,000 men in the Union army, so many that the federal War Department ceased recruiting. But it soon saw its mistake, and the recruiting offices in Wisconsin, closed in April, 1862, were reopened in June. In August President Lincoln asked the states for 300,000 men, and if they were not forthcoming a draft for the deficiency was to be made. In the first draft Wisconsin sheriffs and their deputies were the enrolling officers, and the governor appointed a draft commissioner and an examining surgeon in each county. Some resistance was offered to enrolling officers in the late summer, and as the actual draft approached, trouble was predicted, especially in regions with a large foreign population. After all, many of these immigrants had left Europe to escape compulsory military service. The most serious rioting occurred at Port Washington in Ozaukee County on November 10, where a mob attacked the draft commissioner, threw him down a flight of steps, scattered his papers, and then, stimulated by whiskey, began looting. Federal troops were marched into the county, and about eighty people were arrested as resisters. The draft was to begin in Milwaukee nine days later and trouble was expected there, too, but after a warning proclamation from Governor Salomon and a show of military force, the drawing of names passed off without violence. It was the spring of 1863 before all the supplementary drawings were done. In five months this first draft, managed by the state of Wisconsin, produced about 750 men.

In March, 1863, the federal Congress passed a Conscription Act that set up draft machinery entirely in federal hands. At the head of it in Washington was the provost marshal general, Colonel James B. Fry. In each loyal state there was an assistant provost marshal general, the one in Wisconsin being Lieutenant Colonel Charles S. Lovell. The congressional districts, of which Wisconsin then had six, were the units of administration, and in each there were a provost marshal, a commissioner, and a physician. Three drafts during the years 1863 to 1865 produced something less than 11,000 conscripted men.

The federal draft law of 1863 was not an ideal one. A drafted man would be released from one draft if he paid $300, and he could gain exemption for the entire war by procuring a substitute. A huge business, nefarious in many of its methods, sprang up to find substitutes. Naturally the poor, unable to buy freedom, felt that the law unjustly favored the rich. In wealthy communities large sums, raised by taxation or popular subscription, were offered as bounties to stimulate volunteering. A man was credited to the place where he enlisted and not to the town where he had lived most of his life. Poor country districts were in consequence denuded of their able-bodied young men, who went to the wealthier communities to get bounty money or to become substitutes. Draft insurance companies were formed; a man who thought he might be drafted paid a certain sum, often $50, and if his name was drawn the insurance company paid the $300 that gained him exemption. Able-bodied men in great numbers either took to the brush or fled to Canada. This was called "skedaddling," and in Wisconsin more than 11,000 men, notified that they had been drafted, failed to report. Neither the federal nor the state authorities seemed to be able to take any effective steps against the skedaddlers. The only good thing that can be said for the draft was that it stimulated volunteering; as each draft drew near there was a rush to enlist.

Many things were done to persuade the volunteer that neither his business interests nor his family would suffer during his absence in the army. Ordinary business and legal processes were delayed or suspended in favor of the enlisted men. Mortgages could not be foreclosed or mechanics liens executed against their property while they were in service. If they were in process of buying land from the state of Wisconsin, the transaction would remain *in statu quo* while they served in the army. For a short time at the close of the war, the lands of volunteers could not be sold for taxes.

The war called away the chief and often the only wage-earner of the family. Posters urging men to enlist promised that the members of their families would not come to want. From May, 1861, onward, the state of Wisconsin paid $5.00 a month to the family of each enlisted man. The legislature authorized towns and villages to tax themselves for various war purposes, and more than $7,000,000 were paid in bounties to volunteers, and in many cases the man paid it over at once to his family; it is estimated further that at least a third, or nearly two and one-half million dollars, was paid directly to dependents of the man in service. Of the fifty-eight counties in existence at the close of the war period there were only three in which relief was not given either by the county or by its subdivisions. Soldiers at the front might allot all or part of their pay to their families, and Wisconsin sent three commissioners to travel about in the armies of the North to collect allotment orders from the men. The state of Wisconsin then received the allotted funds from the federal government, in all more than $1,000,000, and distributed them to the designated families.

WISCONSIN REGIMENTS

Wisconsin is credited with slightly more than 91,000 enlistments during the Civil War. A regiment normally contained about 1,000 enlisted men, and the officers raised the total to about 1,050. In the latter part of the war, however, some regiments left the state with less than nine hundred men. The list of Wisconsin infantry regiments runs from the First to the Fifty-third, but the Fifty-third was only partially recruited when it was consolidated with the Fifty-first. Three cavalry regiments were raised in 1862, and during 1863 the Fourth Infantry was mounted and thereafter was known as the Fourth Wisconsin Cavalry. There was one artillery regiment. Thus, there were fifty-six regiments in all.

One may ask how 91,000 men could be put into fifty-six regiments. The length of enlistments varied greatly, and many men enlisted not once but two or three times. The First Wisconsin began as a three-months' regiment, and as such proceeded to Virginia in May, 1861. It was back in Milwaukee in August to be mustered out. In the fall it was reorganized as a three-years' regiment, with Colonel Starkweather again commanding and with several other officers continuing. In 1864 three regiments of 100-day men left Wisconsin. Hence, the total number of enlistments was increased. Besides loss of men due to expiry of enlistment, regiments were depleted by desertion, death, and permanent incapacity due to wounds or disease. It was the policy of the state to keep existing regiments up to full strength, and consequently many men entered old regiments as replacements. Thus were the men contained in fifty-six regiments. Some of the short-term regiments were disbanded before the end of the war, and when the end came there were less than 40,000 men to be demobilized. No one knows exactly how many individual citizens of Wisconsin participated in the war. The Adjutant General's office later compiled and published a list of 82,000 names, but acknowledged that defective records made the list incomplete. Wisconsin men who died in the army, whether in battle or from disease, numbered about 12,000.

Recruits were usually grouped in companies near their homes and then taken to one of the camps established by the state for rendezvous. In or near Milwaukee were camps named in honor of General Winfield Scott, ranking officer in the United States Army when the war began; Franz Sigel, a German-American of New York and a commander in the northern army; and Cadwallader C. Washburn, who organized and at first commanded the Second Cavalry. At Madison the grounds of the Wisconsin Agricultural Society were offered to the state for military purposes, and were promptly accepted and named Camp Randall. This site was particularly acceptable because of its buildings for exhibition purposes which were easily converted into barracks. A generation later this tract was purchased by the University of Wisconsin. There were also Camp Utley at Racine, named for the adjutant general of the time, Camp Bragg at Oshkosh, and one or two others. At these camps the regiments were cared for by the state of Wisconsin until mustered into federal service.

Each regiment had a history and something of a character of its own. The Second, Sixth, and Seventh, along with a regiment from Indiana and one from Michigan, made up the famous Iron Brigade, commanded at one time by General Rufus King, formerly editor of the Milwaukee *Sentinel,* and at another time by Lucius Fairchild. All these regiments had a very high percentage of loss from deaths in battle. The Ninth was composed largely of Germans and was commanded by Colonel Frederic Salomon, brother of the governor. The Twenty-sixth was also a German regiment, and nearly equaled the Sixth in the severity of its losses in battle. The Fifteenth was largely Norwegian, and was commanded by Colonel Hans Heg, whose statue stands at the east corner of the Capitol Square at Madison. The Eighth is remembered because it carried through many battles an eagle captured in the Chippewa Valley. This remarkable bird, called "Old Abe," was kept in the basement of the capitol after the war, was exhibited at Philadelphia at the Centennial Exposition in 1876, and did not die until 1881.

The military and naval operations of the Civil War provided a setting for many deeds of courage and ingenuity. There was a memorable exploit in northwestern Louisiana in the spring of 1864 that could probably have been performed only by northern lumbermen. The authorities at Washington planned what came to be known as the Red River expedition to encourage loyalty to the Union in Louisiana, overawe Texas, and counter French activities in Mexico. From the Mississippi River, which the North had held for some time, General Nathaniel P. Banks of the Union army, with 27,000 men, marched northwestward up the Red River valley while a supporting fleet of gunboats and transports under Admiral David D. Porter proceeded upstream on the spring floods, which alone made the river navigable. The army under Banks met with reverses, his troops were needed elsewhere, and when the expedition was still southeast of Shreveport, the whole enterprise was abandoned and army and fleet began to retire downstream. Unfortunately the Red River fell much more rapidly than had been anticipated, and since some of the boats required seven feet of water, it was apparent that they would not be able to descend a stretch of the river near Alexandria filled with rocks and dangerous rapids. Rather than permit the boats to fall into the hands of pursuing Confederate soldiers, it had been decided to destroy the fleet, when Wisconsin came to the rescue. Colonel Joseph Bailey of the Fourth Wisconsin Cavalry laid his plan before the other officers. Only because the alternative was the destruction of the fleet was he given permission to make the attempt. He obtained from the Twenty-third and Twenty-fourth Wisconsin regiments men who had worked in the pineries, and some other help, and soon had 3,000 men at work. They put a dam across the Red River, at that point about 750 feet wide, backed up the water, and increased its depth. In the midst of their work part of their dam went out, but without rebuilding it they built two wing dams higher up and so accomplished their purpose. On May 12, 1864, the last of the gunboats was saved. Congress voted Colonel Bailey its thanks for saving property worth $2,000,000; and the sword and loving cup presented to him by the officers of the rescued boats may still be seen in the museum of the State Historical Society at Madison.

Banking and Other Business During the War

In the years just before the Civil War some provisions of Wisconsin's banking system were not particularly sound. If one wanted to start a bank, he bought the bonds of one of the states or of the United States, and deposited them with the state bank comptroller, whereupon that official gave permission to issue state currency equal in value to the bonds just deposited. Unfortunately the would-be bankers were permitted to buy the cheapest state bonds on the market, which meant in practice that they bought those that expert opinion judged to be least safe.

On January 1, 1860, there was on deposit with the comptroller a little over $5,000,000 in bonds, but $3,000,000 were bonds of five heavily indebted southern states. The banker got a double income on his investment. He received the interest on the bonds from the states which had issued them, and he received interest from those to whom he loaned the currency. Banks were supposed to serve the community in many ways, and there were many strong banks that did so; but there existed also "wildcat" banks founded merely to issue currency. They had their offices in inaccessible or unknown places, and in a crisis were quite unable to redeem in specie the currency they had issued. The stronger banks had organized in 1857 the Wisconsin Bankers' Association, which had great influence in behalf of sound banking. One of its leaders was Alexander Mitchell, Wisconsin's greatest pioneer banker.

As the Civil War approached, the value of the bonds of the southern states sank. In obedience to law the comptroller, between October, 1860, and June, 1861, made several "depreciation levies"; each time this was done, it forced some banks to admit that they were unable to meet the levy, and thus, in effect, to confess themselves insolvent. In April, 1861, too, the stronger banks in Wisconsin, as well as some in Chicago, refused to receive the notes of wildcat banks in the state. Much of the repudiated currency was in the hands of workingmen; in fact, while adjustments were being made, many employers paid their men in currency of suspected soundness. On Monday, June 24, 1861, there was a serious riot in Milwaukee directed against the banks, and the furniture of several of them was burned. State officials and the legislature, advised by the officers of the bankers' association, found a way back to sound currency. Since Wisconsin was just then issuing bonds to finance its war effort, Wisconsin war bonds and federal bonds were substituted for the securities of southern states. The amount of state currency in circulation was diminished from $4,500,000 at the beginning of 1861 to about $1,590,000 at the end of the year. This rapid contraction worked great inconvenience, not to say hardship, on business. After that year, however, the soundness of the state currency did not again come into question.

Thus the worst hindrance to business, that of a currency with inadequate security behind it, was overcome in 1861. The difficulties that remained—one of them a great shortage of small change—annoyed rather than imperiled business. Soon after the war began, not only did gold disappear from circulation, but so did all coins representing fractional parts of a dollar, even down to the copper pieces. Checks for less than a dollar passed from hand to hand until the banks forbade their use. Token money of many sorts, called shinplasters, appeared. It was issued by banks, municipalities, merchants, hotel-keepers, and as the Milwaukee *Sentinel* complained, by "one-horse auctioneers, butchers, saloon keepers, boot-blacks, loafers and every one who is without money." Government postage stamps were used, too, mostly in the three-cent denomination. The ordinary gummed stamps were rather inconvenient, but in the autumn of 1862 the government issued postal currency, unglued and in the shape of miniature bank-notes, and when these became available, Wisconsin shinplasters rapidly disappeared. Furthermore, the federal legal-tender act of February 25, 1862, and subsequent acts of the same sort provided an ample supply of legal-tender notes or greenbacks. By the middle of the war period, therefore, currency troubles ceased to hamper the ordinary processes of trade.

A national banking act was passed in 1863 and was largely recast in June of the following year. It was hoped that national banks would furnish a currency more uniform and better secured than that of the state banks. Those establishing national banks were required to deposit federal bonds, and this rule would promote the sale of federal securities. Results came very slowly, however. By the end of 1863 there were only six new national banks in Wisconsin under the act; a year later, only fifteen; and it was much the same in other states. One reason for this in Wisconsin was that bankers were loaded with state bonds which could then be sold only at a sacrifice, and consequently they could not buy federal bonds. On March 3, 1865, Congress hastened matters by laying a tax of 10 per cent on all state bank notes, to be paid by any bank either issuing or using them. State banks in actual practice had to give up their note-issuing function, and many were indirectly compelled to become national banks. There had been sixty-four state banks in Wisconsin in 1862; by 1869, only thirteen remained and most of these were in Milwaukee. National banks in 1869 numbered thirty-four.

Wisconsin had gone through a boom period from 1852 to 1857. The panic of 1857 was felt most in the East in that year, but in Wisconsin, bankruptcies were considerably more numerous and severe in 1858, and conditions continued rather bad during the two following years. The outbreak of war precipitated the "panic of 1861," which was marked in the North as a whole by losses aggregating about two-thirds of those of 1857. In this second panic Wisconsin's losses through bankruptcies almost equalled those of 1858, but Wisconsin was spared some of the griefs of the manufacturing East. She had done comparatively little business with the seceding states, and so was not greatly affected when the latter repudiated debts owed to creditors in the North. Wisconsin was also fortunate in having in 1860 the greatest wheat crop in her history; this meant a large purchasing power for farmers and for almost all classes in the state.

Wisconsin at this time was still so largely agricultural that she was scarcely conscious of any industrial problems or labor troubles. The first half of the war period was marked by business depression, the latter part by considerable expansion. Hence for some time the movement of men into the army was not accompanied by any labor shortage. More than half the men at the time of their enlistment were mere boys and had not yet made a place for themselves in industry, though if they came from farms their loss was felt keenly. Yet on the farms, man power was in considerable part replaced by the increased use of the reaper, the harvester, and other new farm machinery. The wartime was not prosperous for mechanics and laborers in Milwaukee and the other industrial centers. "It has been estimated for the North as a whole that during the war prices advanced approximately 100 per cent, while wages rose only 50 to 60 per cent," [1] and this statement is probably true for Wisconsin except that wages rose a little more. Merchants, farmers, and employers stood to gain much more from the prosperity of the years 1863 to 1867 than did mechanics and laborers.

THE DEMOCRATIC PARTY; THE RYAN ADDRESS

The homage paid to Abraham Lincoln at the present time is so great and so unanimous that we find it hard to believe that many could have opposed him; we forget the numbers and ability of those who continued to call themselves Democrats throughout the period of the Civil War, and for a long time after that. Two-fifths of those who voted in Wisconsin in 1860 preferred Douglas to Lincoln, the Republicans leading by about 19,000. In the election for governor in 1863, in a much lighter vote, the Republicans won by some 23,000. In 1864 the state again preferred Lincoln, but only by about 16,000, and four years later in the next presidential election there were 108,000 Republicans and 84,000 Democrats. For two decades after that, as the population of the state grew, so too did the Democratic party, and while it seldom won elections in the state at large, it continued to have a fair representation in the state senate and assembly.

Thus throughout the period of the Civil War the Democratic party maintained its organization, offered its opinions on public questions, contested all elections, criticized the administration, and claimed that it was no whit behind the Republicans in loyalty. A state convention of the party held in Milwaukee, September 3, 1862, approved and issued an "Address to the People by the Democracy of Wisconsin." It was largely the work of Edward G. Ryan, and came to be known as "the Ryan Address." While

---

[1] Frederick Merk, *Economic History of Wisconsin During the Civil War Decade* (Madison, 1916), p. 162.

Republicans called it "that Bible of copperheadism," the Democrats accepted it as the best statement of their political faith. Couched in language always clear and at times of great beauty, it expressed the political thought of nearly half the voters of Wisconsin.

In war as in peace, wrote Ryan, the constitution was the object of the citizens' greatest loyalty. The Republican administration had invaded the rights secured to the citizen by the Constitution. "The Administration may err, but the Constitution does not change. And when the Administration violates the Constitution, loyalty to the Administration may become disloyalty to the Union. . . . In days of civil discord and convulsion, there is danger of patriotism being blindfolded, mistaking the object of its faith and transferring to the servant of the altar the devotion due only to the altar itself." [2]

The Democratic party was nationwide in its scope; it was not, like the Republican party, the representative of sectionalism. Because of its nonsectional character it would be able to render great service in the trying days of reconstruction that were to come. "The people of the South will return to the Union, when they do return, wounded in their pride and embittered in their feeling. When they return they will return as brethren and merit the treatment of brethren. The law may demand its victims, but those guiltless of the war, and those forgiven by the law, will again be our political brothers." [3] Only the Democratic party would be disposed to give them a brotherly reception.

The blame for the outbreak of the Civil War was laid on the two parties of sectionalism, the Republicans in the North and the Breckenridge Democrats in the South. If Douglas, the great Douglas, had been elected, there would have been no war. The nullification sentiments of the Republicans in Wisconsin in the

---

[2] Madison *Evening Patriot*, September 6, 1862, p. 2. The Ryan Address appeared in contemporary newspapers and in pamphlet form. See Selected Bibliography for this chapter.

[3] *Ibid.*

years before the Civil War were recalled as proof of their sectional-ism. The abolition movement was wholly evil, exemplifying as it did both sectionalism and fanaticism, Ryan wrote.

Of the peculiar institution of the South, the address said: "The democracy has no apology to make for southern slavery. We regard it as a great social evil. But we regard it as a misfortune, not a crime. The crime is the presence of the African race upon the continent. That is a crime of the past, not the present." Now that the Negroes were here, their perpetual inferiority, their fitness only for the status of slavery, had to be recognized, the address declared.

"The defeat of the Democratic Party," Ryan wrote, "has been followed by the revolt of several of the States from the Union and by the present terrible Civil War. . . . We reprobate that revolt as unnecessary, unjustifiable, unholy. Devoted to the Constitution, we invoke the vengeance of God upon all who raise their sacrilegious hands against it, whether wearing the soft gloves of peace or the bloody gauntlets of war." At another point in the address he stated: " . . . the war is not only expedient but necessary; not only justifiable but holy. It is a defensive war. It is a war of self-preservation. Disunion, once successful, would be a recurring evil. . . . We know and love the blessings of union; but no human eye can penetrate the dark and terrible picture which lies beyond the grave of the Constitution. The war for the preservation of the Constitution has all our sympa-thies, all our hopes and all our energies."

Finally Ryan recited his complaints against the conduct of the federal government by the Republicans, the suspension of the writ of habeas corpus by executive order, the censorship of the press, and the dangerous extension of the definition of treason. Jury trial and the necessity of indictment by a grand jury had been suspended and superseded by military tribunals. Ryan did not blame Lincoln for all these acts of tyranny; indeed, he was most respectful to the President. The address concluded: "We will not surrender our rights nor forsake them. We will maintain our constitutional liberty at all hazards, and as a necessary step toward that end we will maintain the Union in like manner. . . . We are for the Constitution as it is, and the Union as it was."

What judgment shall we pass on the address after seventy-five years? Its discussion of slavery is, of course, simply obsolete, and some would dissent from its pronouncement about the whole Negro race. But its condemnation of wartime tyranny, which did occur, even in some particulars in Wisconsin, was rooted in an inherited love of justice, centuries old. The whole address was marked by devotion to the Constitution, loyalty to the Union, and zeal to prosecute the war. The Republicans by no means had a monopoly on patriotism. As to the opinion of Ryan's generation, it is significant that when it was necessary to choose a United States Senator in 1863, as Doolittle's first term was drawing to a close, seventy-three votes were cast for Doolittle and fifty-three for Ryan.

POLITICAL AFTERMATH

The victory of the northern forces brought in its wake several difficult questions. On what terms were the states recently in rebellion to be restored to their place in the Union? What would be the status of the recently enfranchised Negroes? President Lincoln's plans were just taking shape when he was assassinated. Andrew Johnson followed in general the lines indicated by his predecessor, but he lacked tact and political skill. He appointed provisional governors and directed the southern states to set about making new constitutions, and before the end of 1865 all but one of them had followed his suggestions.

In 1860 the party that elected Lincoln called itself Republican, but as the war went on it chose to be known as the Union party. Its leaders looked with alarm at what Johnson had brought to pass with such speed. If the Democrats of the North united with those of the South, they might well be in a majority, and the Republican or Union partisans would lose control of the nation's destiny and be ousted from all federal offices besides. Taking their stand on the ground that the admission of the former Confederate states was a function of Congress and not of the President, the Union men in Congress presented their own program of reconstruction, and entered upon a fierce struggle with Andrew Johnson that reached its culmination in the impeachment trial in the spring of 1868. The aims of this congressional party combined vindictiveness toward the southern whites with insistence on the full rights of the Negroes to social and political equality. The recent leaders of the South were to be punished as traitors, plantations were to be confiscated, and the freedmen were at once to exercise the right of suffrage. The proponents of this program were called radicals; Republicans who rallied to the President were labelled conservatives, and this cleavage appeared in all the Northern states, Wisconsin included. Wisconsin's United States Senators at the time were Timothy O. Howe of Green Bay (1861-1879) and James R. Doolittle (1857-1869). Howe was strong in the councils of the radicals, Doolittle a tower of strength to Johnson.

The issue was clearly joined in the spring of 1866, and by June the friends of Johnson, realizing that the President was no longer in control of the Union party of the North, began a separate organization with a view to winning the congressional elections in the autumn. They called themselves the National Union party, thus occasioning considerable confusion in party nomenclature. Senator Doolittle was on their executive committee, and when their convention assembled in Philadelphia in August, he was chosen to preside. In the election of 1866, which determined the composition of the Fortieth Congress, the radicals won a sweeping victory. They were able to complete the undoing of presidential reconstruction and press on with their own program. In the Fortieth, as in the preceding Congress, Wisconsin was represented by five Republican or Union men, all radicals, and one

Democrat, Charles A. Eldredge of Fond du Lac, who in all questions touching reconstruction and the interpretation of the constitution stood staunchly behind President Johnson.

As the struggle waxed hotter at Washington, the Wisconsin legislature frequently expressed its opinion in joint resolutions. In March, 1866, it approved Congress' action in excluding representatives from the rebellious districts, and expressed "pain and disappointment" over President Johnson's course of action. A month later Senator Doolittle was informed that it was his duty to resign. In January, 1867, he was again requested to resign as "totally unworthy of further confidence and support." But Doolittle continued steadfastly to advise and help President Johnson, acting in the impeachment proceedings as one of his most constant advisers. With many of the Republicans who had supported Johnson, he soon passed over to the Democratic party, favored Seymour against Grant in 1868, and afterwards for many years remained a leader of the Democrats in Washington. But it turned out that he had committed political suicide. In 1869 his seat in the Senate was given to Matthew H. Carpenter. In the years that followed he ran twice for Congress, once was the Democratic candidate for governor, and sought various elective judicial offices; but always he was defeated. Ex-Governor Randall, too, stood by Johnson and filled the office of Postmaster-General from July, 1868, to the end of Johnson's term.

But Doolittle and Randall were in the minority in Wisconsin, where, as in most of the North, the radical faction prevailed, and radical and Republican became interchangeable terms. The Congressional policy of reconstruction was approved by the great majority of Republican voters. Why this was so is a moot question. The simplest explanation is that they believed the South merited what she received during reconstruction, and that such treatment of the South was the proper conclusion of the war. But there were other reasons that were almost certainly of considerable weight at the time. When it became clear that the radicals were to dominate the Republican party, and through it the federal government, it was expedient for Wisconsin to fall into line. Only by so doing could she share in federal money and in land grants for internal improvements; only thus could Wisconsin politicians hope for appointment to federal offices. At any rate, the Republican party, still young and perhaps impermanent when the Civil War began, was by the war and its immediate sequel made into a tough, lasting, and even revered institution. It was normally to command the allegiance of the majority in Wisconsin until the end of the nineteenth century.

Selected Bibliography

The period of the Civil War is dealt with in Reuben G. Thwaites, *Wisconsin* (Boston, 1908), pp. 326-370; Milo M. Quaife, *Wisconsin, Its History and Its People* (4 vols., Chicago, 1924), Vol. I, pp. 555-582; *Wisconsin in Three Centuries* (4 vols., New York, 1906), Vol. III, pp. 139-329; and in Charles R. Tuttle, *An Illustrated History of Wisconsin* (Boston, 1875), pp. 344-628. The last two mentioned take up the various regiments one by one and give the names of hundreds of officers.

The Roster of Wisconsin Volunteers, War of the Rebellion, 1861-1865 (2 vols., Madison, 1886), published by the state, is arranged by military units. The state also published *Wisconsin Volunteers: War of the Rebellion, 1861-1865, Arranged Alphabetically* (Madison, 1914). This contains about 82,000 names. The legislature of 1911 ordered the reprinting of two volumes with separate titles: *Annual Reports of the Adjutant General of the State of Wisconsin . . . 1860-1864* (Madison, 1912); and *Annual Report of the Adjutant General . . . for . . . 1865* (Madison, 1912). *Civil War Messages and Proclamations of Wisconsin's War Governors* (Madison, 1912) acquaints us with the administrative procedure of the period.

Two works on military history were issued soon after the war: E. B. Quiner, *The Military History of Wisconsin . . . in the War for the Union* (Chicago, 1866); and William De Loss Love, *Wisconsin in the War of the Rebellion: A History of All Regiments and Batteries* (Chicago, 1866). The latter well illustrates public opinion from sermons and other speeches. Two short sketches of military leaders are: General Charles King, "Rufus King, Editor and Statesman," *Wisconsin Magazine of History,* Vol. IV, pp. 371-381 (June, 1921); and Theodore C. Blegen, "Colonel Hans Christian Heg," *ibid.,* pp. 140-165 (December, 1920).

The great fear of Indians is discussed by Milo M. Quaife, "The Panic of 1862 in Wisconsin," *Wisconsin Magazine of History,* Vol. IV, pp. 166-195 (December, 1920). The author also gives much about the Indians in the state at the time. The history of the Sioux outbreak in Minnesota, which so alarmed Wisconsin residents, may be read in William W. Folwell, *History of Minnesota* (4 vols., Minneapolis, 1924-1931), Vol. II, pp. 109-264.

Lynn I. Schoonover, *A History of the Civil War Draft in Wisconsin,* MS thesis (Ph. M., Madison, 1915), is a good account of its subject. John W. Oliver, "Draft Riots in Wisconsin During the Civil War," *Wisconsin Magazine of History,* Vol. II, pp. 334-337 (March, 1919), is valuable though brief. Carl Russell Fish, in "Social Relief in the Northwest During the Civil War," *American Historical Review,* Vol. XIII, pp. 309-324 (Jan., 1917), has much about Wisconsin conditions. Reuben S. T. Brown, *The War Administration of Alexander Randall,* MS thesis (M. A., Madison, 1921) is useful.

Carl Russell Fish wrote "Phases of the Economic History of Wisconsin, 1860-1870," Wisconsin Historical Society *Proceedings, 1907,* pp. 204-216. The work of Frederick Merk, *Economic History of Wisconsin During the Civil War Decade* (Madison, 1916), can hardly be praised too highly. The history of banking for this period may be studied in Clarence B. Hadden, "History of Early Banking in Wisconsin," Wisconsin Academy of Science, Arts, and Letters, *Transactions,* Vol. X (1894-1895), pp. 159-197; and in Leonard B. Krueger, *History of Commercial Banking in Wisconsin,* University of Wisconsin Studies in the Social Science and History, No. 18 (Madison, 1933), pp. 56-107.

The Ryan address was issued in pamphlet form, *Address to the People of the Democracy of Wisconsin, adopted in state convention at Milwaukee, Sept. 3d, 1862* (n. p., 1862, 8 pp.). There are extensive quotations from it in Love, *Wisconsin in the War of the Rebellion,* pp. 162-167, and the whole of it appeared in many newspapers of the time. See the bibliography of Chapter XIII for estimates of Ryan's whole career. James L. Sellers wrote a sketch entitled, "James R. Doolittle," which appeared in five installments in the *Wisconsin Magazine of History,* Vols. XVII and XVIII (1933-1934).

CHAPTER X

THE BUILDING OF WISCONSIN RAILROADS

DURING most of Wisconsin's history as a state the railroads have been the chief means of communication. They have formed an integral and very important part of the economic structure of the community. Their operation was the first "big business" of the state, unless one includes the fur trade; and the fur trade scarcely touched the lives of the Anglo-Saxon settlers. The men who promoted railroads thought in terms of millions of dollars and showed a tendency to consolidate, while logging and lumbering were in comparison still small and scattered enterprises.

In 1837, while George Wallace Jones was territorial delegate, he presented to Congress a petition from Sinipee, a village in Grant County, for the survey of a railroad route from Milwaukee through Sinipee and Dubuque to San Francisco, California. The petition "produced a great laugh and hurrah in the house." In the following year, however, Jones did get an appropriation of $2,000 for a survey from Milwaukee to the Mississippi River at Dubuque, the idea being that such a road would serve the lead region. For a time Wisconsin public opinion divided its favor between railroads and canals. The first railroad company actually to build was chartered as the Milwaukee and Waukesha in 1847, changed its name soon afterwards to the Milwaukee and Mississippi, and began train service between Milwaukee and Waukesha in 1851.

From these beginnings until nearly the close of the sixties, progress in railroad construction was not rapid. By the end of

1860, there were 891 miles of railway in operation in Wisconsin. The Civil War naturally made labor scarce, and a depreciated currency caused wages and the prices of materials to rise. Milwaukee capitalists, moreover, who might have been expected to build railroads in this state, took a longer view and preferred to extend their enterprises into regions farther west. Consequently, by 1867 the total had risen to only 1,030 miles. Then

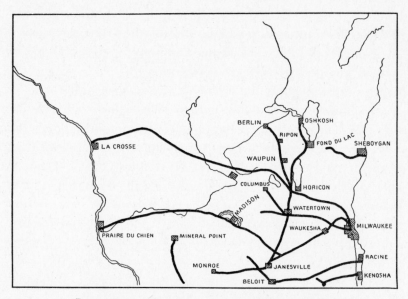

RAILROADS IN OPERATION AT THE END OF 1860*

came six years during which railroads in Wisconsin were doubled. The panic of 1873 caused a temporary cessation of building, but between 1875 and 1890 the mileage doubled again, reaching 5,583 in the latter year. The last decade of the nineteenth century and the first decade of the twentieth each saw the building of about 950 miles of primary track. After 1910 additions were small. A peak, probably for all time, of 7,693 miles was reached in 1916; since that time there have been small decreases almost every year,

* By courtesy of Frederic L. Paxson and the Wisconsin Academy of Sciences, Arts, and Letters.

until at present about 7,000 miles of railroad are operated in Wisconsin.

FACTORS IN EARLY FINANCING OF RAILROADS

In the early days of Wisconsin railroad building, much of the state was still in the frontier stage. The new communities needed the railways desperately to get their surplus products to market. At the same time the frontier was poor. The constitution forbade the state to lend money or credit for internal improvements, whereby Wisconsin was spared some of the woes experienced by Michigan, Illinois, and Minnesota. Yet, if the state might not help, there were still local agencies on the one hand and the federal government on the other. There was no prohibition or effective limitation resting on counties and towns, villages and cities. When a railroad was projected, the localities along the route were expected to borrow to pay for it; and for the most part they did so, readily and rather recklessly. For example, when, in the winter of 1860-1861, the North Western extended its line from Oshkosh to Appleton, a distance of some twenty miles, the company issued $184,000 of Appleton Extension first mortgage seven per cent bonds and $30,000 in common stock in exchange at par for city bonds of Appleton and Neenah. Eastern capitalists were often interested in Wisconsin roads, but regarded them as highly speculative, and until after 1870 they never carried more than a small part of the investment; the localities and individuals served by the road paid for it.

Besides the municipalities the railroad companies exploited private citizens, especially the farmers who so much desired their facilities. Between 1850 and 1857 some 6,000 Wisconsin farmers mortgaged their farms for a total of nearly $5,000,000. The agents of the companies gave stock certificates to the farmers in exchange for the mortgages which they immediately sold to investors in the eastern states. Then in the panic of 1857 every railroad in the state went into bankruptcy, and the farmers were left with a lot of worthless paper. Compromise and legislation did something to remedy this situation during the decade of the Civil War, but it has remained one of the most painful episodes in the history of Wisconsin railroad finance.

The federal government had a great reservoir of wealth in the public domain, and, since the lands belonged to the people and the people wanted railroads, Congress made large grants of these lands to aid in financing railroads. These grants were all made between 1850 and 1872. Sometimes they were made directly to the railroad companies; at other times the lands were given in trust to the state governments. The grants were in some cases not well administered by the states or honestly earned by the companies that received them, and only a third of the lands granted were finally patented to the railroads. Yet the railroads received in all the United States some 49,000,000 acres, and in Wisconsin they ultimately got 2,874,000 acres, or nearly one-twelfth of the area of the state.

In the days before the railroads, land grants had been made for the Milwaukee and Rock River canal and for the improvement of the Fox and Wisconsin rivers. On June 3, 1856, Congress offered land in Wisconsin for two lines of railroad. One was to be built north from Fond du Lac to the state line. The other, according to the federal statute, was to run from Madison or Columbus by way of Portage City to the St. Croix River and on northward to the western end of Lake Superior, with a branch to Bayfield. The legislature met early in September to dispose of the grants, and by October 11 it had made its decisions. The privilege of earning the land set apart for the northeastern line went to a company that ultimately coalesced with the Chicago and North Western system. When this company completed its line to Marinette, in 1872, the fact was reported by the proper state authorities, and the federal government patented to the company something over 546,000 acres of land along its route.

The land offered for the railway into the northwestern part of the state amounted to more than a million acres, and the prize was awarded to the La Crosse and Milwaukee Railroad, which was then building a line across the state.   Byron Kilbourn, president of the railroad, used methods which were later the subject of legislative investigation.   He distributed packages of stocks and bonds, mostly bonds, as follows: to fifty-nine members of the assembly, $355,000 worth; to thirteen senators, $175,000; to Governor Coles Bashford, $50,000; to other state officials, including one judge of the supreme court, $50,000; and to the governor's private secretary, $5,000.   Several persons who had acted as lobbyists received similar gifts.   The total face value of the securities given away was almost $900,000.   The La Crosse and Milwaukee Railroad went bankrupt within two years after these gifts were made, so that most of the recipients never got much money for the company's paper.   Coles Bashford was forehanded enough to call at Kilbourn's office to exchange bonds for cash, and actually received $15,000.   He later moved to Arizona.   The purchase of the legislature of 1856 united with the matter of the railroad farm mortgages to create a belief, destined to a long career in Wisconsin politics, that railroad companies could not be honest.

The second great federal land grant came in 1864.   The details of the disposition of land under it will appear as we proceed to sketch the histories of the principal railroads of the state.   The Wisconsin Central received about 837,000 acres, and the Omaha lines, a part of the North Western system, gained about 1,288,000 acres.

The Chicago, Milwaukee and St. Paul

All of the young Wisconsin cities along Lake Michigan thought of themselves as the future marts of the great areas to the west so rapidly filling up with settlers.   Each wanted to be the terminus of a railroad that would capture the trade of the future.   The map of 1860 shows railroads starting westward, none of them very long as yet, from Sheboygan, Kenosha, and Racine.   In this competition, however, Milwaukee easily out-distanced all of its Wisconsin rivals.   By 1860 it had sent three lines toward the West, and two of them had already reached the Mississippi River.   And after 1855 Milwaukee was also linked with Chicago.

The first railroad out of Milwaukee had begun as the Milwaukee and Waukesha, chartered in 1847.   Growing more ambi-

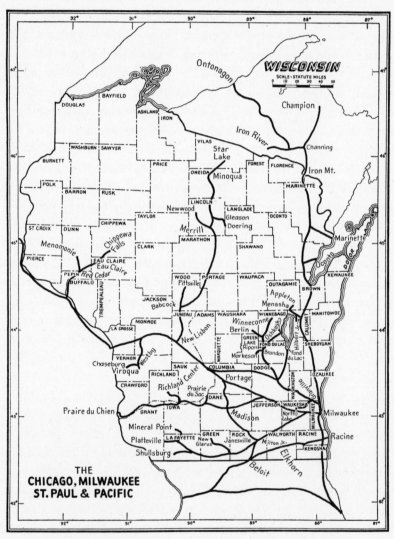

THE CHICAGO, MILWAUKEE, ST. PAUL AND PACIFIC RAILROAD

tious, the company became the Milwaukee and Mississippi in 1850, and the next year it began train service, the first in the state, as far as Waukesha. It reached Madison in 1854 and Prairie du Chien in 1857. The original plan to cross the lead region having been abandoned, the western third of its course followed down the valley of the Wisconsin River, which furnished a uniform and easy grade. The second line to cross the state, the La Crosse and Milwaukee, was built by a company formed in 1854 by the consolidation of several predecessors, and from 1858 onward it, too, could give service to the Mississippi. It was Byron Kilbourn, the president of this company, who distributed so many "pecuniary compliments" in 1856 to legislators and other public officials. The panic of 1857, and gross mismanagement besides, ruined the company, whose affairs were involved in litigation for many years. Finally the new Milwaukee and St. Paul Railway Company, organized in 1863, secured in 1867 control of the entire line, and under its able president, Alexander Mitchell, and equally able superintendent, Sherburne S. Merrill, it achieved a solid financial and business success. Mitchell remained its head from 1865 to his death in 1887; Merrill was its manager from 1865 to 1884.

Like its northern neighbor, the Milwaukee and Mississippi went into bankruptcy and had many troubled years. In 1867, however, the Milwaukee and St. Paul purchased most of the stock of its rival to the south, and the two lines were thenceforth under the same management. The third line striking westward from Milwaukee before the Civil War was the Milwaukee and Watertown, which divided at Watertown, one branch running toward Madison and the other to Columbus and eventually to Portage. This, too, was absorbed into the Milwaukee and St. Paul system.

In 1867 the Milwaukee and St. Paul joined with a railroad in Minnesota to give St. Paul its first railroad connection with the outside world, and in 1868-1869 Alexander Mitchell bought a majority interest in the Racine and Mississippi, which had an outlet on the Mississippi at Dunleith, now East Dubuque. Thus, for the moment, he controlled all the routes across Wisconsin from Lake Michigan to the Mississippi River. In 1874 his company purchased a road from Milwaukee to Chicago, and the name of the corporation became the Chicago, Milwaukee and St. Paul Railway Company. During the next few years its lines were rapidly extended westward to gather in the wheat of the prairie states. The system as a whole is the monument of Alexander Mitchell. At the time of his death in 1887 the company was operating 5,669 miles of road, much of it of course beyond the limits of Wisconsin. Steady careful growth continued until 1905, when the mileage was slightly under 7,000.

For a good many years the Milwaukee turned traffic to and received traffic from the two great railroads of the Northwest, the Northern Pacific and the Great Northern. When the two united in purchasing, through the Northern Securities Company, the Chicago, Burlington and Quincy, the latter became the link with Chicago for the two purchasing companies, and the Milwaukee road was faced with a serious loss of business. It therefore resolved to build to the Pacific Northwest, and in 1905 the construction began. Ten years later came electrification in the Rocky Mountains. The western extensions and improvements proved very expensive, and the new line had to meet sharp competition from those already in the Northwest. The result was bankruptcy, and in 1925 a reorganization began with the appointment of receivers. In 1927 a new corporation, the Chicago, Milwaukee, St. Paul and Pacific Railroad Company, was formed, and early in the next year it assumed charge of the system, now grown to more than 11,000 miles.

THE CHICAGO AND NORTH WESTERN

The North Western of today is the result of many consolidations. Its first construction in Wisconsin, in 1854, ran southwest from Fond du Lac some eighteen miles to Horicon Lake. Several short lines consolidated in the Chicago, St. Paul and Fond du Lac Railroad Company, which by the close of 1859 could offer continuous service from Oshkosh to Janesville, where it made connec-

tions for Chicago.   But consolidation had not saved this line from
bankruptcy.   It was an association of its bondholders that in 1859
first assumed the name, "Chicago and North Western Railway
Company."   William B. Ogden, one of the most active financiers
of Chicago in his day, was president of the North Western from

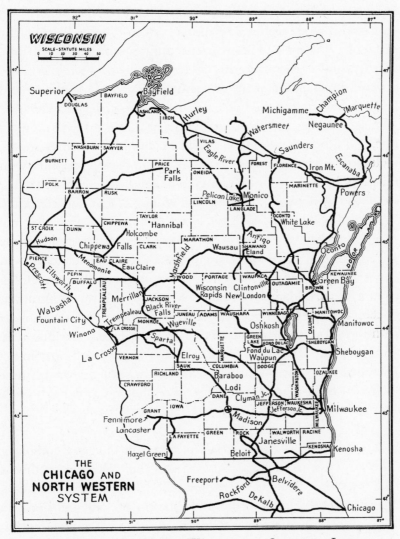

THE CHICAGO AND NORTH WESTERN AND SUBSIDIARY LINES

1859 to 1868.   By 1864 the company could give continuous service from Chicago by way of Janesville to Fond du Lac, Oshkosh, Appleton, and Green Bay.   Early in 1864 it took over a bankrupt line, the Kenosha and Rockford, which represented Kenosha's hope of a connection with the Mississippi.   This brought the trackage up to 315 miles.

The next consolidation, and one of the most important, was with an Illinois rival, the Galena and Chicago Union.   The nucleus of this line had been chartered in 1836, began construction in 1847, and is therefore the oldest part of the North Western system.   At the time of the consolidation in 1864 the Galena road had one line, the original one, that ran from Chicago to Freeport, a branch west to the Mississippi, where it linked up with an Iowa line, and a branch to Janesville and Madison.   The Galena road, including what it held by leases, brought the system up to 800 miles.   The name, North Western, was retained and Mr. Ogden continued as president.

At this time the officers of the North Western were awake to the opportunities in Upper Michigan, where there were developments in copper, iron, and lumber.   The Peninsula Railroad Company, officered by officials of the North Western, built a line northward from Escanaba, Michigan, to Lake Superior.   Construction began in 1863 and soon reached Negaunee, where connection was made with the port of Marquette, twelve miles to the east, by means of the Marquette, Houghton and Ontonagon Railroad.   For many years this was a mere spur about twenty-five miles in length running west from Marquette to Negaunee and on beyond to a point later called Champion.   This and the Peninsula Railway were the only ones in Upper Michigan as late as 1870.   In October, 1864, the Peninsula Railway became a part of the North Western system.   To bridge the gap between this and its railhead at Green Bay, the North Western maintained a line of steamers that plied thence to Escanaba.   At the end of 1872 the two towns were linked by rail.   This made the second all-rail route to Lake Superior.   By building from Green Bay to the state line at Marinette the North Western fulfilled requirements with reference to the eastern part of the land grant in 1856, and ultimately acquired title thereby to 546,446 acres of land.

In 1882 the North Western bought the majority of the stock of the Chicago, St. Paul, Minneapolis and Omaha, commonly called the Omaha road, which is still maintained under its own name but is intimately connected with the North Western system. When it was acquired in 1882 it already extended in a great curve from Elroy, Wisconsin, northwest and then west to St. Paul and Minneapolis, and thence southwest to Omaha. With its branches it had 1,147 miles of track. We are concerned here only with its Wisconsin lines.

The Omaha was the result of a process of growth too long and involved to be detailed here. In 1854, in anticipation of the first federal land grant, the St. Croix and Lake Superior Railway was organized to receive from the La Crosse and Mississippi a conveyance of granted lands. The lands were later conferred by the state legislature upon the Tomah and St. Croix Railroad Company, incorporated in 1863. In 1866 this became the West Wisconsin Railway Company. Between 1868 and 1872 this company built the line already mentioned from Elroy to St. Paul by way of Black River Falls, Merillan, Eau Claire, and Hudson. In 1873 the North Western, having built to Elroy, made a traffic agreement whereby it and the West Wisconsin offered through service between Chicago and St. Paul, thus ending the six years' monopoly of the Chicago, Milwaukee and St. Paul. In 1878 the West Wisconsin Railway Company was purchased after virtual bankruptcy by a group including Philetus Sawyer, and with William H. Ferry as president. In 1880 the North Wisconsin, reaching northeast from Hudson, was absorbed, and the corporate name became the Chicago, St. Paul, Minneapolis and Omaha Railway Company.

The lines of the Omaha on a map of northwestern Wisconsin at any time after 1883 have the form of a great letter X with a line across the bottom of it, and Lake Superior at the top. The line across the bottom is the West Wisconsin line from Elroy to Hudson, built in 1868 to 1872. The lines composing the letter X were built between 1871 and 1883. The lower left-hand line started its slow progress northeasterly from Hudson in 1871 as the North Wisconsin, and the upper ends were completed in 1883, when both Superior and Bayfield were reached. The lower right-hand line, from Eau Claire to Spooner, was finished in 1882. Since that time two branches have been struck off to the eastward, one to Hannibal and one to Park Falls. The several parts of the Omaha group received under federal land grants no less than 1,288,000 acres, most of it valuable timber land.

The North Western acquired still another outlet in the western part of the state. Back in 1857 a company had been chartered, called the La Crosse, Trempealeau, Fountain City and Prescott, to build a line joining the cities named in its title. Before any construction was done the local company passed into the hands of D. N. Barney and Company of New York, who had also obtained the Winona and St. Peters road in Minnesota. In 1867 the Chicago and North Western bought the Barney interests, and a part of the line projected in 1857 was built, from La Crosse as far as the mouth of the Trempealeau River, just across the Mississippi from Winona, Minnesota. At the same time the North Western built what was called the Baraboo Air Line, 126 miles long from Madison by way of Lodi, Baraboo, and Elroy to La Crosse. This line came into use in September, 1873, and not only made the connection with the West Wisconsin at Elroy already mentioned, but gave another route into Minnesota.

In 1893 the North Western purchased a majority of stock in the Milwaukee, Lake Shore and Western, commonly called the Lake Shore lines, which not only served the cities along Lake Michigan, but ultimately traversed the great pine forests of northeastern Wisconsin and tapped the iron and copper resources of both Wisconsin and Michigan. The man who had most to do with the inception of this road was Joseph Vilas of Manitowoc, and its principal promotor was F. W. Rhinelander. A charter was se-

cured in 1870, and in 1873 the road was finished from Milwaukee
to Manitowoc. From the beginning there was coöperation with
the North Western. The latter was just then sponsoring the
North Western Union, a new and more direct line joining Milwaukee and Fond du Lac, and this and the Lake Shore line used
the same station and the same trackage along the lake shore
within Milwaukee.

In 1866 the Appleton and New London was chartered, but
accomplished nothing until in 1871 and 1872 it built from Manitowoc to Appleton. In the latter year this property was absorbed
by the Milwaukee, Lake Shore and Western. A few years after
the panic of 1873 the line was built northwest from Appleton.
New London was reached in 1876, and there was construction
almost every year thereafter. At Eland, on the western edge of
Shawano County, the direction was changed from northwest to
north, and by way of Antigo, Monico, and Eagle River, the state
line and Watersmeet, Michigan, were reached in 1883. There
connection was made with the Vieux Desert and Lake Shore, a
line built in a general east and west direction to tap the iron and
lumber resources along the boundary between Wisconsin and
Michigan. This line was united with the Lake Shore and Western in 1883, and so became a part of the North Western in 1893.

In 1883 a number of lines, some of them already mentioned,
ended their separate existence by being completely absorbed in the
North Western. One was the line that Sheboygan had undertaken to build to the Mississippi, which reached Fond du Lac in
1869. Another was the Chicago and Milwaukee, a subsidiary
company since 1865. Still another was the North Western Union,
built from Milwaukee to Fond du Lac in 1872 and 1873. Lastly
there was the line from Milwaukee to Madison built in 1882.
Within the twentieth century the North Western has completed
two more lines into Upper Michigan, one from Monico to Hurley
and the other from near Green Bay to Saunders, Michigan. The
last significant addition to the system was the line partly rebuilt,

but largely new, from Milwaukee northwest to Sparta, a distance of about 170 miles.

William B. Ogden was president from 1859 to 1868. Then within five years there were three presidents, one of them being Alexander Mitchell of the Milwaukee; for nine months in 1869 and 1870 Mitchell controlled almost all of the railways in Wisconsin. Albert Keep was president from 1873 to 1887, and he was followed by Marvin Hughitt (1887-1910). Today the North Western system boasts of more than 10,000 miles of its own lines, and by means of intimate connections with the Union Pacific it is able to give service to the Pacific Coast. Including the Omaha lines, which now amount to nearly 800 miles, the North Western system has about 3,000 miles in Wisconsin, or about three-sevenths of the railways in the state.

THE WISCONSIN CENTRAL AND THE SOO

The Wisconsin Central railway was a belated result of the land grant of 1864. The federal act stipulated that a road should be built from Portage City, Berlin, Fond du Lac, or Doty's Island (Neenah-Menasha) to Bayfield and Superior. Several companies, formed between 1866 and 1871 with ambitions to earn the offered lands, consolidated in July, 1871, as the Wisconsin Central Railroad Company, and Gardner Colby, a capitalist from Boston, became president. Actual construction of the main line from Menasha by way of Stevens Point to Ashland extended over a six-year period from 1871 to 1877. This was the first railway to cross northern Wisconsin and reach the Wisconsin shore of Lake Superior, although it had two predecessors in attaining Lake Superior. In Minnesota a line had joined St. Paul and Duluth in 1870, while in Upper Michigan Escanaba and Marquette had been linked in 1863-1864, and Escanaba was connected by rail with Green Bay at the close of 1872.

To fulfil the conditions of the land grant as interpreted by the state government the Wisconsin Central also built a line from Portage to Stevens Point, and to get connections with Milwaukee the company, in November, 1873, leased the Milwaukee and Northern. This line had been completed in June of that year and ran from Milwaukee east of Lake Winnebago to Green Bay, with a branch to Menasha. In 1882 the Wisconsin Central terminated this lease, and instead built a line along the west side of

THE MINNEAPOLIS, ST. PAUL AND SAULT STE. MARIE RAILWAY—
INCLUDING WISCONSIN CENTRAL RAILROAD

Lake Winnebago and on down to Schleisingerville, now Slinger, whence it leased trackage into Milwaukee. This southward line was afterwards continued from Schleisingerville to Chicago.

From the main line laid down in 1871 to 1877 various branches were subsequently built, the most important being the one from Abbotsford in Marathon County almost straight west by way of Chippewa Falls to St. Paul, built in part in 1880 and completed in 1884. Another went from Mellon eastward to Hurley and Bessemer to supply the iron country in the western part of Upper Michigan.

From an early period the Wisconsin Central worked in coöperation with the Northern Pacific. This company had terminals in St. Paul, and, after 1885, one in Ashland. Since the Wisconsin Central offered a natural connection with Chicago, in 1889 the Northern Pacific leased the Chicago terminals of the Wisconsin Central and by a traffic agreement ran its trains out of Chicago for the Pacific Coast over the Wisconsin Central. In 1893 this arrangement was terminated. About the same time the Wisconsin Central Company failed, and after a long delay a new company, called the Wisconsin Central Railway Company, took charge. In 1906 was begun the construction of a new line from Owen, just west of Abbotsford, by way of Ladysmith to Superior and Duluth. This afforded the shortest route from Chicago to the western end of Lake Superior. In 1909, before this line was completed, the Wisconsin Central was absorbed by the Soo. By this combination a distinctively Wisconsin enterprise ended its separate existence.

As the first line in the northern part of the state the Wisconsin Central deserves special attention. Its construction preceded settlement, and there were no communities along the route to buy railroad securities with borrowed money in order to assist construction. Eastern capitalists, of whom Gardner Colby was the chief, put about nine million dollars into the enterprise. The company received about 837,000 acres of government land; in fact, the line was built to get the land. The railroad promoters sold the land to lumbermen almost at once and did not receive for it what they might have received if they had held it longer. The two men who, more than any others, developed the Wisconsin Central system were Charles Colby, son of Gardner Colby, and long a leading citizen of Milwaukee, and Edwin H. Abbot.

The Minneapolis, Sault Ste. Marie and Atlantic Railway Company was organized in 1883, and during the next four years it built its way across north central Wisconsin. It ran from Minneapolis, by way of Cameron and Rhinelander, to Escanaba and Sault Ste. Marie. From 1888 onward the Canadian Pacific had a controlling interest in the company. In 1900 it became the Minneapolis, St. Paul and Sault Ste. Marie, the "Soo" of popular parlance. In 1909 it absorbed the Wisconsin Central and completed that company's line to Superior and Duluth. The last significant addition to the Soo was a line built by a separate company from North Crandon, now called Argonne, southward by way of Shawano to Appleton and Neenah, where it connected with the main line of the old Wisconsin Central to Chicago. This line, which was projected as early as 1906, was completed in 1918 and purchased by the Soo in 1921. It was built chiefly to bring wood to the pulp and paper mills of Appleton and vicinity.

OTHER LINES

The Green Bay and Western is the longest independent line entirely within the state of Wisconsin. It was chartered under another name in 1866, and in 1871 was constructed from Green Bay to New London. During 1873 it reached the Mississippi River, and by arrangement its trains crossed from Marshland, Wisconsin to Winona, Minnesota by the North Western tracks. The company was rather frequently in financial difficulties, and there were successive foreclosures, reorganizations, and changes of name, the present title dating from 1896. In the early 1890's it fathered two subsidiary companies whereby it provides the only railway facilities for the counties of Door and Kewaunee.

Several railroads, great in other states, have entered Wisconsin only in a small way. The Chicago, Burlington and Quincy has 222 miles of tracks in Wisconsin, its main line in this state following the Mississippi River rather closely from the border of Illinois to Prescott, whence it crosses into Minnesota. This line was completed in 1866. The Illinois Central has a line coming north from Freeport. It soon divides, the eastern branch going to Madison and the other to Dodgeville.

The Northern Pacific and the Great Northern both aspired to open up the Northwest and link the western end of Lake Superior with the Pacific Coast. The Northern Pacific was chartered in 1866, and was supported by the great banking firm of Jay Cooke and Company of Philadelphia. It was built westward from Duluth across Minnesota, and plans had been made for building eastward into Wisconsin when Jay Cooke failed and the panic of 1873 came on. A line was at length built out of Duluth and Superior to Ashland in 1884, a great bridge across the St. Louis River was finished in 1885, and in 1898 a branch was run to Washburn on the western shore of Chequamegon Bay. The Great Northern Railway was the life work of James J. Hill, who presided over its destinies, from its small beginnings about 1876, until 1907, and built it from Duluth to the Pacific Coast. It operates only about forty miles in Wisconsin. In 1885 it bought a large tract of land at West Superior to be used for terminals to connect with lake shipping, and large grain elevators and ore docks were built. The Duluth, South Shore and Atlantic, a subsidiary of the Soo, has 108 miles in Wisconsin and more in Upper Michigan. It runs from Duluth eastward by way of Iron River and crosses the Montreal River into Upper Michigan a little north of Hurley.

Selected Bibliography

F. L. Paxson tabulated the growth of railroads, with sketch maps for each year to 1860, *Transactions of the Wisconsin Academy of Science, Arts and Letters,* Vol. XVII (1914), part 1, pp. 243-274. The information there given dovetails into that found in Frederick Merk, *Economic History of Wisconsin During the Civil War Decade* (Madison, 1916), pp. 238-343. The frontispiece map shows the railroads in operation in 1865. *The First*

Annual Report of the Railroad Commissioners of Wisconsin (Madison, 1874) furnished statistics at that time. Annual reports on the *Statistics of Railways in the United States* have been issued by the Interstate Commerce Commission since 1889.

Two Wisconsin railroads have their official histories. W. H. Stennett wrote *Yesterday and Today: A History of the Chicago and North Western Railway System* (third edition, Chicago, 1910). John Watson Cary prepared *Organization and History of the Chicago, Milwaukee and St. Paul Railway Company* (Milwaukee, 1893). Richard L. Canuteson, *Railway Development of Northern Wisconsin,* is a very useful manuscript thesis (M. A., Madison, 1930). Besides the text, it contains a series of maps showing railway construction in northern Wisconsin for each year from 1851 to 1929.

The important work of Balthaser H. Meyer is found in two parts: "A History of Early Railroad Legislation in Wisconsin" (to 1853), *Collections of the State Historical Society of Wisconsin,* Vol. XIV, pp. 206-300; and "Early General Railway Legislation in Wisconsin, 1853-1874," *Transactions of the Wisconsin Academy of Science, Arts, and Letters,* Vol. XII (1898), pp. 337-388. Federal assistance to railways during the time when Wisconsin was receiving such assistance is dealt with by Lewis H. Haney, *A Congressional History of Railways in the United States, 1850-1887* (Madison, 1910, Bulletin of the University of Wisconsin, No. 342).

CHAPTER XI

PINE LUMBERING IN WISCONSIN

The Importance of Pine

IN HER forests Wisconsin had a magnificent endowment. For three-quarters of a century many Wisconsin men found their livelihood in laying these forests low, and some few gathered great wealth in the process. Now these forests virtually belong to the past, and in their stead are pleasant tillable fields or else the unkempt wilderness of cut-over land. Though lumbering has thus been but a passing phase in the history of the state and one that will never be repeated, it must remain to succeeding generations an episode of great interest and significance. Novelists have exploited its heroic and picturesque aspects and doubtless will continue to do so. The necessities of lumber operations fixed the location of cities and villages throughout northern Wisconsin and determined the routes of many of the railways; this impress on the geography of the state is indelible. In their time the lumbermen strongly influenced politics and legislation; in their passing they have bequeathed to us problems of no mean dimensions.

With the exception of scattered prairies of small extent, all of Wisconsin was originally forested. The deciduous trees of the southern counties, however, played almost no part in the development of the lumber industry. Through several decades the only merchantable timber in Wisconsin was pine. Its wood was strong, yet light and easy to work, and it satisfied the carpenters and builders as nothing else could do. So the early loggers set themselves to the task of getting out white pine, and along with it the much less frequent Norway pine. Naturally the industry could develop only where the pine grew, and the only area of pine land in southern Wisconsin was a triangle along Lake Michigan from the tip of Door County to the northern end of Ozaukee County and touching Lake Winnebago on the west. But in the north, most of the state north of a line drawn from the lower end of Lake Winnebago to St. Paul, Minnesota, or Hudson, Wisconsin, was pine land. Yet the predominance of pine was always a matter of degree, and even in the typical pineries it seldom amounted to more than 60 per cent of the growing trees. At the beginning the rivers were perforce the highways of the lumber industry, and each river basin was a natural unit in its development. As time passed, the era of water transportation shaded almost imperceptibly into the railway age, and in its later decades lumbering was rather completely reorganized around railway transportation.

Along Lake Michigan and on the Eastern Rivers

Logging, accompanied by rather primitive sawmill operations, began at about the same time on Lake Michigan and its tributaries on the one hand, and on the lower courses of streams emptying into the Mississippi on the other. With the exception of the land about the upper course of the Menominee River, the eastern areas were exhausted first. This was partly because they were smaller and partly because the Chicago market developed before the trans-Mississippi plains which absorbed the logs and lumber of western Wisconsin.

The triangle along Lake Michigan, which contained the pine nearest to Milwaukee and Chicago, was naturally the first to be thoroughly exploited. Sheboygan County had its first sawmill in 1835, and Manitowoc and Kewaunee counties soon followed suit. By 1860 there were more than forty sawmills in these three counties. The product was taken southward, at first by sailing vessels and later by steamboats. Daniel Wells, Jr., a Milwaukee financier, was prominent in lumbering in this area. The exploitation

of the whole region from Ozaukee County to the northern tip of
Door County took about forty years, and by 1875 the pine was
practically exhausted. Of the mills some were dismantled and
some were adapted to hardwoods.

Green Bay is bordered on the west today by the counties of
Marinette, Oconto, and Brown, and through them into the waters
of Green Bay flow a number of streams on which early sawmills
were built. Some early mills had been constructed near the city
of Green Bay, one in 1809 and another in 1814, but their products
were merely for local use. In 1827 John P. Arndt of Green Bay
built a sawmill on the western shore of Green Bay about twenty
miles north of Fort Howard; and in 1834 he sent a raft of lumber
to Chicago. In 1854, after Brown County had been reduced to
its present limits, 80,000,000 feet of lumber were manufactured
within it, in addition to many shingles. Indeed, a few years later
Green Bay was for a short time the leading shingle market in the
United States. By 1875 forests in Brown County were nearly
exhausted.

Meanwhile mills had appeared farther north on the Pensaukee,
Oconto, Peshtigo, and Menominee rivers. In 1845 the first mill
was built on the site of Oconto. Sometimes there would be
twenty-five or thirty schooners waiting at the mouth of the Oconto
River for cargoes of lumber. The most important river emptying
into the Bay was the Menominee, with the twin cities of Menominee, Michigan, and Marinette, Wisconsin, at its mouth. Most
of the logs on this river were handled by the Menominee River
Boom Company, and its records show an increase from 62,000,000
feet in 1868 to 500,000,000 feet in 1881. So vast was the amount of
timber on the Menominee that log driving continued until 1911.
Among the lumber kings in this northeastern area after the Civil
War were Isaac Stephenson and Nelson Ludington. Stephenson
later played an important role in Wisconsin politics.

Rising near the source of the Wisconsin on the borders of Upper
Michigan, the Wolf River makes its way southward through what

was originally some of the finest pine land in the state, flows into and through Lake Poygan, and joins the upper Fox about ten miles west of Oshkosh. In 1835 logs were cut on the Wolf for the erection of government buildings at Neenah, and lumbering as a private enterprise began seven years later. Shawano and Winneconne were the chief sawmill towns on the Wolf River itself, but the greater part of the cut of the Wolf River area was made into lumber at Oshkosh and Fond du Lac. Above Shawano the Wolf has a very troubled course, but below that point it has few obstructions and is an excellent logging stream. Lake Poygan made an admirable reservoir for logs, and a boom was constructed at its outlet. Forty million feet of lumber were manufactured out of logs from the Wolf River district in 1854. Twenty years later, at the peak of production, the cut was 205,000,000 feet, and there were about eighty lumber camps in the woods of the upper Wolf. By 1890, however, the pine was exhausted; production had been declining for fifteen years.

Towns around Lake Winnebago sprang into being to manufacture and market Wolf River pine. In 1842 a small raft of logs was sent to a little mill at Taycheedah, just east of Fond du Lac. The first sawmills appeared in Oshkosh, which came to be called the "Sawdust City," in 1847. By 1856 Oshkosh had no less than fifteen sawmills, and by 1872 there were twenty-four besides a number of factories using lumber. In 1850 Philetus Sawyer undertook to manage a sawmill at Oshkosh at a definite rate per thousand feet, and this enterprise was the beginning of one of the greatest business careers in his generation. Fond du Lac had its first mill in 1845, two years before Oshkosh. At the time of its greatest activity it had eighteen lumber and shingle mills. During the 1870's mills began to be closed, and between 1880 and 1890 Fond du Lac actually decreased in population. Neenah, Menasha, and Appleton received logs from the Wolf River, and, though each had several sawmills, they never approached Oshkosh and Fond du Lac in the amount they manufactured.

STREAMS FLOWING INTO THE MISSISSIPPI

Four main logging streams in the state were tributary to the Mississippi: the Wisconsin, the Black, the Chippewa and the St. Croix. Lumbering on all these streams was at first carried on by men of small means, and fire and destructive floods and financial disaster were frequent. Prosperity and larger enterprise came first between 1852 and the panic of 1857, and after the Civil War progress was amazingly rapid.

We shall here sketch the beginning and early progress of pine lumbering on each of these streams, and first on the Wisconsin River. As a result of the "Winnebago War" of 1827 it was determined to build Fort Winnebago, and the logs for it, the first cut on the Wisconsin River, were floated down to Portage in the spring of 1829. By permission of the War Department, Daniel Whitney of Green Bay built a mill near what is now Plover in 1831-1832; from this mill came the materials for the first house in Madison. By similar permission Amable Grignon and Samuel Merrill put up a mill near the present Port Edwards in 1836.

When Henry Dodge made the treaty with the Menominee at Cedar Point in 1836, he bought all the region between the Wolf River on one side and Lake Winnebago, the Fox River, and Green Bay on the other, and northward into Upper Michigan. Besides this he purchased a strip on the Wisconsin River six miles wide and forty-eight miles long. This area ran from Point Bas (often Englished as Point Bass) some six miles below Wisconsin Rapids, up to Big Bull Falls (Wausau). Here was the southernmost pine land on the Wisconsin River, and its acquisition was evidently a clever bit of "dollar diplomacy." The federal surveyors did their work here in 1839, and several small mills were begun immediately. By the end of 1841 every available millsite in the forty-eight miles had passed into private hands. Within three or four years almost all the cities and villages on this part of the Wisconsin River were begun. Some farming was undertaken, but lumbering long continued to be the chief attraction. In 1848 the region had twen-

ty-four mills operating forty-five saws, and by 1857, 107 mills were
turning out more than one hundred million board feet a year,
while logging and lumbering together gave employment to more
than three thousand men.   This development marks the beginning of the present counties of Wood, Portage, and Marathon.
Because of its many bends and frequent rapids the Wisconsin
River in the pineries was ill adapted to rafting and large-scale
logging.   Consequently, lumbering in the upper part of the Wisconsin valley, from Merrill northward, waited on the coming of
the railroads.

The basin of the Black River lies between the larger Wisconsin
and Chippewa basins.   The stream is about 140 miles long, and
on its upper course in the present counties of Taylor, Clark, and
Jackson, it was once bordered by the finest pine lands.   The
mouth of the La Crosse River, which comes from the east, is
within a few yards of the mouth of the Black, and there the town
of La Crosse was begun.   Some forty miles up the Black River is
a considerable waterfall, and at this point the city of Black River
Falls is located.

In 1839 a company of twenty men, headed by Jacob Spaulding,
built a sawmill near the falls, and for twenty years, save when the
Mormons had it, Spaulding managed this mill.   The Mormons
had bought Spaulding's mill in order to get lumber for their
temple at Nauvoo, Illinois, but upon Joseph Smith's death (1844),
they returned the mill to Spaulding.   The O'Neill brothers came
to the valley in 1839 and later (in 1845) settled at Neillsville, now
the county seat of Clark County.   In 1845 there were from 175 to
200 men on the Black River, and four years later there were between five and six hundred.   Experienced lumbermen from
Maine settled along the river in 1853, and after that more of the
logs were driven down the river instead of being sawed near the
spot where they were felled.   William T. Price had begun logging
north of Neillsville in 1845; his activities grew with the years and
from 1881 to 1886 his company's average annual cut was 60,000,000
feet.

The founder of the city of La Crosse was Nathan Myrick, who settled there in 1841 and had an interest in many of the lumbering enterprises on the Black River. The first sawmill at La Crosse was built in 1852, and by 1857 the little city had ten saw and three shingle mills. Two lawyers of Mineral Point, Cyrus Woodman and Cadwallader C. Washburn, who had invested in pine lands and a sawmill at La Crosse, dissolved partnership in 1855, Woodman taking money and Washburn retaining the mill and the lands. A year later Washburn's holdings were valued at half a million dollars.

The population of La Crosse was about 3,800 in 1860 and over 25,000 by 1890. It took from Green Bay the primacy as a shingle market. The lumber cut on the Black River reached 100,000,000 feet in 1869 and fell below that amount only twice during the next twenty-six years. The period of greatest activity was in the fifteen years ending in 1890, during which the annual cut often approached and sometimes exceeded 200,000,000 feet. By the end of the century the mills were closing: the pine was gone.

The Chippewa River with its many tributaries drains an area of some 10,000 square miles, or one-sixth of the state. The main stream rises about twenty-five miles south of Lake Superior, in Ashland County, and enters the Mississippi at the lower end of Lake Pepin, and a little above Wabasha, Minnesota. The largest tributaries on the east are the Flambeau, Jump, Yellow, and Eau Claire rivers; and the principal affluent on the right or west side is the Red Cedar or Menomonie River, which comes down through Barron and Dunn counties.

By permission of the Indians and the War Department, James S. Lockwood, a merchant of Prairie du Chien, built a mill on the site of Menomonie on the Red Cedar River in 1831. By June of that year he had 100,000 feet of lumber sawed, about half of which he ultimately succeeded in getting to St. Louis. The chief sawmill town on the Chippewa River was Chippewa Falls. Continuous history of lumbering there began in 1836, when Jean Brunet erected a mill for Hercules L. Dousman and several others,

mostly men of Prairie du Chien. Dousman ran the mill until
1842 and then sold it to H. S. Allen. During the next half century several owners in succession had this mill. Allen persevered
through many early hardships, and in 1848 formed the Chippewa
Falls Lumber Company, which lasted until the panic of 1857.
After an interval, the mill and the pine lands that Allen's company had acquired came into the hands of Thaddeus C. Pound
and his associates. First they were Pound, Halbert and Company,
and then, from 1869, the Union Lumber Company. They enlarged the mill and acquired further pine lands; then, after ten
years their property was sold in bankruptcy. The activities that
centered around this historic mill were only the best known of
many enterprises in or near Chippewa Falls.

Twelve miles down the Chippewa River from the Falls, where
the Eau Claire River joins the larger stream, is the city of Eau
Claire. The first sawmill there was built in 1846, and the second
one, erected two years later, became the property of Nelson C.
Chapman and J. G. Thorp, the firm that later expanded into the
Eau Claire Lumber Company. By 1890 five lumber companies
in Eau Claire were each producing between twenty and forty
million feet of lumber a year, and there were many other firms of
smaller resources.

On the Red Cedar River there were many small beginnings in
lumbering, but the group that came to dominate in that part of
the Chippewa valley was Knapp, Stout and Company. This firm
began in 1846 with a partnership between Captain William Wilson and J. H. Knapp. Mr. Stout, who had considerable capital,
entered the firm in 1853. By 1890 this company was cutting
nearly 90,000,000 feet a year in its three mills. The company was
dissolved in 1904, having nothing left but its water power rights,
which were sold to an electric light and power company.

The leadership in lumbering on the St. Croix River was taken
by Minnesota men. It is related that as soon as the treaty with
the Chippewa was signed, on July 29, 1837, a party left Fort Snelling in a canoe and traveled almost without rest until they reached

the falls of the St. Croix, where they staked out a pre-emption claim that would give them control of the water power there. The leader in this enterprise was Franklin Steele, long prominent in business and politics in Minnesota. Largely because of persistent pressure by this group of men, a land office was opened at St. Croix Falls (1848), and Steele and his associates were finally able to make sure of the water power, both at this place and at the Falls of St. Anthony, now within the city of Minneapolis. Along with water power sites they bought much good pine land. By the outbreak of the Civil War the annual cut in the St. Croix valley was about 80,000,000 feet, half of which may be credited to Wisconsin. The chief mill towns on the Wisconsin side were St. Croix Falls, Hudson, and Prescott.

In this rapid review of the beginnings of pine lumbering the state seems to fall naturally into seven areas, each having its main extent in a north and south direction. Exploitation began in all seven areas in the 1830's and proceeded northward, either up the Lake Michigan or Green Bay shore, as in the case of the first two, or else up the valley of a river. In this survey we proceeded from east to west across the state, but the real direction of progress was northward. The lumbermen pushed up the rivers so that their frontier was not a straight line across the state, but was more like an open hand and fingers, with the northernmost operations on each of the several rivers as the fingertips.

Grand Finale: The Weyerhaeuser Interests

The chief market for pine from Wisconsin's westward-flowing rivers was the great treeless plain of Illinois, Iowa, and other states westward to the Rocky Mountains. From the beginning it was a question whether it was better to float the pine out of the pineries in the form of logs or of sawed lumber. If you owned a mill at Eau Claire or somewhere else on the edge of the pine country, you believed in sawing it in Wisconsin. But if you had invested in a sawmill on the banks of the Mississippi in Illinois or Iowa, at the head of a railway leading westward, you wanted a supply of logs. After the Civil War, the mill owners on the Mississippi looked to the Wisconsin pineries for their raw material, and began to invest in Wisconsin pine lands. To assure the delivery of logs from the Chippewa to the Mississippi was a business opportunity, seized by an association of men from Michigan, Oshkosh, and Fond du Lac who formed the Beef Slough Booming Company, with headquarters at Alma, Wisconsin. Beef Slough was really one of the mouths by which the Chippewa emptied into the Mississippi, and it was the plan of the company to turn logs out of the main stream of the Chippewa into this channel by means of a boom. The new company entered into a contract to deliver 60,000,000 feet of logs to the Mississippi in the spring of 1868. The sawmill owners on the Chippewa had dams and booms to control their own logs, but these were only slight impediments to the men intent on getting logs to the Mississippi. By the simple if lawless method of cutting all the booms and opening up all the storage ponds along the Chippewa, the new company fulfilled its contract. Exasperation rose to such a pitch along the way, and especially at Eau Claire, that bloodshed was narrowly averted, and the incident is known as the "Beef Slough War." The successful delivery of the logs induced the Mississippi capitalists to continue using logs from the Chippewa, though never again was there such recklessness and disregard of others' rights as in 1868.

The greatest consolidation of interests to appear in the history of Wisconsin lumbering was that headed by Frederick Weyerhaeuser, whose career as a lumberman began in Illinois and ended in Minnesota, but included, in the middle period, an invasion of Wisconsin. Weyerhaeuser was born in Germany in 1834. He came to the United States at the age of eighteen, and in 1856 he was employed in a sawmill at Rock Island, Illinois. Soon he acquired a small mill for himself, and in 1860 he took his first partner. At first he and his associates purchased logs from river jobbers, but later they invested heavily in lands along the Black and Chippewa rivers.

In 1870 Weyerhaeuser led in forming the Mississippi River Logging Company, which leased the boom and storage rights from the Beef Slough Company and two years later bought a majority of its stock. Weyerhaeuser next made peace along the Chippewa by arranging a great "pool" whereby each firm got out of the annual drive a definite share proportionate to what it had put in; it meant a gigantic exchange of logs. The Mississippi River Logging Company bought great amounts of pine lands; in 1875 they purchased 50,000 acres of Chippewa lands from Cornell University, which had received them from the federal government. Up to 1881 the company merely furnished logs to its members. In that year, however, it bought a majority of the stock in the Chippewa Lumber and Boom Company, which had recently been formed at Chippewa Falls. The latter company continued under its old name, but with Weyerhaeuser as president. It owned, among other things the properties of the defunct Union Lumber Company, which had gone into bankruptcy in 1879, and which owned the old mill built by Brunet, already enlarged and rebuilt several times. The old mill burned in 1886, but was immediately rebuilt, and became, so it was said, "the largest mill in the world," with a capacity of 2,000,000 feet a week. Thus the Mississippi River Logging Company became a manufacturer of lumber in Wisconsin. In 1887 the company bought out the Eau Claire Lumber Company for something over a million dollars. By this and other purchases its resources in pine lands became enormous, and it controlled the water highways for transporting logs as well. In 1887 it made it a rule to ship all sawed lumber by rail.

The Beef Slough began to choke up with sand and so the West Newton Slough was acquired. This was in Wabasha County, Minnesota, and opened into the Mississippi about six miles below the outlet of Beef Slough. Logs from Wisconsin were towed across the river for storage and sorting there. West Newton first supplemented and then supplanted Beef Slough. In 1890 both were used to handle more than a billion feet of logs which the company was moving for its own mills and for outside purchasers. For years a thousand men were employed at the West Newton Slough to handle upwards of half a billion feet of logs annually.

At length even the resources of the Chippewa were exhausted. In 1909 the original Mississippi River Logging Company was dissolved. The next year saw the last drive down the Chippewa, and in 1911 "the largest mill in the world" sawed its last lumber. By that time the chief Weyerhaeuser investments were in Minnesota. From 1890 onward, Weyerhaeuser resided in Minneapolis, and there in 1911 he died. Large Weyerhaeuser mills are still operated at Cloquet and Virginia, northwest of Duluth, and the Weyerhaeuser syndicate has great holdings in the Pacific Northwest.

How the Work Was Done

The standing pine of Wisconsin 100 years ago is said to have amounted to 129 billion feet, and to fell, saw, and bring to market all this lumber was a colossal task, one that demanded long-continued effort and no little hardship. It called into existence a manner of life which the younger generations in Wisconsin can recreate in imagination only.

In its very nature logging required the coöperation of many men. The early logging crews consisted of only a dozen or twenty men, but after 1870 a camp usually contained from fifty to two hundred men. A season's work began in the late summer or autumn and lasted until the spring drive. The first task was to erect shelters for the men and animals, and, until the opening of the present century, camp buildings were always of logs. Another preliminary duty was the laying out of roads, and after winter had set in water was applied to them until they had a coat of ice several inches thick. This practice was an innovation of the 1880's.

Many of the larger pine trees were 120 feet in height and three or four feet in diameter. In the earliest days trees were felled with axes, but after the Civil War it was customary to begin the task with the axe and then do most of it with the crosscut saw. The tree once on the ground, "swampers" cut off the branches and the top down to where the diameter of the trunk was about twelve inches. The scaler then measured it and decided how it could be cut to the best advantage, and sawyers cut it into various lengths, usually varying between ten and sixteen feet. The next task was to take the logs to the bank of a stream to await spring floods. There was usually a short haul to the side of the logging road, where the logs were temporarily piled or "decked," and a longer one, often of several miles, along the carefully iced road to the river bank. Before the Civil War the hauling was done almost everywhere with oxen, the Maine loggers in particular taking great pride in the skill and quietness with which they handled their oxen. Later, horses were used, especially for the longer hauls. The size of the loads on these iced roads is almost incredible; they ran sometimes to more than twenty thousand feet and even the finest and largest logs averaged about five tons to the thousand feet. With smaller logs the weight per thousand was greater. Beside the river the logs were carefully decked so that in the spring they could be quickly released and allowed to roll into the water.

During the winter most of the men were felling, sawing, or hauling, but there were several men in a camp with special duties. There was always a cook and sometimes he had helpers called "cookees." The fare offered was always generous, though at times coarse and monotonous. Cattle were driven into the pineries to furnish fresh meat, and venison was often obtained. The blacksmith shod the horses and oxen, kept tools in repair, and he or a filer sharpened the saws. "Toters" drove "tote teams" in and out over "tote roads" to fetch supplies.

Before the railroads were built the supply roads would lead out to some point on a navigable river, or would connect with some coach road, of which there were many; there was, for example, a road from Milwaukee to Stevens Point, another from Prairie du Chien to Black River Falls. After rivers had frozen they could be used as highways. The keel-boat, a flat-bottomed craft built like a Durham boat and propelled with poles, was much used to move heavy supplies upstream. When the railroads began to penetrate the pineries in the early seventies, they were at first counted on to get supplies in, rather than to get lumber out.

The lumberjacks had to be hardy men, inured to the severest toil for long days in the northern winters. Before 1860 they were mostly of native American stock, the New England states furnishing many men with previous logging experience. In the seventies and eighties there was a strong admixture of Europeans, especially Irish and Scandinavians, with some Germans. Both early and late there was a sprinkling of men of French-Canadian stock, doubtless descended from *voyageurs*. Many of the settlers on the fringe of the farming frontier in the central part of the state found employment in the logging camps during the winter. Hard work in the winter was often followed by hard drinking and carousing in the spring.

The climax of the year's work came in the spring drive. By April there were great piles of logs beside the streams, each log stamped with the owner's name or sign. When the freshets caused by the melting snow and ice had reached the necessary height, props were knocked from under the logs and they began their hurtling journey to the sawmill, which might be on one of the Wisconsin rivers or far down the Mississippi. The best of the logging crew followed their harvest downstream, their sole task to keep the logs in motion.

Sometimes an obstruction in the stream caused a jam, and whenever this seemed about to happen, the greatest efforts were made to prevent it. Once the way was blocked the logs coming on behind rapidly increased the mass. Jams of from two to four miles in length were not infrequent, and there was one famous jam on the Chippewa River when the river was covered for fourteen miles. To break a jam the key logs had to be located and worked out with pikes or peavies, or dynamited, or, in the later days, pulled out with a chain and a traction engine. In the smaller streams far in the woods there was often not enough water to float the logs, but the needed depth of water could be secured by building dams. If logs went aground on the bank of a stream or started floating off into a slough, they had to be rescued and started on their way again. The cook and his supplies followed in the wake of the drive in a boat. The drive and the season's work ended either when the logs were in the storage pond of a sawmill, or when they were delivered at some designated point on one of the larger rivers, whence they would be rafted farther by some milling or jobbing company.

With a whole year's harvest coming into the larger streams within a few weeks in the spring, it was necessary to find storage room for vast amounts of logs until they were needed in the mill. They could be held in a certain part of the river by a boom, or stored in some slough or lake for a time, as at Lake Poygan above Oshkosh, or in Half Moon Lake near Eau Claire. A boom was a string of logs or squared timbers joined end to end with chains. An Eau Claire lumberman in the sixties invented the sheer boom or fin boom. This device had fins underneath made of planks, which could be made more or less upright by means of ropes operated from the shore; and thereby the position of the boom in the river could be altered. This invention soon came to be used in logging streams all over the United States to shunt logs out of a river into some channel or reservoir beside the main stream. Because it was movable, it did not permanently interfere with navigation as something attached to the river bottom would have done.

There was a constant improvement in sawing methods and machinery. The earliest lumber was made with a whipsaw. One end of the log rested on the ground and the other on a framework. If one man worked he stood below the elevated end; if two, one above and one below. Sometimes a shallow hole was dug in the ground for the sawyer to stand in. An improved whipsaw was often set in a light frame to keep it taut and to aid in making a straight cut. When the first water-power mills were built, the power from the water wheel was transmitted to an arm that gave back-and-forth or up-and-down strokes and drove what was really just a whipsaw in a frame. This was the beginning of the muley saw, which in various forms held the field, at least in the smaller mills, for half a century. In the late fifties or early sixties the circular saw was just coming into general use. Then came the double rotary consisting of two circular saws, one cutting into the log from above and the other from below. The rotary saws were for a long time exceedingly wasteful of lumber, cutting out a half inch kerf. This type was eventually superseded by the band saw, a thin ribbon of flexible steel driven like an endless chain. After the Civil War steam power quite eclipsed water power, the sawdust and other mill refuse serving as fuel. Steam carried the logs from the storage pond into the mill, shot the logs on a carriage against the saws, drove the saws themselves, planed the lumber after sawing it, and carried it out to the seasoning yard or loading sheds.

As the lumber industry grew, the loggers on each river felt the need for improving their highway and controlling its floods as far as possible. For example, the Black River Improvement Company was formed while the Civil War was going on. Ten years later this group was declaring a 50 per cent dividend and was planning to spent fifteen or twenty thousand dollars within a year in improving the Black River and in increased facilities for handling logs. Similar organizations appeared on all the large rivers to remove obstructions, build dams, and sometimes to sort, store, and exchange logs. Since the rivers were navigable highways, these companies had to get charters from the legislature, and in the case of the Menominee and the St. Croix, which are interstate boundaries, their operations had to be authorized by two states. The number of permissive acts passed for the benefit of such companies during the second half of the nineteenth century must number many score.

Until the 1880's a good deal of sawed lumber was transported down Wisconsin rivers to market. For the journey the lumber was piled in cribs twelve to twenty courses (inches) deep and

measuring sixteen by thirty-two feet; each crib thus contained
from six to ten thousand feet.   Several cribs fastened together end
to end made up a "string" or "rapids piece."   In quiet waters from
two to four strings would be lashed together side by side in a raft;
but in descending rapids or waterfalls the rivermen took one string
down, tied it to the river bank, and returned for another.   Each
string had two huge oars, one at each end, for steering, and in
shooting rapids each oar required the services of four or five men.
Chippewa Falls made rafting difficult on that river, and the Wisconsin River from Point Bass up to Wausau was almost a con-
tinual succession of rapids.   The work of the rivermen was therefore strenuous in the extreme; often they had to be in and out of
the water many times a day.   The Chippewa saw more rafting
than any other stream in Wisconsin, and opposite the mouth of
the Chippewa, on the Minnesota side at Read's Landing, the Mississippi rafts were made up.   Many strings, sometimes as many as
eighteen, were placed side by side, until the raft had a surface of
three or four acres and contained more than two and one-half
million feet.   On the top were cabins for the crew and a top
loading of shingles, lath, and pickets.   After the Civil War these
Mississippi rafts were pushed downstream by steam tugs.   This
method gave very cheap transportation, but the lumber arrived at
its destination covered with silt and partially water-soaked.   In
the vast yards at St. Louis or in the Iowa towns it had to be given
time to dry out and season.

Pine lumbering in Wisconsin had about it much that was picturesque and even thrilling.   It was an episode in Wisconsin
history in which many strong men strove mightily to convert
nature's gift into wealth.   Those who succeeded gained positions
of leadership in the economic and political life of the state.   Too,
the pine from Wisconsin and its neighbors was a factor in the
making of all the states westward and southwestward to the Rocky
Mountains.   As the railroads crossed the Mississippi and carried
the bearers of European civilization into the upper half of the
Louisiana purchase, millions called for shelter.   Their houses

were built of Wisconsin lumber and roofed with Wisconsin shingles. If these throngs had been forced to bake brick or quarry stone, settlement on the treeless plains would have been far different, much less attractive, and surely much less rapid.

When the pine was gone it did not mean the end of lumbering in Wisconsin. It was discovered during the last decade of the nineteenth century that hemlock could be used as rough lumber. And there were the hardwoods. But maple, birch, and oak will not float; and in floating hemlock the percentage of loss is almost prohibitive. So hemlock and the hardwoods were harvested in close connection with the railroads. The old methods and the old life were gone.

SELECTED BIBLIOGRAPHY

In 1897 Filibert Roth, an expert of the forest service of the Department of Agriculture, spent three months inspecting the northern woods, after which he wrote: *On the Forestry Conditions of Northern Wisconsin,* Bulletin 16, U. S. Department of Agriculture (Washington, 1898), also published as Bulletin 1, Wisconsin Geol. and Nat. Hist. Survey, 1898. Another study made while lumbering was in its prime is George W. Hotchkiss, *History of the Lumber and Forest Industry of the Northwest* (Chicago, 1896). Frederick Merk, *Economic History of Wisconsin During the Civil War Decade* (Madison, 1916), pp. 59-110 is excellent. Joseph Schafer has a chapter on lumbering in *A History of Agriculture in Wisconsin* (Madison, 1922), pp. 130-149.

For lumbering in separate localities there is not as much in print as one could wish. "Shaw's Narrative," by Col. John Shaw, *Collections of the State Historical Society of Wisconsin,* Vol. II, pp. 197-232, deals with early lumbering on the Black River. Ellis B. Usher speaks with first-hand authority of the same region in his *Wisconsin, Its Story and Biography* (8 vols., Chicago, 1914), Vol. I, pp. 153-219. William W. Bartlett, out of lifelong familiarity with lumbering, wrote *History, Tradition and Adventure in the Chippewa Valley* (Eau Claire, 1929).

Much may be gleaned from the biographical articles in the old county histories. Of similar date and make-up, and most valuable, is *History of Northern Wisconsin* (authors unknown, Chicago, 1881).

On the subject of river transportation one may read J. M. Holley, "Waterways and Lumber Interests in Western Wisconsin," State Historical Society of Wisconsin *Proceedings, 1907,* pp. 208-215; and Walter A. Blair, *A Raft Pilot's Log: A History of the Great Rafting Industry on the Upper Mississippi* (Cleveland, 1920).

Ellis B. Usher, "Cyrus Woodman, A Character Sketch," *Wisconsin Magazine of History,* Vol. II, pp. 393-412 (June, 1919), deals with an early capitalist engaged in lumbering. Isaac Stephenson, a lumberman who became a capitalist, gives his autobiography in *Recollections of a Long Life* (Chicago, 1916). Albert H. Sanford, "The Beginnings of a Great Industry at La Crosse," *Wisconsin Magazine of History,* Vol. XVIII, pp. 375-388 (June, 1935), besides introducing Charles L. Coleman, whose business grew to great proportions, has an interesting description of machinery for cutting shingles. John Emmett Nelligan, *The Life of a Lumberman,* a brief autobiography, contains very good descriptions of logging operations. It appeared in three installments in the *Wisconsin Magazine of History,* Vol. XIII (1929, 1930), and was also issued as a bound volume by the author (n. p., 1929).

The following manuscript theses contain valuable material: Richard Lewis Canuteson, *The Lumbering Industry of the Black River* (B.A., Madison, 1925); Robert Francis Fries, *A History of Lumbering in Wisconsin* (Ph. M., Madison, 1936); Victor Linley, *Brief History of the Lumber Industry in the Chippewa Valley* (B.A., Madison, 1925); Genivera E. Loft, *The Evolution of Wood-Working Industries of Wisconsin* (M.A., Madison, 1916); Lloyd D. Miller, *The History of Lumbering in the Wisconsin River Valley* (B.A., Madison, 1914); Catherine E. O'Neil, *History of the Lumber Industry of Chippewa Falls* (B.A., Madison, 1917); and Donald W. Snell, *An Introduction to the History of Lumbering in Minnesota* (M.A., Minneapolis, 1926).

CHAPTER XII

A CENTURY OF AGRICULTURE

When Wheat Was King

WHEAT was the principal crop on Wisconsin farms until after the Civil War. For this there were several reasons. Half of the early American settlers were from New York state, and most of the others were from New England, Ohio, and Pennsylvania, and in all these areas, except possibly New England, wheat was the leading crop. Hence in this period Wisconsin farmers were wheat farmers by reason of their own early training. Wheat culture, too, was suited to the frontier because it required relatively little care and little capital. Further, just when Wisconsin was being settled, the growth of industry and urban life, both in England and in the United States, was creating a market for vastly increased amounts of wheat.

Between 1835 and 1850 most of the land in southern Wisconsin was made into farms, though usually it was several years before all of a farm was improved. Once he had chosen his land, the farm maker erected a shelter and made haste to break a little land and plant some wheat. In 1850 the state produced just under 8,000,-000 bushels. In the following decade the population more than doubled and farm making went on apace. The closing years of the 1850's were rather lean when the expanding acreage is taken into account, the crop amounting to about 15,000,000 bushels a year. Then in 1860 came a golden harvest of 28,000,000 bushels. During the five years of the Civil War Wisconsin's contribution to the world's food supply and to the economic strength of the North was about 100,000,000 bushels of wheat. Of this, 67,000,000 bushels went east as wheat, while the state also shipped nearly 3,000,000 barrels of flour, equivalent to about 13,000,000 bushels. Doubtless some of the wheat shipped from Wisconsin lake ports was produced in Iowa and Minnesota, but even so, Wisconsin's showing is little short of marvelous.

Year after year, in those early times, the Yankee farmers planted wheat in the same fields, until the soil was inevitably depleted and the yield per acre began to decline. This unvarying practice on the American frontier may be regretted, but it is easily explained. Wheat was the crop most easily produced and most readily turned into money. The farmer thought scarcely more of conserving soil fertility than the lumberman did of saving the pine forests. The lands in the public domain were still counted inexhaustible and if a living failed, a new beginning could be made farther west.

It should not be forgotten that by 1860 one-sixth of the people of Wisconsin had come from Germany, and what was true of the Yankees was not by any means true of the German farmers. In their concentration in the eastern part of the state the German settlers gave evidence of their desire to be close to their obvious market, the lake ports. Those who had farmed in southern and western Germany, whence came the majority of the early Germans in Wisconsin, had been accustomed in their old homes to somewhat intensive farming. They knew and cared more about fertilizers than did the Americans. They set to work to clear out the stumps more completely, and hence had to be content with slower progress than the Yankees in their conquest of the forests. As compared with the native Americans they took better care of their livestock, especially in the matter of shelter in the winter, though they had no more idea of the advantages of selective breeding than the average Americans of that time. They used a greater variety of crops from the beginning, and gave more attention to the vegetable garden and the orchard. While Americans were willing to exhaust the soil, the Germans regarded a farm as a permanent possession or estate to be conserved in and for the family. Hence they did not expect to sell, and generally speaking were not speculators in land. When they had money to invest, they either bought land near at hand or took mortgages on farms in their vicinity. Within a few years the Germans were buying the farms of their Yankee neighbors.

When the English-speaking settlers first crossed the Alleghenies and descended into the Ohio Valley, agricultural implements and methods were almost as primitive as in the time of the Roman Empire. The spacious Mississippi Valley invited large-scale farming, which in turn brought a demand for labor-saving machinery. Necessity again proved the mother of invention. In the great states of the corn belt, Ohio, Indiana, and Illinois, originated cornplanters, checkrowers, and all the needed equipment for the cultivation of maize. Similarly, in Wisconsin, one of the great wheat-raising states, the ingenuity of her Yankee settlers turned with distinct success to the invention of machinery for handling wheat.

In the 1830's wheat was still cut with the cradle, a scythe with a frame attached to guide the falling grain. A cradler was followed by two men binding, and the three of them could cut and bind between two and three acres a day. On the average, twelve men would cut and bind about ten acres a day. Many machines were devised to do some of this work, some valuable and others impractical. In 1834 Cyrus McCormick, then of Virginia, patented his reaper, a mower with a platform behind the cutter. One man drove the team and a second raked the grain from the platform with a rake and left it in neat little piles or gavels ready to be made into sheaves by hand. McCormick, who was but the leader of many makers of reaping machines in his day, began to manufacture in Chicago in 1846, and three years later he turned out 1500 machines, of which about one-ninth were sold in Wisconsin. On many farms in Wisconsin the cradle had given place to the reaper by 1861; it was estimated that three thousand reapers of various makes had been sold for the harvest of that year.

In 1843 George Esterly, a native of New York state, began farming near Janesville, and he, after losing a crop for lack of harvest hands, invented "the first successful American harvesting machine." It was of the type later called a header. "It had a wide reel revolving on a horizontal axis, mounted on a box on wheels, which swept the heads of grain against a knife also placed horizontally. The heads fell into the box back of the knife and just in front of the horses, which were hitched in the rear." [1] Esterly contracted with several manufacturers to make his machines, and then in 1858 he set up his own plant at Whitewater, where he came to make not only headers and mowers, but, in the course of time, twine binders.

The goal of all efforts was a machine that would bind. During the Civil War period the Marsh brothers put out their famous harvester. This was essentially a reaper with a platform on which rode two men who there bound the grain by hand. Many men during the next fifteen years devised binding machines to be attached to Marsh harvesters, among them S. D. Locke of Janesville and S. D. Carpenter, a Madison journalist. These two men and many others in different states made contributions to the final solution. Charles B. Withington, also of Janesville, invented a machine that bound the sheaves with a band of wire. The McCormick firm bought the Withington patents, and from 1877 to 1880 made wire binders, selling in all some fifty thousand of them. Other companies were doing the same, but the wire binder was not satisfactory: cattle were killed by wire in the straw they ate, and sometimes wire made trouble in flour mills.

The inventor who drew together the useful ideas of many predecessors and with the insight of genius fused them into one master machine, a practical twine binder, was John Francis Appleby. He was born in New York state in 1840, and at the age of five came with his parents to Walworth County, Wisconsin. As a lad of eighteen he constructed a model that contained all the essential elements of the later perfected Appleby knotter. After

---

[1] Carl W. Mitman, *Dictionary of American Biography*, Vol. VI, page 188.

service in the Civil War he returned to his problem and in 1867 demonstrated a complete machine at Mazomanie, but its performance was not equal to his hopes. Appleby associated himself with a Beloit firm, and along with them gave attention to wire binders. Dissatisfaction with wire drove him back to twine, and in 1878 he patented his knotter, and in the same year he and his partners in Beloit completed what was to be the machine of the future—at least, for half a century. Deering and McCormick soon purchased the right to use Appleby's patents, and today, wherever grain is bound, the Appleby knotter is at work.

After wheat was bound it still had to be threshed. The most famous manufacturer of threshing machines in Wisconsin, and one of the greatest in the United States, was Jerome Increase Case. When he was preparing to leave New York state in 1842 he bought six horse-powered threshers and brought them to Racine. There he sold five but kept the sixth, for he meant to make his living as a thresherman. Two years later at Rochester, Wisconsin, he designed, built, and put into operation a combined thresher and separator, thus making unnecessary a separate fanning mill. By 1857 he was manufacturing in his plant at Racine no less than 1,600 of these machines a year. After the Civil War he manufactured a great variety of farm machinery. His wealth enabled him to keep a fine racing stable, and he attained some prominence as a philanthropist.

ELEVATORS AND FLOUR MILLS

Wisconsin's surplus wheat went to eastern markets to pay interest on borrowed money and to buy the necessities and simple luxuries of life, many of which could not yet be produced in a frontier state. All the principal lake ports shared in the task of loading and shipping wheat to the eastern markets. Much of it went to New York and some of it ultimately to Liverpool. Milwaukee's primacy was assured by her leadership in railway building. She made a small shipment of wheat from her port in 1841, and when railway connection with the Mississippi was made in

1857 and 1858, the day of great business began to dawn. Before 1857 all wheat was shipped in bags, but in that year Milwaukee erected her first elevator, and thenceforth handled grain in bulk. By 1866 she had seven or eight elevators with a combined daily capacity of 1,100,000 bushels. A number of the elevators were the property of the railroad companies, and for a time the railroads refused to deliver grain to any elevators but their own. In 1864, however, an act of the legislature required them to deliver to any elevator in Milwaukee equipped with proper tracks.

Indispensable in the early days of farming in Wisconsin were the grist and flour mills. If someone bought a millsite from the government and failed to make use of it, he was compelled to sell it at a fair price to someone who would meet the needs of the community. Farmers brought their own wheat to the mill and took it home again in the form of flour and feed. Many cities and villages, especially in southern Wisconsin, had their location determined by an available water power, though that power has long since ceased to be used for milling. According to the federal census, there were 117 such mills in the state in 1849, and their great number, reaching 705 in 1879, shows how they spread over the state with the culture of wheat. Within the twentieth century their number has declined: the present-day Wisconsin farmer plants little wheat, and even if he has planted some he is content to sell it and use the products of Minneapolis and other milling centers.

The Indians and sometimes the earliest settlers made wheat into flour with something fashioned like a mortar and pestle, but in the mills set up by early settlers the grinding was done by two stones, the lower one concave and the upper fitting into it and revolving in it. At Prairie du Chien as early as 1818 there was a crude mill worked by horsepower, but almost all early mills were driven by water. The granite stones of the earliest mills were replaced by French burr (*buhr*) stones and the change effected a considerable improvement in the product. Modern milling methods, however, are fundamentally different from those of the mid-nineteenth century and did not grow out of American practice at all. Today the wheat is first broken and then ground by several pairs of rollers in succession, the first pair corrugated and the later pairs smooth, and each pair set closer than its predecessor. Alternating with these steps in gradual reduction are numerous siftings and purifyings by means of many devices such as sieves, brushes, and air currents. The idea of the successive purifying processes was first applied in the early seventies, still in connection with millstones, and the use of rollers in place of stones began in 1880. The capitalist-miller who pioneered in both innovations was Cadwallader C. Washburn, a resident of La Crosse, governor of Wisconsin, and leader in developing the great Washburn-Crosby mills at Minneapolis. The very complicated purifying process was developed by a French mechanic in his employ after 1870. As for the rollers, Washburn sent one of his technical experts to Hungary to study developments there, and the first milling with rollers in the United States was done in an experimental mill in a corner of the Washburn plant in Minneapolis in 1880, and the rollers used were imported from Hungary. With the old millstones about 25 per cent of the product was first grade flour; by the new process, about 90 per cent. The profits to millowners who made the change were enormous, but they accrued only to those who could bear the expense of installing the new and elaborate machinery. Washburn's leadership was followed, however, in the larger mills of Wisconsin, and the making of "patent" flour was soon a matter for pride in Milwaukee and many other milling centers in Wisconsin.

That the great shipping centers, by reason of their location and early railway development, should also become centers for the growing milling industry was only natural. Milwaukee, although all the lake ports made promising beginnings, soon outdistanced the others. Her fourteen mills produced 202,810 barrels of flour in 1860, and nearly twice that amount in 1870. Indeed, with a product valued at $3,400,000 in 1870 and $4,200,000 ten years later, Milwaukee's leading industry until almost 1880 was flour milling. The peak of the city's flour production, 2,000,000 barrels, came in 1892; by 1909 the number had decreased to 1,500,-000, and within the following decade she had ceased to make flour at all. The mills of the present day make oatmeal and corn products.

Many other communities had their day of flour milling, and some of them were widely known for their product: the cities on Lake Winnebago and the lower Fox; La Crosse, where the steamboats brought wheat from the upper Mississippi towns to the railroads; Janesville, Racine, and Madison. In most of these towns no flour has been made for many years because, as Wisconsin farmers ceased to raise wheat, the milling industry, except locally and in a very small way, moved northwest nearer to the sources of its raw material. The mills of Wisconsin have almost entirely ceased to compete with Minneapolis and Duluth. The city of Superior, Wisconsin, however, has had some part since 1889 in milling the wheat of the great Northwest, and in loading both flour and wheat to go by way of the Great Lakes to the eastern markets.

DIVERSIFIED AGRICULTURE AND DAIRYING

Wheat, for most of the farmers of early Wisconsin, was the chief cash or export crop, and the only thing that would lure them away from wheat was a conviction amounting to certainty that a different sort of farming would give them a better living. Eventually Wisconsin farmers abandoned wheat almost entirely, and the key to the change was the hope of greater profits, or, what is probably nearer the truth, the hope of climbing out of the slough of debt and poverty in which soil depletion and the declining yield of wheat had left them.

As we look back over a long period of years, we see that some alternatives to wheat farming were but temporary, while others were destined to be relatively permanent. While the Civil War was in progress, the products of the South were largely lacking in the markets of the North. The shortage of cotton stimulated

wool growing, and Wisconsin's sheep were multiplied from 332,-
000 in 1860 to 1,260,000 in 1865, with wool production rising from
one to four million pounds. This annual amount was then maintained until 1870. A beginning was also made in raising flax, but
the cost of linen manufacture in the United States could not be
brought down to a point where it could compete with cottons.
African sorghum or sugar cane had a momentary popularity, but
Wisconsin's northern climate did not permit permanent competition with the South. Just after the war (from 1868 to 1872),
sugar beets and the making of sugar from them had a temporary
vogue.

One of the most curious episodes in Wisconsin agriculture was
the hop "craze," which rose gradually from about 1861 to its zenith
in 1865-1867. The crop had failed temporarily in New York state
as the result of a visitation of vermin, and this, together with an
increase in the national consumption of beer, caused prices to rise
from twenty-five cents in 1861 to fifty, sixty, or even seventy
cents a pound by 1867. Wisconsin's production rose from a mere
trifle to between 6,000,000 and 7,000,000 pounds valued at $4,200,-
000 in 1867. Sometimes the product of a single acre would bring
$1,000. Sauk County was the heart of the hop-raising area, and
Kilbourn had temporarily the distinction of being "the greatest
primary hop district in the United States." The initial expense
of poling an acre for hops was large, and many farmers, dazzled
by the sudden wealth held out before them, went heavily into
debt to enlarge their acreage, while they and their families reveled
in unaccustomed luxury. Then, in 1868, came the crash: New
York was able to raise hops again, the louse came to Wisconsin,
prices fell, and many farmers were left only with their memories
of wealth that had come and gone—and their debts.

While these were only temporary vagaries, a more permanent
and important change, slowly working its way from the southern
part of the state northward, was proving to be the real solution of
the farmers' problem. Little by little the place of wheat in the
fields was being taken by the feed crops for animals—corn, oats,

and hay—while at the same time the number of horses, cattle, sheep, and swine was slowly increasing. By 1879 wheat had dropped into a position of minor importance in perhaps fifteen counties in the southern part of the state. Grant County was leading in corn and Dane County in oats, and a million bushels of one or the other grain was recorded in several southern counties. The production of corn in the whole state in 1879 was 34,000,000 bushels and of oats, 32,000,000. Nearly 2,000,000 tons of hay were cut that year. These figures may not be impressive when compared with those of the twentieth century; they do show, however, that wheat was rapidly being relegated to a minor position, for the wheat that year amounted to but 24,000,000 bushels.

Some tobacco was produced in Wisconsin before the Civil War, but the real development of this specialty came in the last three decades of the century. At the end of the century about three-fourths of the tobacco grown in the state came from the south-eastern part of Dane County and the adjacent part of Rock County. Some seven thousand farmers were raising tobacco in 1899, and the crop of 45,500,000 pounds was valued at almost $3,000,000.

Although the numbers of Wisconsin farm animals at census periods are available, one cannot be so certain about their quality in the early days. The Wisconsin Agricultural Society was founded and began its series of annual state fairs in 1851, and while farmers were greatly interested in the livestock exhibits, one gets the impression from the limited number of entries that the purebred stock in the state was restricted in amount and was owned by very few people. Until about 1880 the horses displayed were of the racing and fancy driving types. There was a general interest in horse racing, and every city of any size had its driving association and its "fair grounds" with a race track. This racing stock, however, was not generally crossed with horses on farms, and so there was little improvement in the latter. After 1880 prizes were offered at the state fair for heavy draft horses of several different breeds, and soon Clydesdales, Percherons, and other heavy types were being raised throughout the state and Wisconsin was exporting them to western states. This stock was frequently crossed with the farmers' work horses, and the improvement effected in them by the end of the century was great and general.

The rise in the number of sheep during the period of the Civil War has been mentioned. Well-to-do Wisconsin farmers were giving much attention to the breeding of improved sheep, and since wool and not mutton was their object, Merinos and Saxons were preferred to the English types. After about 1870 wool production ceased to be profitable, and interest in sheep gradually shifted to mutton. At the same time, as might be expected in view of the amount of corn produced, a pronounced movement began in favor of better hogs. Where before there had been only the "prairie racers," driven up in droves from Indiana and southern Illinois, now on the farms of Wisconsin's corn belt appeared the Poland-Chinas and other breeds that quickly transmute corn into ham and bacon.

Wisconsin is today the greatest dairy state in the Union, but the beginnings of dairying were small and growth was very gradual. The early Wisconsin farmer frequently used oxen for draft animals, and however poor he was, he usually managed sooner or later to have one or more cows. In 1850, when there were 41,000 farmers, there were 64,000 cows in Wisconsin. On most farms they were likely to be of nondescript breed and they merely supplied milk for home use. Occasionally there might be a little butter to use in trade at the general store. There was also a certain amount of home cheese making. Cheese was produced in quantity in New York state in the forties and fifties, and many immigrants brought their skill from the Empire State to Wisconsin. A Swiss colony was begun at New Glarus in Green County in 1845, and as soon as they could buy cattle these people began making Swiss cheese at home. Increased resources came with the years and some of their cheeses were sold, but there was no factory among them for many years.

In 1851 the factory system of cheese making was begun in New York, and as the Civil War was drawing to a close it had its beginnings in Wisconsin. A number of farmers would join to erect a little building, and they and perhaps others would agree to bring in the milk of their herds. Someone would be employed as a cheesemaker, and the new enterprise was launched. Detailed statistics are lacking, but by 1870 there were probably about fifty cheese factories in Wisconsin scattered through sixteen counties and producing about a million pounds of cheese. In February, 1872, the Wisconsin Dairymen's Association was organized. The first president was Chester Hazen of Fond du Lac County, who is generally credited with starting the first cheese factory in the state. The association established a market day at Watertown, where Wisconsin makers could meet the eastern buyers. It also arranged for the shipment of Wisconsin cheese to New York by the Star Union Line, the first railroad refrigerator service in the United States.

Dairying and dairy manufacturing have since grown to be of the greatest importance in the economic life of the state. Few farmers in those early years had a vision of this great future, and the conversion of the many to a belief in dairying was the result of years of patient persuasion. This leadership came from farmers actually engaged in successful dairying, like Chester Hazen and Hiram Smith; from editors of the agricultural journals; and in the last two decades of the century from the staff of the University of Wisconsin College of Agriculture.

Among the confident leaders was William Dempster Hoard, who as a youth in New York state had the good fortune to work for a successful farmer who taught him the current New York practice in making butter and cheese. Hoard came to Wisconsin in 1857 and married. After service in the Civil War he returned to Wisconsin and settled at Columbus. He made some money in the nursery business, but lost it all, and more, growing hops, and it took him twenty years to pay his debts. In 1870 he started the *Jefferson County Union,* a county newspaper. He helped organize the Jefferson County Dairymen's Association and a year later he became the first secretary of the Wisconsin Dairymen's Associa-

tion. He was constantly urging the farmers of Jefferson County
to substitute the cow for the plow. In 1885 he started the weekly
Hoard's Dairyman, then a little four-page sheet; today it is one of
the largest and best publications of its kind. Hoard was not only
a convincing writer, but a vigorous and popular public speaker.
With pen and voice he insisted on the value of dairying. He
urged the elimination of the "dual purpose" cow and the substitution of a type bred definitely and solely for milk production. He
preached the use of the silo and all other means of reducing the
cost of feeding, advocated the closest coöperation between farmers and the agencies of government, and encouraged the farmers to
avail themselves of all the resources of science. His election as
governor of Wisconsin in 1888 was evidence of widespread approval of his message and appreciation of his long devotion to the
cause of better farming. Toward the end of his life the state legislature paid tribute to him by voting him the most distinguished
citizen of the state. Yet, William D. Hoard was only one of a
score of great agricultural leaders. Hiram Smith, a successful
practical dairyman who became a member of the Board of Regents
of the State University, had much to do with the improvement of
the Agricultural College, and there were great leaders in that college, such as Dean William A. Henry, head of the institution from
1881 to 1907.

Three important additions were made to the available equipment of dairy farming and dairy manufacturing and came into
general use in the latter part of the nineteenth century: the silo,
the Babcock milk tester, and the cream separator.

The silo grew out of experiments in Europe. If green fodder
is put into a pit in the ground and covered from the air, it will,
under favorable conditions respecting drainage and moisture,
come out months later fit for animal food. In the meantime it
has gone through a certain fermentation and chemical change not
unlike what occurs in the making of sauerkraut. A Frenchman
named Goffart made a thorough study of this phenomenon during
a quarter of a century, and his book on the subject, published in

1877, introduced the subject to practical agriculture. A few silos were built in Wisconsin as early as 1880. Little by little improvements were made as to size, shape, building materials, and methods of filling, and prejudice yielded to confidence. In 1904 there were 716 silos in operation in Wisconsin, and twenty years later there were more than 100,000. They have aided greatly in solving the dairymen's problem of cheap winter forage, and there is an obvious relation between the facts that Wisconsin has more than twice as many silos as any other state and that she is the leading dairy state in the Union.

The milk tester was perfected by Dr. Stephen M. Babcock, head of the department of dairy husbandry of the University of Wisconsin College of Agriculture. It measures accurately the amount of butterfat in milk. To a definite amount of milk taken as a sample is added sulphuric acid of known strength. The acid releases the globules of fat and when the bottle containing the mixture is whirled in a machine, centrifugal force brings all the fat together into a column in the neck of the testing bottle, where it can be measured. The method of the test has remained for fifty years exactly as when Dr. Babcock gave the process to the public in 1890.

The advent of the cream separator was a great boon to dairying. In its fundamentals it was not an American invention, but was developed almost simultaneously about 1878 in Denmark, Sweden, and Germany. A large power-driven separator became part of the equipment of most American cheese factories and creameries in the early eighties, and farmers brought whole milk to the factories or skimming stations, returning home with a proportionate amount of skim milk. About 1892 small machines for use on individual farms were offered for sale, but the farmers were apparently content with existing methods, for only between 1900 and 1910 did they come into general use in Wisconsin.

The federal census of 1900 measured the progress made in dairying by the end of the century. According to its definition, a farm was a dairy farm if 40 per cent of its income came from the sale of dairy products; by that test more than 25,000 Wisconsin farms, one-seventh of the total number, were dairy farms. There were in the state nearly a million dairy cows, and the farmers sold milk to the value of nearly $16,000,000, and butter worth $4,500,-000. When we turn to the industries, we find the manufacture of dairy products standing fourth in the state. Butter, cheese, and condensed milk were made to the value of more than $20,000,000. The faith of the founders of Wisconsin dairying had been amply justified, and the twentieth century was to show still greater developments.

NORTHERN WISCONSIN

In the days of the Indians and the fur traders, the Fox and Wisconsin rivers were a part of the principal route of travel between Canada and the whole Mississippi Valley. When the time came for the Wisconsin wilderness to be transformed into farms and villages, a region southeast of the old water highway was naturally settled first; it is convenient to call this area "southern Wisconsin," and the part of the state to the north and west of it "northern Wisconsin." By 1850 ordered life based upon agriculture had been established throughout southern Wisconsin, and there was even a small fringe of farming settlement beyond the old highway. By this time, too, agriculture was definitely more important than mining in the old lead-mining areas in the southwest, while around Green Bay and Kaukauna members of the old *voyageur* families were taking to farming alongside of the Anglo-Saxons and the Irish. Practically the whole life of the territorial period was lived within southern Wisconsin. Representatives of this region wrote the constitution, and its settlers established the customs and traditions of the state. By 1860 the agricultural population had reached the saturation point in many of the southeastern counties; increase in population since that time has been in the urban areas alone.

Agricultural settlement had by 1860 filled up several counties north and northwest of the Fox and Wisconsin rivers. Joseph

Schafer in his *History of Agriculture in Wisconsin* (1922) suggested the name, "the Old North," for the part of northern Wisconsin settled before the Civil War. It includes one line of counties along the western border from Vernon to St. Croix, and an-

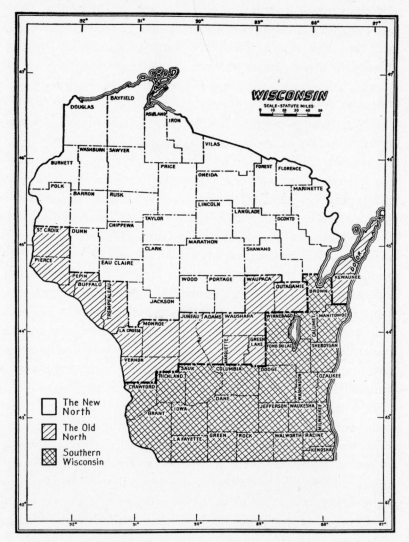

THE OLD NORTH AND THE NEW NORTH*

*From Joseph Schafer, *Agriculture in Wisconsin* (1922). By courtesy of the State
Historical Society of Wisconsin.

other irregular row extending from La Crosse on the Mississippi to Outagamie, Kewaunee, and Door on the east. This Old North, which takes in seventeen of the present counties, had a population of 122,000 in 1860, or about one-sixth of the total of the state, and 205,500 in 1870. By this time it was so well settled and had made such progress in farming as to be counted agriculturally merely an extension of southern Wisconsin, participating in all the new movements there. Its growth was undoubtedly stimulated by the fact that several lumbering and sawmill towns lay within it.

Beyond all this to the north lay the region called by Schafer "the New North." A line from the city of Green Bay to Hudson on the St. Croix, with a considerable sag in the middle, divides the two regions fairly well. The counties of Portage, Wood, Jackson, and Eau Claire are in the New North; that is, the line must pass south of Stevens Point, Wisconsin Rapids, Black River Falls, and Eau Claire, all familiar towns in the early history of lumbering. In terms of the present map, this New North embraces twenty-nine counties, and in area is considerably more than half the state. With the exception of the pine-covered triangle along Lake Michigan, it is roughly equivalent to the original pine land of the state. The federal surveyors did not complete their work there until 1865, and many of the present counties were at that time still unorganized. The census of 1860 showed for the whole state a population of 776,000, but only 31,000, or one twenty-fifth of the whole, lived in this as yet undeveloped North.

For a long time prospective farmers shunned the forest lands of the northern part of the state, partly because of an erroneous belief that they were not fertile, partly to avoid the toil of clearing the land. The New North got its first railroads in the early seventies; the North Western built from Green Bay to Marinette, the West Wisconsin (later part of the Omaha) from Elroy by way of Eau Claire to Hudson, and the Wisconsin Central from Menasha to Ashland. This did much to dispel false ideas about the North. Farmers found in the lumber camps markets at their very doors, and by the time production outran the needs of the lumbermen the

railroads were there to carry their surplus products to Milwaukee
and Chicago.   Meanwhile, the farmers found work in the camps
during the slack winter months.   Life in northern Wisconsin was
thus marked for some decades by a mutually advantageous combination and interplay of lumbering and farming, and the two advanced northward together.   By 1890 the population of the New
North had reached 361,000.

The natural trend of agricultural migration in the United States
was not northward but westward.   Soon after 1890, it being then
apparent that pine lumbering was drawing to a close, the state
legislature authorized a definite effort to attract farmers into northern Wisconsin.   A state board of immigration was established
with headquarters at Rhinelander.   A book by Dean William A.
Henry of the state College of Agriculture, called "Northern Wisconsin, a Handbook for the Home Seeker," was published in 1896
and widely circulated.   During the twenty years from 1900 to
1920, while the agricultural population of southern Wisconsin was
stationary or (in some areas) declining, that of the twenty-nine
northern counties increased by 140,000.   By 1920 the total population of the New North was just under 703,000, or about 26.7 per
cent of the population of the state.   In sixty years it had grown
from one twenty-fifth to have more than one-fourth of the people
of the state.

The census of 1930 told a somewhat different tale.   Of the
twenty-nine counties, sixteen had suffered an actual if small decline during the decade.   For the group, there was an increase
of 4,281, or six-tenths of one per cent.   Yet in the same decade
the other forty-two counties of the state showed an increase of over
300,000, or a little over 15 per cent.   The extremely small increase
in the northern part of the state seemed to indicate that the decline of lumbering had seriously affected the confidence of the
people there, and, even in the decade before 1930, many of them
were removing elsewhere.   As the depression of 1929 continued
and grew worse, there was an enormous increase of public relief,
and a crushing financial burden fell on the counties and other

units of local government. It was in these northern counties that the percentage of those on relief was largest, and the local financial resources proved quite inadequate, so that the state had to make special grants; the south had to bear part of the burden of the north, while the federal government assisted both. The details of these financial readjustments will be found in a later chapter.

AGRICULTURE IN THE TWENTIETH CENTURY

Wisconsin agriculture toward the close of the 1930's resembled in a general way that of 1900. The number of farms rose from 170,000 at the turn of the century to almost 200,000 in 1935. On these farms were living in 1935 about 930,000 people, or about 32 per cent of the estimated population of the state. Dairying was the most important branch of farming throughout the period, and the list of leading crops did not show much variation. Yet farm life underwent great changes. In 1938 there were automobiles on 92 per cent of the farms, motor trucks on 60,000 of them, and roads were constantly improving throughout the state. The value of farm machinery was in 1930 five or six times what it had been in 1900, and in 1938 about 61,000 farms were equipped with tractors. There were telephones on about 60 per cent of the farms in 1928, but this was a convenience that could be dispensed with during the depression: in 1938 telephones were found on but 37 per cent of the farms. In the latter year, about 35,000 farms were lighted by electricity. Only about nine per cent were equipped with milking machines.

Dairying became more and more important as the years passed. The number of cattle on Wisconsin farms came to exceed two millions for the first time in 1901. Of this number 996,000 or forty-six per cent were "cows or heifers two years old and over kept for milk." The number of all cattle reached three million in 1920 and after that climbed very slowly until 1934, when they numbered 3,331,000. The drought of that year caused a diminution during the following winter, after which the slow climb was resumed, and the peak of 1934 was slightly exceeded in 1939.

Milk cows have numbered more than two million since 1930.

The greatest number of swine ever recorded was in 1923, when there were 1,960,000. Drought conditions in 1934 combined with the government program of restriction led to an especially rapid decline, and at the beginning of 1935 there were but a little more than a million. In 1939, a preliminary estimate reported 1,454,000. Swine are most numerous in the southwestern part of the state, in the old lead-mining area, "where the agriculture is essentially of the corn-belt type"; but hog raising is fairly widespread wherever there is a supply of whey and skim milk on which they thrive. Both horses and mules increased somewhat in numbers during the World War only to decline again when it was over. During the 1930's they have been fairly stable at a little above a half million, but with a tendency to decline rather than to increase. Sheep exceeded a million in 1900, but after 1912 were always less than half a million, except for the year 1936, when they numbered 502,999.

Wisconsin farmers, it appears from the foregoing, must feed more than three million cattle, from one to one and one-half million hogs, and almost another million horses, mules, and sheep. This necessity gives its character to the cultivation of Wisconsin's fields. Nine-tenths of the cropped land is used for the production of feeds, among which the most important are tame hay including alfalfa, corn, oats, and barley. Forty or fifty per cent of the corn is used to fill silos, which by 1937 numbered about 122,000. The production of oats in 1899 was 84,000,000 bushels, and since then the amount has occasionally reached a hundred million. Over 90 per cent of the hay, corn, and oats is fed to livestock on the farms where they are produced, and nearly as large a part of the barley raised in the state is used in the same way.

One should consider not only the number of dairy cattle but their value and the value of the products sold. Before the depression the figures were impressive. Dairy cattle were valued at almost two hundred million dollars in 1930. In each of the three years before that Wisconsin farmers sold butter, cream, and milk worth $225,000,000. These milk products furnished, indeed, more than half the total farm income. Wisconsin dairymen also sold livestock to other states and to foreign countries, often as many as 70,000 head a year. These, along with cattle and calves sold within the state for slaughter and herd-building, produced another $50,000,000 or more a year. The dairy herds altogether yielded about 65 per cent of the total farm income. While the number of cattle and the share of farm income derived therefrom have remained fairly stable since the depression began, values went down with the depression and then regained much of the loss. Cattle worth $200,000,000 in 1930 were in 1934, with but a slight reduction in numbers, valued at $77,000,000; but by 1938 the value had mounted again to $188,000,000. Throughout this period the physical production, the amount produced to sell, varied surprisingly little, in spite of some drought years, but because of low prices received the farmer's income varied much as did the value of his livestock.

During the ten years, 1927-1937, hogs produced about ten per cent of the gross farm income, and eggs and chickens another ten. Among Wisconsin's cash crops tobacco just about held its own for the first thirty years of the century, and then declined. The production was 45,000,000 pounds in 1899 and almost the same twenty years later. The World War brought some increase in amount, while the value of the crop temporarily multiplied fourfold. From 1933 to 1936, inclusive, because of drought and government crop limitation, the yield varied between twelve and eighteen million pounds, but after that recovered partially; it exceeded 32,000,000 pounds in both 1938 and 1939. The potato crop since 1900 has been fairly stable, varying usually between twenty and thirty million bushels a year, though it too has shown a tendency to decline since 1930. Peas for canning rose from something over two thousand acres in 1899 to become fairly stable at about 100,000 acres for the period since 1930.

Further details would not greatly alter the picture as a whole. Wisconsin agriculture is diversified in the sense that numerous field crops are raised; and yet, in it all, the cow has the chief place. It may fairly be said that the faith of William D. Hoard and other dairy leaders of the past century has been justified.

Wisconsin as a state has done much to promote better farming and has aided the farmers in matters of finance and marketing. A department of agriculture and markets was established in 1929, a consolidation of many previously existing agencies. Various divisions of the department gather statistics, inspect seed and fertilizers, strive to control insect and weed pests and plant and animal diseases, and impose and maintain standards of quality in production. Many of these services are rendered in coöperation with the federal government. When the dairy herds were being threatened by bovine tuberculosis some years ago, both governments joined in the work of testing herds and removing infected animals. From 1917 to 1930 more than 8,000,000 cattle were tested in Wisconsin, and about two per cent were found diseased. By examining more than a million animals a year, the authorities continue to test all the cattle in the state once in three years. Similar care is being used in the battle against Bang's disease or contagious abortion in cattle. To preserve the home market for butter, high taxes and license fees have practically excluded oleomargarine from Wisconsin. Processes in cheese factories, creameries, condenseries, and ice-cream factories are regulated and inspected to maintain inviolate the reputation of Wisconsin dairy products, built up through more than half a century. The state is both the leader and the servant of every one engaged in agriculture.

SELECTED BIBLIOGRAPHY

The most comprehensive book on the subject of this chapter is Joseph Schafer, *A History of Agriculture in Wisconsin* (Madison, 1922), which was written as an introduction to the Wisconsin Domesday Book. Each of the subsequent volumes in the series (*see* Selected Bibliography of Chapter V) has much on the history of agriculture in the region of which it treats. Frederick Merk, *Economic History of Wisconsin During the Civil War Decade* (Madison, 1916), pp. 15-58, offers a valuable chapter on agriculture. Oliver E. Remey, "A Half Century of Agricultural Development," was contributed to Milo M. Quaife, *Wisconsin, Its History and Its People* (4 vols., Chicago, 1924), Vol. II, pp. 41-72. Two excellent special studies are: Benjamin H. Hibbard, *The History of Agriculture in Dane County, Wisconsin* (Bulletin of the University of Wisconsin, No. 101, Madison, 1904); and John Griffin Thompson, *The Rise and Decline of the Wheat Growing Industry in Wisconsin* (Bulletin of the University of Wisconsin, No. 292, Madison, 1909).

On the subject of farm machinery, a very informative book with many illustrations is Robert L. Ardrey, *American Agricultural Implements* (Chicago, 1894). Two accounts of the development of the reaper are: William T. Hutchinson, *Cyrus Hall McCormick* (2 vols., New York, 1930, 1937); and Cyrus McCormick, *The Century of the Reaper* (Boston, 1931). F. B. Swingle described "The Invention of the Twine Reaper," in *Wisconsin Magazine of History*, Vol. X, pp. 35-41 (September, 1926). In the *Dictionary of National Biography* are brief accounts of inventors and early manufacturers under the names of John F. Appleby, Gael Borden, Jerome I. Case, William Deering, George Esterley, and Elijah H. Gammon. There is much information about the changes in methods of milling flour in Gaillard Hunt, *Israel, Elihu and Cadwallader Washburn, A Chapter in American Biography* (New York, 1925).

N. S. Fish wrote "The History of the Silo in Wisconsin," *Wisconsin Magazine of History*, Vol. VIII, pp. 160-170 (December, 1924). Halbert W. Hoard, *Historical Survey of Hoard's Dairyman,* is an interesting MS thesis (B.A., Madison, 1923) by the grandson of the founder of the periodical. Material on the early history of the cheese industry is to be found in the following; John Luchsinger, "The Planting of the Swiss Colony at New Glarus, Wisconsin," *Collections of the Wisconsin State Historical Society,* Vol. XII, pp. 335-382. The same author wrote "The History of a Great Industry," Wisconsin Historical Society *Proceedings, 1899,* pp. 226-230. J. Q. Emery added "The Swiss Cheese Industry in Wisconsin," *Wisconsin Magazine of History*, Vol. X, pp. 42-52 (September, 1926). There is further material on the history of cheese making in *Collections,* Vol. VIII, pp. 411-439; and Vol. XV, pp. 292-337.

For current conditions in agriculture there is available the *Wisconsin Crop and Livestock Reporter* (monthly since 1921), which contains statistics and brief comment. It is issued by the Wisconsin department of agriculture and markets in coöperation with the United States Department of Agriculture. Under the same auspices appear about once in four years crop reporting service bulletins entitled *Wisconsin Agriculture,* and taken in series they constitute an excellent source for the history of agriculture. The latest, Bulletin No. 188, appeared in 1938. Similar and equally valuable is *Wisconsin Dairying* (Bulletin No. 200, 1939). Walter H. Ebling, senior agricultural statistician of the Wisconsin Department, directs the preparation of the *Reporter* and the Bulletins. Mr. Ebling has also written the following: "The Development of Agriculture in Wisconsin," *Blue Book,* 1929, pp. 51-75: "Changes in Wisconsin Agriculture Since the Last Census," *Blue Book, 1933,* pp. 133-139: and "The Situation in Agriculture," *Blue Book, 1935,* pp. 45-57.

CHAPTER XIII

AGRARIAN DISCONTENT AND FARM ORGANIZATIONS

CLAIM ASSOCIATIONS AND LAND LIMITATION

IN ONE generation after another the farmers of the Middle West have had their griefs and grievances, and, realizing their helplessness as isolated individuals, they have repeatedly organized to defend their rights, confront their enemies, and reserve to themselves a larger share of the fruits of their toil. Such organizations have had many forms and diverse aims, they have often been impermanent, and they have not always been successful. But they have again and again expressed the mind of an important share of the population, and on several occasions they have had considerable weight in determining the results of elections. Especially after 1900 there have been formed organizations which, because of their coöperative features, have had no small part in securing or maintaining that degree of well-being which Wisconsin farmers have enjoyed during recent decades.

From early in the year 1836 Yankee farmers were choosing good lands in southeastern Wisconsin and squatting on them, expecting to purchase as soon as the government was ready to sell. They feared lest claim jumpers should dispossess them or in their absence seize their lands. They feared also that moneyed men whom they called speculators might outbid them at the land sale. So in March, 1837, they organized a claim association. This registered each man's claim, protected him in its possession, and prepared to help him purchase it despite the speculators. Under the rules of the association each member was obliged to give evidence of good faith and intent to settle by erecting a building on his claim and bringing under cultivation a part of the land that he expected to buy. Such claim associations were not peculiar to Wisconsin, but were a feature of the westward-moving frontier at many different times and places. The great land sale was finally held at Milwaukee in February and March, 1839, and the association secured for its members the lands they had chosen. This does not of course mean that capitalists had no part in this sale, for they did buy much land; but they were not able to dispossess or even bid against members of the association, who almost without exception secured their land at the minimum price of $1.25 an acre.

The association apparently regarded 160 acres as a normal amount of land for one man, and would protect no claim larger than 640 acres. This idea of the proper size of one man's holding is akin to the principle or policy of "land limitation" which George Henry Evans, editor of a New York newspaper called the *Workman's Advocate,* was upholding about this time. Thus, when the Free Soil party of Wisconsin drew up its platform in 1848, it included such planks as exemption of homesteads from forced sale, the limitation of the amount of land to be held by one person, and the disposal of the national domain in small parcels to actual settlers only. It is impossible to know how many were attracted by these ideas in 1848; it is usually assumed that other issues were decisive in the campaign. It may be noted, however, that in the southeast, where this particular claim association had functioned nine or ten years before, the Free Soilers triumphed and sent Durkee to Congress.

First Conflicts with the Railroads

The building of the railroads began, as we know, about the time Wisconsin became a state. To the wheat farmers of that time the raising of the crop was not so perplexing as the problem of transport to market. So long as they were without railroads the settlers looked upon them as the greatest of blessings, but once the roads were built the farmers came almost immediately to have grievances against them. Something was told in a previous chapter of how the farmers pledged their farms, taking railroad stock for themselves, while the railroad companies sold the farm mortgages to eastern investors. About six thousand farmers in southern Wisconsin were involved to the amount of about $5,000,000. The panic of 1857 threw every railroad in the state into bankruptcy and their stock became worthless. Then the mortgages began to fall due and the easterners started to foreclose.

The imperiled farmers organized a league in 1860, established a weekly paper, secured lawyers, and took what steps they could to save their homes. They were able to elect county officers in sympathy with their cause, but their main hope, a vain one as it turned out, lay in securing remedial legislation. From 1858 to 1863 all Wisconsin legislatures, with one exception, passed laws designed, "either to render impossible the foreclosure of the mortgages or to compel the reorganized railroads to cancel them." [1] All these laws, however, were declared unconstitutional by the state supreme court, and thus the effort of the legislature to give relief came to naught. In 1861, Chief Justice Orsamus Cole, and in 1863 Justice Dixon, had to stand for re-election. The League of Farm Mortgagors tried to replace them with judges in agreement with their own position, but in both instances failed of their purpose by a narrow margin.

Some of the farmers lost their homes by foreclosure; this seemed particularly hard where a member of the family had been killed in the Civil War. Sometimes lawyers who had come to arrange the details of foreclosure were hustled out of town. The various Wisconsin laws passed in this connection discouraged the holders of mortgages, and often compromises were effected at less than fifty cents on the dollar. Some of the federal land grants were, with the consent of Congress, sold for the benefit of the mortgagors.

---

[1] Frederick Merk, *Economic History of Wisconsin During the Civil War Decade* (Madison, 1916), p. 255.

In these and other ways a settlement was reached in most cases before 1870. Eastern investors had been shocked at the relief laws, which seemed to them nothing short of repudiation, and one result of the episode was that for years they were very chary of lending money in Wisconsin.

In settling the rates for their services the railroads had the wheat farmers almost at their mercy. Parts of Minnesota and Iowa were by 1860 coming to be important wheat-producing areas, and the adjacent parts of Wisconsin were developing rapidly in the same way. There were five railroads connecting the Mississippi with Lake Michigan in Wisconsin and Illinois, and every year or oftener their representatives met and amicably fixed rates for hauling wheat. A few short rate wars made but brief discords in the usual harmony. Along the Mississippi and its larger tributaries steamboats and barges bore the crop to the various railway terminals on the Mississippi. A through rate was fixed from each point on the river to Milwaukee and Chicago, and the steamboat companies divided receipts with the railroads. In 1862 and 1863, moreover, the steamboat lines on the upper Mississippi were consolidated into one exclusive corporation, controlled and largely owned by railroads or railroad officials, and the railroads refused to handle wheat brought down by independent boats. The fruits of monopoly were at once apparent. For example, in 1860 the combined steamboat and railroad freight rate on wheat from Prescott or Hudson to Milwaukee was ten cents per bushel. In the spring of 1863 it was fixed for all points above La Crosse at eighteen cents, in the autumn it was increased to twenty-five cents, and in 1865 it rose to thirty-five cents from Hudson and thirty-four cents from Prescott. The towns in inland Wisconsin paid even higher proportionate transportation charges than those on the Mississippi River. It sometimes cost more to ship from Madison or Ripon to Milwaukee than from points on the Mississippi River.

For two or three years (1864 to 1866) there was widespread agitation on the part of the farmers along the Mississippi. Their delegates aroused sympathy in the eastern part of the state, and chambers of commerce in Milwaukee and even in Chicago passed resolutions in their favor. Many regulatory bills were introduced in the Wisconsin legislature, but the railroad lobby prevented the passage of any one of them. The end of the Civil War was followed by a resumption of wheat traffic down the Mississippi, and this was more effective than any indignation meeting. The railroads reduced their rates, but not enough to satisfy the farmers. The largest meeting of protest, the St. Paul Anti-Monopoly Convention, was held in February, 1866, and was attended by many Wisconsin farmers. The convention sent delegates to the Wisconsin legislature to ask for remedial action, and considered ways and means to increase wheat transport down the Mississippi. By April of 1866 the rates from Hudson and Prescott to Milwaukee were down to nineteen cents per bushel, and six years later they had declined to twelve. Cities in the interior of Wisconsin, however, experienced less relief, and where there was no competition they were treated with scant consideration.

The year 1871 marked the end of two decades of railroad history in Wisconsin. None could deny the decisive and helpful part the railroads had come to have in the economic life of the state. Yet, the manner of their financing and the methods of their rate making had not inspired confidence in the honesty and public spirit of the management. The episodes just recounted had naturally left an aftertaste of suspicion and in some quarters of deep distrust and hostility.

The Granger Movement and the First Railroad Regulation

After the Civil War the Republican party was in office in Wisconsin with but one short interruption until 1891. As was natural in the case of a party long entrenched in power, the platforms of the party and the messages of the governors expressed great satisfaction with the condition of the nation and the state. This satisfaction, however, did not extend to all citizens. The Democratic party was always ready to capitalize discontent. In addition, there was a succession of independent movements of protest, most of them built upon the grievances of the farmers.   The first of these, after the short-lived and rather local anti-monopoly convention in St. Paul in 1866, was the Granger movement.   Though this label was derived from the popular name of a farmers' secret society, in a wider sense it covered an upsurge of agrarian discontent that manifested itself in many ways for at least a decade, and was much more important than that society.

Oliver Hudson Kelley, who had been a farmer in Minnesota, was a clerk in a government department in Washington when, in 1867, he founded the order of the Patrons of Husbandry.   He believed that the farmers needed intellectual stimulus and more social intercourse.   The order had a ritual modeled after that of the Masonic Lodge, and each local body was called a grange, a name that came to be widely used for the society as a whole. After a slow start the organization took root and spread rapidly in Minnesota and Iowa; there the promoters discovered that economic grievances gave them the greatest leverage.   They argued convincingly that only in combination with each other could the farmers effect any relief against railroads and other corporations. Coöperative buying by the agent of the Grange was a feature bound to save members a great deal of money.   The order was introduced into Wisconsin in Adams and nearby counties in 1871, but a quarrel among officials led to the breakup of most of these granges.   In the following year efforts were more successful, especially in the southeastern counties, and in December, 1872, twenty-eight granges were represented at the first annual meeting. Two years later, when the order had reached its highest point, there were over five hundred granges in the state with a membership of about 20,000.   It should be borne in mind, however, in estimating the strength of the Grange, that its membership counted not only farmers, but wives, and also children over fourteen who cared to join.   At that time there were well over 100,000 farmers in Wisconsin.

The only instance between 1855 and 1891 when the Republicans failed to elect their candidate for governor occurred in the fall of 1873, when Cadwallader C. Washburn, the incumbent, was defeated for re-election by William R. Taylor, a Democrat. It was formerly assumed that Washburn fell a victim to the Granger movement, but, in view of all the attendant circumstances, this is doubtful. Washburn had alienated the German element by approving a law regulating the saloons and had antagonized Alexander Mitchell and other railroad capitalists, who supported Taylor. It appears, further, that the rural vote at this election was unusually light, while in the larger cities the vote was heavy and, especially where there were Germans, markedly against Washburn. Moreover, even at its maximum, which had not been reached in 1873, the numerical strength of the order of the Patrons of Husbandry was not impressive.

Governor Taylor was in a quandary as to what course he ought to pursue with regard to the railroads. As a Dane County farmer he was something of a local leader among farmers. He had been chosen chairman of the county board of supervisors and at different times had sat in the assembly and in the state senate. He was also a member of the Grange. Altogether his background made him an excellent representative of the farmers, who, whether they had joined the Grange or not, and whether they went to the polls in 1873 or not, were universally desirous of the downward adjustment of railroad rates. On the other hand Taylor knew that the railroads had played no small part in placing him in office.

The group supporting Taylor had a majority in the assembly, but, with only sixteen out of thirty-three in the senate, was at the mercy of the Republicans there. Several bills providing for the regulation of the railroads originated in the lower house but made no progress in the upper. The bill that finally became a law was introduced by Robert L. D. Potter, a Republican of the senate, and had been prepared by the friends of the railroads. It had been made so extreme that even the Grangers were expected to reject it as unreasonable and obnoxious; but, faced with the alternative of this bill or no regulation, the Grangers elected to pass this bill. It was bound to drive a wedge between the Democrats and the capitalists interested in railroads.

The Potter law divided the railroads of Wisconsin into three classes according to the volume of business, and fixed maximum passenger rates for each class. It divided freights into classes, fixed maximum rates for some, and provided that rates on other classes should be fixed by a commission provided by the act. The railroad commission was to consist of three members, and would have powers of investigation, with right to demand the attendance of witnesses and the production of papers. Agents who charged more than the rates set by the law or by the commission were guilty of a criminal offense and liable to civil suits as well. A separate law forbade certain abuses in railroad practice such as discrimination, consolidation of competing roads, and the giving of free passes to public servants. These laws were to go into effect in April, 1874.

The two leading railroads, the Milwaukee and St. Paul and the Chicago and North Western, announced through their presidents, Alexander Mitchell and Albert Keep, that because they considered the Potter law unconstitutional they would not obey it. Governor Taylor announced by proclamation that they would. The matter was brought before the supreme court of the state, and in September, 1874, the court decided in favor of the state. The chief justice of the supreme court had resigned in the spring of that year, and it fell to Governor Taylor to fill the vacancy by appointment. He offered the place to a very able young lawyer named William F. Vilas, destined later to be United States Senator, but he declined. He then preferred it to the veteran lawyer and Democratic leader, Edward G. Ryan, who accepted. The railroad cases were the first he heard on the bench.

The action took the form of injunctions against the two railroad companies brought by the attorney general of Wisconsin. The judgment given covered both cases. Legal writers give it unstinted praise. About eighty pages were given over to a careful restatement of arguments of counsel, and about 100 more pages to the opinion of the court. The state was amply justified in proceeding against the railroads. "In our day the common law has encountered in England as in this country a new power unknown to the founders, practically too strong for its ordinary private remedies. The growth of great corporations, centers of vast wealth and power, new and potent elements of social influence . . . has been marvelous during the last half century." But if they chose to commit wrongs, they were too great for the ordinary citizen to meet in litigation. It was the duty of the courts of justice to change in a changing age, hence the procedure by injunction as in this case. Having established the rightfulness of its jurisdiction, the court went on to declare that the "Potter Law" was constitutional and must be obeyed. To reduce their income was not to confiscate the property of the railroads. The court had no leanings toward communism, "that horror of doctrine." So long as this law was the law of the state, the court existed to make it clear. The court could not criticize the law or join in any outcry against it. If it worked unfairly against the railroads they had their remedy; they might present their case in legislative halls and the law might there be changed.

Ever since this famous decision was handed down in September, 1874, the principles enunciated in it have stood unimpaired; in fact, they furnished a basis for Wisconsin's later regulation of railroads. The enactment which had occasioned the great opinion, however, had but a short life. It had gone into effect in April, 1874. The next governor, Harrison Ludington, and the legislature elected with him in the autumn of 1875 were well-disposed towards the railroads, and in February, 1876, the Potter law was repealed. The commission of three men was replaced by one commissioner, who had no power to determine rates. Certain abuses, indeed, such as discrimination and unreasonable charges, were forbidden. Better times came, the Granger movement declined, and the railroads had learned to be cautious or considerate. With the return of the Republicans to power, the railroads were given a long respite.

LESSER PROTESTS, 1875 TO 1900

The part played by discontented farmers in ousting the Republicans and putting Taylor into office has sometimes been exaggerated. The first legislation regulating railroad rates was repealed within two years of its passage. Yet, despite all comment of this sort, Taylor's election and the passage of the Potter law are important if only as proof of discontent. A majority did, for once, vote against the Republicans, and probably considerably more than a majority believed that railroads should be regulated. Fifteen years were to pass before the Republicans again failed to elect a governor, but as these years went by there was an undercurrent of dissatisfaction still manifest. The Democrats were victorious in the election of 1890, and it is significant that the decline in Republican votes as compared with 1888 was several times the increase in Democratic votes.

The first protest of this period was the Greenback movement, whose history in Wisconsin falls within the years 1875-1884. At its height it made serious inroads into the Republican ranks, and many farmers saw in its proposals a relief from their economic distress. During the Civil War the federal government had issued legal-tender notes, commonly called greenbacks, which could not be exchanged for gold or silver. These notes depreciated in value, at their lowest point in 1864 being worth less than forty cents on the dollar. The panic of 1873 was the beginning of a depression that lasted almost to the end of the decade. In 1875 Congress set January 1, 1879, as the date when the United States would be prepared to redeem the greenbacks "in coin" on demand. The depression and the Specie Resumption act were the background of a widespread movement whose leaders asserted that the precious metals were inadequate and undesirable as currency and maintained there should be a paper currency, secured not by gold or silver, but by the credit and resources of the nation. In the East those chiefly interested were apparently urban workingmen, but in Wisconsin, as throughout the West, many farmers desired expansion of the currency in the belief that it would enhance the value of their products. Ranged with the farmers were many thoughtful business and professional men. The most prominent and respected leader of the movement in Wisconsin was Edward P. Allis of Milwaukee, a successful manufacturer of iron and steel products, who employed at that time about 1,800 men. Another who sought to lead was a journalist named Marcus M. Pomeroy, who cultivated the nickname of "Brick" Pomeroy. During the Civil War he had conducted a Democratic newspaper at La Crosse, and after 1863 he had abused Lincoln most violently. By 1868 he claimed to have 300,000 subscribers to his newspaper and was urging the repudiation of the national debt. At that time he established himself in New York City, where one edition of his paper called the New York *Democrat* was issued. In 1875 he removed to Chicago and during the next few years spent much time in Wisconsin and neighboring states establishing Greenback clubs. Some remarked that he made subscriptions to a Pomeroy newspaper a condition of membership.

In the presidential election of 1876 the Greenback vote in Wisconsin was but 1,509; in the following year, with Allis as their candidate for governor, they polled more than 26,000 votes. William E. Smith, the Republican candidate, was elected, but the Democratic and Greenback vote combined amounted to considerably more than Smith had received. In 1878, four Greenback and three Fusion (Democratic and Greenback) candidates for Congress polled 57,000 of a total of 206,000 votes, but none of them was elected. This election was the high water mark of the movement. Good crops and good prices in 1879 and 1880 took the heart out of protest, and when prosperity and not catastrophe accompanied the resumption of specie payment, the party's day was over. In the federal election of 1880 the Greenbackers were the main support of a "National" party led by General Weaver of

Iowa, who in Wisconsin received 7,980 votes. In 1884 the Green-backers had their own candidate for governor, but the party strength had sunk to about 4,000 votes.

The 1870's were marked by the Granger movement and the more successful part of the Greenback movement; during the 1890's the farmers' protest took the form of Populism. Between the two—in the 1880's—several great societies of dissatisfied farmers were founded. The Farmers' Alliance, originating in Texas, and a National Agricultural Wheel, originating in Arkansas, united in a Farmers' and Laborers' Union of America. A somewhat similar organization began in Cook County, Illinois, and was led by Milton George, editor of the *Western Rural* of Chicago. The group soon spread over several states, and took the name of the National Farmers' Alliance, although to distinguish it from the southern organization it was often called the Northwestern Alliance. Its object was "to unite the farmers of the United States for their protection against class legislation, and the encroachments of concentrated capital and the tyranny of monopoly; to oppose, in our respective political parties, the election of any candidate to office . . . who is not thoroughly in sympathy with the farmers' interests." This society was most popular in Kansas, Nebraska, Iowa, and Minnesota, but by 1883 there were state organizations in Wisconsin and Michigan as well. The order was most active about 1887, yet it seems not to have disturbed the Republican dominance in Wisconsin, which continued throughout the decade.

In the nation as a whole the next expression of agrarian discontent was the Populist movement, which had its greatest strength in the states west of the Missouri River. Robert Schilling, who had appeared in Milwaukee in 1878 as an organizer for the Knights of Labor, was the secretary of the national executive committee of the Populist party in 1891, charged with the duty of sending out publicity to several hundred newspapers. In 1894, the banner year of the party in the nation, it showed a strength of about 25,600 votes in Wisconsin. So many of these, however, were cast in the counties containing the larger industrial cities that it may be doubted whether more than ten or twelve thousand farmers voted Populist. The Wisconsin farmers were not in such a plight as those of Kansas, Nebraska, and the Dakotas, and though not without grievances, especially against the railroads, they were not attracted by the radical Populist proposals.

More significant than Populism for Wisconsin was the political overturn accomplished at the election of November, 1890, in which George W. Peck, a Democrat, defeated the Republican farm leader, William D. Hoard, who sought a second term as governor. All but one of the ten Congressmen chosen at the same time were Democrats. These changes were due to a variety of causes more fully discussed in the next chapter. One was a controversy about foreign language instruction in parochial schools occasioned by the passing of a law innocently meant as a forward step in education and child welfare. Probably more important than this law was the widespread dissatisfaction with the latest Republican tariff. A surprising abstention from voting resulted in a total poll of 45,000 less than in 1888. There was a decline of 43,600 in the number of Republican votes cast for governor, but an increase in Democratic votes of less than 5000. The Democratic vote increased in only twenty-seven counties, or less than half of them, and the largest increases were in the lake shore counties containing the manufacturing cities. Summed up, this indicated that while the farmers might not be satisfied with Republican rule, there had been few new converts among them to the Democratic party. Two years later Peck's plurality was greatly reduced and the Republicans captured four of the ten seats in the House of Representatives. In the elections of 1894 the Republicans won easily: the short Democratic era was over.

The most important change of the 1890's was one that was taking place within the Republican party itself. Old leaders and old methods were repudiated, and out of the ferment came the progressive movement, with its many aspects, one of them its appeal to farmers. For a generation progressivism was a mild agrarian crusade, in which the state came to the aid of the farmers in many ways.

AGRICULTURAL SOCIETIES IN THE TWENTIETH CENTURY

The early decades of the present century were marked by the rejuvenation of the Grange and the appearance of several new organizations of farmers in Wisconsin. Springing from economic causes and for the most part declaring economic purposes, these groups frequently sought legislation as a means toward the ends they had in view; their impress on the politics of Wisconsin was greater than their numbers might lead one to expect. Occasionally, indeed, the farmers and the organized workingmen of the cities, in spite of some fundamental divergencies of purpose, recognized each other as actual or potential allies.

The order of the Patrons of Husbandry or the Grange had over 20,000 members in Wisconsin in 1875, but after that it fell rapidly in numbers and influence, both in Wisconsin and in the nation. For twenty years, 1891 to 1911, it had less than 1,000 members in the state. There is only one local grange with a continuous history since the seventies. New activity began in 1912, but while many granges were organized, relatively few survived. The order in 1938 had about sixty granges and some 4,500 members in the state. It was localized in three areas, one about Walworth, one about Winnebago, and one about Oneida County. The southern and central groups do some cautious coöperative buying for their members. The northernmost group in the first flush of new organization after 1912 attempted to manage insurance companies and to conduct coöperative stores, but these ventures uniformly failed. In having a long past which the members revere, in its secret ritual, and in its greater emphasis on social intercourse, the Grange resembles a lodge more than it does the other agricultural societies.

The strongest farmers' organization to appear in Wisconsin has been the American Society of Equity. The credit for originating the society in Illinois about 1902 is given to J. A. Everitt, who had written a book, called *The Third Power,* to show that the farmers, if organized, might hold a place beside capital and labor. It encouraged farmers to combine and hold out for "dollar wheat." Prices went up to about that point, and it was counted a great victory. The society also started successful coöperative marketing of tobacco in Kentucky. Introduced into Wisconsin about 1905, the society soon had ten thousand members, and increased its membership rapidly during the World War. In 1920 it reached its peak with over nine hundred local societies and a membership of almost 29,000, fairly well distributed over the southern two-thirds of the state; since that time it has declined considerably.

While there were some coöperative enterprises among farmers before the equity society was organized, it has undoubtedly done much to educate rural America in the benefits of coöperation both in buying and selling. The society as such is not in business, but a group of Equity members frequently forms a corporate group to conduct a retail store and gain the advantages of buying in quantity. Even more characteristic of the society are the many combinations for marketing products. For example, the Wisconsin Cheese Federation, which was begun in Sheboygan County in 1912, was handling 28,000,000 pounds of cheese a year by 1924. Similar organizations exist for selling butter. There are four or five hundred livestock shipping associations in Wisconsin, nearly half of them originating within the equity society. Pools dealing in wool and tobacco have also been very successful. There were, to be sure, some failures: farmers who were members of the equity society set up seven meat-packing establishments with great loss to themselves. An attempt, in conjunction with the state federation of labor, to set up a store in Milwaukee proved an expensive fiasco.

Not all coöperation carried on by farmers should be linked with the equity society. Many groups that the Equity fostered still continue to do business, sometimes even with "Equity" in their firm name, even though none of the associates has been a member of the parent society for years. According to the federal census of 1930 about one-fourth of the 180,000 farmers in Wisconsin sold some of their produce through the instrumentality of coöperative societies; and this group of farmers sold but one-third of the total produce of their farms by this means. Today the value of coöperative marketing is a commonplace, urged in all the schools and aided by state and federal governments. Yet it is but a few years since it was a new gospel; the American Society of Equity did much to spread the evangel.

The constitution and by-laws of the American Society of Equity originally provided that no officer of the society, state or national, might be a candidate for political office, but after a few years this restriction was removed. Ordinarily the society puts what pressure it can on the legislature and is content merely to have a legislative committee for this purpose. In 1918, however, J. N. Tittemore, then president of the society in Wisconsin, ran for governor on a farmers' ticket nominated at a mass meeting of organized and unorganized farmers and laborers. He polled 46,000 votes at the primary. The only man endorsed at that meeting to be elected was J. J. Blaine, candidate for the office of attorney general, who had support in other quarters as well.

The American Farm Bureau Federation resembles and competes with the equity society. The movement began in the East as a coöperative effort of farmers and county agricultural agents, and spread through the United States. In Wisconsin it began in 1920, and by the close of the following year it had risen to its greatest strength of more than nine thousand members, only to fall within three years to but a third as many. It was most popular in the tier of counties adjoining Illinois. The farm bureau serves its members, as does the equity society, in purchasing in quantity farm necessities such as fertilizers, sprays, fencing, and binding twine, in addition to urging farmers' needs before the legislature.

The Nonpartisan League was a farmers' movement that originated in North Dakota about 1915. The American Society of Equity had prepared the way by its insistence upon coöperation and combination, but professed to keep out of the political field. The Nonpartisan League, on the other hand, intended to become the political master of the state, and in North Dakota, where farmers and their families made up 80 per cent of the population, their plan was feasible.   The farmers felt that the state should rescue them from the necessity of giving all their profits to the businessmen with whom they dealt.   As matters stood the farmers could not avoid doing business with certain big corporations, and they felt that these organizations squeezed all the profits out of farming.   Moreover, these same big interests controlled the machinery of state government.   The program of the Nonpartisan League as worked out in North Dakota, therefore, was to have the state own terminal elevators, flour mills, stockyards, packing houses, and cold storage plants.   The state should manage the grading of grain, finance hail insurance, and conduct rural credit banks operated at cost.   The burden of taxation should be readjusted to the farmers' advantage.   The league sought not to found a new party but to take control of the dominant party in each state.   In North Dakota it seized the machinery of the Republican party; in Montana, of the Democratic; in Minnesota it shaped up the Farmer-Labor party; and in Wisconsin, where it never became numerous enough to control the state, it affiliated with the La Follette progressive group.

In 1917 an organizer from North Dakota invaded Wisconsin, and until the end of 1920 the league grew rapidly.   At its height it claimed over 22,000 members.   For most of the year 1920 it published a weekly paper.   Those who joined the league were supposed to pay a fee of $18 for their first two years, but many never paid this amount in full.   Almost its only expression of political power in Wisconsin occurred in 1920, when it, along with the La Follette progressives, endorsed John J. Blaine for governor, and claimed great influence in shaping the Republican platform. After that it disappeared as rapidly as it had risen.

No organization of farmers since 1920 has had a prominence in politics equal to that temporarily enjoyed by the Nonpartisan League.   In recent years the farmers, while still in politics, have pinned their hopes of economic betterment more and more on coöperative organizations. As we have seen, these had long been known in some form in Wisconsin. The state has increasingly helped in their formation. A Wisconsin statute of 1911 so defined the rights of coöperative groups that it was widely copied. A law of 1921 said that the department of markets might give assistance in the formation of coöperatives, and one of 1929 directed the giving of such aid. Pursuant to the law of 1929, the department of agriculture and markets, which had been formed in the meantime, not only encouraged local organization, but also helped initiate several state-wide marketing organizations, each concerned with a single product. Large bodies were created to handle milk, wool, livestock, potatoes, and other commodities. It is admittedly impossible for such groups either to limit production or to attain a monopoly and thereby fix prices. They can benefit the farmers, however, in several ways. By holding back a seasonal or an annual surplus and carefully feeding the market, they can improve the farmers' bargaining power and stabilize prices. They may also tap credit resources not accessible to the individual farmer and arrange loans secured by commodities held in association warehouses. By means of advertising they enlarge existing markets, and they teach farmers to grade and pack their products the better to attract the buying public.

Consumer coöperatives seek to buy to advantage for distribution or resale to members. The purchase of machinery and other farm necessities by the equity society and similar groups early in the present century has been mentioned, and some of the marketing coöperatives have regularly bought in quantity for their members. There are at present perhaps seventy coöperatives in Wisconsin conducting general stores or groceries. The most numerous group is the oil coöperatives, which numbered 163 at the end of 1936. Some of them are in urban centers but nearly all are composed of farmers. As retail outlets grow more numerous, wholesale plants are established to serve them. About sixty-five oil coöperatives in Wisconsin in 1936 held stock in and were served by the Midland Coöperative Wholesale, which had its principal office in Minneapolis and a warehouse in Milwaukee. The Central Coöperative Wholesale of Superior, Wisconsin, whose main business is groceries, is the largest institution of its kind in the United States.

Several other kinds of coöperatives exist. More than 80 per cent of all farm fire insurance risk in Wisconsin is carried by about two hundred town mutuals, which are regional coöperative organizations of farmers. Their rates are only half those of the stock companies, partly because there is no expense for solicitation and much of the managerial work is done without charge. From 1936 onward automobile insurance and urban property fire insurance were to be had on a coöperative basis. Credit unions— small coöperative banks—first appeared in Wisconsin when two were founded in Milwaukee in 1922. In 1930 the state banking commission sent out a credit union field organizer, and after that growth was so rapid that Wisconsin led all other states in the field. In 1935 the headquarters of the Credit Union National Association (CUNA) was moved to Madison. By the end of 1938 there were in Wisconsin 552 credit union banks, which are the only type of coöperative that has flourished more in urban centers than among farmers. Especially since 1933, encouragement from state and federal authorities has led to the formation of many coöperative groups, some to borrow money through the Farm Credit Administration or other government agency, others to deal with the Rural Electrification Administration, which lends money to bring electric service to farmers. The facilities of the two last-named organizations are not available to urban coöperatives.

Coöperatives have come to play a very important part in rural life. As can be imagined from the foregoing pages, many farmers are members of more than one coöperative group. It is not possible to say just how many farmers are and how many are not members, but the best estimate available in 1938 was that about 85 per cent had joined at least one coöperative society. Forty per cent of all cheese factories in Wisconsin are owned coöperatively, and two-thirds of Wisconsin's butter comes from coöperative creameries. With many differences of detail, the coöperative has become for the farmer what the trade union is to the urban worker, a very present help in trouble and a tool for every purpose. A state law of 1935 added coöperative marketing to the list of subjects that must be taught in every common school and required all institutions engaged in teacher training to provide "adequate and essential instruction in co-operative marketing and consumers' co-operatives."

In 1928 many existing groups of farmers formed the Wisconsin Council of Agriculture. The Grange and the Farm Bureau Federation were included, but nearly all of the thirty-four ordinary member societies in 1938 were coöperatives. The alphabetical list began with the Antigo Milk Products Coöperative and ended with the Wisconsin Swiss and Limburger Cheese Producers' Coöperative Association. There were also six *ex officio* members, headed by the College of Agriculture of the University of Wisconsin. The purpose of the council is to express the collective mind of the farmers of the state. It seeks to influence legislation in the interests of farmers, but it has no intention of promoting a political party.

SELECTED BIBLIOGRAPHY

The claim association of southeastern Wisconsin is described in Joseph Schafer, *Four Wisconsin Counties* (Wisconsin Domesday Book, Madison, 1927), pp. 69-80. Benjamin F. Shambaugh generalizes about such associations over a wider area in "Frontier Land Clubs and Claim Associations," American Historical Association *Report, 1900,* Vol. I, pp. 67-84. The best account of the railroad farm mortgage troubles and the anti-monopoly movement of the Civil War period is found in Frederick Merk, *Economic History of Wisconsin During the Civil War Decade* (Madison, 1916).

Solon J. Buck, *The Granger Movement* (Harvard Historical Studies, Cambridge, 1913), besides the valuable text has an extensive bibliography and copious footnotes. The same author's *The Agrarian Crusade* (Chronicles of America, Vol. 45, New Haven, 1920), covers the same ground more briefly and carries the narrative to 1896. Agricultural conditions and the Potter law are discussed in *Wisconsin in Three Centuries* (4 vols., New York, 1906), Vol. IV, pp. 103-121. Lawyers' estimates of the work of Edward G. Ryan may be found in Parker McCobb Reed, *The Bench and Bar of Wisconsin: History and Biography* (Milwaukee, 1882); *History of the Bench and Bar of Wisconsin,* prepared under the direction of John R. Berryman (2 vols., Chicago, 1898); and John B. Winslow, *The Story of a Great Court* (Chicago, 1912). Ryan's decision in the Potter law cases is given in *Wisconsin Reports,* Vol. XXXV, pp. 425-608.

Orin G. Libby wrote "A Study of the Greenback Movement, 1876-1884," *Transactions* of the Wisconsin Academy of Science, Arts and Letters, Vol. XII (1898), pp. 530-543. More detailed is Ellis B. Usher, *The Greenback Movement of 1875-1884 and Wisconsin's Part in It* (Milwaukee, 1911). There is a chapter on the same subject in Fred L. Haynes, *Third Party Movements since the Civil War with Special Reference to Iowa* (Iowa City, 1916). John D. Hicks, *The Populist Movement* (Minneapolis, 1931), though necessarily dealing more largely with other states, has some data on Wisconsin.

Much information about coöperatives is to be found in the *Biennial Report of the Department of Agriculture and Markets,* 1930-1932, pp. 50-61; and in the same report, 1935-1936, pp. 309-311. Dean Chris L. Christensen and others from the staff of the College of Agriculture, University of Wisconsin, prepared a manual, *Coöperation Principles and Practices* (Madison, 1936, 128 pp.), which has excellent reading lists. Harold M. Groves gives a very inclusive survey in "Consumer Coöperation in Wisconsin," *Blue Book, 1937,* pp. 209-228.

CHAPTER XIV

REPUBLICAN RULE, 1866–1901

How the Republicans Ruled

O N THE political stage in Wisconsin during the last third of the nineteenth century, the chief role was played by the Republican party. After the Civil War it claimed great credit for saving the Union. It was able to reward its members with federal office, and every postmaster and internal revenue collector worked zealously for the hand that fed him. In each locality the Republican rank and file met in caucus and chose delegates to county conventions; these in turn chose delegates to the state convention; and this body named the candidates on the state ticket and approved a platform.

But the business on the floor of the convention was not conducted at mere haphazard. There were leaders who met in consultation and made decisions beforehand; the results of their deliberations were merely ratified by the convention. Some of these leaders made up the state central committee. This group, which grew in thirty years from about twelve to more than twenty men, was the executive staff of the party. It carried on the work from one annual convention to the next, settled questions of election strategy, and often had a large part in shaping the platform and making up the list of candidates. The committee naturally kept in close touch with the Republican part of the Wisconsin delegation at Washington, which was usually the larger part. It also had the task, not always an easy one, of raising funds for party use, although it assessed without hesitation office holders elected with its assistance. The Democratic party had a similar organization, except that it did not have the spoils of office to distribute, and most of the time no hopes in that direction.

To outsiders the men highest in the councils of the Republican party in Wisconsin constituted a political "machine." In the late sixties three men were called the "Regency," so great was their influence. One of them, Horace Rublee, went as minister to Switzerland; another died; the third, who remained in Wisconsin, was Elisha W. Keyes, long known throughout the state as "Boss" Keyes. He was a native of Vermont and came to Wisconsin with his parents when he was nine years old. After studying law he held various offices, among others those of district attorney of Dane County and postmaster at Madison. In 1869 he became chairman of the state central committee, and his power was greatest during the ensuing eight or ten years. With the aid of the Republicans at Washington he dispensed a good deal of the federal patronage, and had large influence in deciding upon nominations for state and local offices. His very power, however, tended to rouse hostility. Ex-Governor Washburn called him "a most unscrupulous ring politician."

Several things occurred in the later seventies to lessen Keyes' power. In the winter of 1874-1875, Benjamin H. Bristow, the energetic Secretary of the Treasury in President Grant's cabinet, began uncovering an intricate criminal organization known as the "whiskey ring," composed of distillers and others engaged in the manufacture and sale of spirits and acting in collusion with dishonest revenue officers and politicians. Its chief purpose was to escape the payment of legal duties on whiskey and other spirits, and undoubtedly it defrauded the federal government of several million dollars. Along with St. Louis and Chicago, Milwaukee was the scene of much of the dishonesty. In June, 1876, a number of the guilty men from Milwaukee, in testifying before a congressional committee in Washington, asserted that assessments had been made upon them by "Boss" Keyes, specifically, in one case, to aid in securing the re-election of Senator Carpenter. Keyes and Carpenter both claimed that these witnesses had perjured themselves, but the matter had been widely commented upon in the newspapers, and Keyes' power was undermined. The whole episode, together with the lenient attitude of President Grant toward some of the culprits, clouded the reputation of the Republican party, and there was a rising demand for the end of "machine" control.

In June, 1877, President Hayes issued his famous "Order No. 1," which forbade federal office holders to direct political organizations and prohibited the assessment of them for political purposes. Keyes, rather than give up the postmastership at Madison, resigned from the chairmanship of the Republican state central committee. In 1879, and again two years later, he was a candidate for the United States senatorship, but was not chosen. These defeats marked the end of his period of great power and relegated him to a place of local rather than state-wide leadership. No one man definitely fell heir to his scepter, but until the triumph of the progressive movement in 1900, the most influential Republican leaders were Philetus Sawyer of Oshkosh, Henry C. Payne of Milwaukee, and John C. Spooner of Madison.

After each federal census from 1850 to 1900 Wisconsin's representation in the lower house of Congress was increased. During the fifties Wisconsin had three Representatives. Beginning with the Congress elected in 1862 she had six, and then decade by decade, the number rose to eight, to nine, and to ten. From 1860 to 1900 Republicans won seven-tenths of all the congressional elections. Up to the election of 1894 there were usually two or three Democrats in the Wisconsin delegation, Milwaukee and the district around Fond du Lac being most persistently Democratic. Only three times—in 1862, in 1890, and in 1892—did the Democrats gain a majority. From 1894 until 1902 no Democrat was elected to Congress.

The two highest prizes that the dominant party could bestow were the offices of United States Senator, throughout this period still filled by election in the legislature. Wisconsin sent able men to the Senate; James R. Doolittle, supporter of Andrew Johnson, was followed by Matthew H. Carpenter, a flashing orator who sometimes made bold to prick the dignity of the great Sumner of Massachusetts. But Carpenter was thought to be a defender of the corruption of the Grant regime, and was not re-elected in 1875, in spite of all "Boss" Keyes could do for him. In this result ex-Governor Washburn had a hand. Timothy O. Howe held a seat in the Senate from 1861 to 1879. His greatest ambition was to be appointed to the Supreme Court of the United States, but an odd turn of fate denied him this honor. When Chief Justice Chase died in May, 1873, President Grant offered the vacant post to Howe, but this happened to be one of the rare occasions when the Democrats were in power in Wisconsin, and Howe was loyal enough to his party not to give Governor Taylor the opportunity to appoint, nor the legislature the chance to elect, a Democrat in his place. Howe was named Postmaster General by President Arthur and died in office in 1883. Philetus Sawyer, wealthy lumberman and capitalist, who had served ten years in the lower house, was sent to the Senate in 1881, and served two terms. His great wealth solved some of the troubles of the Republican campaign chest, and only gradually was it realized that the impact of great wealth was altering political life. The Republicans had an exceptionally able man in John C. Spooner, a railroad attorney and polished orator, who was first chosen for the Senate in 1885, and then again in 1897.

Fairchild and Washburn

Beginning in 1866, and for a third of a century, governors of Wisconsin were, with but few exceptions, chosen from among those who had served in the Civil War. The first of these ex-soldiers was Lucius C. Fairchild. He was the second son of Jairus C. Fairchild, a merchant who came to Madison in 1846, already a man of means, and engaged in business there until his death in 1862. The elder Fairchild was the first treasurer of the state of Wisconsin, serving under Nelson Dewey for two terms, and was also the first mayor of Madison.   His son Lucius was in the California gold diggings from 1849 to 1855, and there accumulated a competence.   During the war he commanded one of the regiments of the Iron Brigade, losing an arm at Gettysburg.   In 1863 he was elected secretary of state for Wisconsin, and in January, 1866, when but thirty-four years old, he began his six years as chief executive.

During Fairchild's governorship the state closed many matters of wartime business.   Railroad building was resumed, but popular discontent with railroad rate making was increasing, and Governor Fairchild repeatedly asked for a commission to study the apparently conflicting rights of the railroads and their patrons, the public.   The state established an immigration commission, and its activity both in the United States and in Europe, aided by the Homestead Law of 1862 and the natural movement of population, brought in a new stream of home and farm makers, so that by 1870 the population had risen to more than a million.   The legislature spent much time with bills relating to private business enterprises, and there was considerable logrolling, and talk of wicked lobbying and bribery.   In 1871 a bill to incorporate the Chippewa Improvement and Booming Company, commonly called the "Dells Bill," passed both houses.   The lumber interests of Eau Claire had sought to get this bill through the legislature at several sessions.   Governor Fairchild vetoed it, however, giving as his reason his conviction that it had been passed only by the help of purchased votes.

Governor Fairchild was still a comparatively young man in 1872 when his six years as governor were ended.   For nine years he represented the United States abroad: first as consul at Liverpool, then as consul-general at Paris, and finally for a short time as the United States Minister at Madrid.   After his return home he was not a candidate for office again.   He would gladly have gone to the United States Senate, but the Republican politicians of the eighties decided otherwise.   He was active in the Grand Army of the Republic, served on a commission to negotiate with the Cherokee Indians, and in other ways continued a beneficent semi-public life until his death in 1896.

Cadwallader C. Washburn, who followed Fairchild as governor, like him had given distinguished service in the Civil War. A native of Maine, he was probably the ablest of seven brothers, four of whom went to Congress from as many states, and two of whom became governors, one in Maine, he in Wisconsin. Self-supporting from the age of eighteen, he had by the time he reached his majority clerked in a store, taught school, and read some law. After living for three years at various points along the Mississippi River in Illinois and Iowa, he established himself as a lawyer at Mineral Point. In 1844 he entered into partnership there with Cyrus Woodman, and the two of them acquired a good deal of pine and mineral land in Wisconsin. This proved to be the foundation of Washburn's considerable fortune. After the Civil War his business interests expanded greatly, and at the time of his death in 1882 his property was valued at between two and three million dollars. He served six years in the lower house of Congress before the Civil War and four after it. During the war he rose to the rank of brigadier general, and won nation-wide respect.

When Lucius Fairchild declined a fourth term as governor, Washburn was the choice of the party, and was easily elected. He brought wide experience and recognized integrity to the governorship and might have been expected to hold office for two or three terms. Two acts of his administration, however, raised up political enemies against him: the passage of the Graham law, and the veto of the La Crosse Bridge bill.

Another wave of anti-alcoholic sentiment was at its crest. The most earnest organization for forwarding this movement was the Lodge of Good Templars, which was widespread in Wisconsin, especially of course among those of Puritan traditions. A member of the assembly from Rock County, Alexander Graham, introduced the bill commonly called by his name. It required the deposit of a bond of $2,000 for the issue of a license to sell liquor, contained a civil damage clause with a long list of possible claimants, and imposed a heavy penalty for drunkenness. The bill passed both houses by ample majorities and was signed by Governor Washburn. In the following year, 1873, the requirement that the Graham law be regarded as a part of every city charter made it still more stringent and difficult of evasion. In passing the law and thus standing by it, the Republican party in Wisconsin came into collision with the opinions of large numbers of citizens, particularly those of German extraction. It seems probable, though absolute proof is lacking, that brewers and distillers furnished considerable money in 1873 to finance Taylor's campaign against Washburn.

The second legislature of Washburn's term passed a bill authorizing the Milwaukee and St. Paul Railroad to construct a bridge across the Mississippi River at La Crosse. Washburn vetoed it because such a bridge might interfere with navigation on the Mississippi; he maintained it should be built, if at all, with the permission of the federal government and under the supervision of the War Department. Alexander Mitchell, president of the railway company, had long been a leader in the Democratic party and was especially eager to defeat Washburn.

When, as in the case of Washburn's defeat by Taylor, several factors enter into an election, it is difficult to say which is most important. The Republican party was suspect in some quarters and there was a Liberal Reform organization in the nation which had a Wisconsin branch. This supported Taylor in 1873, but it probably appealed to the zealous few rather than to the masses. As indicated in the preceding chapter, it used to be taken as a matter of course that Washburn fell a victim to the Granger movement. Apparently, however, the reaction against the Graham law was more fatal than the griefs of the farmers. Washburn had written a day or two before the election: "The combined powers of darkness, Whiskey, Beer, Railroads and a sprinkling of Grangers, have been on my trail and are confident of my defeat." His single term as governor proved to be Washburn's last public office. He died, a very wealthy man, in May, 1882.

THE HEYDAY OF THE REPUBLICAN PARTY

After the Democratic-Reform regime of William R. Taylor, the Republicans recaptured the governor's chair and held it for fifteen years (January, 1876-January, 1891). Harrison Ludington, member of a successful business family of Milwaukee and mayor of that city when the Graham law was greatly troubling the German element, won their special favor by delaying the enforcement of that law and temporarily defying the state authorities. As Republican candidate for governor in the fall of 1875 he defeated Taylor, who sought re-election, by less than a thousand votes. As noted in the preceding chapter, the Potter law was repealed and the railroad commission was reduced to one man and a secretary and had no power to control railroad rates. Because of the three-cornered contest and the good showing of Edward P. Allis, the Greenback candidate for governor, William B. Smith, the victorious Republican candidate in the election of 1877, was placed in office as the choice of a minority of the voters. Two years later, however, he was supported by a majority.

Jeremiah Rusk was governor of Wisconsin for seven years, beginning in January, 1882. In order to bring the election for state offices into the even numbered years, along with congressional and presidential elections, his first term was made three years. At the same time the regular sessions of the legislature were changed from annual to biennial. Rusk, or "Uncle Jerry," as he was familiarly called, had been a farmer, hotel-keeper, sheriff of Vernon County, a colonel during the Civil War, member of Congress, and bank controller before he was elected governor. Weighing about 250 pounds, with abundant gray hair and beard, he was a patriarchal figure. He spoke his mind with unadorned directness; once he had chosen his course, he acted with vigor and promptness. Many temperance advocates were in 1881 in the process of final withdrawal from the Republican party, and the Republicans, in the hope of holding them, put in their platform an ambiguous statement on the temperance issue. After his nomination Rusk announced in a public letter that the question of prohibition was purely a moral one and should not be permitted to enter into politics.

A railroad company, the Chicago, Portage and Superior, was engaged in construction work in the northwestern part of the state. It went into bankruptcy owing several months' wages to more than a thousand laborers. The men refused to seek work elsewhere until they were paid. While some remained in the construction camp, others paraded the streets of Superior, and, since they were without resources, they had to be fed at public charge. To emphasize their claims some of the men set fire to a railway bridge. The authorities of Superior in alarm asked the governor for soldiers to maintain order and protect property. Governor Rusk replied that bread was needed, not bayonets, and at the same time promised the men that their just claims would be met. He also made an arrangement with the Omaha company that they should complete the line and take over the land grant of the defunct corporation, but should also deposit with the state $75,000 to be used in paying the men and those who had furnished provisions for them. This plan was immediately embodied in an act by the legislature (February, 1882), the men soon found work elsewhere, and the crisis passed.

In May, 1886, Milwaukee was in the throes of labor difficulties. The mayor and the sheriff of Milwaukee County both informed the governor that disorder and destruction of property were imminent. Rusk soon had seventeen companies of militia on the ground to preserve order, declaring that the working men had full right to strike and to bargain, but that they must operate within the limits of the law. The most serious trouble occurred at the plant of the Illinois Steel Company at Bay View. The plant was protected by a company of the National Guard drawn from Milwaukee. Angered particularly by opposition from these soldiers, many of them workingmen from their own city, the strikers attacked them. Warnings and a harmless volley proving ineffective, the soldiers fired and seven persons were killed. Rusk took full responsibility, simply making the oft-quoted comment: "I seen my duty and I done it." The laboring element of some of the cities bitterly condemned Rusk, but throughout the state there was as yet little sympathy with or understanding of labor's aims, and Governor Rusk's re-election six months later by an increased majority showed the general approval of his firmness.

Rusk was the first governor to occupy the house that for more than half a century has been the executive mansion. Interesting associations from an even earlier date attach to the house, which was erected by Joseph G. Thorp, a wealthy lumberman of Eau Claire. There Thorp's daughter was courted by the famous Norwegian violinist, Ole Bull, and in 1870 she became his second wife. Henry Wadsworth Longfellow, while a guest in this house, wrote the beautiful little poem entitled "The Four Lakes." Rusk bought the house, made it his home for several years, and in 1885 sold it to the state for $20,000.

After his long service as governor, Rusk became, under President Harrison, the first secretary of the newly created Department of Agriculture. He died in 1893.

William D. Hoard, dairy authority and editor, was the candidate of the Republican party for governor in 1888. Opponents spoke of him as the "cow candidate," but his election was really a recognition of the growing importance of dairying in the state. Governor Hoard's message to the legislature called attention to the needs of farmers and dairymen, and several enactments of 1889 were for their benefit. The office of dairy and food commissioner was created, and laws were passed forbidding the imitation or adulteration of milk, butter, and cheese. Milk to be sold must have a certain amount of butter fat. Other matters that were made the subject of legislation were: the increase of the National Guard from thirty-six to forty-two companies; the acquisition of land at Camp Douglas in Juneau County for a permanent camp and rifle range for the National Guard; and provision for the general adoption throughout the state of the "Australian" system of secret voting.

No law passed in 1889 provoked as much subsequent discussion as the so-called Bennett law. It was entitled: "An Act concerning the education and employment of children." The law required every child between the ages of seven and fourteen to attend some public or private school "in the city, town or district in which he resides" for a period of not less than twelve weeks in each year. "No school shall be regarded as a school unless there shall be taught therein . . . reading, writing and arithmetic and United States history in the English language." The employment of children under thirteen years of age was forbidden, except in cases of necessity, and in those cases a permit was to be secured from the county judge. The whole was designed simply as a forward step in the interests of youth. Democrats as well as Republicans voted for it, and no one, apparently, foresaw what a tempest it was to unloose.

Between the enactment of the law in April, 1889, and the elections in the fall of 1890, the Democrats discovered that they had in it an excellent weapon to use against the Republicans. The requirement of attendance in the district of the child's residence angered the supporters of parochial schools; both Lutheran pastors and the Roman Catholic hierarchy used their influence against the Republicans. The Democrats also asserted that the law was an attempt to legislate against instruction in a foreign tongue, and sought the votes of the Germans and Scandinavians on this issue. Governor Hoard, who was seeking re-election, met the challenge squarely, proclaiming his loyalty to the "Little Red Schoolhouse," and to what a later generation called "One hundred per cent Americanism."

There is reason to believe, however, that bitter as was the feeling against the Bennett law among some groups in Wisconsin, the Republicans would have been defeated in 1890 had there been no such law. Another wave of protest against Republican rule was running high throughout the West. In some quarters the Populist movement was taking shape, in others the people were turning to the Democratic party. The currency question was up again, this time in the form of "free silver," while the passage of the McKinley tariff in October, 1890, was sharply condemned by the farmers. In Wisconsin the congressional delegation was changed from seven Republicans and two Democrats to one Republican and eight Democrats. The same thing occurred in all the neighboring states. Wisconsin, Michigan, Illinois, Iowa, and Minnesota taken together chose forty-seven Republicans and nine Democrats in 1888, fifteen Republicans and forty-one Democrats in 1890. Clearly the political overturn in Wisconsin had causes other than the Bennett law.

The End of the Century and the Close of an Era

For fifteen years the Republicans had had things pretty much their own way in Wisconsin. The last ten years of the nineteenth century, however, offer something of a contrast to what had gone before. Democratic control lasted for four years, and the six years that followed show a different temper from what had prevailed during the heyday of the Republicans. Thirty-five years had passed since the Civil War, and old loyalties were failing to bind the younger generation. The Democratic victory of 1890 was due largely to economic ills, and when the hard times of 1893 showed that the Democratic party had no magic formula for prosperity, the majority, still at heart Republican, returned to its traditional moorings, but in a critical frame of mind. In the closing years of the century the Progressive movement led by the elder La Follette was getting under way. The whole movement meant, of course, that many were dissatisfied with things as they were. This attitude, even on the part of many Republicans, must be borne in mind as an ever-present factor in the time of Governors Peck, Upham, and Scofield.

George W. Peck, governor from 1891 to 1895, came to Wisconsin as a child and began learning the printer's trade in Whitewater at the age of fifteen. Except for his service in the Civil War and his tenure of the governor's office, he was engaged in newspaper work most of his life. In 1874 he started a paper of his own at La Crosse called the *Sun,* and a few years later moved it to Milwaukee, where it gradually grew into a thriving enterprise with 80,000 subscribers. All this while Peck was winning recognition as a humorous writer, his best-known production being *Peck's Bad Boy,* which first appeared serially in the *Sun.*

The two incidents of the Democratic administration that occasioned the most discussion and partisan feeling were the treasury suits and the reapportionment of the districts of state senators and assemblymen. For many years it had been the practice of the state treasurer to deposit in various banks the state funds not actually needed from day to day. The banks paid interest on the deposits; from this source, in the 1880's, the treasurers were receiving from $25,000 to $30,000 a year which they retained as personal gain, subject only to heavy assessments for party expenses. Those who knew the facts had occasionally criticized the practice, and the Democrats not only determined to end it, but, asserting that money earned by state funds belonged to the state, they brought suit against a number of former treasurers and their bondsmen to compel them to pay these profits of many years into the state treasury. The first cases, which were tried in the circuit court of Dane County, went in favor of the state. A few months later, in January, 1893, on appeal, the supreme court confirmed in almost every detail the opinion of the lower court. The judgments in all amounted to $725,000, and of this sum about $373,000 was actually turned back to the state. Not all the suits were finished when, as a result of the election of 1894, the Republicans returned to control, both in the governor's office and in the legislature. In spite of election pledges to the contrary, the legislature in 1895 passed an act discontinuing the pending suits. One former treasurer was released from a balance due of some $50,000, and two others who had been ordered by the lower courts to restore $228,-000 escaped altogether.

There had been no reapportionment of the state into senate and assembly districts since 1877, and this fact, together with the fresh statistics of population furnished by the federal census of 1890, called for a new deal. The apportionment act that was passed, however, was a flagrant gerrymander designed to perpetuate Democratic power. In areas known to be strongly Republican the districts were made to contain three times as many people as where they were Democratic. Furthermore, the law violated the constitution by running district boundaries across counties instead of always following county lines. The Republicans brought the matter before the supreme court, and the court declared the first reapportionment act unconstitutional. In a special session in June, 1892, a second reapportionment was made, not much better than the first, and it too was declared unconstitutional. Again the legislature was called together, and this time it passed an act that was allowed to stand for four years. At that time the secretary of state was Thomas J. Cunningham, and the cases brought before the supreme court are commonly referred to as the Cunningham cases.

During the years when the Democrats were in power the legislature named two United States Senators. For their first they had in William Freeman Vilas one of the national leaders of the party. Already eminent in Wisconsin as a lawyer, he achieved national fame as an orator by a speech given at a banquet tendered to General Grant in 1879. He was made Postmaster General in Cleveland's first cabinet and then in 1887 was transferred to the Department of the Interior. In 1891 he took the place of John C. Spooner in the Senate. Though that body had a Democratic majority, it was not in entire harmony with Cleveland, and, since Senator Vilas was recognized as a counsellor and mouthpiece of the President, he was scarcely a leader in the Senate. In 1893 the legislature chose John L. Mitchell, son of Alexander Mitchell, to succeed Philetus Sawyer. During the early nineties the free silver doctrine was gaining ground among the Democrats, but Vilas, like President Cleveland, believed strongly in maintaining the gold standard. In 1896 Bryan made his "cross of gold" speech and the party accepted the free silver doctrine. This meant that Vilas' leadership was repudiated, and when his term as Senator expired his political career was ended.

The cause of the Republicans was admittedly almost hopeless in 1892, but they chose John C. Spooner, whose first term in the United States Senate had ended the year before, as their candidate for governor, and embarked on a campaign of education. Wisconsin's twelve electoral votes were cast for Cleveland that year, but the Democratic tide had already begun to recede. Ten Congressmen were chosen; four of them were Republican, instead of but one, as two years earlier. The hard times of 1893 discredited the Democrats throughout the North, and in 1894 Wisconsin returned to the Republican fold, sending ten Republican Congressmen to Washington and capturing the governorship and both houses of the state legislature.

William Henry Upham, a native of Massachusetts, came with his widowed mother to Racine when he was twelve years old. In 1861 he entered the Union Army, and at the first battle of Bull Run he was wounded and left for dead. President Lincoln appointed him to West Point and after graduating there he remained in the artillery service of the regular army until the end of 1869. Ten years later he settled at Marshfield, in Wood County, Wisconsin, and there, beginning with a saw and shingle mill, he set up one by one a number of business enterprises. After the first mill came a furniture factory, a general store, a machine shop, a flour mill, and the First National Bank. In fact, he was the maker of the town. In 1887, he suffered a great loss by fire, and while he was able to rebuild at once, his properties carried heavy mortgages until he retired from business many years later.

While in 1894 Democratic strength almost vanished for the time in Wisconsin, a cleavage was beginning to appear in the Republican ranks. Against the leadership of former Senator Sawyer, Henry C. Payne of Milwaukee, and others, new forces were rising. In the Republican convention of 1894 the younger men supported, as their nominee for governor, Nils P. Haugen, a lawyer of River Falls, a Norwegian by birth, and the only Republican Congressman not defeated in 1890. But the "machine" men prevailed and Upham was their choice. He was elected by an unprecedented majority of over 50,000. Functioning at this time was a society called the American Protective Association, or popularly, the A. P. A., devoted to the preservation of native American institutions and violently anti-Catholic. Obviously a recurrence of the nativism of earlier generations, this society was active in Wisconsin during the nineties and claimed to have brought about Upham's victory, though Upham himself gave it little credit.

The new governor had to take up the administration at a time when the Republicans had been out of office for four years. Hard times had turned an unusual number of Republicans into office seekers. Upham had to deny the requests of most applicants and his lack of political experience made the task very irksome to him. Nevertheless, the legislature carried out many of his suggestions. A school for the feeble-minded was established at Chippewa Falls. The first steps were taken towards the erection of a fire-proof building for the State Historical Society. The legislature also ended the suits against the former treasurers. This bill Upham signed against his own better judgment and frankly in deference to the considered opinion of the majority of the legislature and of several party chiefs, Sawyer among them. For this the governor was severely criticized. In a special session in 1896 a reapportionment act was passed that replaced the handiwork of the Democrats under Governor Peck. As his term drew to a close Upham decided that he must devote himself to his private business affairs.

Edward Scofield was the last of the honorable line of Civil War veterans in the governor's chair. Some time after the war he became the foreman of a lumber mill at Oconto, and eventually he established his own lumber business there. Four years as state senator (1887-1891) had given him some familiarity with the administration and politics of the state. Like Upham he was a "machine" candidate. The younger men tried to gain the nomination for Robert M. La Follette, but to no avail; Scofield was nominated and elected. The year 1896 was marked by the free silver campaign. William J. Bryan charmed Wisconsin audiences, but many "Gold Democrats" bolted and formed a separate organization; and many others voted for McKinley.

The administration of Governor Scofield was admirably businesslike. He discovered that the state treasurer was accustomed to ask the railroads to pay their taxes in advance, and that only by securing what was in effect a loan was a deficit avoided. A special tax in 1897 and 1898 met the deficit and ended a practice that put the state officers under what might be an embarrassing obligation. A corrupt practice act required candidates and party committees to file statements of campaign expenses. The legislature of 1897 passed a bill laying certain taxes on express and sleeping car companies. Alleging that in its haste the legislature in passing these tax laws had not proceeded as required by law, Scofield vetoed the two bills. His critics asserted that he cared for the corporations more than for the interests of the people.

A rising tide of dissatisfaction gave increasing strength to the protesting or reforming group in the Republican party. In 1898 the old element named the candidate for governor again, desiring that Scofield should succeed himself, as he did, but the platform was written by the reformers. During his first term Scofield had used railroad passes; in his second, in recognition of public feeling, he returned those sent to him; and in May, 1899, he signed an anti-pass law. Taxes were laid on the property, but not on the income, of express and sleeping car companies. And as a step in preparation for equalizing taxes, a tax commission of three members, intended at first to be merely a temporary body, was authorized by the legislature and appointed by the governor. An act was also passed to diminish the evils of lobbying. In comparison with what was to be accomplished early in the twentieth century these measures seem small, but they show the setting of the current toward new conditions. In 1900 Robert M. La Follette captured the Republican nomination and was elected governor.

During Governor Scofield's administration the war with Spain occurred. This brief and unequal struggle lasted from April 19, 1898, to the signing of a preliminary peace or protocol at Washington on August 12, though there was fighting thereafter in the Philippine Islands. The final treaty of peace was concluded at Paris on December 10 of the same year. Wisconsin's four regiments of the National Guard were called in the order of the seniority of their commanders in the Guard. First came the Third Regiment from the region north and west of the Wisconsin River. The Second, which was called next, was from the various points in the eastern half of the state from Beaver Dam northward, excluding Milwaukee and Green Bay. These two regiments went to Chickamauga in May, then to Florida, and in August formed a part of the force led to Puerto Rico by General Nelson A. Miles. The Americans were still in process of taking possession of the island when word came of the preliminaries of peace. The two Wisconsin regiments left Puerto Rico in October, and were home within the same month. The two other regiments, the First, and the Fourth which happened to include all the eight companies from Milwaukee, saw no active service. One of them spent some months in a camp in Alabama and the other did not leave Wisconsin. The four regiments and Wisconsin's one battery of artillery contained in all some 5,400 men. There were two deaths in battle in Puerto Rico and 129 men died from disease in camp. The adjutant general of Wisconsin, at the direction of the governor, expended about $140,000 in equipping and maintaining these troops until they entered federal service, and the quartermaster some thousands more. The federal government reimbursed Wisconsin for its outlay, over $100,000 being received before the end of the Scofield administration.

SELECTED BIBLIOGRAPHY

There are two narratives of Wisconsin politics by men who had personal contacts with political leaders toward the end of the period. The more detailed is by Alexander M. Thomson, *A Political History of Wisconsin* (Milwaukee, 1902), pp. 163-294. The other is a chapter by William J. Anderson, "Politics Since the War," in *Wisconsin in Three Centuries* (4 vols., New York, 1906), Vol. IV., pp. 255-342, which deals with the years 1865-1904. R. G. Plumb, *Badger Politics, 1836-1930* (Manitowoc, 1930), pp. 55-121, provides a good summary. Nils P. Haugen, *Pioneer and Political Reminiscenses* (reprinted from the *Wisconsin Magazine of History,* Vols. XI, XII, and XIII) pp. 46-125, writes as an active participant in politics, especially in the decade of the nineties. Reuben G. Thwaites, *Wisconsin* (Boston, 1908), pp. 400-416, and Milo M. Quaife, *Wisconsin, Its History and Its People* (4 vols., Chicago, 1924), Vol. I, pp. 582-602, both discuss some parts of the history of this period. Isabel Bacon La Follette (Mrs. Philip F. La Follette) wrote very interestingly of the "Early History of the Wisconsin Executive Residence," *Wisconsin Magazine of History,* Vol. XXI, pp. 139-150 (December, 1937).

Herman Julius Deutsch wrote *Political Forces in Wisconsin 1871-1881* as a Ph. D. thesis (MS, Madison, 1929). Much of this appeared in the *Wisconsin Magazine of History,* Vols. XIV, XV, and XVI, in a series of six articles (1931-1932). Dorothy Ganfield's Ph. D. thesis, *The Federal Influence of Wisconsin 1880-1907* (MS, Madison, 1928), was summarized in "The Influence of Wisconsin on Federal Politics, 1880-1907," *Wisconsin Magazine of History,* Vol. XVI, pp. 3-25 (September, 1932). The facts about the Whiskey Ring may be read in Ellis Paxson Oberholzer, *History of the United States since the Civil War* (5 vols., New York, 1917-1937), Vol. III, pp. 144-159. For the evidence on the whiskey frauds see 44th Cong., 1st Sess., House Misc. Doc. No. 186 (Serial number 1706), testimony taken in June, 1876.

Louise P. Kellogg, in "The Fairchild Papers," *Wisconsin Magazine of History,* Vol. X, pp. 259-281 (March, 1927), gives a clear portrait of Fairchild. Joseph Schafer edited *California Letters of Lucius Fairchild* (Madison, 1931). A most interesting study of ability in a family is Gaillard Hunt, *Israel, Elihu and Cadwallader Washburn, A Chapter in American Biography* (New York, 1925). Joseph Schafer, "Washburniana," *Wisconsin Magazine of History,* Vol. XIV, pp. 314-321 (March, 1931), adds interesting details about Governor Washburn. Joseph Schafer also wrote short sketches of all the governors of this period for the *Blue Book, 1927,* pp. 33-48. Henry Casson, *"Uncle Jerry," Life of General Jeremiah M. Rusk* (Madison, 1895) is the work of an admirer. William W. Wight, *Henry Clay Payne, A Life* (Milwaukee, 1907) is written in a very friendly tone.

William F. Whyte, "The Bennett Law Campaign," *Wisconsin Magazine of History,* Vol. X, pp. 363-390 (June, 1927), should be read in conjunction with editorial comment by Joseph Schafer, *ibid.,* pp. 455-461. The text of the Bennett law is in *Session Laws, 1889,* chapter 519 (April 27, 1889).

Accounts of Wisconsin's part in the Spanish-American War are to be found in *Wisconsin in Three Centuries* (4 vols., New York, 1906), Vol. IV, pp. 239-252; and in Ellis B. Usher, *Wisconsin, Its Story and Biography* (8 vols., Chicago, 1914), Vol. III, pp. 443-454. Additional details are given in the *Report of the Adjutant General* (of Wisconsin) dated September 30, 1900.

CHAPTER XV

LA FOLLETTE

Early Career

IN ANY history of Wisconsin Robert M. La Follette must have an important place. Throughout the nation he is generally regarded as the most distinguished political figure that has yet appeared in the state. Rising by dint of industry, perseverance, and pluck, and at times meeting with bitter opposition, he attained the highest offices that the state could bestow. Thrice he was elected governor and four times he was chosen United States Senator. But La Follette reached an eminence above that of the ordinary governor or senator; he made for himself a special place among the political leaders of his day.

A great battle was raging in the later nineteenth century to prevent the dominance of American political and social life by the masters of great wealth. America had thought she was a democracy, with a government of, by, and for the people; she discovered that in many of its actions government, both in state and nation, was the servant of private wealth. La Follette did not begin this struggle, nor did he end it; but he took his place in the front line as a champion of the common man. He had initial successes in Wisconsin and helped the progressives into power there. Transferred to the national scene, he failed to become President of the United States; but he was nevertheless a significant national figure and came to have a loyal following far beyond the limits of his own state. At Washington he sought to apply the principles he had championed in Wisconsin, and, in a

ROBERT M. LA FOLLETTE*

certain sense, his later no less than his earlier career belongs to the history of Wisconsin.

Robert Marion La Follette was born in Dane County, Wisconsin, June 14, 1855. He could not remember his father, and as the youngest of four fatherless children he had a boyhood not unacquainted with want. In 1873 the family took up its residence in Madison, and in due time Robert entered the state university. All through his course there he partially supported his mother and one of his sisters. Under the strain of all the work he assumed, his health, naturally robust, gave way, and for several years he suffered recurrent illness. While still a student at the university he showed himself an insurgent by defying certain student organizations that tried to capture all the offices of honor. He won a state and an interstate contest in oratory, and in June, 1879, at the age of 24, he was graduated Bachelor of Arts. He was the first Wisconsin governor to be born within the state, and if we except Major Upham's years at West Point, the first to have a college training.

In February, 1880, after five months' study of law, La Follette was admitted to the bar. He decided to seek the office of district attorney of Dane County, and while Keyes, the Republican "boss," tried to dissuade him, his own attitude is summed up thus: "I was asking the people for an office of public service which they had the full power to give me." He gained the office and held it for four years. Late in 1881 he married a college classmate, Miss Belle Case of Baraboo; thereafter he always acknowledged that much of his political success was due to her aid and counsel. In the fall of 1884, after another conflict with the bosses, he was elected to the House of Representatives, where he was to remain for six years. While he could not be called a standpat Republican, he usually voted with the party and did not at this time show the tendency to insurgency that marked his later career. He was quite a friend and admirer of William McKinley, serving with him on the Committee of Ways and Means. He lost his seat in the Democratic landslide of 1890 and in the following spring returned to Madison and resumed the practice of law.

While La Follette was in the House the two Senators from Wisconsin were Philetus Sawyer and his brilliant protégé, John C. Spooner. On more than one occasion La Follette thwarted plans of Sawyer and his friends by preventing their access to natural resources on Indian lands. Twenty years later, in the *Autobiography,* La Follette wrote:

It seems to me now . . . that most of the lawmakers and indeed most of the public looked upon Congress and the government as a means of getting some sort of advantage for themselves or for their home towns or home states. . . . At the time I was in Congress . . . the onslaught of these private interests was reaching its height. . . . Even then the two diametrically opposed ideas of government had begun a death grapple for mastery in the country. Shall government be for the benefit of the private interests. . . ? Or shall government be for the benefit of the public interest? [1]

These words were not written until about 1912, and La Follette himself admits that his ideas had clarified since 1891; but they set forth clearly one of the chief points in La Follette's appeal to his generation.

In September, 1891, La Follette had an experience with Senator Philetus Sawyer, whom he considered a representative of the "interests," that crystallized his thoughts on American public life as nothing else had done. The Democratic administration of Wisconsin had just begun to collect interest from former state treasurers. Sawyer was one of the bondsmen and he was liable, if all the suits were pressed to a successful conclusion, to the amount of about $300,000. The cases were to be tried in the Circuit Court of Dane County. The judge of that court was Robert G. Siebecker, La Follette's brother-in-law and former law partner. According to La Follette, Sawyer attempted to hire him to see Judge Siebecker off the bench and persuade him to get the cases decided

---

[1] Robert M. La Follette, *La Follette's Autobiography* (Madison, 1913), pp. 86, 88-90.

"right." Sawyer's version was that he did not know that Siebecker was La Follette's brother-in-law and that he offered La Follette a retainer. It became a conflict of veracities that was known in the remotest corners of the state. Twenty years later La Follette wrote of the effect of this incident upon himself:

So out of this awful ordeal came understanding, and out of understanding came resolution. I determined that the power of this corrupt influence, which was undermining every semblance of representative government in Wisconsin, should be broken. . . . I knew that Sawyer and those allied with him were allied with the railroads, the big business interests, the press, the leading politicians of every community. I knew that the struggle would be a long one, but my resolution never faltered.[2]

Thus La Follette entered upon the road of insurgency in Wisconsin; doubtless in the beginning he did not know how far it was to lead him. It was not until January, 1901, that he held public office again, and it was several years more before he had a legislature that would carry out his wishes. In 1892 the Republican leaders attempted to ignore him, but when he indicated that otherwise he would speak independently, they grudgingly accepted him as one of the campaign speakers for the party. Two years later he and other rebels against the bosses attempted to secure the Republican nomination to the governorship for Nils P. Haugen, whom La Follette persuaded to make the race; they gained about a third of the Republican convention, but Upham was nominated. La Follette sought the nomination for himself in 1896, and believed that he would have been nominated had not money been used to buy supporters pledged to him. Not long after this he delivered a notable speech, "The Menace of the Machine," and began to advocate the direct primary as the best means to take away the power of wealth and privilege wrongfully exercised in caucuses and conventions, and restore it to the people. La Follette and his friends acquired a newspaper and his platform assumed more definite shape. Besides the direct primary he desired

[2] *Ibid.*, pp. 164, 165.

equality of taxation, an anti-pass law, and legislation against lobbying and against bribery and corruption.

In the presidential election of 1896 Wisconsin was again overwhelmingly Republican after the Democratic victory of four years before. For the victory of McKinley both in Wisconsin and in the nation, great credit was accorded to Henry C. Payne of Milwaukee. Payne had built up a great influence with Republicans in Wisconsin during the eighties, becoming chairman of the state central committee in 1888, and in the nineties he came to be well known in the national field. He was counted one of the foremost strategists of the Republican party, being in the opinion of some of the inner circle abler than Mark Hanna, and he helped manage the campaigns of 1896, 1900, and 1904. He was appointed Postmaster General by President Roosevelt and when Mark Hanna died he succeeded him as chairman of the Republican National Committee, of which he had previously been vice-chairman. He died in October, 1904.

Payne was of the same political group as Sawyer and Spooner. Sawyer was a real influence in Wisconsin until his death in March, 1900. Spooner was again in the Senate for ten years beginning in 1897. He was not only a powerful debater but a great constitutional lawyer. Roosevelt called him his right-hand man, and he was one of the recognized leaders in the United States Senate. Another Wisconsin politician very important at Washington was Joseph W. Babcock, Congressman from 1893 to 1907. He became chairman of the Congressional Campaign Committee, was said to know the political peculiarities of every congressional district in the United States, and under his management five successive congresses were Republican. During the years while La Follette was climbing to power all these men threw the weight of their great influence into the scale against him.

In the state campaign of 1898 La Follette sought the Republican nomination a second time, but the old leaders again placed Scofield at the head of the ticket. The La Follette partisans, however, had much to do with writing the platform, and the party was now pledged to an anti-pass law, a corporation tax, and election reforms. The first pledge was redeemed, but bills to raise the assessments on railroads and to institute primary elections were passed by the assembly only to be rejected by the senate. The other small reforms of the second Scofield administration seemed to the eager reformers but a meager part of what they desired and what they had been promised. The legislature of 1899 chose Joseph V. Quarles as United States Senator. One of the defeated aspirants was Isaac Stephenson, a millionaire lumberman of Marinette, and, displeased with the dominant element for not electing him, he came over to La Follette and was a powerful supporter of the insurgent group for many years.

La Follette as Governor

In 1900 La Follette gained the Republican nomination and was elected governor by a plurality of 102,000. His supporters were in the majority in the assembly, but not in the senate, and because of the complexion of the upper house, the record of the legislature of 1901 was, from the reformers' point of view, a comparatively barren one. Not one of La Follette's cherished plans, for which he felt he had a mandate from the people, was carried out. The tax commission, set up as a temporary body in 1899, was made permanent, and Nils P. Haugen was appointed to the commission, where he was to serve the state for twenty years.

By this time the adherents of the old leaders were commonly called Stalwarts, while they in turn dubbed La Follette's partisans Halfbreeds. In the spring of 1901, after the adjournment of the legislature, fifty-nine of its Stalwart members organized the Wisconsin Republican League, which because of the location of its headquarters in Milwaukee came to be called the Eleventh Story League. It sent out great quantities of literature calling the Governor "demagogue," "socialist," and "Populist," and denouncing his as "unsafe." The Milwaukee *Sentinel,* while not entirely committed to La Follette, had up to this time been friendly to him. In March, 1901, however, it was purchased by

Charles F. Pfister, a Milwaukee capitalist, and was henceforth aligned with the Stalwarts. In June the La Follette forces launched a newspaper of their own, the Milwaukee *Free Press,* supported financially by Isaac Stephenson.

In the election of 1902 La Follette bent his efforts to gaining a legislature that would carry out his plans. The Stalwart leaders, including John C. Spooner, placing a high value on party unity, told their followers to vote for La Follette. They still had almost complete control of the federal patronage, while La Follette was building up a small corps of political lieutenants out of the state game wardens and oil inspectors. Many who wanted particularly to defeat La Follette supported the Democratic candidate for governor, David Rose, the mayor of Milwaukee. La Follette continued to carry his appeal personally to as many people as possible, for the first time using an automobile to get from place to place, and in November won an easy victory.

In the legislature of 1903, two important measures were enacted on which La Follette had long insisted, the primary election law and the ad valorem railway tax. The primary election law was passed with the proviso that it should be referred to the people, and it was approved by referendum. The new system was first used in municipal elections in 1905 and for state and congressional elections in September, 1906. The primary election was designed to end the caucus and the convention, which, according to La Follette, thwarted the real desires of the people and served as instruments of corruption wielded by great industrial and financial interests. He believed, for example, that he had really been preferred by the majority of Republicans in 1896 as their candidate for governor, but that he had been supplanted by Scofield in a convention controlled by "the bosses" or "the machine."

The new law provided that a man might offer himself as a candidate for an office, and if a sufficient number of signatures to a petition in behalf of his candidacy was secured, his name was placed on the list of the candidates of his party for the office he sought. At the polls, the voter was presented with several ballots, one for each party, and of these ballots he used whichever one he chose, but only one. The voters of each party thus selected one candidate for each office. From the passage of the law until 1932, nomination by the Republicans to a state office was usually equivalent to election. Sometimes during this period there were five or six candidates for the Republican nomination for some of the state offices, and since a plurality gained the nomination, it frequently happened that a man was nominated and then elected who was before the primaries the choice of rather a small minority. An attempt to amend the method was made by the legislature of 1911. Voters were asked, when choosing an officer, to indicate a second choice; four-fifths of the voters, however, did not make any second choice, and after four years of trial, the act was repealed.

The act of 1903, still the law of Wisconsin, also provided certain new ways of carrying on party business. After the September primaries, those nominated in each party for state offices and for senate and assembly meet as the state platform committee of their party. Besides drafting a platform, they name a state central committee made up of five from each congressional district. These in turn choose a chairman and an executive secretary, and the chairman chooses a small group to compose, with him and the secretary, an executive committee. This system was supposed to do away with conventions and the rule of bosses. Yet the custom soon arose in each party or faction of having a pre-primary gathering which prepares a platform and a list of candidates, quite after the manner of the old-time conventions, although the actual choice among the candidates, of course, remained with the voters.

The ad valorem tax law of 1903 remedied an inequity of long standing, the removal of which La Follette had made a leading feature of his program for many years. Almost from the beginning of railroads in Wisconsin they had been taxed a certain percentage of their gross earnings: in 1900, four per cent for most lines. The tax commission set up under Governor Scofield had reported that railways yielded less than half as much taxes as property of the same value belonging to private persons. The first step under the new legislation was an evaluation of railroad properties in the state. The market price of railroad stocks and bonds was used in making the new assessment, but the estimate on this basis was checked by engineers' estimates of the cost of replacement, and the valuations thus reached were not greatly less. After 1904 railroads paid taxes as did other business enterprises in the state, and, during the six-year period 1904-1909, railroad taxes on the ad valorem basis were four million dollars more than they would have been at the old rate and by the old method. The legislature of 1903 also established an inheritance tax. There had been such a tax by a law of 1899, but the Wisconsin Supreme Court had declared it unconstitutional. The law of 1903 stood the test of constitutionality.

By 1904 the unity of the Republican party in Wisconsin had become a very transparent fiction. In the previous session of the legislature all the Stalwart strength had been thrown against Governor La Follette's measures. Representative Joseph W. Babcock had returned from Washington to direct the fight against the primary law, and the opposition to the new railroad taxation had been just as open. Early in 1904 La Follette made several speeches in an attempt to end Babcock's career in Congress, but he was nominated in his district convention and ultimately reelected. Both factions put forth their best efforts to gain control of the party machinery, which was as yet unaffected by the new primary election law. Contesting delegations to the state convention appeared from a number of counties and from some of the wards of Milwaukee, but there seems no reasonable doubt that the majority of the Republicans of the state desired to support La Follette. Two of the contests were decided unanimously in La Follette's favor by the state central committee, and these decisions gave him a clear majority of all delegates, 535 out of 1065, without reference to contests in which the committee was divided. The convention met in the university gymnasium at Madison, May 18, 1904, and is remembered in Wisconsin history as the "gymnasium convention." Irvine L. Lenroot presided and called attention to the fact that because of the new primary law it would be the last of the state conventions.

Various considerations caused the breach in the Republican party that now occurred. The old-time leaders were not disposed to submit tamely to changes that spelled the end of their power, while other citizens, conservative by nature, felt that La Follette was a dangerous radical who was in a fair way to alter the foundations of government and society. At the gymnasium convention, after roll call, Marvin L. Rosenberry voiced a protest from the minority against the way in which the roll had been made, and proposed the substitution of Stalwart delegations. The presiding officer would not put his motion. Soon after this a meeting of "Anti-Third Term delegates" was announced and most of the Stalwarts left the gymnasium, retiring in quiet and orderly fashion. The gymnasium convention then proceeded expeditiously with its business. At the opera house the bolters similarly did all the things that a convention had to do. The state was now presented with two Republican platforms, two state central committees, two lists of candidates for state offices, and two groups of four men each who claimed to be delegates-at-large from Wisconsin to the national convention. The four from the gymnasium convention included Governor La Follette and Isaac Stephenson. The four from the opera house convention were United States Senators John C. Spooner and Joseph V. Quarles, Congressman Joseph W. Babcock, and Judge Emil Baensch of Manitowoc.

In the matter of the delegates-at-large each side engaged lawyers to present its case to the national committee. The acting chairman, Henry C. Payne, because of his connection with Wisconsin, absented himself while the case was presented and considered. The decision went in favor of the opera house group, perhaps because some of the men included in it were expected to play leading parts in the national convention. A few days later the committee on credentials and then the whole convention accepted the decision. President Roosevelt refused to interfere in any way, merely regretting that there had been a bolt in a presidential year. La Follette's friends felt that Roosevelt, if a sincere reformer, would have influenced the national organization in La Follette's favor. As a matter of fact, John C. Spooner was more of an adviser to Roosevelt than La Follette ever was.

In Wisconsin it fell to the secretary of state to determine which list of candidates should be printed on the ballots in the column headed "Republicans," and he decided in favor of the La Follette group. The Stalwarts took the matter to the supreme court, and lost. They then decided to use the name "National Republican." Their candidate for governor until October was S. A. Cook of Neenah. After the decision of the supreme court, Cook withdrew, and the Stalwarts turned to ex-Governor Edward Scofield. The Democratic candidate was former Governor George W. Peck. As the campaign drew to a close Scofield himself was advising his audiences to vote for Peck as the only hope of defeating La Follette. Roosevelt carried the state by 150,000, but La Follette's plurality over Peck was only about 50,000.

One of the early actions of the legislature of 1905 was to choose Governor La Follette as United States Senator to succeed Joseph V. Quarles. But La Follette was determined to bring his work in Wisconsin a stage further before resigning as governor. In 1903 he had secured the ad valorem taxation of railroads, but unless the state controlled charges for services the railroads would shift the payment of the increased taxes to their patrons. La Follette had desired a law regulating rates in 1903, but had failed to secure it. This had been one of the chief issues in his campaign for the governorship in 1904, and his victory was a mandate for regulation. Accordingly the railroad commission was established in 1905, with authority to control rates and the quality of service and to prevent discrimination. One of the men who had most to do with formulating the original law in 1905 was William H. Hatton, a member of the state senate and chairman of its committee on transportation. As he stated the guiding principle of the law, "it was as much the duty of the state to furnish transpor-

tation as it ever had been to make roads or build bridges, and
. . . if the function was delegated to any one, it was the duty of
the state to regulate it so that the agent should be required to
furnish adequate service, reasonable rates and practice no discrimination." Senator Hatton also said: "I want this procedure
so simple that a man can write his complaint on the back of a postal card, and if it is a just one, the state will take it up for him."
When the railroad commission was two years old, there was added
to its duties the regulation of all utilities operating in the state,
whether privately or municipally owned.

During the Civil War the state of Wisconsin spent over a million dollars in equipping soldiers, borrowing the money for the
purpose. The federal government refunded the principal without interest, about three-fourths of it almost at once, and most of
the rest at intervals before the end of 1875. But as the money was
returned it was not used to pay off the indebtedness, but was put
into the general fund of the state. When the last few thousands
were paid in the time of Governor Hoard, it was supposed that the
account was closed, but toward the end of the 1890's it was cal-
culated that Wisconsin was entitled to recover interest and losses
incurred by selling state bonds below par during the Civil War.
The federal government admitted the new claims, and accordingly
Wisconsin received about $458,000 in 1903 and $727,000 in 1905.
These sums were put into the general fund, and the La Follette
administration was enabled thereby to demand less in taxes than
it otherwise would have done. At the time there was a state
debt, originating in the Civil War operations, of more than $2,-
000,000, on which interest was regularly paid. Some of La Follette's critics were of the opinion that the money received from
the federal treasury should have been used to retire certificates of
indebtedness.

It fell to Governor La Follette to take the first steps toward
the erection of the present capitol building. The first small capitol had been begun in 1837. The construction of the second extended over the years from 1857 to 1869, part of the building

coming into use during the Civil War; and there were additions
to it in the eighties.   In the early morning of February 27, 1904,
fire destroyed about half of this capitol, but by good fortune the
loss of records was small.   The legislature of 1905 determined on
a new building and established a capitol commission of six members including the governor.   Four governors, of whom La Follette was the first, served in succession on the commission.   Actual
construction of the present capitol began in the autumn of 1907
and continued for ten years.   The cost was met by the state as the
enterprise progressed, and amounted in all to about $7,500,000.
It is one of the boasts of Wisconsin that no financial corruption
stained the record here.   The extreme length of the building is
426 feet and the height from the terrace to the top of the figure
on the dome is 280 feet.   The exterior is of Vermont granite, while
the stone used inside was brought from many parts of the world.
The whole building is a fitting symbol of the greatness of the
state and is a worthy monument of the generation that built it.

The legislature of 1905 also passed a state civil service act, and
set up a state board of forestry whose duty it should be to prevent
forest fires and manage the state forest reserves.   A fuller discussion of conservation and reforestation will appear in a later
chapter.

On the first of January, 1906, La Follette's resignation from the
governorship took effect and he went to Washington as Senator,
while James O. Davidson, the lieutenant governor, advanced to
take his place in Wisconsin.   La Follette was not, however, to
lose touch with his home state, and many times during the next
nineteen years his leadership was felt in the political life of Wisconsin.

An Insurgent in the United States Senate

When La Follette entered the Senate, Roosevelt had been president for a little more than four years, and had made a name for
himself as a champion of the people against big business.   In the
Northern Securities case the national government had begun suit

to dissolve a monopolistic holding company. A federal law of 1908 forbade rebates in interstate commerce. The Department of Commerce and Labor was created with a bureau to watch the corporations in the interest of the public. What La Follette had begun in Wisconsin was also in process in the nation at large. It might well be expected that La Follette would fall into line as an able lieutenant of Roosevelt, but this was not to be.

In the spring of 1905 the Hepburn Act was passed to regulate railroads and give the Interstate Commerce Commission more power over them. The law prescribed the manner of railroad accounting, made their books continuously open to government inspection, and forbade the issuance of private passes. La Follette, both in conference with the President and on the floor of the Senate, insisted that the bill was inadequate. He desired a physical valuation of the railroad properties as the basis of regulation and taxation. He offered a succession of amendments which were voted for usually only by himself and a few Democrats. The New York *Tribune* remarked in May, 1906: "Mr. La Follette's manners and methods have so far antagonized his party colleagues that they refuse to examine into or listen to his propositions."

For some time La Follette continued to be a rather lonely crusader in the Senate, even though personally respected and considered charming by those who came to know him. In the spring of 1908 he tried to organize a filibuster against the Emergency Currency Bill, speaking nineteen hours without rest himself. When the Republican National Convention was considering its platform in 1908 a minority report was presented embodying La Follette's ideas. It criticized as insufficient several accomplishments of the Republican Congress, and advocated among other things publicity of campaign expenses, physical valuation of railroads, the eight-hour day for persons employed on public works, and the election of United States Senators by direct popular vote. This report was defeated by 952 votes to 28, the twenty-eight consisting of the Wisconsin delegation of twenty-five and three others.

In January of 1909 the publication of *La Follette's Weekly*

Magazine was begun. The first issue gives his impression of the state of the nation and its government about three years after he entered the Senate:

Open-eyed at last we are startled to find our great industrial organizations in control of politics, government and national resources. They manage conventions, make platforms, dictate legislation. They rule through the very men elected to represent the people.

It was generally understood in 1908 that the tariff would soon be revised downward, and when in the Payne-Aldrich tariff the schedules were revised upwards, ten Republicans in the Senate, led by La Follette, voted with the Democrats against it. This is usually regarded as the beginning of the national insurgent movement. President Taft approved of the new tariff and so did Roosevelt after his return from Africa, but the country in general was displeased with it. The elections of 1910 gave the Democrats a majority in the House of Representatives, and in the Senate the insurgents held the balance of power. Taft called this new Congress in special session in April, 1911, and the Democrats and insurgents began to revise the tariff downward schedule by schedule, but the President vetoed all their bills.

In January, 1911, the National Progressive League was formed at the La Follette home in Washington and for a time La Follette had hopes of becoming the Republican nominee for president. In October a National Progressive Conference of three hundred men from thirty states endorsed him as their candidate. Yet, Progressives who were also experienced politicians naturally wanted the candidate with the best chance to win, and when they found Roosevelt advocating progressive reforms, and came to believe that he could be persuaded to become a candidate, they deserted La Follette for him. On February 2, 1912, La Follette made a speech in Philadelphia before the Periodical Publishers' Association of America which led some of his hearers to believe that he was near a physical breakdown and could not be seriously considered as a candidate; after that the movement to Roosevelt became even more pronounced. On February 24, Roosevelt announced that he would accept the Republican nomination. La Follette always felt that Roosevelt had treated him unfairly in taking the leadership of the Progressive movement away from him, particularly as La Follette had gone forward on the strength of Roosevelt's repeated statements that he would not again be a candidate. Roosevelt's friends asserted that in his candidacy lay the only hope for the triumph of progressive principles.

Roosevelt had hoped to receive the Republican nomination, but when the convention assembled in June, he had the support of but a little more than 400 delegates out of 1078, and President Taft was renominated. Roosevelt and his friends decided to hold a separate convention and later organized the Progressive party. La Follette and the Wisconsin delegation participated in the regular Republican convention to the end. A member of the delegation offered the name of La Follette as a candidate, and in 1912 as in 1908 a platform was presented embodying the La Follette reform proposals, but it was again voted down overwhelmingly. Yet La Follette did not join the Progressives. Roosevelt invaded Wisconsin in October of 1912, and was shot by an insane man in Milwaukee, but fortunately was able to resume campaigning within a few weeks. The governor of Wisconsin, Francis E. McGovern, declared for Roosevelt, but La Follette, while advising his followers to vote for McGovern, counted Taft a reactionary and Roosevelt a compromiser and untrustworthy. He stated that he did not intend to vote for Taft, Roosevelt, or Wilson, but hoped that Wilson would prove a leader whom he could follow and assist in progressive reform. At the polls in November the combined vote for Taft and Roosevelt was 193,000, but Wilson with 164,000 had more than either, and Wisconsin's electoral vote was cast for a Democrat for the second time since the Civil War.

La Follette spent nineteen and one-half years in the Senate and during that time he supported, within the Senate and outside of it, a great deal of legislation. He wanted the government to be more and more a servant of the people, and he advocated parcel post and postal savings. He believed in a separate Department of

Labor long before it was established. He insisted on the eight-
hour day in government offices and on public works. Two laws
in the interests of workingmen he especially counted his own: one
to give seamen better conditions aboard ship, the other providing
that railwaymen should not be compelled to work for more than

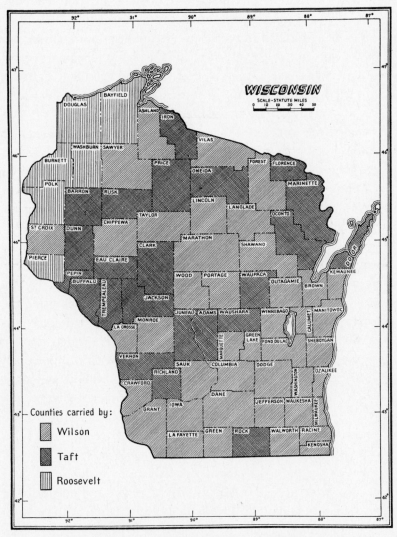

THE PRESIDENTIAL ELECTION OF 1912 IN WISCONSIN

sixteen hours without rest. He supported the right of the men to form unions and to strike, and often assailed the use of the injunction in the interests of employers. He did all that he could to correct the evils of child labor through federal power, warmly supporting the child labor amendment to the constitution. He was an early champion of woman suffrage, and he wished to bring the primary election from Wisconsin into the federal system. The tariff had its value in assuring work to American workingmen, but he was deeply dissatisfied with every tariff passed while he was in the Senate. He distrusted the great bankers and combinations of bankers, did not think the Federal Reserve system would help matters much, and voted against it. He looked at all these problems from the angle of the workingmen and the farmers, not from that of the employers and the wealthy.

The World War and After

Whatever one may think of the correctness of Senator La Follette's attitude during the World War, there can be no doubt of his courage and sincerity. The war sprang from causes deep-rooted in the history of Europe. President Wilson, as the spokesman of the nation, declared the neutrality of the United States and all thoughtful Americans were glad that their country was not involved. Yet slowly America had to recognize that war was drawing near. The sinking of the *Lusitania* in May, 1915, turned many Americans against Germany and raised acutely the question of our right to travel the ocean ways in safety. In view of the possibility of war, steps were taken during 1916 greatly to strengthen the army and navy. These measures La Follette vigorously opposed, holding that Americans ought not to take the risk of ocean travel. Americans in general were still intent on peace, and in Wilson's second campaign the Democrats captured many votes with the slogan, "He kept us out of war." At the end of January, 1917, Germany practically forbade Americans to use the seas about the British Isles. The President severed diplomatic relations with Germany, and a few days later the Senate by a vote of 73 to 5 approved of what he had done. One of the five dissenters was La Follette. He maintained that war should be undertaken only to repel actual invasion, and after a popular referendum. Toward the end of February President Wilson asked Congress for authority to arm merchant vessels, and a measure conferring such authority passed the House by a vote of 405 to 13. The bill failed in the Senate because of a filibuster by a small group of Republican Senators, of whom La Follette was the most conspicuous. Wilson's rebuke was stinging: "A little group of wilful men representing no opinion but their own have rendered the great government of the United States helpless and contemptible."

The President's fateful message of April 2, announcing that Germany's recent actions meant war, was followed by joint resolutions in both houses that a state of war existed. In the Senate there was an opposition of six, including La Follette, and in the House there was an adverse vote of fifty, of whom nine were Wisconsin representatives in agreement with La Follette. Senator Paul Husting and Representative Lenroot supported the administration.

La Follette continued his independent position with reference to subsequent war legislation, approving, opposing, or offering amendments as seemed to him good. He voted against the selective service act, but urged the conscription of wealth. He always favored measures designed to bring greater care and comfort to the men in service. He was bitterly criticized for his course, but the greatest deluge of abuse descended upon him after a speech in St. Paul, September 20, 1917, in which he said, as reported in the *Pioneer Press* of that city:

I wasn't in favor of beginning the war. We had grievances. The German government had interfered with our rights to travel on the high seas—as passengers on the munition ships of Great Britain.

On these grievances, which were insignificant considering the consequences and rights involved, chiefly that of our citizens to ride on foreign munitions ships, we went to war. We had a right to ship munitions, but I wasn't for the riding.

The Associated Press had no representative at the meeting, but its St. Paul editor secured a copy of the *Pioneer Press's* version of the speech, and in sending it out inserted the word "no," changing the second sentence quoted to "We had no grievances." [3] Whether this was done by accident, or by design as La Follette's defenders claimed, is unknown; the garbled version of this bit of the speech appeared in many newspapers. Speaking at Toledo a few days later, La Follette himself declared that his remarks at St. Paul were misconstrued and that he was deliberately misquoted throughout the country, but the false version was not easily overtaken by the true one. Eight months later the Associated Press admitted its mistake.[4]

During the next few days a perfect torrent of abuse began which continued more or less as long as the war lasted. A committee of the United States Senate held a sort of trial to determine whether La Follette should be expelled in answer to popular clamor. From a stenographic version of the speech in which the offending "no" did not appear, the committee considered the tenor of the speech as a whole; he was not expelled. But over the country generally, he was called a pro-German, a neo-Copperhead, a slacker; he was hung in effigy; he was assailed with everything in the vocabulary of abuse. His old rival Roosevelt was particularly vehement in denouncing him. An educator of national reputation asserted that he would rather give children poison than La Follette's words. He was expelled from the Madison Club, was disowned by the state senate and by the University of Wisconsin. It was not pleasant to be an outcast, and yet La Follette never changed his opinion of war, nor of America's entry into this war. In January, 1918, he wrote: "I would not change places with any living man on the record as it stands today." During the spring of 1918 he stated more clearly that since we were involved the war should be prosecuted with all possible vigor. Yet when it was all

---

[3] There were other slight changes in wording and punctuation which did not affect the sense. I am indebted to the Minnesota Historical Society for checking the quotation from the *Pioneer Press* of September 21, 1917.

[4] *The New York Times,* May 24, 1918, page 14, col. 1.

over he could not give his approval to the Treaty of Versailles. "I challenge any man," he said, "to name one new privilege, one added right, which the common people of this or any of the Allied countries are to gain as a result of the war."

In 1920 the Farmer-Labor convention wanted La Follette as their presidential candidate, but he declined. In 1922 the people of Wisconsin sent him to the Senate for the fourth time by a vote of 379,000 in a total of 470,000. When Congress assembled in December, 1923, the Progressive bloc with La Follette at its head again held the balance of power in the Senate. In uncovering the oil scandals, which were revealed in that Congress, La Follette had no small part. In 1924, at the age of 69, he became an independent candidate for President. He was supported by a Conference for Progressive and Political Action and endorsed by the American Federation of Labor. The Socialists did not count him one of their party, but he announced himself as favoring government ownership of railroads. The Socialists did not nominate a candidate of their own and supported him. An affection of the heart had become apparent the year before, and La Follette's speech-making was severely curtailed at the orders of his physicians. He received some 4,800,000 votes or about one-sixth of those cast. In Wisconsin he had 453,000 votes or about 50 per cent more than Coolidge. He gained the electoral vote from no other state. When the next Congress assembled, La Follette and three other Senators who had supported the independent movement were expelled from the Republican party. In June, 1925, he died.

We stand too close to La Follette's great career to pass judgment upon it with any hope of finality. The passions aroused in the course of his political battles are still running strong throughout Wisconsin, and all the documents are not yet open to the historian. According to custom there was a memorial service in his honor in the United States Senate, and another in the House of Representatives; in the two of them thirty-four speeches were made about him, chiefly by political friends and lieutenants. The qualities of character most emphasized in these tributes were sincerity, an utter lack of financial self-seeking or ambition, a sympathy that winced at human suffering everywhere, and loyalty to that which he conceived to be the right, whatever the cost to himself. Though he bound many to him in close ties of friendship, he often seemed a solitary man. Senator Shipstead of Minnesota found him great by Ibsen's measure: "He is strongest who stands most alone." Many of the great decisions of his career were not the fruit of consultation but were made alone. Several of his friends, altering Henley's well-known lines, said of La Follette:

> He was the master of his fate;
> He was the captain of his soul.

One great secret of La Follette's political strength was his constant touch with the masses of the people. He had respect for their understanding and, once he had determined upon a policy, he laid it before the voters at length with all the arguments in support of it. He made them feel, too, that he and the people were together facing the enemy, the privileged and the wealthy, who in the very nature of things were bent on exploiting the poor. His speeches were notoriously long but they dealt with things that the hearers counted important and built up a lasting confidence in the speaker. The common people heard him gladly, year after year. Furthermore he did not shirk the drudgery of detail in organizing his political following, marshalling his supporters, distributing literature, and writing personal letters. This could be done in Wisconsin with measurable success, but it was physically impossible in the national field.

The highest office La Follette sought was the Presidency, and this he failed to attain in 1912 and again in 1924. Perhaps he was too much of a prophet for such a success. The list of political and social reforms that he fathered or favored is a long one, and he lived to see many of them enacted into law, proving that he was an able leader and forecaster of social progress. But his cargo of reforms was too heavy for good political navigation. He had most success in getting things done when he was governor of Wisconsin, and in those early days his program was much shorter than in later years. The word prophet may mean and does most properly mean one who "speaks forth" the truth; a prophet in this sense usually creates opposition and undergoes persecution. It was this aspect of La Follette's career that had most impressed Albert Eustace Hayden, the noted divine who delivered the funeral sermon in the capitol at Madison.

Always the prophet must suffer; always the people have been slow to appreciate and understand the men who make of themselves the spearpoint of a new era. . . . In those terrible days of war madness, when the minds of men were befogged, when the fires of persecution were lit, it was then that he stood true. . . . With quiet courage he stood forsaken, forsaken though his heart reached out to lay hold of the masses of the common people. . . . Almost alone he held his vision true.[5]

The legislature was in session when La Follette died, and it named him one of "Wisconsin's immortals" by authorizing the erection of a statue of him in the Hall of Fame at Washington, along with that of Father Marquette.

Selected Bibliography

Ernest W. Stirn has prepared *An Annotated Bibliography of Robert M. La Follette* (Chicago, 1937). In this are given all references to La Follette in the *Congressional Record,* and in the only available indexes of metropolitan newspapers in the United States, those to the *New York Daily Tribune,* 1875-1906, and to *The New York Times,* 1913-1936. It covers also the periodical literature from 1900 to 1936 and lists the available secondary material in printed books. The whole is a valuable aid to the study of half a century of Wisconsin history.

After La Follette's death his accumulated papers were deposited with the State Historical Society. As they will not be available to historical students until 1941, there can be no definitive biography until after that date. La Follette himself, with assistance from Ray Stannard Baker, wrote *La Follette's Autobiography: A Personal Narrative of Political Experience* (Madison, 1913). Unfortunately it ends with 1912. The famous speech at the publishers' banquet at Philadelphia is included, pp. 762-797. An account

[5] Dr. Hayden's entire address was printed in 69th Congress, 1st Sess., Senate Doc. No. 157, pp. 9-13.

of the delivery of that speech by an eyewitness with a shrewd estimate of the strong and weak points of La Follette is found in Ray Stannard Baker, *Woodrow Wilson, Life and Letters* (8 vols., New York, 1927-1939), Vol. III, pp. 267-277. Along with the *Autobiography* should be mentioned *La Follette's Weekly*, 1909-1930, which was discontinued only after Mrs. La Follette's death. Frederic L. Paxson wrote the excellent article on La Follette in the *Dictionary of American Biography*.

One of the best accounts of La Follette's earlier career is Fred L. Holmes' chapter, "The Triumph of the Progressive Movement," in Milo M. Quaife, *Wisconsin, Its History and Its People* (4 vols., Chicago, 1924), Vol. II, pp. 3-39. R. G. Plumb gives his narrative of La Follette's governorship in *Badger Politics 1836-1930* (Manitowoc, 1930), pp. 122-138. The remainder of the book shows La Follette's continuing influence in the political life of the state after he went to Washington. Albert O. Barton, *La Follette's Winning of Wisconsin* (Madison, 1922), is the work of a discriminating admirer. With it may be read *The Political Philosophy of Robert M. La Follette as Revealed in His Speeches and Writings*, compiled by Ellen Torelle (Madison, 1920). Two one-time supporters of La Follette who later parted from him have much about him in their memoirs: Isaac Stephenson, *Recollections of a Long Life* (Chicago, 1916); and Nils P. Haugen, *Pioneer and Political Reminiscences* (reprinted from the *Wisconsin Magazine of History*, Vols. XI, XII, and XIII). See especially pp. 149-153 of the reprint, or *Wisconsin Magazine of History*, Vol. XII, pp. 278-281, for Haugen's final judgment of La Follette.

Two books overflowing with the enthusiasm of the earlier years of progressivism in the state are: Charles McCarthy, *The Wisconsin Idea* (New York, 1912); and Frederic C. Howe, *Wisconsin, an Experiment in Democracy* (New York, 1912). Benjamin Parker DeWitt, *The Progressive Movement* (New York, 1915), pp. 54-88, tells the story of La Follette's rise to power.

Joseph Lincoln Steffens was one of the first writers to call the attention of the nation to the progressive movement in Wisconsin. See his *Struggle for Self-Government* (New York, 1906), and a chapter entitled "Wisconsin and Bob La Follette," in the *Autobiography of Lincoln Steffens* (one-volume edition, New York, 1931), pp. 454-463.

The following are short pen-pictures or estimates of La Follette: E. G. Lowry, *Washington Close-Ups* (Boston, 1921), pp. 233-242; Chester C. Platt, *What La Follette's State is Doing* (Batavia, New York, 1924), pp. 102-113; O. G. Villard, *Prophets True and False* (New York, 1928), pp. 187-201; Bruce Bliven, "Robert M. La Follette's Place in our History," *Current History*, Vol. XXII, pp. 716-722 (August, 1925); Charles H. Crownhart, "Two Wisconsin Immortals," (Marquette and La Follette) *Blue Book, 1927*, pp. 5-20; and Frederick A. Ogg, "Robert M. La Follette in Retrospect," *Current History*, Vol. XXXIII, pp. 685-691 (February, 1931).

The hearings on the matter of the expulsion of La Follette from the United States Senate may be read in 65th Cong., 3d Sess., Senate Report 614, 2 parts, Committee on Privileges and Elections (Serial number 7453). The memorial services in the Senate and the House are printed in 69th Cong., 1st Sess., Senate Doc. No. 157 (Serial number 8582).

CHAPTER XVI

THREE CRUSADES

WISCONSIN AND THE WORLD WAR

THREE events of great moment came upon Wisconsin almost simultaneously: the World War, the inauguration of prohibition, and the attainment of woman suffrage. The war originated in Europe, and Americans living in the interior of the continent hoped longer than those on the Atlantic seaboard that the United States might avoid being drawn into the conflict. Eventually Wisconsin, along with the rest of the Middle West, came to regard America's participation as an inescapable duty, and threw herself with all her energy into the task of winning the war, believing that she was fighting for the coming of a better world. The United States became an active belligerent in April, 1917, and so continued until the armistice more than one and a half years later. In July, 1919, Wisconsin, together with all the other states still "wet," became "dry" in obedience to a federal statute enacted as a belated war measure. This remained in effect until it was superseded by the Eighteenth Amendment and the federal act for its enforcement. Woman suffrage, which was attained in August, 1920, like prohibition, was the fruition of many years of crusading effort in state and nation. The successful conclusion of both these domestic crusades was undoubtedly hastened by the war.

The soldiers of the United States in the World War were of three sorts: the regular army, the national guard mustered into federal service, and the national army made up of those called under the selective service law. The Wisconsin National Guard formed the larger part of the Thirty-second Division and also contributed three companies to the Forty-second or Rainbow Division. About 91,000 Wisconsin men were selected or drafted, of whom only a part reached France. If the Wisconsin men in the regular army, the navy, and the marine corps are included, it appears that the state had in all nearly 125,000 men under arms in the World War.

Wisconsin looks with special pride upon the career of the Thirty-second Division. The four thousand men of the Wisconsin National Guard who had served on the Mexican border were all mustered out by March, 1917. Shortly afterwards one regiment of the guard, the Third Wisconsin infantry, was called to protect plants engaged in war manufacture. In August all the Wisconsin guard assembled again at Camp Douglas, their numbers already raised by new enlistments to fifteen thousand. From September onwards they trained at Camp McArthur near Waco, Texas. There, along with eight thousand of the national guard of Michigan, they became the Thirty-second Division. Shortly before they left for France four thousand national army men from Wisconsin and Michigan were added to the division. Until they left for France all the equipment for the Wisconsin men was furnished by the state of Wisconsin at a cost of about $780,000. In January, 1918, they crossed the Atlantic, and by May they were ready to enter front-line trenches in a quiet sector in Alsace, not far from the Swiss border.

Marshal Foch began his memorable forward movement July 18, and the Thirty-second, commanded by Major-General William G. Haan, moved into the region about Soissons. July 26 they were billeted at and near Chateau Thierry, which had fallen to other American divisions five days before. Their first great battle came July 30 to August 5, when they carried on the task of reducing the Marne salient and straightening the line from Soissons to Rheims. It was here that a French general named them "Les Terribles." In its second great battle experience, August 27 to September 1, the Thirty-second pierced the enemy line in such fashion that a red arrow was made the insignia of the division.

In October it took part in the Meuse-Argonne offensive, and after the armistice it held the bridgehead east of the Rhine beyond Coblenz. The division lost nearly three thousand killed and almost eleven thousand wounded. Among twenty-nine combat divisions it stood seventh in total casualties and fourth in the number of battle deaths.

The general features of the federal "draft" law of May, 1917, were known before its passage, and Wisconsin early addressed herself to the task of registering all her male population of suitable age for possible military service. On June 5 all men between the ages of twenty-one and thirty inclusive were registered, and at four o'clock the next morning Wisconsin reported, first of all the states, the number of her registrants. Later on, all men from eighteen to forty-five were listed, and Wisconsin registered in all nearly half a million men. In the precinct or registration area each man who registered was given a serial number. In Washington a great "lottery" or drawing of numbers took place in July, and this determined the order in which these men should be called for service in every registration area in the United States, number 258 coming out at the head of the list. In September the "drafted" men began going into training camps. It was impossible for the wealthy to buy exemption as they had done in the time of the Civil War. The selected men of the national army were for the most part not organized according to their place of origin, and the achievements of Wisconsin men cannot be singled out for separate narration.

While soldiers were going to the camps and across the ocean there was devoted effort on the part of those who remained at home. Ten days after the declaration of war the legislature of Wisconsin authorized the governor to appoint eleven persons to act with him as the State Council of Defense, which operated as a war cabinet. It made investigations, informed and educated the public, and directed a host of enterprises. The idea of such a council originated with Professor A. L. P. Dennis of the state university, who was the secretary for the first six weeks. Magnus

Swenson, a capitalist interested in water-power development, was chairman from the beginning until a month before the armistice. Each county had its council of defense officered by the chairman of the county board, the county clerk, and the county treasurer. The counties laid taxes to carry on the local work, and spent in all about a third of a million dollars. The state council coördinated and directed the local work, issuing a weekly, later a bi-weekly bulletin or newspaper for that purpose. The expense of the state council amounted in twenty-five months to about $75,000.

The farmers were urged and aided, partly through the agricultural committee of the council of defense, to produce more food. The state bought and resold seed potatoes and seed corn with excellent results. The wheat acreage was multiplied threefold, and there were increases in all field crops. From 1917 to 1918 the increase in canned peas was a million cases, reaching nearly 11,000,000. The state helped the farmers in marketing and in handling many products, and middlemen's charges were eliminated to the advantage of both producers and consumers. Ten thousand boys were given instruction in school about farming and sent out to help the farmers, and nine-tenths of them made good. Altogether the farmers increased production about 25 per cent.

Under right of eminent domain the legislature specifically authorized the council of defense to seize and control supplies of food and fuel, and the council was giving its attention to food conservation before the establishment in September, 1917, of the federal food control. When this came, Magnus Swenson directed it for some months in addition to presiding over the State Council of Defense. Wheatless days and meatless days both originated in Wisconsin. Housewives signed a pledge to save food, hoarding was prevented, and hotels and restaurants were closely supervised. There was a similar regimen for fuel. The state council urged the federal government to take over and manage the anthracite coal mines, so that Wisconsin's war industries might not be stopped for lack of fuel. At home it devised ways of saving fuel.

People were urged to burn wood, and "Cut a Cord" was a slogan of the hour. To conserve material and labor a committee of the council of defense assumed control of building operations, and in the last two months of the war refused permits for 125 buildings planned to cost more than $2,500,000.

The Red Cross organization was wholeheartedly supported by the people of Wisconsin, its membership exceeding 500,000 at the close of 1917 and 700,000 a year later. State headquarters were in Milwaukee and local chapters were organized in over two hundred cities and villages. In the chapter workrooms and at home, women of the state made half a million knitted articles and incredible numbers of surgical dressings. About four hundred and fifty Red Cross nurses came from Wisconsin, and other women served as hut hostesses or did canteen or clerical work behind the lines in France or elsewhere. In Wisconsin the Red Cross looked after the families of soldiers or sailors whose allowances were delayed or inadequate.

The women of the state to the number of eighty thousand had their organization for war work, though many of the matters which they took into their charge pertained really to peace as much as to war: health, thrift, the care of little children, and education. At the head of this large group was Mrs. Henry H. Morgan of Oshkosh, who represented the women of the state on the council of defense.

Wisconsin again, as at the time of the Civil War, provided for the dependent families of the men in service, paying $30 a month for one dependent, $40 in the case of two, and so on. More than six hundred families were thus aided at a cost to the state of about $110,000. An attempt was made to give all Wisconsin men in service a chance to vote, but the federal military authorities decided against trying to reach the soldiers overseas. Those in this country were able to vote in the senatorial election in April, 1918. In November following, when there were about 22,000 Wisconsin men in the camps in the United States, about 4,500 availed themselves of the opportunity to vote. The Wisconsin legislature also granted to Wisconsin soldiers immunity from civil suits for three years, though in one case that arose it was decided that civil suits might be brought in certain circumstances under federal statutes.

The war greatly altered university and college life. Most of the able-bodied male students went into service, some in the ranks and some in the officers' training camps. The call for experts in military and other government departments depleted the teaching staffs. The normal schools, private colleges, and the state university all entered into arrangements with the federal government to train the Students' Army Training Corps. This was made up of men not yet of age who were to receive instruction preparatory to their becoming army officers, should they later be needed. It was found in practice that the demands made upon these students in the strictly military part of their training left little time or mental energy for classroom work. At the state university in the first quarter of 1918-1919 there were about three thousand S.A.T.C. men, a few more than two thousand woman students, and between four and five hundred civilian men.

When the World War was over, Wisconsin wished to show her gratitude and in some measure redeem her obligation to those who had served on the field of battle or in camp. Appropriating $500,000 for the purpose, the legislature of 1919 began by establishing a board to relieve sick, wounded, or disabled ex-service men. Whenever an individual began to receive care from the federal government, aid from the state ceased. County relief for needy soldiers and their dependents was also authorized, and was administered by the county judges. By an act of the same legislature the state offered to each soldier, sailor, marine, or nurse who had resided in Wisconsin before the war a cash bonus computed at $10 for each month of active service. The money was provided partly by an addition to the general property tax and partly by a surtax on incomes. June 30, 1933, was eventually set as the latest date for claiming this bonus, and by that time about 116,400 claims had been paid amounting to a little less than $16,000,000.

Provision was also made, in September, 1919, for an "educational bonus." A resident of Wisconsin who had been in service three months or more might have $30 a month while attending school, college, or university. A maximum of $1,080 (thirty-six months) was set for each individual. Nearly six thousand took advantage of this offer during the first year and over four thousand in the years that followed; up to June, 1936 the state had paid out about $4,611,000 for the education of its ex-service men. One-third of the money came from a graduated surtax on incomes; the rest, from a special levy added to the general property tax.

The funds collected for paying the cash bonus and the educational bonus were more than these purposes required, and with the surplus several things were done. The legislature in the special session of 1920 authorized the construction of the Wisconsin General Hospital "as a memorial to those who served in the World War." The amount appropriated for the hospital building, nurses' home, and equipment was $1,350,000, all of this out of bonus money. The hospital was opened in October, 1924. Its erection enabled the medical school of the University of Wisconsin to offer a full course of four years.

Even as late as 1923 not all the ex-service men were getting the care they should have from the federal government. By a Wisconsin law of that year the rest of the bonus money, at that time about $1,800,000, was set apart as the Soldiers' Rehabilitation Fund, and with the income from this fund hospital care and medical attention were to be given to ex-service men who needed it. To administer the law the Soldiers' Rehabilitation Board was set up and began its work in July, 1924. During the next six years nearly a thousand persons were cared for.

In 1925 a sum of $75,000 was taken from the fund for a rehabilitation camp for ex-service men at Tomahawk Lake in Oneida County, an enterprise sponsored by the American Legion. At the same time something over $800,000 was transferred from the rehabilitation fund to the University of Wisconsin and was used to provide classrooms and laboratories for the medical school.

In 1927 a sum of $175,000 was used for erecting a hospital at the Wisconsin Veterans' Home at Waupaca. By these various drafts upon the fund it has been reduced to about three quarters of a million dollars.

It was inevitable that the Americans in the World War should form some organization of veterans. In February and March, 1919, important first steps to this end were taken at Paris. In May there was a meeting at St. Louis, where a tentative draft of a constitution was hammered out and the name "American Legion" was chosen.

As men returned home in the spring of 1919, local clubs of veterans were formed in several Wisconsin cities. Representatives of some of these clubs were at St. Louis in May, and were requested by those managing the new organization to proceed with the work in Wisconsin. The first state convention assembled in Milwaukee in September, and this really marked the beginning of the "Department" of Wisconsin. When the first national convention met in Minneapolis in November, there were forty-one posts organized in Wisconsin, and by June of the following year, 1920, there were 285 posts and 23,000 members. Growth continued for many years; there were about 31,000 members in 1932 and 34,000 in 1938.

The federal government, in caring for those who served in the World War, extended its hand into Wisconsin in many ways. To the old National Home for Disabled Volunteer Soldiers near Milwaukee, built after the Civil War, additions were made in 1922 and 1932. A hospital with 240 beds was begun in 1919 at Waukesha for veterans suffering from mental and nervous diseases. The Waukesha establishment was eventually placed under the same management as the one near Milwaukee. In 1937 the combined plant was rechristened Wood, Wisconsin, and by that time had a capacity of 1,304 hospital and 1,801 "domiciliary" beds.

The Wisconsin Memorial Hospital was authorized by the Wisconsin legislature of 1921 and was located just west of the Mendota State Hospital. For many years it was under the authority of the

State Board of Control, while the expenses of patients were borne largely by the United States. For a time, beginning in 1933, federal support was almost entirely withdrawn, and the number of patients sank to about forty-five. In 1936-1937 the federal government acquired title and took over the management, and the capacity was rapidly increased until it came to exceed 600. This hospital has always been maintained exclusively for mental patients. In the year ending June 30, 1937, about 2,400 individual veterans of all past wars received hospital or domiciliary care in these several federal hospitals and homes in Wisconsin. It may be added that in the same year about 9,500 World War veterans residing in Wisconsin received pensions to the amount of $4,-250,000.

During the World War, American soldiers were receiving about $30 a month, while those who remained in civilian occupations were paid very high wages. In 1924 Congress sought to make up for this discrepancy by the Adjusted Compensation Act. This gave each ex-service man an endowment and insurance policy computed on the number of days he served, the rate being $1.25 for each day overseas and $1.00 for each day in the United States. The average value of these policies was about $1,000, and they were to mature in 1945. When the depression came great pressure was brought to bear to have these policies paid at once, and in January, 1936, Congress so enacted. About 88,000 veterans in Wisconsin applied for their "bonus" and in June they received it, mostly in bonds which with a few exceptions they promptly converted into cash. The whole operation, besides extinguishing debts which were liens against the endowment policies, brought more than $40,000,000 into the hands of the veterans in Wisconsin.

The Rise and Fall of Prohibition

Twice before in this narrative attention has been directed to the temperance movement. A crusade against the use of alcoholic beverages reached a high point in Wisconsin, as in many other parts of the United States, in the 1850's and subsided only as Civil

War issues came to monopolize the public mind. A second wave reached its crest in Wisconsin with the enactment of the Graham law in the time of Governor Washburn, but this was repealed within two years. After that neither Democrats nor Republicans cared or dared to support drastic legislation. Yet the enemies of alcohol continued their propaganda. There were three organizations in the forefront of the fight: the Prohibition party, the Woman's Christian Temperance Union, and the Anti-Saloon League. Each of these, while carrying on a nation-wide activity, found support and sought its coveted ends in Wisconsin.

The national Prohibition party was born in 1869 and presented its first candidate for the presidency three years later. The movement was at its zenith in the eighties, and in New York in 1884 it gained enough votes among those normally Republican to throw the state to Cleveland and thus decide the national election. Wisconsin gave the party two of its distinguished leaders, both at different times candidates for the governorship. The first was Samuel Dexter Hastings, who as a Republican had been state treasurer during the Civil War. For years he was a member of the executive committee and treasurer of the national Prohibition party. In his tours on behalf of prohibitory legislation he visited not only all parts of the United States, but England, Australia, and New Zealand. The other was Eugene Wilder Chafin, who was born and lived nearly half a century in Wisconsin. He, like Hastings, held high office in the temperance lodge or Order of Good Templars and was a leader in the Prohibition party in Wisconsin. About the turn of the century he removed to Chicago, ceased practicing law, and gave all his time to temperance work. He stood as the Prohibition candidate for President in 1904 and again in 1908. For some time after the Graham law (1872), the temperance advocates in Wisconsin hoped for further favors from the Republican party, but the attitude of the German element made the Republicans very cautious. Finally, in 1881, the Wisconsin Prohibitionists affiliated with the national party. The largest prohibition vote ever cast in the state was that for John

M. Olin, candidate for governor in 1886, when he was the choice of 17,000 or about six per cent of those who voted.

The Woman's Christian Temperance Union began in Ohio about 1873. Its national membership was some 26,000 by 1879 and rose to about 300,000 in 1914. As a continuing organization well and successfully managed entirely by women, it was evidence of their changing status, and the Union early made woman suffrage one of its goals. In its habits of thought it was deeply imbued with evangelical religion and worked in close union with the Protestant churches. Through its widely ramifying educational work it undoubtedly sowed the seed in the nineteenth century that bore fruit abundantly in the early twentieth. To this society Wisconsin contributed its greatest leader, Frances Willard. Born in New York, she came in early childhood with her parents to a farm near Janesville. She received her later education in the Milwaukee Female College, and in the Northwestern Female College at Evanston, Illinois, where she also taught for a time. From 1874 onward she gave her whole time to temperance work; she became the national president of the W.C.T.U. in 1879, and held the office until her death in 1898. A tomboyish girl, she developed into a winsome and compelling personality, a great public speaker, and a tireless worker.

The Anti-Saloon League was not a society of individuals but a league of existing temperance organizations to make more effective their efforts toward the common goal. It was launched at Oberlin, Ohio, in 1893, and by 1901 was organized in twenty-four states. The league had the support of some prominent Roman Catholics, but essentially its work was the political expression of the temperance sentiment long nurtured in the Protestant denominations. Its officers, recognizing that legislators wish to keep the favor of their constituencies, held over the lawmakers the whip of defeat in the next election, and mobilized and increased the anti-saloon vote with incredible skill and persistence. They also drafted the bills they desired, lobbied in behalf of them, and built up a public opinion in their favor. The Wisconsin

State Anti-Saloon League was organized in 1897, with the Rev. Henry Coleman, a leading Methodist minister, as the first superintendent.

At the close of the nineteenth century only three states—Maine, Kansas, and North Dakota—were dry to stay dry until the coming of national prohibition. Yet the nation at large was half converted, and one by one, especially after 1907, the states enacted prohibitory laws or wrote prohibition into their constitutions. At the end of 1914 there were fourteen dry states; by the end of 1916 there were twenty-three; and two years later there were thirty-two. Many states permitted local option in advance of state-wide prohibition.

In Wisconsin after 1885 a vote might be taken on the question of "license" or "no license" in any town, village, or city, and by 1905 about 11 per cent of the population were living in areas that had voted dry. Progress was more rapid between 1914 and 1919, and by the latter date about 45 per cent of the people of Wisconsin were living in dry territory. Superior voted saloons out in 1916, but Milwaukee and most of the larger cities continued to have them. In this movement Wisconsin may fairly be said to have lagged behind the country as a whole, for, before the World War broke out in Europe, 71 per cent of the area and more than half the population of the United States were dry through local choice or state prohibition and there were large gains between 1914 and 1919. In the South it was desired to keep the Negro sober; in industrial areas employers and others favored prohibition to increase efficiency and diminish industrial accidents. Most of all, however, prohibition came as the triumph of the Puritan conscience in rural and semirural America.

The issue received nation-wide attention in December, 1914, when there was an eight-hour debate in the House of Representatives on a resolution for submitting to the states a prohibition amendment to the federal constitution. Congressional delegations from forty-two states gave majority votes in favor of the proposal, and the total vote in the House was 197 for and 190 against it. One of Wisconsin's representatives on this occasion voted for the resolution, nine voted against it, and one did not vote. As the two-thirds required by such a resolution was lacking, the matter went no further in that Congress.

The advent of prohibition in the United States was the fruit of a generation or more of education and propaganda which had created a majority in favor of such legislation. This result came, in the nation at large, quite apart from the occurrence of the World War, with which it is often joined in popular memory, although the war undoubtedly hastened the final steps. As a war measure the use of grain for the manufacture of distilled liquors was forbidden in June, 1917. In the second half of the same year both houses of Congress agreed to submit the prohibition amendments to the states. Senator La Follette voted for this submission, not as a supporter of prohibition, which he never approved, but because as a consistent democrat he believed in leaving important matters to the decision of the whole people. In the House of Representatives six of the Wisconsin delegation voted for submission and five against it. The six included five who had voted "Nay" three years before. The states ratified speedily; by January 18, 1919, the necessary thirty-six states had signified their approval, and within a few weeks the number had risen to forty-five. Wisconsin's was one of the unnecessary final ratifications, her approval finishing its legislative course on January 22. Meanwhile, before the Eighteenth Amendment went into effect, a further federal war measure was passed, after the armistice, under which the manufacture and sale of intoxicants ceased at midnight June 30, 1919. At that time nearly ten thousand saloons and 137 breweries were closed in Wisconsin.

In the history of prohibition in Wisconsin it seems that the state of war that existed after April, 1917, was more notable a factor than in the nation as a whole. The legislature that ratified the Eighteenth Amendment was chosen, all save half the senate, in the fall of 1918. In this campaign the Anti-Saloon League devoted $67,000 to obtaining a legislature pledged to ratification, and in the outcome about two-thirds of each house did vote to ratify. This same legislature, in July, 1919, passed the Mulberger Act, which made the manufacture, sale, or transportation of intoxicants for beverage use illegal within the state, and provided for a new officer, the state prohibition commissioner, to enforce the state law. In the autumn of 1920, by a vote of more than two to one, the people indicated in a referendum that they wished the act continued, and at the same time a new legislature was elected that soon after in obedience to this mandate passed the Severson Act, which was in effect a repassage of the Mulberger Act in a more detailed and stronger form. During the first two years the commissioner and his staff had an appropriation of $15,000 a year; from 1922 onwards, of $60,000. He was most successful during the year 1922, when he secured over four thousand convictions and the payment of fines amounting to more than $500,000. The total of fines collected down to the end of 1927 was a little more than $2,500,000.

Though Governor Blaine had signed the Severson act in 1921, he soon led the way in voicing the sentiment of the majority of the people against prohibition. In addressing the legislature in 1923 he bitterly attacked the Eighteenth Amendment and the federal enforcing act, the Volstead Act. In 1926 a referendum favored a change in the Volstead Act to permit the manufacture of beer. By this time the prohibition commissioner had come to feel that his work was increasingly hampered by the way in which the courts limited him in securing evidence. In April, 1929, there was a referendum on the Severson act, and 350,000 Wisconsin citizens favored its repeal, while only about 200,000 wished to retain it. In May the legislature repealed the law, abolished the office of prohibition commissioner, and left the people of the state to be restrained from the buying and selling of intoxicants only by federal law and federal officers.

In Wisconsin prohibition was the desire of a minority, a vigorous and growing body with a continuous history since the foundation of the state. But it was only a minority. In view of what happened afterwards, the victories of prohibition in 1918 and the years immediately following cannot be taken as revealing a conviction on the part of the majority in favor of prohibitory legislation. Wisconsin's position in those years was rather delicate. It had become the fashion throughout the United States to belabor Wisconsin on account of La Follette's attitude on the war, supported, as his attitude frequently was, by a majority of Wisconsin's representatives. In April, 1918, the detractors counted it a further cause for reproach that a fourth of Wisconsin had voted for Victor L. Berger, a Socialist candidate for United States Senator. In the fall of 1918, when the majority of the United States seemed to desire prohibition, and when the war was at its fiercest and grimmest, a vote for liquor would have been interpreted as a vote for something German, as a vote against the war-time conservation of foodstuffs; and the majority in Wisconsin at that time were protesting their loyalty with a vehemence that outweighed their anti-prohibition feelings. Similarly, in 1920, a refusal to stand by some state enforcing act would have been counted, both within and without the state, as disrespectful to a part of the federal constitution, or as a gesture in favor of nullifying a federal statute; so through four bienniums Wisconsin legislatures voted appropriations to maintain a prohibition commissioner and his staff. Thus the governor who had signed the Severson act in 1921 could give a shrewd blow to the Volstead Act in 1923 without imperiling his political future; and by 1929 the whole prohibition structure was razed insofar as it could be accomplished by a single state. At no time in this generation were a majority of citizens of Wisconsin converts to the "temperance" movement; never would they calmly and under normal conditions have voted to place prohibitory laws on the statute book. That there were such laws in Wisconsin was due to the conjunction of three factors: a genuine prohibition sentiment embraced by a majority in the United States and a militant minority in Wisconsin, skillful "pressure politics" on the part of this minority in Wisconsin engineered by the Anti-

Saloon League, and, most decisive of all, conditions incident to the World War.

The repeal of prohibition in Wisconsin, like its coming, had to be accomplished by federal action. The platform of the Democratic party in 1932 declared for the immediate legalization of light wines and beer and the repeal of the Eighteenth Amendment, and Franklin D. Roosevelt came to office pledged to accomplish these things. Congressional action for repeal was started on its course by a resolution offered, December 6, 1932, by John J. Blaine, onetime enemy of the Severson act in Wisconsin and now United States Senator. The Twenty-first Amendment was duly laid before the states. The legislature of Wisconsin in March, 1933, provided for a special convention to pass on it. The repeal candidates, who were chosen on April 4, captured 82.1 per cent of all votes cast and carried every county in the state. In a session of about forty minutes, on April 25, they gave their unanimous decision for repeal; Wisconsin was preceded only by Michigan in officially announcing its acceptance of the new amendment. On December 5, Utah, the thirty-sixth state, ratified it, and on the same day President Roosevelt proclaimed that prohibition was at an end.

In the meantime a federal act of March, 1933, had legalized the sale of light wines and beer, and after midnight of April 6, it was again possible to buy and sell these commodities without breaking the law. The Wisconsin legislature passed one law providing for the licensing of taverns and tavernkeepers on April 4, and another of the same sort in July. On December 11, five days after the President's proclamation, a special session of the Wisconsin legislature convened, and in about two months it laid down the main lines of regulation, control, and taxation of the manufacture and sale of liquor, substantially as they have continued to the present. Local areas have great powers: licenses are granted by town boards, village boards, and the common councils of cities; local option elections are easy to obtain and may be held frequently. In the fiscal year ending June 30, 1937, taxes on liquor yielded $3,500,000 to the local governments and $500,000 to the state, while malt beverages paid nearly $3,000,000 to the state. In addition taverns that dispense hard liquor, as practically all of them do, are required to pay a federal tax of $25 each. In the two fiscal years 1937 and 1938, the federal government under this law collected in Wisconsin a little more than $335,000 each year. This shows that the taverns numbered about 13,400, or approximately one to every 225 people.

WOMAN SUFFRAGE AND WOMEN'S RIGHTS

The World War, though of great importance, was but a short episode in American history; and the experiment of nation-wide prohibition lasted only fourteen years. The elevation of women to political and legal equality with men, on the other hand, represents a permanent accomplishment. It is rather amazing that the subordination of women continued so long; when they received the right to vote, and certain other privileges were assured to them about the same time, another relic of medieval custom vanished forever.

The rejected Wisconsin constitution of 1846 provided, with what was then daring innovation, that married women might hold property apart from their husbands; and while that clause was omitted from the instrument of 1848, the same end was effected soon after by legislation. Coeducation was the announced policy of the state university from 1851 onward, though it was not a reality in all departments until a quarter of a century later. Women were made eligible to school district offices soon after the Civil War, and before the end of the century many were serving on city school boards and as county superintendents.

In 1869 a Woman Suffrage Association was formed that was to last until its goal was attained fifty-one years later. In 1885 the presidency of this body was assumed by the Reverend Olympia Brown, nationally known as a feminist leader. She is said to have been the first woman to graduate from a theological seminary.

She occupied the pulpit in several Wisconsin churches in succession, in 1878 becoming pastor in Racine. Her presidency of the association was destined to last for twenty-seven years. By a legislative act (1885) approved by referendum, women were given the right to vote at "any election pertaining to school matters." The Rev. Olympia Brown and others insisted that they now had the right to vote for any officials who had anything to do with the schools; for example, for the mayor and aldermen of Racine. The state supreme court, however, showed that the intent of the legislature had been to give women merely the right to help choose officials in school districts. The act of 1885 remained practically a dead letter for many years.

An act was passed in 1911 providing for the extension of suffrage to women, subject to referendum as required by the constitution. Besides the association there was organized a Political Equality League, whose president was Miss Ada L. James. The American Suffragettes also appeared in Milwaukee, and a mass meeting held under their auspices was addressed by Miss Emmaline Pankhurst of England. At the polls, in November, 1912, woman suffrage was lost by more than 90,000 votes. After this defeat the association and the league united, retaining the old name of Woman Suffrage Association. Its president during the next eight years was Mrs. Henry Youmans of Waukesha. Early in 1919 the Wisconsin legislature authorized another referendum; but this was rendered unnecessary by the Nineteenth Amendment to the federal constitution. The Wisconsin legislature ratified this in June, 1919, and its ratification was the first to be received in Washington. The amendment went into effect in August, 1920. The Woman Suffrage Association thereupon became the League of Women Voters.

A further step in giving equality with men to the women of Wisconsin was a bill passed in 1921, usually called the Equal Rights Bill. Its most important sentence runs: "Women shall have the same rights and privileges under the law as men in the exercise of suffrage, freedom of contract, choice of residence for voting purposes, jury service, holding office, holding and conveying property, care and custody of children, and in all other respects." By an amendment approved at the election of November, 1934, the right of women to vote was written into the constitution of Wisconsin.

SELECTED BIBLIOGRAPHY

For the study of Wisconsin's part in the World War two books are available: Fred L. Holmes, *Wisconsin's War Record* (Madison, 1919): and Rutherford B. Pixley, *Wisconsin in the World War* (Milwaukee, 1919). "Wisconsin's War Activities," in the *Blue Book, 1919,* pp. 301-438, gives both military statistics and data about the home front. There is a chapter, "The World War and After," in Milo M. Quaife, *Wisconsin, Its History and Its People* (4 vols., Chicago, 1924), Vol. II, pp. 73-106. *The Thirty-second Division in the World War, 1917-1919* (Madison, 1920), was issued by the Joint War History Commissions of Michigan and Wisconsin.

The beginnings of the American Legion are narrated in Marquis James, *A History of the American Legion* (New York, 1923). Its later development in Wisconsin may be followed in the semi-monthly publication, *The Badger Legionnaire,* published at Appleton since 1922. Details about the federal care of veterans in the various states may be found in the *Annual Report of the Administrator of Veterans Affairs.*

Delos Sackett Otis, *The Rise of National Prohibition, 1865-1919* (Ph.D. thesis, MS, Madison, 1929), is excellent. There are articles on Eugene Wilder Chafin and Samuel Dexter Hastings in the *Dictionary of American Biography.* Peter H. Odegard, *Pressure Politics: the Story of the Anti-Saloon League* (New York, 1928) finds some typical activities of the league well illustrated in Wisconsin. *The Year Book of the Anti-Saloon League* (Westerville, Ohio, annual beginning 1908) has maps showing wet and dry territory. The Mulberger act is Chap. 556 of the *Session Laws* of 1919; the Severson act is Chap. 441 of the *Session Laws* of 1921; the latter was repealed by Chap. 129 of 1929. The activities and griefs of the state prohibition commissioner of Wisconsin are described in the *Blue Book, 1927,* pp. 263-268, and the *Blue Book, 1929,* pp. 303-305.

President Hoover's National Commission on Law Observance and Enforcement, often called the Wickersham Commission, issued as the first part of its findings, "Report on the Enforcement of the Prohibition Laws of the United States," 71st Cong., 3d Sess., House Doc., No. 722. A report on conditions in Wisconsin under prohibition may be found in 71st Cong., 3d Sess., Senate Doc. No. 307 (Serial number 9341), Vol. IV, pp. 1097-1116.

In the monumental *History of Woman Suffrage,* edited by Susan B. Anthony, Ida Husted Harper, and others (6 vols., Rochester, New York,

1881-1922), sections devoted to Wisconsin are found in Vol. IV, pp. 985-996, and Vol. VI, pp. 699-708. The decision of the state supreme court in the case of Olympia Brown is given in *Wisconsin Reports,* Vol. LXXI, pp. 239-255 (1888). Mrs. Theodore W. Youmans, one of the leaders in the crusade, contributed "How Wisconsin Women Won the Ballot" to the *Wisconsin Magazine of History,* Vol. V, pp. 3-32 (September, 1921). Chester C. Platt included a chapter, "The Legal Status of Women," in *What La Follette's State is Doing* (Batavia, New York, 1924), pp. 149-166.

CHAPTER XVII

MODERN LIFE AND THE GROWTH OF INDUSTRY

THE history of English-speaking Wisconsin began when Southerners came to work the lead mines in the southwestern part of the state and Yankee farmers came to choose farms in the southeastern section. They brought with them the tools and appliances to which they had been accustomed in their former homes. Since that time mechanical inventions and the progress of science have so changed the manner and tempo of American life that virtually a new civilization has come into being. During the past half-century the United States has become outstanding, even among the more advanced nations of the world, by reason of the degree to which applied science and new inventions have been made available to most of our population. Life with such things as telephones, electric light and power, and modern means of transportation is infinitely richer and less toilsome than it would be without them.

But the progress of science and invention did more than merely make life easier for the individual. As machinery came to the farm, a smaller percentage of the population was sufficient to produce food for all, and an increasing number of men and women turned from agriculture to industry. Wealth accumulated rapidly. Wisconsin became a great manufacturing state, but in so doing came face to face with the problem of readjustment that usually confronts industrial nations. Farmers continued to be important in economic and political life, but alongside them arose a class of urban laboring men. Politicians sought their votes and legislation was passed to aid and care for them.   At the same time the masters of accumulated capital, whether bankers or lumber "barons" or the owners of railroads and factories, gained great political power, and quite naturally and often with complete honesty sought such legislation in state and nation as would conduce to their own greater profit.   We may picture as existing at the foundation of the state a simple agricultural economy and its expression in political life, but an economy which began almost at once to change into something different, until eventually we have the complicated pattern of the present, with its many conflicting interests and antagonistic pressure groups.

WATERWORKS AND ELECTRICAL EQUIPMENT

There is in common use today a number of the appurtenances or conveniences of life which were lacking during the childhood of many now living.   Among them is the central water supply. In early Wisconsin, water was usually secured in villages and cities much as it is on farms today, either from a spring or by means of hand pumps, with windmills added a little later.   Central waterworks in all the United States numbered only eighty-three in 1850.   Even cities like Buffalo and Cleveland were at that time without them.   Milwaukee long secured water for household purposes from springs and wells.   In 1873 a temporary pumping station began to send water from the Milwaukee River through the newly laid mains, while in the following year the North Point Station went into operation, drawing its water from an intake 2,000 feet out in Lake Michigan.

Waterworks appeared in most Wisconsin cities between 1880 and 1900, in many cases beginning as private business enterprises. Often it was well into the twentieth century before measures were taken to provide uncontaminated and filtered water.   By 1935, 318 communities were served by central waterworks.   About two-thirds of them derived their water from deep or rock wells, and most of the rest from shallow or drift wells.   A few systems used the water of lakes, springs, or rivers.   In the great majority of

Wisconsin communities, the waterworks are municipally owned. In 1939 there were 302 communities which owned waterworks, and but 14 where the waterworks were privately owned. In the latter group were a number of moderate-sized cities: among them, Beloit, Merrill, and Superior. The state board of health now inspects all waterworks and must approve the plans for new construction.

Before the Civil War candles furnished light for Wisconsin homes. About 1865 kerosene became available, and was the chief illuminant until it was displaced either by gas or electricity. By 1875 there were plants to furnish gas manufactured from coal in many Wisconsin cities. The invention in 1885 of the Welsbach incandescent gas mantle gave gas a new lease on life in its struggle against electric lighting; but ultimately electricity was the victor almost everywhere. Gas, however, found a new use in cooking and heating, and in this field seems able to hold its ground.

Alexander Graham Bell first demonstrated his invention, the telephone, on March 10, 1876, and exhibited it at the centennial exposition in that year. The inventor and his financial associates formed a succession of Bell telephone companies that controlled the business in many ways until the expiration of Bell's most important patents in 1893 and 1894. The Bell companies sold telephones and licensed the use of them, and their monopoly tended to limit early development to the cities.

Within two or three years of its invention, however, the telephone was in use in several places in Wisconsin. In 1877 a banker of Appleton named Alfred Galpin connected his office with his residence; early in the following year there was a small exchange in operation in Appleton. Richard Valentine of Janesville also built a private line in 1877, and in 1878 installed telephones for other people in Janesville, Berlin, and elsewhere. Charles H. Haskins formed a company in Milwaukee which became the chief representative of the Bell interests in the state, and ultimately developed into the Wisconsin Telephone Company, which today handles about three-fifths of Wisconsin's telephone business.

After the principal Bell patents had expired, a great many independent telephone companies were formed and the use of the telephone became more common, especially in rural areas. Within the twentieth century there has been much consolidation of companies, many of the independents having sold out to the Wisconsin Telephone Company. In 1890 there were in Wisconsin about three telephones for each one thousand inhabitants. In 1929 there were more than 550,000 telephone subscribers among a population of less than three millions.

Arc lights had been in use for illuminating streets for many years when Thomas A. Edison invented the incandescent lamp in 1879. Within a short time a company was formed, with headquarters at Chicago, to promote the new system in the Middle West and to sell and install the necessary machinery. The first customers were a group of men, most of them factory owners, of Appleton. The water power of the Fox River, already harnessed for the paper mills, was used to drive the dynamos, and the first light was produced September 30, 1882. Within a few weeks it was found best to remove the dynamos from the two mills where they had first been installed and place them in a small building erected especially for them. Primacy in commercial lighting is denied to Appleton because earlier in the same month an electric lighting plant run by steam power had come into operation in New York City; Appleton must rest content with the distinction of having had the first hydroelectric plant in the world. Between 1882 and the end of the century electric lighting became an integral part of American civilization.

Streetcars drawn by horses appeared in New York City in 1832, and horses remained the chief motive power for urban transportation in spite of some competition from steam until they were supplanted by electricity in the last decade of the nineteenth century. Horsecars were found in many cities in Wisconsin in the eighties and nineties. The dynamo to furnish heavy electric current was perfected by a German inventor, Werner von Siemens, about 1867. He and his partner, Halske, constructed an electric car for exhibition in 1879. Two years later in a suburb of Berlin, Germany, they began the operation of the first commercial electric streetcar in the world. Meanwhile, in the United States, Thomas A. Edison built a demonstration car in New Jersey in 1880. Electric streetcars were operated for profit at Cleveland, Ohio, in 1884, and at Kansas City, Missouri, in the following year, and by 1887 there were electric streetcars at a dozen widely scattered places in the United States. Appleton again led the way in Wisconsin by having such a streetcar in operation in August, 1886, though service was not continuous from that early date. The electric streetcar was introduced in most Wisconsin cities during the decade of the nineties; and in the first ten years of the twentieth century interurban electric lines were built in the more densely populated parts of the state. Between 1920 and 1940, however, these lines were almost all replaced by motor bus service, and by the latter year streetcars were still in use only in the cities of Milwaukee and La Crosse. Besides these, a few interurban lines were still maintained.

In generating electricity, water power and steam are the chief rivals; oil burning engines are of little consequence. About two-thirds of the possible water power in Wisconsin has already been harnessed, and the streams that floated logs half a century ago now give wealth in another form. Most of Wisconsin's water power is developed by means of about 190 dams, about three-fourths of it by the thirty-eight largest dams. It costs considerably more to install a hydroelectric generating plant than a steam plant of the same capacity, and the promoter chooses between interest charges in the case of a hydroelectric power plant and the cost of fuel for a steam plant. In 1929 water power furnished a little less than forty per cent of the electricity developed in Wisconsin.

MOTOR VEHICLES AND HIGHWAY IMPROVEMENT

The advent of the railroad brought a great change in transportation, a change, indeed, in man's whole economic life; from about

1850 until near the end of the nineteenth century railroads monopolized the interest and the financial resources of society in the field
of transportation to the almost utter neglect of other means.   The
ordinary highways were badly maintained by local authorities and
were used either for purely local traffic or as feeders to the railroads.
The popularity of the bicycle after about 1880 brought some loud
demands for better roads, and the paving of city streets made
some progress in the last two decades of the century, but country
roads in Wisconsin remained in the care of the towns and generally speaking were in bad condition.

It was the automobile that changed all this.   The internal com-
bustion engine burning oil or gasoline was developed in Germany
in the 1880's, the leading inventors being three men named Otto,
Daimler, and Benz.   In 1895 a Frenchman drove a primitive
automobile, equipped with one of these engines, from Paris to
Bordeaux and back again, a distance of 744 miles, and averaged
fifteen miles an hour.   In 1899, 3,700 automobiles were manufactured in the United States, and in 1904 more than 21,000.

Automobiles had appeared in Wisconsin by 1900, and in 1905,
when licenses were first required, there were 1,492 of them in
the state.   Annual licenses were first required in 1911-1912, and by
that time there were more than 20,000 automobiles in Wisconsin.
Their widespread use came with the World War.   The number
first passed 100,000 in 1916, 200,000 in 1919, and 300,000 in 1921.
Eight hundred and seventy-one thousand motor vehicles were
licensed in Wisconsin in 1937, including 712,000 automobiles, 141,-
000 trucks, and 5,000 trailers.

The automobile brought with it a new era in highway building,
and the construction and maintenance of roads has become one of
the chief functions of government.   A Wisconsin law of 1907
(the county aid law) provided that a town might tax itself for
road improvement, whereupon the county must match the funds
provided by the town.   During the next four years twenty-four
counties and some of the towns within them spent about $300,000
under the law.

The constitution forbade the use of state funds for works of internal improvement, and this prohibition had to be removed by a constitutional amendment, finally approved in 1908. The legislature of 1911 passed the first state aid law and appropriated $350,-000 to aid counties and towns. The sum was inadequate to the demand, and the legislature of 1913 raised the annual appropriation to $1,200,000. As a part of Governor Philipp's retrenchment program the annual appropriation was cut down to $785,000 in 1915 and there it remained for ten years. In 1911 the Wisconsin Highway Commission was set up. It was this body that originated in 1918 the system of marking highways with numbers and letters and of issuing corresponding highway maps.

In 1916 federal grants to the states to aid in highway construction began. During the fourteen years 1917-1930, Wisconsin's share of the federal gifts exceeded $23,000,000, and in 1931-1932 the annual grant exceeded three million dollars. Partly to comply with the conditions of the first federal grant, a law of 1917 (the state trunk highway law) authorized definite planning for a system of five thousand miles of roads to join together all county seats and all places of considerable population. In subsequent years the plan was extended until it now includes 10,000 miles of roads. At first counties had to share the burden of matching federal gifts, but in 1923 the state government assumed the whole task. Between 1919 and 1923 many counties voted large bond issues to pay for road building.

Expenditure on highways by the state and its subdivisions increased steadily until it reached about $70,000,000 a year in 1930 and 1931; these totals included the interest on money borrowed by the subdivisions and the retirement of some bonds. Such an outlay placed the highways, temporarily at least, alongside of education, so that before the recent increase of public relief the two stood as the most expensive enterprises of government in Wisconsin. At the beginning of 1931 there were some 80,000 miles of roads in Wisconsin. About 50,000 miles were unsurfaced dirt roads kept up by the towns with a little help from the state. Of the 30,000 miles of surfaced roads, 10,000 miles were regularly patrolled and maintained as state or federal trunk lines, and the rest were either city streets or county roads. The investment in Wisconsin highways made during the quarter-century ending in 1931 by the federal, state, and local governments exceeded the total cost of all the railways in the state.

The automobile and modern highways have effected far-reaching changes in our way of life. The horse has practically disappeared from the cities and from the principal highways. Save among the genuinely rural population, the younger generation knows little of the noble animal that was long man's faithful helper. The new transportation has brought bankruptcy to many railroads. It has greatly altered country life in such matters as education, social activities, and marketing. It has made larger cities possible and has given the city dweller and the commuter a new freedom.

Mining and Smelting

At present the principal economic activities of Wisconsin are agriculture and various forms of manufacture. Though less important than either of these, mining and smelting have played some part in the enrichment of the state. The first considerable English-speaking group in Wisconsin came to the southwestern part of the state to work the lead mines there. This region has been predominantly agricultural since about 1850, but some lead and zinc are still extracted by modern methods. In 1927 the zinc produced was valued at more than four million dollars. The five years 1933-1937, however, showed Wisconsin producing only about a third as much as it had done in the years 1925-1929.

There are four regions in Wisconsin where iron has been mined in quantity, two in the south-central and two in the northern part of the state. The earliest iron mining was done at Mayville and at Iron Ridge in Dodge County, where in 1849 there were both a mine and a small charcoal furnace. Before the panic of 1873 this region was sending ore to Chicago and St. Louis, to points in

Michigan and Ohio, and to three or four places in Wisconsin where smelting furnaces had been erected. In 1893 the North-western Iron Company of Milwaukee opened a mine at Mayville which in the next thirty years produced a million and a half tons of ore. The other south-central region was in Sauk County. Mining was begun in 1904 on the "Baraboo range," and during the next twenty years this area shipped something over half a million tons. The ore is good in quality and considerable in quantity but, since it lies nearly five hundred feet beneath the surface of the earth, the mining is too expensive for it to compete with that of more favored regions.

The iron ore of Dodge and Sauk counties, small in amount or difficult of access, has proved much less important commercially than Wisconsin's share in the deposits about Lake Superior. Three areas in Upper Michigan yield iron in paying quantities: the Marquette, the Menominee, and the Gogebic ranges. The richest and most accessible deposits of all are in Minnesota, which, though later developed, easily outdistanced anything in Michigan or Wisconsin. The presence of iron near Marquette, Michigan, was known to the prospectors who sought copper in that vicinity from 1845 onward, and regular shipments of ore from the Marquette range began in 1856, by way of the canal around the rapids at Sault Ste. Marie completed the year before. The Menominee range included mines at Vulcan, Cyclops, Norway, and Quinnesec, and the Chapin mine near Iron Mountain, all of these in Upper Michigan. The engineer who developed all these properties, beginning with the Vulcan mine in 1873, was Nelson Powell Hulst, who was employed first by a succession of companies with headquarters at Milwaukee. It was soon known that the ore deposits continued westward into Wisconsin, and in 1881 the railroad along the range crossed the Menominee River into what was soon to be Florence County, Wisconsin. The first mine there, the county, and the county seat were all named Florence in honor of Mrs. Hulst. The ore was shipped by the Chicago and North Western Railway to Escanaba, and thence by boats to ports on the lower lakes. Between 1881 and 1923 about seven million tons of ore were mined in Florence County. This area has not been able in recent years to meet the competition of the Minnesota ranges. Insignificant amounts of ore were mined in 1929 and 1930, and after that none at all. Florence County has become emphatically a "depressed area," as the English say. It has by quite a margin the smallest population of any county in the state, and of late (1936 to 1939) more than half of its people have been on relief.

The continuation of the Gogebic range of Upper Michigan into Wisconsin is called the Penokee range. It extends for some forty miles westward from the interstate boundary across Iron, Ashland, and Bayfield counties. The eastern third of this range is the only part thus far developed. Hurley, the chief town of the region in Wisconsin, was founded in 1885, and shipments of ore began that year, by rail to Ashland and thence by boat to the lower lakes. The opening of the Gogebic and the Penokee ranges was accompanied by a speculative mania, the "booming of the Gogebic," during which the prices of mining stocks rose to fantastic heights. The bubble burst in August, 1885, and while many lost in the gamble, the excitement made capital available for rapid development. During the fifteen years 1923-1937, Iron County has been the only one in the state to mine the ore in significant quantity. The value of Wisconsin iron ore at the mines in 1900 was more than $2,000,000. By 1910 this had risen to $3,500,000; and in 1919, when wartime prices still prevailed, the value exceeded $4,000,000. In 1929 the mines produced 1,500,000 tons, but by 1933 the figure had fallen to just over 250,000, and it did not again pass a million tons until 1937. The price at the mine is usually about $3.00 a ton.

Wisconsin businessmen took steps after the Civil War to develop the smelting industry. The timber of the virgin forests could be made into charcoal and used for fuel, while the railroads then being rapidly built brought ore to the furnaces and carried the pig iron to market. Between 1868 and 1874 eleven blast furnaces were constructed in Wisconsin: one at Green Bay, two at De Pere, two at Appleton, one at Fond du Lac that was never put in blast because the panic of 1873 came on, and three at Bay View, Milwaukee. These furnaces continued in most cases until the forests in their vicinity were exhausted. The two enterprises at De Pere each had charcoal kilns in connection with the furnaces and together produced nearly 2,500 bushels of charcoal a day, using daily the timber from two and one-half acres of forest lands. The Milwaukee furnaces either began with anthracite coal or were remodeled to use it, and thus were able to continue after the exhaustion of the forests.

MANUFACTURING

Fifty-three per cent of the people of Wisconsin is now urban; that is, this percentage lives in communities of more than 2,500 population; and the rural population is in the minority. Of 1,129,000 "gainful workers" found by the census takers in 1930, less than 300,000 were returned as farmers or farm laborers. Factory operatives and factory laborers numbered about 167,000, and these were but a part of a larger group, engaged in what were called "manufactures and mechanical industries," that counted nearly 376,000.

While the total value of manufactures in Wisconsin increased steadily until 1929, there have been constant changes in the relative importance of the various industries. The statistics issued by the federal government after each decennial census show these movements. In the following summary the figures in parentheses give the value for the year indicated in millions of dollars.

According to the census of 1880, which reports the manufactures for the year 1879, flour and grist mill products were first (27) among Wisconsin's manufactures, lumber and timber stood second (18), leather was a long way behind as third (nearly 9), and then close together came liquors, iron and steel, and meat packing (all 6) in the order named. Ten years later lumber and timber had risen to first place (60), the flour and grist mills were second (24), malt liquor was third (14), leather fourth (11), and foundry and machine shop products were fifth (8). Meat packing was sixth (8), and butter, cheese, and condensed milk were seventh (nearly 7). At no time before or after 1890 did liquor rank so high.

Lumber and timber held first rank for three decades without much change in values (1890, 60; 1900, 57; 1910, 57). In 1900 flour and grist mill products held second place (26), and after them stood foundry and machine shop products (22), butter, cheese, and condensed milk (20), leather (20), and malt liquors (19). Ten years later the order was the same except that flour and grist mill products had dropped from second to sixth place, and consequently the other four items just named for 1900 each rose one place in the list. In the decade the value of each of the four had more than doubled.

When reading the figures furnished in the census report of 1920, which were based on manufactures during 1919, we must remember the high prices that prevailed during the World War and through 1919. Butter, cheese, and condensed milk had multiplied in value fourfold since 1909 and had taken first place (221), while lumber and timber, though of greater value (88) than in 1910, had fallen to seventh place. Foundry and machine shop products were second (198), motor vehicles not including motorcycles stood third (119), and meat packing was fourth (104). Thus four industries each manufactured products valued at more than $100,000,000. Two items destined to a great increase in the decade to follow were paper and wood pulp, which stood eighth (80), and electrical machinery, which was twentieth (23).

The last available decennial report is for 1929. By the close of that year the depression had begun, but it probably affected the figures reported but little except in the group of dairy products, where low prices had already set in. Butter, cheese, and condensed milk had fallen to second place and to a lower total (203) than in 1920. First place had been taken by motor vehicles (210), while the sixth item in the list was motor vehicle bodies and motor vehicle parts, and the twelfth was rubber tires and tubes; these three together had a value of $355,000,000. Third and fifth places, respectively, were held by foundry and machine shop products (149) and engines, turbines, and tractors (96).[1] Paper and wood pulp had risen to fourth place (129). Places seven to eleven were held by wholesale meat packing, boots and shoes, knit goods, electrical machinery (48), which had doubled during the decade, and lumber and timber (44), which was but half as valuable as ten years earlier. Other industries of some importance were the production of canned goods (35) and aluminum (21), which seemed to be increasing, and agricultural implements (27), which showed a decline. The list of Wisconsin's manufactures thus exhibited the greatest diversity.

Besides the decennial reports, from which the foregoing figures were drawn, the federal government publishes a biennial census of manufactures. The volumes for 1935 and 1937 show Wisconsin business climbing out of the great depression. In comparing the conditions of 1935 with those of six years earlier, one notes some changes in the order of the industries, but most striking was the shrinkage of values all along the line. The value of motor vehicles was not given for either 1935 or 1937, in order not to reveal even approximately the production of a single plant; almost certainly they no longer headed the list. Of industries for which figures could be given, butter, cheese, and condensed and evaporated milk stood first (156 in 1935, 168 in 1937), paper and wood pulp second (94 in 1935, 128 in 1937), and motor bodies and parts third (68 in 1935, 90 in 1937). The reborn brewing industry had a product valued at $44,000,000 in 1935 and $51,000,000 two years later. No data were collected where the product of a plant was worth less than $5,000 a year, but the establishments covered by the census of 1935 produced goods valued at $1,314,-000,000. In 1937 the total was $1,772,000,000, and at that time Wisconsin ranked tenth among all the states in the value of her manufactures.

While some industries wax, others wane. Underneath the sta-

---

[1] Figures in parentheses represent millions of dollars.

tistics of growth and decay lies the throbbing life of our people, the endless striving for profit, for economic betterment. Industry must be in a constant state of transition as it readjusts itself to the demands of a nation-wide and even a world-wide market. On the one hand, looking to agriculture for materials, Wisconsin has developed the manufacture of butter, cheese, and condensed milk and has built up meat packing and leather industries. On the other hand, as the forests have declined, she has created new industries based largely on metal work, carried on by a combination of scientific knowledge and engineering skill. Changes of emphasis are certain to come in the future. But Wisconsin's accomplishments during the first third of the twentieth century point to success in the years to come.

SELECTED BIBLIOGRAPHY

Eliot Jones and Truman C. Bigham, in *The Principles of Public Utilities* (New York, 1931), though chiefly concerned with contemporary organization, give valuable bits of history about the utilities. Louise P. Kellogg told of beginnings in "The Electric Light System at Appleton," *Wisconsin Magazine of History,* Vol. VI, pp. 189-194 (December, 1922). Harry Barrantee wrote "The History and Development of the Telephone in Wisconsin," *ibid.,* Vol. X, pp. 150-163 (December, 1926). In the *Wisconsin Regional Planning Committee Report* (Madison, 1934), pp. 148-154, there is a brief discussion of public and private water supply systems. Adolph Kannenberg has written ably of "The Water Power Situation in Wisconsin," in *Blue Book, 1929,* pp. 75-96.

The development of public highways in the twentieth century may be studied in a chapter by Francis A. Cannon, "The Highway System," in Milo M. Quaife, *Wisconsin, Its History and Its People* (4 vols., Chicago, 1924), Vol. II, pp. 453-480; and in M. W. Torkelson, "Wisconsin Highways," in the *Blue Book, 1931,* pp. 9-29.

Joseph Schafer, *The Wisconsin Lead Region* (Madison, 1932), pp. 92-109, describes the methods of lead mining, chiefly before 1860. William Stuart Smith wrote, as a B.A. thesis, *The Development of Iron Mining in Wisconsin* (MS, Madison, 1923). Ellis B. Usher, in "Nelson Powell Hulst, the Greatest American Authority on Iron," *Wisconsin Magazine of History,* Vol. VII, pp. 385-405 (June, 1924), tells how iron mining was begun in Florence County. A good account of mining around Lake Superior is given in William W. Folwell, *History of Minnesota* (4 vols., Minneapolis, 1924-1931), Vol. IV, pp. 1-60. Statistics of mineral production are given in the reports of the Bureau of Mines, since 1924 called the *Mineral Year-book*, and before that *Mineral Resources* (Washington, annual).

The standard work on its subject is Victor S. Clark, *History of Manu-factures in the United States* (4 vols., New York, 1929). Statistics about industry in Wisconsin may be gathered from each decennial census of the United States beginning with the seventh census, 1850. There is also a quinquennial census of manufactures from 1904, and a biennial one be-ginning with 1921. See, for example, *Biennial Census of Manufactures, 1935* (Washington, 1938). A good deal of material from these federal reports is repeated in the biennial Wisconsin *Blue Books*. See J. H. H. Alexander, "A Short Industrial History of Wisconsin," *Blue Book, 1929,* pp. 31-49; and Edwin E. Witte, "Wisconsin in the 1930 Census," *Blue Book, 1933,* pp. 103-132. Pages 123-129 are devoted to manufactures and page 132 to mining. Statistics of manufactures in counties and the larger cities are given, *ibid.,* pp. 696, 697. The *Wisconsin Regional Planning Committee Report* (Madison, 1934), pp. 291-350, presents much statistical material about manufacturing and electric power in interesting graphs and charts.

CHAPTER XVIII

POLITICS SINCE 1906

PROGRESSIVES IN POWER, 1906-1915

THE history of Wisconsin politics from 1906 to 1940 falls into several rather clearly marked periods. (1) The first of these is a continuation of the movement that elevated Robert M. La Follette to the governorship. It lasted on through five years under Governor Davidson and four under McGovern. (2) In the election of 1914 the Stalwarts or conservative Republicans elected Emanuel L. Philipp to the office of governor, which he held for six years. In his time the flow of progressive legislation was checked, but no great measure of the preceding period was repealed. (3) Then came six years (1921-1927) under John J. Blaine, during which the influence of La Follette and the progressive wing of the Republican party was again paramount. La Follette died in June, 1925. (4) After Blaine came Zimmerman and then Kohler, each of whom had one term. Though Zimmerman had long adhered to the senior La Follette, he gained the Republican nomination in 1926 against the wishes of Blaine and Robert M. La Follette, Jr., and the four years of Zimmerman and Kohler form an interruption in the progressive dominance over the state. (5) At the election of 1930 the "regular" Republicans such as Hoover and Kohler could be blamed for the depression, and Philip F. La Follette captured the Republican nomination and was elected. His tenure of office was interrupted by the Democratic landslide of 1932, which made Schmedeman governor. During Schmedeman's last year the progressives finally abandoned the Republican party and formed their own Progressive party. Under its banner Philip La Follette was twice chosen governor. In 1938 he sought a fourth term, but was not elected. (6) A Republican administration began with the inauguration of Julius P. Heil in January, 1939.

When the elder La Follette resigned the governorship and entered the United States Senate early in 1906, the lieutenant governor, James O. Davidson, succeeded him in Wisconsin. Davidson was a native of Norway. After coming to America, he was a farm hand, learned the tailor's trade, and kept a general store. For six years he was in the legislature and then for four years he was state treasurer. One of Wisconsin's leading writers on politics thus described him: "Mr. Davidson was a kind-hearted, good-natured, and well-meaning man with a dash of natural shrewdness. He had not had the opportunity for education, he did not have a grasp of economic and governmental problems, but he had a high sense of justice." [1]

During Davidson's governorship the progressive legislation begun under La Follette was continued. All public utilities were made subject to the railroad commission, and they and the railroads were restrained from stock-watering. A two-cent railway fare law was passed and insurance companies were regulated. Several steps were taken looking towards the conservation of natural resources. In accordance with Wisconsin practice, a constitutional amendment authorizing the imposition of an income tax was passed by two successive legislatures and approved by popular vote.

In the spring of 1907, United States Senator John L. Spooner resigned his office to take up the practice of law in New York City. The legislature chose as his successor Isaac Stephenson, a millionaire lumberman of Marinette. This vigorous man had been born in New Brunswick in 1829. During the 1880's he had sat in the House of Representatives, and the goal of his ambition, long before

---

[1] Fred L. Holmes, in Milo M. Quaife, *Wisconsin, Its History and Its People* (4 vols., Chicago, 1924), Vol. II, p. 34.

1907, had been a seat in the Senate. In 1899 Stephenson was encouraged, he says, to believe that he might succeed Senator John L. Mitchell, but the seat was given to Joseph V. Quarles, and Stephenson at the age of 70 began to "realize for the first time the power and devious ways" of the machine! The result was that he joined in La Follette's crusade. He maintained that he persuaded La Follette to run for governor in 1900 when the latter was disposed not to do so. He financed the Milwaukee *Free Press* and helped the progressives with many gifts of money. He later asserted that he had spent no less than half a million dollars in the cause. Surely such zeal should have its reward.

Stephenson would have been glad to succeed Quarles in 1905, but La Follette was elected. When Spooner resigned, the legislature in choosing his successor was deadlocked for many weeks. Besides Stephenson, the leading candidates were Congressman Esch and State Senator William H. Hatton of New London. Finally, on May 17, 1907, Stephenson was elected for the remainder of Spooner's term, which ran until March, 1909. In the fall of 1908 he announced himself as a candidate for re-election. To win out in the preferential primary, which was taken to guide the legislature in its choice, some of the other candidates spent large sums of money, but Stephenson spent far more. In 1907 Senator La Follette had been noncommittal about Stephenson; now he was openly opposed to him. The result of the primary was not very decisive, though Stephenson had a plurality.

When the legislature met, a state senator, John J. Blaine of Boscobel, called for an investigation into the recent campaign. An inquiry was conducted during which another state senator, Paul O. Husting, a Democrat, displayed great energy and ability, so becoming favorably known throughout the state. Stephenson admitted having spent more than $107,000. Governor Davidson believed, however, that Stephenson was the choice of the people and should be elected, and, in spite of the great expenditures which had been brought to light, he was finally chosen by the legislature on March 3, 1909—just a few weeks before his eightieth birthday.

After the Wisconsin investigation there was another by a committee of the United States Senate. Its decision was that, while there had been a foolish waste of money, nothing illegal had been done. This report was approved by the Senate, with La Follette voting against accepting it. Stephenson's election by the legislature was taken as evidence that La Follette was not in control of the state.

Francis E. McGovern, Davidson's successor, was born on a farm in Sheboygan County in 1866. After some years spent in alternate teaching and studying, he established himself as a lawyer in Milwaukee. For four years (1901-1905) he held the appointive office of assistant district attorney in Milwaukee County, and thereafter he was twice elected district attorney. In these positions he distinguished himself by a crusade against dishonesty in municipal politics in which more than two hundred people were indicted. He was an unsuccessful candidate for the United States Senate in 1908, but two years later he was elected governor. That same autumn, by means of the preferential primary, La Follette was indicated as the choice of the people for Senator and duly reelected. This was the last time the legislature of Wisconsin chose a United States Senator.

McGovern's first message to the legislature of 1911 was a well-presented statement of the progressive program. "Few legislatures," he said, "have convened in Wisconsin with equal opportunity for doing good." Calling attention to the consolidation or concentration taking place in finance and industry, he urged forcefully but without bitterness that these great combinations be regulated but not destroyed. Under McGovern's leadership the legislatures of 1911 and 1913 passed an unusual number of epoch-making laws. The recent episode of the Stephenson election occasioned a new corrupt practices act. The old requirement of reports of expenditures was retained, and in addition limits were set to the amount candidates might spend. An industrial commission was established and compensation for accidents in industry was made certain and speedy. The income tax was put in force, and important steps were taken in a great highway building program. A unique project for vocational education was inaugurated. A minimum wage law for women was passed. These were but the more outstanding of many measures enacted under McGovern.

The national election of 1912 was made memorable by the Bull Moose campaign and the split in the Republican ranks. McGovern declared his support of Roosevelt, and by that act parted company with La Follette. In the field of Wisconsin politics the whole progressive point of view was challenged anew by the Stalwarts, chiefly on the ground of the expense connected with progressive measures, whether to the state or to industry. After McGovern gained the Republican nomination, conservatives of both parties gravitated towards the Democratic candidate, Judge John C. Karel of Milwaukee, who made a vigorous campaign, attacking especially the new income tax. This was the year of Wilson's first election, and the movement in his favor doubtless aided Judge Karel. The outcome of the election was in doubt for days, and McGovern won at last by the narrow margin of about 12,000 votes. The progressives were thus given two more years of power.

The election of 1914 was an important one in Wisconsin. A close study of the campaign reveals a scene of great confusion. Woodrow Wilson had entered the White House in March, 1913, and what the Democratic party had accomplished by the summer of 1914 in national affairs had given new heart to Democrats everywhere. "The faded parade of Wisconsin democracy has taken on new life." Yet, as there were Republican Stalwarts and progressives, so there was a similar cleavage among Democrats. In 1914 they again nominated for governor Judge Karel, a conservative. This campaign was also the occasion for the first election of a United States Senator by popular vote under the new Seventeenth Amendment to the federal constitution. For this office the Democrats nominated Paul Oscar Husting, a bachelor lawyer of Mayville, who had distinguished himself in the Stephenson investigation. His father had been a German-speaking immigrant from Luxemburg; his mother was a daughter of Solomon Juneau, founder of Milwaukee. Throughout his public career Husting had favored progressive measures.

The Republicans at the primaries had to choose from a list of six candidates for governor. Two men were known as La Follette progressives, A. H. Dahl, whom Senator La Follette himself favored, and William H. Hatton of New London, long a leader in progressive legislation. Fifty thousand votes were divided almost equally between these two men. Conservative Republicans held a pre-primary gathering and organized behind Emanuel L. Philipp, with the result that he secured the Republican nomination by a plurality, having received 44,000 votes, or but little more than a third of all cast by the Republicans. The other nominations on the Republican state ticket all went to progressive candidates. When the platform committee met, after the primaries, progressives were in a majority and produced a platform not altogether to Philipp's liking. Senator La Follette had been very much displeased with McGovern because he had supported Theodore Roosevelt for President in 1912; when McGovern gained the Republican nomination for United States Senator, he did it in spite of vigorous opposition from the senior senator.

When the primaries were over, McGovern faced Husting, while devoted progressives lamented that for governor they could but choose between two conservatives, Philipp and Karel. They were offered a third choice by the launching, on October 6, of the independent candidacy of John J. Blaine of Boscobel. Blaine had been a member of the state senate for two terms in 1909 and 1911, and like Husting had played a leading part in investigating the expenditures of Stephenson. In 1912 he had campaigned for Woodrow Wilson, though nominally a Republican. Now, in 1914, it was hoped that he would gain the support of progressives, both Republican and Democratic. Senator La Follette came on from Washington after a serious illness to speak in his behalf.

The final election was as confused as its antecedents. The Republicans carried their whole state ticket with the Stalwart Philipp at its head, while all the other state offices went to progressives. The vote for Blaine was but 32,500, or about one-tenth of the total poll. McGovern was defeated by Husting in a contest so close that the result was in doubt for several days. In a state still Republican by every other test, this can be explained either by the weight of Senator La Follette's influence against McGovern or by the personal popularity of Husting. The Democrats elected twenty-six members to the assembly and ten to the senate.

It might be difficult to say, since Philipp was opposed by a Democrat who was also counted a conservative, that his election meant that Wisconsin had had enough of progressivism for the time; but that this was the case seems indicated in another way. In 1914 a vote was taken on no less than ten constitutional amendments. Two of them were to make amendment of the constitution easier. One provided for the recall of officers, except judicial, by popular vote, and another gave the people the right of initiative and referendum. Still another provided for a larger measure of home rule for cities and villages; this was particularly desired by Milwaukee. All these proposals and some others had received the approval of the two preceding legislatures, which had passed so much progressive legislation under McGovern. Yet to the mood of 1914 they seemed too extreme, too "Socialistic," and they all went down to defeat together.

GOVERNOR PHILIPP, STALWART

Emanuel L. Philipp was born in Sauk County in 1861 of mixed Italian-Swiss and German-Swiss ancestry. At the age of twenty he began work as a telegraph operator. He became a train dispatcher for the Chicago and North Western Railway and later a contracting freight agent for the same company. For a time he managed a lumber enterprise in Mississippi, where a small town is named for him; finally he came to own and manage a Wisconsin company that built and operated refrigerator cars. He was active in the Republican party, at first supporting La Follette, but he early separated from him politically because he disapproved of

La Follette's plans for taxing railways. In 1904 he published a book called *The Truth about Wisconsin Freight Rates,* and in 1909 another called *Political Reform in Wisconsin.* In these he took issue with some of La Follette's statements and conclusions. He came to be one of the leaders of the Stalwart wing of the party, supporting Taft in 1908 and again in 1912.

During the campaign of 1914 Philipp had promised to consolidate offices and boards, eliminate useless machinery, and effect great economies. Much was done to redeem the governor's promises. A new department, that of agriculture, was erected with a single commissioner at its head, and under his authority were gathered several services, some of which dated back into the nineteenth century. A conservation commission had been set up in 1911, but upon the establishment of a new body with the same name in 1915 a wide-reaching consolidation was effected. Philipp was of the opinion that the operation of the state institutions of learning might be much improved on the business side. Here he secured but a small part of the changes he had in mind. A central board of education was created to present the needs of these institutions to the legislature, and it was continued for eight years. Governor Philipp failed to get a state board of public welfare. While a candidate he had advocated the abolition of the tax commission, but he became convinced that he had been mistaken. In his second campaign he was able to assert that while the state had spent $30,000,000 in McGovern's second biennium, expenses were reduced to $26,000,000 in his own first term.

In June, 1916, Wisconsin along with other states was asked to send her National Guard to the Mexican border to aid the regular army of the United States in controlling Villa and his marauders. Wisconsin sent south about 4,100 men organized in these regiments. In September a cavalry unit of ninety men was added. Governor Philipp called a special one-day session of the legislature to make it possible for these soldiers to vote in the fall elections; and about two-thirds of them, probably most of those who were of age, did vote. The homeward movement began in November and the last Wisconsin troops were mustered out early in March, 1917. The value of the training received on the Mexican border became apparent when the crisis of the World War came upon the country.

In the campaign of 1916 La Follette was again the Republican nominee for United States Senator. Governor Philipp was the Republican choice to succeed himself. This time Philipp was in control of the platform convention, and it was counted significant that the platform made no reference to Senator La Follette. It turned out to be a Republican year. Charles Evans Hughes carried the state as presidential candidate, the Republicans gained all the state offices, and La Follette was sent to the Senate for his third term.

As the World War drew near, the American people became more and more wrought up against Germany, and, after the United States entered the war, hatred of the enemy became in the popular mind the touchstone of loyalty. Senator La Follette's attitude met with widespread criticism. From time to time newspaper writers and public speakers asserted that Wisconsin was not loyal to the American cause—a hasty deduction from the attitude of Senator La Follette and most of the Wisconsin Congressmen, and from the presence of the large German element in the population. It fell to Governor Philipp, in speeches and in writing, to defend the state. He asserted most forcefully that Wisconsin was loyal, and urged the people of the state to make a war record that would support his statement. Their response was all that could be desired.

For many years Senator La Follette had enjoyed a large and eager political following in Wisconsin. His partisans now had to choose whether they would agree with him or join in the hue and cry against him. Those who continued to stand with him by their choice condemned the Wilson administration and to a certain extent the vigorous war measures taken under the direction of Governor Philipp. They also became the object of some of the criticism directed against their leader. The most official Wisconsin censure of La Follette was known as the Wilcox resolution. Originating in the state senate and receiving the concurrence of the assembly on March 6, 1918, the resolution condemned Senator La Follette for his pacifistic ideas, his failure to see the righteousness of the cause of the United States, and his failure to support President Wilson.

In October of 1917, Senator Paul O. Husting was accidentally shot while on a hunting trip in northern Wisconsin, and there were special elections to choose his successor, the primary in March, and the final on April 2, 1918. The Democratic candidates were Joseph E. Davies,[2] who had just resigned from the Federal Trade Commission, and Charles McCarthy of the Legislative Reference Library, both of them pro-Wilson and pro-war men. There were at first three Republican candidates: Francis E. McGovern, now called a conservative, Congressman Irvine L. Lenroot, a progressive who believed in the war, and James Thompson of La Crosse, a La Follette candidate. McGovern withdrew before the primaries, and Republicans in choosing between Lenroot and Thompson had a clear issue. The primaries narrowed the field to Davies, Lenroot, and the Socialist candidate, Victor L. Berger. Those who wished to voice their disapproval of the war, and of the treatment meted out to Senator La Follette, voted in many cases for Victor Berger, who received a fourth of the poll. Lenroot triumphed over Davies by a safe margin.

Irvine Luther Lenroot was born in Superior, Wisconsin, in 1869. After attending the common schools and a business college, he became first a stenographer in a law office and then a court reporter; at the age of twenty-eight he was admitted to the bar. While La Follette was governor he was twice speaker of the assembly. In 1908 he was elected to the House of Representatives, where he served for nine years. In his last year the House was

---

[2] Davies was appointed United States ambassador to the U. S. S. R. in 1936, and ambassador to Belgium in 1938. In December, 1939, he was brought to Washington, D. C., and assigned to "special duties in the State Department as an adviser on international trade and on war emergency matters." *The New York Times*, December 27, 1939, p. 10.

Republican and he had some support for the office of speaker. Long a loyal lieutenant of La Follette, Lenroot parted from him on the issue of American participation in the war, being one of the two Wisconsin Congressmen who voted for the breach of relations with Germany.

The fall campaign, which came seven months after the election of Lenroot, was much colored by war issues and war conditions. It was also marked by a political movement supported by a numerous body of Wisconsin farmers. In March, 1917, a Wisconsin branch of the Nonpartisan League had been formed, but it did not have the significant place in 1918 that it was to have two years later. Far more important was the longer established American Society of Equity, whose state president at the time was J. N. Tittemore of Omro. A Farmers' Progressive League was formed by several anti-Philipp groups, among them La Follette partisans, leaders of the American Society of Equity, and other farm and labor organizations; of these groups the Equity men were the most numerous and the most important. The league was rapidly developed into a political party, and in convention on May 1, 1918, it nominated a full state ticket with Tittemore as the candidate for governor. The platform, besides listing the wants of the farmers, declared for a basic eight-hour day and was otherwise intended to attract the labor vote. A number of prominent La Follette men declared themselves for Tittemore, but not always for all the candidates of the Farmers' League; Tittemore was generally looked upon as the La Follette candidate.

Those progressives who had repudiated La Follette because of his pacifistic attitude favored Roy B. Wilcox of Eau Claire, author of the Wilcox resolution. Of him Tittemore said that he was "body and breeches in the gizzard of the great corporations and water-power monopolies of the state." [3] Wilcox, for his part, emphasized his services to the progressive cause and his zeal for the war. Governor Philipp in his own behalf pointed to his rec-

---

[3] Edward Paul Halline, *Embattled Farmers* (Madison, B. A. thesis, MS, 1921), p. 52, citing the *Capital Times* (Madison), August 5, 1918.

ord. In the Republican primaries Tittemore carried sixteen counties and received about a fourth of the votes cast. Philipp defeated Wilcox by a scant 440 votes and was again the choice of a minority. The rest of the men on the Republican ticket were of the progressive wing of the party, and some, like John J. Blaine, also had the support of the organized farmers. In the November election Philipp was an easy victor, and the Republicans elected their whole state ticket. The Socialist candidate for governor, Emil Seidel of Milwaukee, received about 57,000 votes, slightly more than half as many as Victor L. Berger had polled in April. The Democratic contingent in the legislature was reduced to two in the senate and five in the assembly.

Between the elections of 1918 and 1920 the World War ended, the nation went dry, and women received the ballot. Issues arising from the war affected politics for a time, but economic questions gradually came to have their old prominence. The farmers were in a state of great discontent; many of them had to meet wartime debts under the conditions of deflation that set in after the war was over. The American Society of Equity fell, for the time being, into eclipse. It was torn with internal dissensions, and was temporarily quite overshadowed by the Nonpartisan League, which was spreading rapidly and was voicing some extremely radical ideas. During the year 1920 the membership of the league in Wisconsin reached 22,000.

Governor Philipp refused to consider a fourth term, and six Republicans offered themselves as candidates to succeed him. Blaine, who was destined to gain the nomination, had the support both of the Nonpartisan League and of the La Follette forces. Roy B. Wilcox, who ran second among the Republicans, again led the progressives who had condemned La Follette in wartime. J. N. Tittemore was also a candidate again, but this time he secured only seven per cent of the Republican vote. The Stalwart candidate, who had the backing of both McGovern and Philipp, was Colonel Gilbert E. Seaman, a soldier in the recent war. Seaman was the most pronounced "wet" among the candidates.

The bitterest issue concerned the nature and purposes of the Nonpartisan League. In North Dakota, the state of its origin, the league had demanded a good deal of state enterprise and state ownership. Its platform of 1920 in Wisconsin did not emphasize state ownership. It did propose a revision of the tax system with a higher rate on the larger incomes and on inheritances, the taxation of idle land held for speculation, and a gradual raising of the exemption from taxation of farm implements and city homes up to $5,000. The state should provide loans to buyers of land and builders of homes. The league asked that the representatives of organized farmers and workers be placed on educational boards. In national affairs it demanded the repeal of the "espionage act" and the release of political prisoners. This was the platform; but many league speakers expressed themselves in much more radical fashion. Blaine himself is quoted as saying: "The railroads, the forests, the shipyards, the mines, the water power must be returned to the people. . . . We do not want to injure any one unrighteously. But those who have not earned what they have must lose it. Regulation is ineffectual. Nothing but ownership by the government will remedy these ills." [4] The league was condemned as communistic and bolshevistic, and many professed to see in it a threat to the very existence of democratic government. Of the six Republican candidates for the governorship four were definitely opposed to the Nonpartisan League, and had the anti-league forces been able to unite, their combined strength as revealed in the primary would have been more than twice that marshalled by the victorious Blaine.

The fraction of a term for which Lenroot had been elected to the Senate was about to expire, and he stood for re-election. La Follette favored James Thompson again, and when Lenroot gained the Republican nomination, Thompson ran as an independent. La Follette attacked Lenroot with great bitterness, both in his speeches and in *La Follette's Magazine*.

---

[4] Chester C. Platt, *What La Follette's State is Doing* (Batavia, New York, 1924), pp. 116, 117.

At the election of 1920 the people of the United States, glad to be done with everything connected with the World War, turned against the Democrats. In Wisconsin, Harding defeated Cox by about four and one-half to one, and all Republican candidates, including Lenroot and Blaine, were swept into office. Lenroot's rival, James Thompson, received 235,000 votes, which were taken to be a gesture of loyalty to La Follette and a protest against the treatment given him during the war. Blaine and his program alarmed many who voted for Harding, and these conservatives voted for the Democratic candidate for governor, Colonel Robert H. McCoy, a veteran of the recent war. He received 35 per cent of all votes cast and more than twice as many as Cox did.

BLAINE, GOVERNOR AND SENATOR

John James Blaine was born on a farm in Grant County in 1870. He finished high school in the neighboring village of Montfort, and there a few years later began the practice of law. In 1897 he removed to Boscobel, some fifteen miles away, where he made his home until his death in 1934. Once in making a political speech to farmers he said: "I was born, raised, lived and worked most of my life on a farm. In my youth shortly after the death of my father, I sustained an injury which, while it will not prevent me from getting into the fight with you, would prevent me from pitching hay. I have always been interested in farming, always had it closest to my heart." [5]

Blaine's rise to prominence has for the most part already been told. As a partisan of La Follette he was present at the famous gymnasium convention of 1904, conspicuous in red suspenders. He served in the state senate for two terms in 1909 and 1911. In 1912 he tried to turn Republicans to Wilson. Two years later he was an independent candidate for governor with La Follette's support. In 1918, with the help of the Farmers' Progressive League, he was elected attorney general.

---

[5] Chester C. Platt, *What La Follette's State is Doing* (Batavia, New York, 1924), p. 115.

Blaine's inauguration as governor, on January 3, 1921, ushered in a second period of progressive control. In his first message to the legislature, Blaine disappointed Nonpartisan Leaguers when he remarked that the constitution prevented the public ownership of storage warehouses. He did recommend the adoption of the initiative and referendum, which had been defeated in 1914. He condemned the concentration of wealth in the hands of great bankers and desired the surplus wealth of Wisconsin to be used for financing Wisconsin industries. He recommended that higher income and inheritance taxes be laid upon the wealthy. In harmony with the program of the state federation of labor, he asked for a law establishing an eight-hour day as basic in industry. He had a good deal to say about encroachments of the federal government upon the liberty of action of the states. By offering to pay part of the expense involved, he complained, the national government was leading the states into many enterprises. Two years later he was using the same formula of iniquitous federal interference in condemning the Eighteenth Amendment and the Volstead act.

Blaine's campaign in 1922 coincided with La Follette's last election to the Senate, and the La Follette-Blaine combination won an easy victory. The Democratic vote at the primary was so small that it did not come up to what was required by law of a regular party, and Bentley, the Democratic candidate, had to run as an independent. Blaine received seven times as many votes as Bentley, and the latter's poll was the smallest made by a Democratic candidate in the present century. There were no Democrats in the state senate and but one in the assembly.

In 1924 La Follette ran for the presidency and carried Wisconsin against Coolidge. Blaine was his loyal lieutenant and was easily re-elected. Whatever Blaine's own appeal to the voters, he had the good fortune in 1920, after being the choice of a minority at the primary, to ride into office on the crest of the Harding wave. In 1922 he profited by La Follette's last senatorial campaign, and in 1924 he was the beneficiary of the same leader's campaign for the presidency. The chief interest in the Republican primary lay in the contest for the office of secretary of state. The incumbent, Fred R. Zimmerman, desired a second term, but Blaine preferred Theodore Dammann. Zimmerman gained the nomination and was re-elected.

In June, 1925, Senator La Follette died, and the state paid him its highest tribute. To succeed to the vacant seat in the Senate there were several candidates. Mrs. La Follette declined the honor to which her services and abilities well entitled her, and the progressive leaders supported Robert M. La Follette, Jr. His leading opponent was Roy B. Cox. "Young Bob" was nominated and elected.

In his first term Blaine had the majority of both houses of the legislature against him, but in his other terms he secured important legislation. Much of it concerned industrial workers and wards of the state of various sorts and will be discussed in later chapters. The department of markets was created out of what had been a subdivision of the department of agriculture. The campaign against bovine tuberculosis was pushed vigorously, and probably as a result of this Wisconsin gained a strong foothold in the Chicago milk market. One amendment to the constitution secured greater home rule for cities and villages, and another provided for the recall of elective public officials. Inheritance taxes were doubled and the income tax was made more productive. During his six years as governor Blaine was face to face with the major problem of all progressive governments: if the state constantly undertakes more tasks and more services to the people, it must find money to pay the cost.

After six years as governor, Blaine sought the office of United States Senator, and in so doing clashed with the desires of Lenroot, who was a candidate for re-election. Lenroot had been long at Washington, nine years in the lower House and nearly nine in the Senate. Originally a supporter and friend of La Follette, he had, after the World War, drawn close to Harding and Coolidge, and had come to be counted a "regular Republican." The group with which he was now identified was in 1926 the target of great and widespread criticism, especially in connection with the wrongful leasing of the government oil reserves to private parties. Lenroot was a forceful campaigner and made a strong defense of his own course. In his last two terms as governor, Blaine had revealed himself as a great enemy of prohibition legislation. In his campaign for the Senate, Blaine caused circulars to be distributed advising that a vote for him would "bring back beer." Blaine secured the Republican nomination and was elected. Thus ended Lenroot's services as a spokesman of Wisconsin. In 1929 he was appointed a judge in the United States Court of Customs and Patent Appeals, and in this capacity continued at Washington in the service of the national government.

In the United States Senate, Blaine continued as an outspoken opponent of prohibition. This phase of his public life reached its culmination when on December 6, 1932, he introduced the Senate resolution which set in motion the process of repealing the Eighteenth Amendment, a process completed just a year later. Blaine also consistently championed the cause of the farmers and the laboring men, especially of organized labor. He so frequently voted against appropriations of public funds that *The New York Times* christened him "Blaine the Blocker." He was at all times opposed to the World Court and the League of Nations. He was the only Senator to vote against the ratification of the Kellogg-Briand Treaty. When his term in the Senate had run its course he sought re-election. In the autumn of 1932, however, the Republican nomination went to John B. Chapple of Ashland. After the primaries Blaine advised all progressives to vote Democratic, just as he had done in 1912 and again in 1928. Chapple was defeated by the Democratic candidate, F. Ryan Duffy of Fond du Lac. This proved to be the end of Blaine's political activity. He died in April, 1934.

ZIMMERMAN AND KOHLER

When Blaine gave up the governor's chair in January, 1927, he was succeeded by Fred R. Zimmerman, a distinctly less radical progressive, and Zimmerman was followed by Walter J. Kohler, a conservative Republican. The four years of their two terms form an interruption in the control of the state by the more vigorous or extreme progressive forces. Zimmerman was born in Milwaukee in 1880. As a young man he served as director of industrial relations for the Nash Motor Company. For ten years he conducted a business in Milwaukee, dealing in building materials and supplies. A member of the assembly of 1909, he later gained political experience and reputation as a member of the Republican National Committee. Always he was a staunch supporter of the senior La Follette. He was secretary of state during Blaine's last two terms, although he did not have Blaine's endorsement in the election of 1924. In 1926 the progressive conference or pre-primary gathering, in which Blaine and Robert M. La Follette, Jr. were leaders, chose Herman Ekern as their candidate for governor. Zimmerman sought the nomination and, despite the fact that he had always been counted a progressive, he seemed to conservative Republicans more moderate than Ekern; with support from that quarter he was nominated and elected. At the same time Theodore Dammann was elected secretary of state. He was destined to hold the office for twelve years, the longest tenure in the history of the state.

Governor Zimmerman stood in a rather peculiar relation to the legislature of 1927. The senate majority was conservative and thought Zimmerman too progressive. The assembly was controlled by progressives who suspected that he was turning toward the conservatives. In spite of the friction inherent in such a situation, a number of important laws were passed. Better provision was made for the education of crippled children and an equalization law authorized state aid to poor school districts. The income tax was made heavier for the more well-to-do. Forest conservation and water-power regulation received attention and more money was made available for highways. Reduction of taxes proved to be impossible.

The second of these one-term governors was Walter Jodok

Kohler, who was born in Sheboygan in 1875. His father, a native of the Austrian Tyrol, began in 1873 the enterprise that grew into the Kohler industry of today. Three thousand men are regularly employed there in the manufacture of plumbing fixtures. At the age of fifteen the future governor began work in his father's plant, and in 1905 he became, by the death of his father, the head of the company. The village of Kohler, near Sheboygan, where the plant is located, is widely famed as a "garden city" and a model industrial town.

Before he ran for governor in 1928, Kohler had been a presidential elector and had served six years on the board of regents of the state university. In the spring of 1928 he was elected one of the four delegates-at-large to the Republican National Convention, a success which drew attention to him as a vote-getter, since he was the only one of the four who was of the conservative wing of the party. This group soon after "drafted" him as their candidate for the governorship. The progressives, who were led by the United States Senators, persuaded Congressman Joseph D. Beck to be their candidate. The progressive leaders besought Zimmerman not to try for the nomination, but he persisted, and though he polled but 82,000 votes and ran a poor third, he probably deflected enough progressive votes from Beck to give Kohler the nomination. The conservatives controlled the making of the platform and pledged their allegiance to Hoover, whereupon Senator Blaine gave his support to Al Smith and A. G. Schmedeman, the Democratic nominee for governor. In the November elections the state went for Hoover, and Kohler was elected. The conservative Republicans were in a majority in both houses of the legislature. At the same time, however, Robert M. La Follette, Jr. was re-elected Senator by an overwhelming majority, and, except for the governor, all the chief state officers were progressives.

Like Philipp fifteen years earlier, Kohler intended to economize by eliminating useless boards and departments, and the legislature of 1929 passed several measures of reorganization, but not so much was accomplished in this direction as the governor had hoped. The "Children's Code" was passed, bringing Wisconsin's practice in the field of child welfare into agreement with the best modern knowledge.

THE LATEST AGE

The eight-year period beginning in January, 1931, consisted of one term under Philip F. La Follette, one under Schmedeman, a Democrat swept into office in the overturn of 1932, and then two more under Philip La Follette. By 1931 the related matters of the depression and relief to its victims had come to have a central place in American life. These will be dealt with in a later chapter; here we continue the personal and political narrative.

In 1930 the progressives were united and their leader, Philip Fox La Follette, defeated Kohler in the Republican primaries. The younger son of Robert M. La Follette, Sr., he was born in Madison in 1897, and was educated in the public schools there and at Washington, D. C. During the World War he went to an officers' training camp and was commissioned a second lieutenant in the infantry. This service divided into two parts his work at the University of Wisconsin, from which he was graduated as a Bachelor of Arts in 1919. Training in the law school of the same university followed, and in 1924 he was elected to the office of district attorney of Dane County, which his father had once filled. Before he became governor he also gave part of his time to teaching law at the University of Wisconsin. In the final election of November, 1930, which made him governor, he received about 65 per cent of the popular vote.

Philip La Follette's first message to the legislature showed that the progressives of his generation had moved far beyond those of thirty years earlier, when the elder La Follette first became governor. He began by drawing attention to the forces that were altering American social and economic life. He called for a better-planned economic order, and challenged the haphazard distribution that characterized our civilization. "We must mobilize for the solution of the critical problems of distribution the ability and experience which have perfected our machinery of production. In the midst of plenty great sections of our population are suffering." As a means towards better planning, the government, he declared, should consult more and more with the representatives of special interests, such as farmers, organized labor, and leaders in industry and commerce, who have special wisdom to offer.

Many of the governor's recommendations were enacted into laws at a regular session. The legal status of labor unions was much improved. The income tax was raised to make possible a lowering of the general property tax, and it was the announced policy of the government for the future not to use the general property tax for expenses of the state at all, but to leave that resource entirely to the counties, municipalities, and school districts. The state forestry program was advanced. The governor desired a law taxing dividends, "the last great exemption under the income tax law," but failed to get it. Electricity, he believed, should be furnished more cheaply as a benefit to industry and also to raise the standard of living, especially in farm homes. With this end in view he asked constitutional amendments, one of them permitting municipalities to exceed their quota of debt to establish power plants, and the other looking toward the time when the state of Wisconsin should establish a state-wide power system. The first amendment, which had originated in 1929, again passed the legislature and was approved by the people in 1932. The other did not meet with favor in the legislature.

Philip La Follette gave much attention during his first term to the unemployment problem. As a project to create work he proposed the elimination of about eighty grade crossings. To provide the six or seven million dollars required for this enterprise the legislature raised the gasoline tax from two to four cents a gallon. Toward the close of 1931, La Follette summoned the legislature in special session. It enacted a permanent plan of unemployment relief. The financial burden was placed upon the employers, as had been done in 1911 in the matter of industrial accidents. The coming into effect of the law was later postponed, but in July, 1934, employers began to put money into a fund and the first benefit payment was made in August, 1936. Another task of the special session of 1931-1932 was to find money for emergency poor relief; for this purpose it added about eight million dollars to the income taxes collected in 1932.

At the primary election in September, 1932, ex-governor Kohler again won the Republican nomination for governor, his majority over Philip La Follette being nearly a hundred thousand. Republican nominations, however, were made of little consequence by the Democratic victory in November.

The year 1894 and the failure of George W. Peck to gain a third term as governor had marked the beginning of a long Republican ascendancy in Wisconsin. Thirty-eight years passed before there was another Democratic governor. Furthermore, very few Democratic Congressmen were sent to Washington in this period: in more than half the congresses there were none at all. And yet one should not hastily assume that the party was without importance during this time. In all the elections for governor from 1900 to 1920 those who voted for the Democratic candidate were never far from one-third of the whole number of those who voted. The vote for President told much the same story. Woodrow Wilson received more than 40 per cent of the vote, both in 1912 and in 1916. In 1912 the split in the Republican party allowed the Democrats to cast the vote of Wisconsin in the electoral college for the only time between 1892 and 1932. Davis was the choice of more than a third of the Wisconsin voters for President in 1924, and Al Smith, because of the prohibition issue, scored 45 per cent in 1928; and in both these years the vote for a Democratic candidate for governor fell but a little below 40 per cent. A change of heart on the part of 12 or 15 per cent of the voters would turn defeat into victory.

In 1921 the Republicans took charge of the national government, and as long as a measure of prosperity continued they remained in power. When the depression came, however, and the government could do nothing to end it and not much to mitigate its accompanying hardships, the people took the first opportunity to turn the Republicans out of office. Wisconsin, by reason of its tradition of criticism and independent thinking, would inevitably join in such an action.

In the election of 1932, Franklin D. Roosevelt carried Wisconsin, gaining about two-thirds of the popular vote. Democrats were elected as governor and United States Senator. Theodore Dammann, the secretary of state, was the only one of the principal state officers to escape the deluge. Among the Congressmen the changes were not so sweeping. After thirty years during which Wisconsin had eleven Congressmen, the state's delegation in the lower house had been reduced to ten. Of this number elected in 1932, five were Democrats, one was a regular Republican, and four were progressives. After the primaries in September many progressive leaders, among them Blaine and Robert M. La Follette, Jr., advised their followers to vote Democratic, and when the Democratic victory was assured, La Follette expressed himself as well pleased with the outcome of the national election. The majority in the Wisconsin assembly was Democratic, but the hold-over element in the senate kept the majority there Republican.

Albert George Schmedeman, the new Democratic governor, was born in Madison in 1864. For many years he engaged in business there as a tailor and purveyor of men's furnishings. In 1912 he showed great enthusiasm for the Democratic cause, and by President Wilson's appointment he was for eight years United States minister to Norway. He became mayor of Madison in 1926, and held the office until his election to the governorship.

The word "progressive" has been used rather frequently in this narrative. Until 1934 it meant simply a group within the Republican party of Wisconsin, sometimes controlling the party and sometimes not. The elder La Follette faced the question as to whether he should leave the Republican ranks and organize a third party. He preferred to take his chances of controlling the old party. A generation later his sons faced the same problem, but chose the other solution. In the spring of 1934, during the second year of Schmedeman's governorship, a Progressive party was founded. It contested the election of 1934, with Philip La Follette as candidate for governor. He carried forty-eight counties, but his popular vote surpassed that of Schmedeman, the Democratic candidate, by only a little more than 13,500 votes, or by 1.5 per cent of the total. Schmedeman's strength lay for the most part in the counties east of the middle of the state and south of Green Bay; La Follette carried Dane and Kenosha counties and almost all those in the northern and western parts of the state. Of the Congressmen three were Democrats and seven were Progressive.

In the summer of 1935 the Wisconsin State Federation of Labor took steps that led to the establishment in December of the Farmer-Labor Progressive Federation (FLPF), whose purpose was "to unite all the state liberal forces." Nine groups coöperated in its formation. Some were economic in character, such as the Wisconsin Milk Pool and the Railroad Brotherhoods; others were political, like the Progressive and Socialist parties. The new body did not accept group membership, but sought to organize individuals in each county. By July, 1936, there were units in half the counties of the state. It sought control of the government to realize such ends as: a chance for all to work at decent wages, limitation of the work day and the work week, the promotion of coöperatives, the elimination of speculation in farm products, and a system of refinancing farm and home mortgages. One purpose stated in the FLPF constitution was the restriction of production for private profits and the eventual substitution of production for use through coöperatives or public ownership.

Milwaukee County was the chief stronghold of the Socialists in Wisconsin, and the continued existence there of both Socialist and Progressive parties would naturally divide the more liberal or radical vote and enable "reactionaries" to win the elections; to some extent this had happened before there was a separate Progressive party. One of the chief purposes of the FLPF was to end this disunion in Milwaukee County. Socialist and Progressive leaders made a "deal." The Socialists ceased to have a slate of state officers and a separate column on the ballot. In return for giving up so much, they were practically allowed to write the statement of principles of the FLPF. Philip La Follette himself did not join the new federation, for the alleged reason that the idea of production for use was "open to misinterpretation." Another reason probably was that many Progressives thought the principles of the FLPF were too extreme, and La Follette could not risk antagonizing them. For the campaign of 1936 the FLPF omitted the production-for-use statement from its platform; instead it said: "We favor the establishment of public corporations similar to the TVA to perform such functions of government as the welfare of the people makes necessary."

Since it was a presidential year, some 320,000 more votes for governor were cast than in 1934. La Follette carried sixty counties and, with a plurality of more than 200,000, did not need the votes of the Socialists in the FLPF. This organization rendered a great service, however, in unseating certain Democratic senators and assemblymen in Milwaukee and Racine, and sending Progressives to Madison in their places. Without these marginal men, there would not have been Progressive majorities in the two houses of the legislature in 1937. Alexander Wiley, a lawyer of Chippewa Falls, was the Republican candidate for governor and ran second. Progressives and Republicans had both gained at the expense of the Democrats, whose share of the total vote for governor had dropped in two years from 37.1 to 21.7 per cent.

During Philip La Follette's last two terms there was a great deal of legislation designed to relieve farmers and others burdened with intolerable debts. Naturally, also, many laws were passed dealing with the various phases of public assistance. Here Wisconsin sometimes imitated the federal government, sometimes arranged to coöperate with it. In 1935 the tax on oleomargarine, which had been set at six cents a pound in 1931, was raised to fifteen cents a pound. Protests against this were received from some of the southern states that produced cottonseed oil, but the Wisconsin law remained unaltered. In April, 1937, a nonprofit corporation was organized and named the Wisconsin Development Authority (WDA), and in July the legislature designated it to handle state funds and other funds and to promote the cheaper production and distribution of light, heat, and power in Wisconsin. The authority was clearly intended to encourage the public ownership of establishments furnishing such services. The newspapers called it the "little TVA." Its field of operations, however, was carefully circumscribed by decisions of the Wisconsin Supreme Court. At a special session of the legislature that began in September, 1937, a similar law designated a similar corporation, to be known as the Wisconsin Agricultural Authority (WAA), which was to improve the standards of production in agriculture and extend the markets for agricultural products. Governor La Follette gave much study, during his last term in office, to the organization of the state government and the interrelation of its various parts. Some changes were ordered by the special session, and the governor was given power to transfer bureaus, boards, or other agencies from one department of government to another, and during his last year he made a number of changes of this sort.

In April, 1938, the Progressive party of Wisconsin invited like-minded political leaders to Madison and at a great meeting held in the livestock pavilion launched the National Progressive party. Philip La Follette made the keynote speech. He could not accept the Socialist plans nor the Socialist philosophy. Neither the waiting for prosperity with Hoover nor the growing federal indebtedness under Roosevelt had led the nation out of the depression. He condemned all policies that discouraged production, whether through the maintenance of artificially high prices or through unduly high hourly wage rates, or through government plans for crop control. Men and women should be put to work, not made to live idly on relief. "Private capital and private business must be afforded opportunity to go to work." It is the task of statesmen to provide that opportunity. It is still too early, as this is written, to know how important this third-party movement will be.

In the primary elections of 1938 Philip La Follette was the choice of the Progressives, while the Republican victor was Julius P. Heil, a German-born manufacturer of Milwaukee. There was a coalition movement designed expressly to defeat La Follette, and the coalition candidate won the Democratic nomination for governor. He then withdrew from the contest in favor of Heil. A caucus of Democratic officeholders and candidates and their state central committee thereupon chose as their leader an elderly state senator, Harry W. Bolens. In the final election in November, Heil won by a handsome majority, polling more than 540,000 votes compared with about 250,000 for La Follette. The Democrats made rather a dismal showing, Bolens receiving about 80,000 votes. At the same time the Republicans elected Alexander Wiley to the United States Senate and eight of Wisconsin's ten Congressmen, the other two being Progressives. This outcome was part of a swing back to the Republican party throughout the northern states. In Wisconsin several reasons were given for the defeat of the Progressives. Progressive government, with its multitude of services to the people, always means high taxes. The business "recession" of 1937 and 1938 made people discontented. The farmers deserted La Follette, it was said, because low prices for milk had prevailed for years. Some simply thought it was "time for a change."

It is too early to comment fully on the months that have passed since Julius P. Heil became governor. The legislative session of 1939 continued from January to October, 269 days in all, and was the longest in the history of the state. The Republicans had a majority in the assembly, but in the senate a group of five Democrats held the balance of power. Heil, in his pre-election campaign, had promised retrenchment and lower taxes. Departmental expenditures were curtailed in some quarters, but these savings were more than counterbalanced by what seemed inescapable contributions for relief and subsidies to the local governments.

After wrangling for months over a long series of taxation bills, the legislature adjourned without imposing taxes adequate to the needs of the biennium.

The Heil administration saw much reorganization of the machinery of government, though not as much as the governor desired. The three-member commission, with staggered terms, was a form often used to manage departments in Wisconsin; in 1935 there were no less than eight such commissions. Philip La Follette had obtained legislation abandoning the three-member commission in the department of agriculture and markets, and had taken the first steps to recast the board of control. Heil and the legislature of 1939 repealed the whole La Follette reorganization plan and undid all transfers of bureaus and changes of function which he had ordered. They then proceeded to abolish two of the three-member bodies, the tax commission and the board of control, and to establish other agencies in their stead. Bills supported by Heil and designed to recast the banking commission, the public service commission, and the highway commission, and to place one man at the head of each of them, failed to pass. The legislature also withdrew all financial support from the Wisconsin Development Authority (WDA) and the Wisconsin Agricultural Authority (WAA), and repealed the acts which had established them as agencies of the state. Laws defining labor disputes and curtailing the use of picketing were passed;[6] these laws pleased employers' associations and certain farm groups but greatly angered the leaders of organized labor. Partly because of vacancies which existed when he was inaugurated and partly because of reorganization laws, it fell to Governor Heil to appoint an unusual number of the higher officials in the state government.

SELECTED BIBLIOGRAPHY

A number of items in the bibliography of Chapter XVI, on the elder La Follette, continue to be of use for the early part of this chapter. Among them are: Nils P. Haugen, *Pioneer and Political Reminiscences,* in the *Wisconsin Magazine of History,* Vols. XI, XII, XIII; Charles McCarthy,

---

[6] For further details about these laws, see p. 394.

The Wisconsin Idea (New York, 1912); and Frederick C. Howe, *Wisconsin, an Experiment in Democracy* (New York, 1912). R. G. Plumb, *Badger Politics* (Manitowoc, 1930), pp. 139-228, covers the years down to 1930.

Isaac Stephenson, in *Recollections of a Long Life* (Chicago, 1916), tells of his election to the United States Senate. The record of the Wisconsin investigation of this episode is *Joint Senatorial Primary Investigation Committee Report, 1911.* The federal investigation is detailed in 62d Cong., 2d Sess., Senate Doc. 312 (Serial numbers, 6149, 6150).

Antoinette Schweke wrote a B.A. thesis on *The Administration of Governor Philipp* (MS, Madison, 1922). The two books by Emanuel L. Philipp, *The Truth About Wisconsin Freight Rates* (Milwaukee, 1904), and *Political Reform in Wisconsin* (Milwaukee, 1909), present the case of the Stalwarts against La Follette. Chester C. Platt, *What La Follette's State is Doing* (Batavia, N. Y., 1924), views the scene with the eye of a Nonpartisan Leaguer. His chapter on Blaine is found in pages 114-127. *Back to Boscobel, A Tribute to the Late John J. Blaine* (privately printed) is the eulogy delivered at Blaine's funeral by Robert M. La Follette, Jr., April 19, 1934. There is an excellent summary of Blaine's career in a Joint Resolution found in the *Session Laws, 1935,* pp. 1216-1220.

For many years reports of departments and officials for a biennium were bound in a series of volumes called *Wisconsin Public Documents.* Each series began with the message of the governor of the following biennium. Thus McGovern's message to the legislature of January 11, 1911, is to be found at the beginning of Vol. I of *Wisconsin Public Documents, 1909-1910.* Governors' messages of later date may be read in the *Assembly Journal.* Blaine's first message of January 13, 1921, is in *Assembly Journal, 1921,* pp. 18-52; Philip La Follette's first, January 15, 1931, in the *Assembly Journal, 1931,* pp. 11-35.

For the more recent years the bibliographer can offer little beyond the raw materials for historical writing. Attention may be called again to the biennial *Blue Books,* which contain election statistics and national and state party platforms. There is an account of the founding in 1935 of the Farmer-Labor Progressive Federation in the *Proceedings of the Forty-fourth Annual Convention of the Wisconsin State Federation of Labor, 1936,* pp. 215-219. In *The New York Times* of April 29, 1938, is a report of the launching of the National Progressive Party of America, with the keynote speech by Philip F. La Follette.

Each session of the legislature produces its volume of *Session Laws,* and when a session ends summaries of its work appear in the newspapers. The article on Wisconsin in the annual *New International Yearbook* is a convenient guide. The Legislative Reference Library in the capitol in Madison is doing an invaluable service to future historians in clipping the newspapers and in preserving other fugitive material.

CHAPTER XIX

LABOR

Trade Union History

FOR several decades after Wisconsin became a state, organized labor was numerically unimportant and but little understood by the agricultural majority. Only three or four labor unions are known to have been formed before the Civil War. The Milwaukee Typographical, No. 23, which began in 1852 or 1853, seems to be the oldest. Between 1850 and 1870 the local unions of many trades were drawn together in "nationals." The printers, for example, had the National Typographical Union. During the Civil War both prices and wages advanced, but prices more rapidly, so that the workingmen lost in real wages. Therefore, a general movement to unionize began, and within three years, 1863 to 1865, there were six or seven new unions in Milwaukee and eight or ten in the various smaller cities throughout the state. There were many strikes, almost all for increased wages, and as prices were rising rapidly, employers usually yielded. Lake shipping was relatively more important than now and strikes of a single crew on board ship were rather frequent. Labor in those days was often paid in scrip, mere promises to pay, and the workmen could get cash only at a discount; or sometimes they were paid in orders good only at a store in which the employer had an interest. Another grievance accentuated by war was the entrance of women into occupations previously confined to man. The printers felt this especially, but protests were unavailing while the Civil War lasted.

The demand for the work of skilled laborers was being constantly diminished by new mechanical inventions. After the Civil War this was especially true of the shoemakers: one process after another was taken from them by machinery. To protect the field still remaining to them the shoemakers united in an association called, after the patron saint of their craft, "The Knights of St. Crispin." This began in Milwaukee and spread throughout the United States. The first lodge was formed March 1, 1867, and was organized by Newell Daniels, who had but recently come from Massachusetts. The cardinal principle was to restrict the number of skilled operatives by refusing to teach "green hands." Daniels carried his gospel to the shoe manufacturing centers in the East, where it was welcomed, and the lodge soon had 50,000 members. The first national meeting was held at Rochester, New York, in 1868, and the movement had a vigorous life of some four or five years. Besides two lodges in Milwaukee, one largely English-speaking and the other German, there were eleven others in smaller places in Wisconsin. Yet most of these lasted only until 1872, and the last one in the state vanished in the panic of the following year. This breakup occurred throughout the United States, although there was a shortlived revival in the shoe towns in the East a year or two later.

Two or three things about which laboring men waxed enthusiastic in the older parts of the United States in the sixties had a slight following in Wisconsin. One was coöperation, in which the Rochdale pioneers in England had offered a successful model to the workingmen of the world. Attempts were made by various small groups of workingmen in Milwaukee to conduct a grocery store, to form a ship-building association, to issue a daily newspaper, to make cigars, and to run a factory that made chiefly sashes, doors, and blinds. Some of these enterprises developed into ordinary business firms and lost their coöperative character; most of them were failures.

Another movement that temporarily attracted the attention of the workingmen was that to secure an eight-hour day. A Labor

Reform Association with this end in view was formed in Milwaukee, and grew into the General Eight Hour League of Wisconsin.
The subject was brought to the attention of the legislature in 1867
by Governor Fairchild, and this was followed by the passage of
the Eight Hour law of that year. This law provided that eight
hours should constitute a day's work in all factories in the state except where a contract was agreed upon to the contrary, and also
contained the first halfhearted attempt to limit the working hours
of women. Children under fourteen were not permitted to work
more than ten hours in any one day. This last clause was probably the only one meant to be effective, "and even this was never
enforced." There were indications that laboring men throughout the state at that time preferred the ten-hour day to the reduction of their wages by one-fifth.

The Noble Order of the Knights of Labor originated in Philadelphia in 1869, and achieved a national organization in 1878.
With the disruption of most of the national trade unions in 1873,
many of the surviving locals affiliated with this new order, which
had a far greater membership than any predecessor. After 1886 it
reached its maximum in the United States of about three-quarters
of a million members. The order was different in many ways
from the typical labor union or combination of unions of today.
It urged the union of all trades and preached the "one big union"
idea. In addition to gathering in many locals already in existence
which were limited to one trade, it formed unions, especially in
the smaller places, composed of men of diverse occupations. The
Knights of Labor believed in coöperative enterprise and its members invested their savings in mines, shoe factories and other ventures. The resulting failures discredited both coöperation and the
order, which, furthermore, did not develop a good technique in
conducting strikes. At the last it turned its energies from the
economic front to politics.

An early organizer for the Knights of Labor in Wisconsin was
Robert Schilling, who came to Milwaukee in 1878. In 1881 there
were only two lodges in the city, but during the next five years

the lodges rose to fifty and the number of members to 16,000, and there was probably half that number in the rest of the state.

Between the Civil War and the end of the nineteenth century arose several movements of protest against the dominant political parties, all fundamentally efforts of debt-laden farmers to improve their economic position. None of them proved to be permanent, even for the farmers. In 1878 a good many workingmen in Wisconsin voted with the Greenback party, then at its zenith; but the movement had little strength in the state thereafter. When the Knights of Labor entered politics, they supported in Wisconsin a Labor or People's party, and John Cochrane, their candidate for the governorship in 1886, polled more than 21,000 votes. Of these more than half were cast in Milwaukee County, while Racine and Winnebago counties each contributed more than a thousand votes. The use of soldiers against strikers at Bay View in May of that year accounted in part for this showing. At the same time Henry Smith, a millwright and labor leader was sent to Congress from the Milwaukee district. Two years later, when Smith tried for re-election, Democrats and Republicans combined and elected a wealthy manufacturer.

Next, a Union Labor party was formed and put forward a national platform in 1888. It favored a graduated income tax, equal suffrage, direct election of United States Senators, and the ownership of the means of transportation and communication by the people. In Wisconsin there was a "Labor" candidate for governor in 1888 and a "Union Labor" candidate in 1890, but each received less than 10,000 votes. Then for two elections the People's or Populist party was on the scene, and in 1894, the banner year of the Populist party in the nation, it showed a strength of 25,600 voters in Wisconsin. Probably about half of these were urban workingmen. Robert Schilling, who had been an organizer for the Knights of Labor, was in 1891 the secretary of the national executive committee of the Populist party. In 1896 this party lost its identity by fusing with the Democrats. In that year, however, appeared a Socialist Labor party, and in 1897 Victor L. Berger of Milwaukee and Eugene V. Debs of Terre Haute, Indiana, led in organizing the Social Democratic party of America.

Contemporaneously with the meteoric rise of the Knights of Labor in the early eighties came the birth of the American Federation of Labor, which was in process of formation from 1881 to 1886. The importance of this new development is apparent from the fact that in 1930 there were some four million men and women in trade unions in the United States, and about four-fifths of them belonged to unions included in the American Federation. As working parts of the national federation, there are state federations, and each considerable city has its central body made up of representatives of all the local unions. In Wisconsin the most important city central body is the Federated Trades Council of Milwaukee, organized in 1887 at the request of the American Federation of Labor. The state federation in Wisconsin was organized and held its first convention in 1893. Its principal officers were a secretary-treasurer and a general organizer; eventually the latter's title was changed to president. Frank J. Weber, the first general organizer or president, held his office for twenty-five years. The number of unions in the state federation varies, as does also the total membership. In 1913, when the federation was twenty years old, there were more than four hundred local unions with a membership exceeding 42,000. By 1920 the membership had reached about 52,000. At that time the four railway brotherhoods, the only important statewide unions not in the federation, had about 10,000 members. Statistics of trade union membership are difficult of attainment because they are based on the payment of dues, and whenever a person is unemployed dues are not required. The best estimate available toward the close of 1938 was that unions in the state federation counted 220,000 members, while the four brotherhoods had about 18,000 members.

As in the national field, so in Wisconsin, there has appeared the disruptive C. I. O. movement. The Committee for Industrial Organization was born in John L. Lewis' office, November 9, 1935, and remained a rebellious subsidiary of the American Federation of Labor until September 5, 1936, when its adherents were expelled from the national body. Efforts to bring the C. I. O. and the A. F. of L. together during the next two years came to naught. The C. I. O. leaders eventually claimed a following of about four million workers, and, being either without hope or without desire for reconciliation with the A. F. of L., they determined to found a permanent national body. At a convention held at Pittsburgh, November 14 to 18, 1938, a constitution was adopted for the Congress of Industrial Organizations. In the details of its organization, the new body copies the A. F. of L. very closely.

The industrial union has arisen gradually to challenge the older craft union, which was "based upon the special skills of clearly distinct organizations." There might, for example, be a coopers' union at a brewery. In its origin the American Federation of Labor was composed of craft unions, and modified craft unionism still remains the backbone of that organization. New machines and new methods have made many special skills obsolete and have rendered those that remain relatively less important in American industry; hence the labor movement has had to adjust itself to these altered conditions. Under fully developed industrialism, a national union would be composed of locals "each of which admits to membership all the workers in and around a given productive unit." There was much industrial unionism within the American Federation before the revolt of 1935 and 1936, but not enough of it, according to John L. Lewis and his followers. The C. I. O. movement has appeared in Wisconsin chiefly in the larger cities along Lake Michigan. Its leaders claim from 80,000 to 100,000 followers, but officials of the state federation assert that these figures are exaggerated. The C. I. O. in Wisconsin, as elsewhere, cites as its chief virtue that it has organized large numbers of workers whom the older state federation had neglected.

Neither the American Federation of Labor nor the state federation nor the C. I. O. is a political party. The purpose of a trade union is to fight on the economic front, to secure better wages, shorter hours, and an improvement in the standard of living. In gaining these ends, especially the last, which is very inclusive, the help of government may be very effective. In contrast to the trade union, a political party seeks the privilege and the responsibility of conducting the government in county, state, and nation. If the trade unionist wishes the government to do something, one party may carry out his will as well as another. Politicians act against the measures desired by the national or state federation at the certain peril of losing the votes that the union can command. The state federation in Wisconsin publishes a list of the bills that it has supported at each session of the legislature with the record of individual senators and assemblymen in connection with each one. The principle is: "Reward your friends, punish your enemies." The aim of organized labor is not to take over the administration of government, but to control those who do legislate and administer. The state federation and the railway brotherhoods, to be sure, gave their wholehearted support to the elder La Follette when he was a candidate for the presidency in 1924, and these same organizations entered into the Farmer-Labor Progressive Federation in 1935. But the difference between trade unions and political parties still exists.

SOCIALISM AND VICTOR BERGER

Modern class-conscious socialism of the European type began with Karl Marx, German refugee in England. Soon after the Civil War his disciples were to be found in several of the larger cities of the United States. This socialism found most of its adherents among immigrant workingmen, many of whom had accepted it before coming to the United States. There was such a nucleus of Socialists in Milwaukee, one of their leaders being Paul Grottkau, who edited a Socialist paper there from 1885 to 1888. The American Federation of Labor, warned perhaps by the history of the Knights of Labor, kept clear of politics and never committed itself to socialism. After the Federated Trades Council was organized in Milwaukee in 1887, there was a struggle between Socialists and Anti-Socialists for its control; finally in the late nineties, the Socialists gained a majority, and in 1898 the whole of the executive committee was Socialist. As a result of this victory, the labor movement in Milwaukee, and to a certain extent in Wisconsin, is somewhat different from that in many other parts of the United States. Most of the trade union leaders of Milwaukee and the officers of the Wisconsin State Federation of Labor have been Socialists. Socialism was able to win its strong position, however, only by altering, if not its aim, at least its methods and its proposed rate of progress. It has become in Wisconsin peculiarly evolutionary and opportunist, willing to use friends in either of the older parties, and to take half a loaf for the present when it can gain no more. Socialism has thus, in the opinion of many, proved its adaptability to American conditions. No one man has accomplished all this, but the outstanding leader of the Milwaukee Socialists was Victor L. Berger. Next to him have been Emil Seidel and Daniel W. Hoan, the two Socialist mayors of Milwaukee.

Victor L. Berger was born in Austria-Hungary in 1860. There he attended the Gymnasium (high school) and the universities of Budapest and Vienna, where his special interests were history and economics. Before his graduation financial reverses came and his family migrated to America. Young Victor did work of various sorts in several places, among other things learning the trade of a metal polisher. About 1881 he became a teacher in the Milwaukee public schools, a vocation he followed for nine years. During this time he also rose to leadership among the Socialists of the city. In December, 1892, he became the editor of the Socialist newspaper formerly edited by Grottkau, and soon changed the name of it to *Vorwärts*. From 1901 to 1913 the Socialists also had a weekly newspaper in English, the *Social Democratic Herald,* with which Berger was connected; this was ultimately superseded by a daily, the *Milwaukee Leader,* which was begun in 1911. Twenty-seven years later, in January, 1939, the *Leader* ceased to appear under its old name. Its successor was the *Milwaukee Evening Post.*

In the spring of 1910 the Socialists elected Emil Seidel mayor of Milwaukee, and seven months later Victor Berger was chosen the first Socialist Congressman in the history of the United States. The nation was startled by these victories, but the election of the mayor in particular was the result of a long preparation. In the municipal campaign of 1898 the Socialists had polled about 2,500 votes, and there had been a gradual increase in strength, most pronounced in 1904 when the Socialist vote reached 15,000. During the period of 1898 to 1910, David Rose, a Democrat, and La Follette's opponent in the race for the governorship in 1902, was mayor for all save two years, when there was a Republican interlude of two years under Sherburn Becker. Both parties thus had shown of what stuff they were made, and, to put it mildly, they had given an unsatisfactory government. The people consequently turned in increasing numbers to the Socialists, who meanwhile had skilfully moderated their tones and had thus made it possible for many professional and business people to join with them at least in voting against the Democrats.

The first Socialist administration of the city was hampered by an antiquated city charter, and by the captious opposition and pettifogging of some influential opponents; yet, it made a good record. It introduced a modern accounting system and greatly improved the city's financial practice, made an expert and very valuable survey of the city and its government, and gave especial attention to public health. Seidel was defeated in 1912, and in November Victor L. Berger likewise failed of re-election to Congress. Daniel Hoan had been elected prosecuting attorney in 1910 for a four-year term and was then re-elected. In 1916 Hoan became the second Socialist mayor of Milwaukee, and has held that office without interruption down to the present. His continuance in office marks the confidence that he has gained. It is notable that never yet has a majority of the city council been Socialist.

Through his various newspapers Berger had a great influence both in spreading socialism and in reshaping it to appeal to American workingmen. Had it not been for his Austrian birth he might well have been the candidate of the Socialist party for the Presidency. The story is told of Eugene V. Debs that one day in 1894, after the Pullman strike in South Chicago when he was in jail charged with contempt of court, he was visited by Victor L. Berger, and that the visitor's conversation, together with a copy of Karl Marx's *Capital,* which he left, worked the conversion of Debs from populism to socialism. Debs was the presidential candidate of his party four times, always with Berger's wholehearted support.

The Socialist always begins by considering the condition of the working classes, stressing their poor food and clothing, their desperate condition in the recurring and apparently inevitable unemployment, and their hopeless old age. All these evils, he points out, exist alongside of the heaped-up riches everywhere visible in industrialized countries. The wealth of the millionaires has been created by the toil of the many, and yet the many are unable to enjoy it. The central idea of the Socialist hope is the abolition of this poverty and of this unfair apportionment. Something is wrong with society, and the Socialist has a plan to set it right. Once, on the floor of the House of Representatives, Berger was asked what the Socialists had in view, what their plan was, and he replied in words which he and other Socialists have made familiar:

The Socialist Party stands for the collective ownership and democratic management of all of the social means of production and distribution. We will start with the national ownership of the country's natural resources, such as mines, oil wells, forests and so forth. With this must go the national ownership of the means of transportation and communication—railroads, telegraphs, telephones. Furthermore, we must carry out everywhere the principles of public ownership of public utilities. . . . The Socialists would go further after these things have been accomplished, but this would do for some time.

Our aim is finally to get hold of all the trusts. The national ownership and democratic management of the trusts is the end of the road as far as I see it.[1]

Berger might have added, for he stated it often enough in other places, that in the meantime the Socialist gives his support to much social legislation that improves the lot of workingmen while the present regime continues. The war against poverty is fought with various weapons and at all times.

One often feels in reading of socialism that it is concerned altogether with economic readjustment, with a change in the distribution of wealth; sometimes, however, Berger went beyond this to speak of the promised land, where the anxiety about daily bread will no longer exist, where bitter competition and personal selfishness will have disappeared among men. Then the strong will be magnanimous towards the weak, and it will be a better world because it is filled with better people. But ere this roseate dawn can break, must come the night of battle. Handworkers and brainworkers are to unite in "mighty class-conscious armies before which exploiters begin to tremble." And yet Berger had no hope of any speedy attainment of his goal nor any desire to reach it by violence. His socialism was evolutionary, not revolutionary.

However warlike their invectives against capitalism, Socialists have always been opposed to international war. Again and again, long before 1914, Berger, like other Socialist writers, both in this country and in Europe, had asserted that wars are of interest or profit only to the wealthy. "It is the working class that has to do the fighting although they have nothing to do with the declaration of war. If the railroad managers and the bankers and the capitalists should have to do their own fighting, a war would not last long." This was written in 1907.

The Socialist party held a convention in St. Louis, April 7, 1917, and, though war had been declared the day before, the convention voiced its opposition to all wars and to this war in particu-

---

[1] Speech delivered February 16, 1924; *Voice and Pen of Victor Berger* (Milwaukee, 1929), p. 43.

lar, "which a capitalist class is forcing upon this nation against its will." The convention pledged itself to "continuous action and public opposition to the war through demonstrations, mass petitions and all other means within our power." Throughout the period of the war this St. Louis platform was the official one of the Socialist party, and Berger approved it at once. Some Socialists, to be sure, and many of them in Milwaukee, did not accept the St. Louis platform and came vigorously to support the war, but Berger continued steadfastly in his original attitude. He sometimes stated that certain things, such as invasion of the country, might justify fighting; he was not a nonresister; but our entry into the World War he could not approve.

Under the so-called "Espionage Act," the Post Office department denied second-class privileges to twenty-two Socialist newspapers in the United States, including four dailies. One of these was the *Milwaukee Leader*. Berger and the other owners fought the matter in the courts, but the courts upheld the postmaster general. The majority of the Supreme Court agreed with the lower courts, but Justices Holmes and Brandeis dissented. Brandeis pointed out that the postmaster general, in denying second-class rates, was in effect imposing a fine of $150 a day, and gave it as his opinion that this imposition was not authorized by law. The *Leader* did not cease publication during the war, but had its circulation curtailed. One curious thing is that *Vorwärts,* the German-language Socialist daily of Milwaukee, continued to have the use of the mails.

In February, 1917, Berger and four other Socialists were indicted under the same espionage act for conspiracy, the main evidence against Berger being his editorial articles in the *Leader,* in which he had among other things denounced the draft law as unconstitutional, arbitrary, and oppressive. It was held that such statements were tantamount to advising disobedience to the law. In December the trial began in Chicago before Judge Kenesaw M. Landis, and in February, 1919, all five men were found guilty and sentenced to twenty years in Leavenworth. The case went up to the federal Court of Appeals and finally to the Supreme Court, which early in 1919 reversed the decision of Judge Landis and thus ended the case.

In the autumn of 1917 the accidental death of United States Senator Paul O. Husting caused a special election to be held in the following April to fill the vacant place. Berger was the Socialist candidate and, while the Republican candidate, Irvine L. Lenroot, was elected, Mr. Berger's showing was, to say the least, remarkable. In a total of 424,000 he received 110,000 votes. Of these about one-third were in Milwaukee County, but in twenty-eight counties he received over a thousand votes and in eleven he was the leading candidate. His vote might be interpreted as a tribute to his character and courage; it may also mean that a fourth of the people of Wisconsin disapproved of the aims or the methods of the Wilson administration. It obviously does not mean their conversion to Socialism.

At the congressional elections in 1918 Berger was chosen in the fifth district, which was by this time limited to a part of Milwaukee County. In the House of Representatives his right to take his seat was challenged because of his attitude toward the war and his recent conviction in Chicago, and ultimately he was excluded. As the seat was thereby declared vacant, a special election was held in 1919; again Berger was the victor, and the 24,000 men who voted for him did so with the knowledge that they would not be represented in Congress. In the following year in that district William H. Stafford, a nonpartisan candidate of Republican antecedents, was supported by both Republicans and Democrats and was elected. Then, beginning in 1922, Mr. Berger gained the seat three times in succession. No further objection was made on account of his stand during the war, and for six years he was the only Socialist in Congress. In the election of 1928 he was defeated. In his valedictory speech in the House he spoke of economic imperialism and its threat to the peace of the world. In the summer of 1929 he was struck by a streetcar in Milwaukee and died of his injuries a few weeks later.

Victor Berger was one of the outstanding leaders of his party. He and his Wisconsin associates did much to make socialism acceptable to American workingmen; even so it has not attracted great numbers, either in the nation at large or in Wisconsin. Debs received more than 80,000 votes in Wisconsin in 1924; Thomas, 53,000 in 1932 and less than 11,000 in 1936. Socialist candidates for governor in five elections from 1926 to 1934 polled each time between 40,000 and 60,000 votes. In 1936, because of their participation in the FLPF, and again in 1938 they had no candidate for governor, throwing their support to Philip La Follette. Sixty per cent or more of the Socialist vote after the World War was always found in Milwaukee County. There were also many Socialists in the northern part of the state. In Polk and Taylor counties, where they made their best showing, they sometimes exceeded 10 per cent of the poll. It seems unlikely that the Socialists will soon have anything approaching a majority in Wisconsin. They have nevertheless made a great contribution to progressive legislation in the state. Many are the projects first broached in Socialist platforms that have in the course of years gained the support not only of both the early and later Progressives but of the older parties as well, and so have become the law of the state.

SAFETY, THE INDUSTRIAL COMMISSION, AND OTHER LABOR LEGISLATION

The industrial revolution began to gather men, women, and children into factories in England and the eastern part of the United States more than a hundred years ago, and it was soon found that the new employment carried with it hazards unknown to the earlier agricultural life. Factories were sometimes burned and employees lost their lives; power-driven machinery was dangerous; pure air, good lighting, cleanliness, and suitable temperature were often wanting; hours of labor were too long. These conditions shocked humanitarian feelings and, other remedies failing, called for the intervention of the state.

In the late seventies the first requirement in Wisconsin of exterior fire escapes on factories was made. In 1883 it became the duty of the labor commissioner, whose office was then created, to inspect factories and to examine their protection against accidents and their means of escape from fire, but actually he did little beyond receiving and compiling statistics. The first really important law was one of 1887 that gave the commissioner and an increased staff of inspectors the right to order the guarding of dangerous machinery of any kind. The legislature of 1899 and its successors passed a number of safety and sanitation laws, but the work was very uneven. There were detailed regulations about cigar factories, sweatshops, and bakeries in the interests of cleanliness and welfare, but many industries were untouched. The task of keeping abreast of conditions in factories was not one that a legislature, meeting once in two years and burdened with a vast assortment of legislative work, could perform successfully.

The legislature of 1911 established the industrial commission. Professor John R. Commons of the state university had made a careful study of European practices in the administration of labor laws and contributed much to the initiation of the Wisconsin plan. The drafting as well as the enforcement of safety legislation was put into the hands of the new commission, and in the drafting of its orders the commission has followed the same procedure in one industry after another. A council or committee is created which includes representatives of employers, employees, and the public. In many cases the state federation of labor has suggested or named the spokesmen of the employees. This composite group then drafts a set of orders or a code which is published in tentative form with the announcement of public hearings for discussing details; at the hearings a wider circle of employers and men interested make their suggestions. After all this preparation the code is published and has the force of law. In this manner have been produced the boiler code, the building code, and a dozen more. The whole process is a continuous one; changes, if called for, can be made much more readily than by a legislature.

The first members of the commission were Professor Commons, Charles H. Crownhart, and J. D. Beck, commissioner of labor until the office was merged in the new commission.

The use of power-driven machinery in modern factories seems inevitably to be accompanied by accidents resulting in the maiming of employees and sometimes in death. To the wage earner and his family a disabling accident is a tragic occurrence that results in suffering, inability to earn, and increased poverty. Such a change in the condition of an individual or a family is also a matter of concern for society as a whole. A productive earner has become a burden; a self-supporting family may be obliged to ask either for private charity or for public assistance. The problem appeared in every country as the industrial revolution advanced. Sometimes the workman felt that the owner of the factory had not taken proper precautions, and according to English and American law there is no wrong without a remedy. But the injured man must sue in court, and the common law put into the hands of the employer in such cases three defenses; the employer escaped liability if the injured man had been negligent, if a fellow workman had been at fault, or if the injured man had voluntarily assumed the risk of accident. Only toward the close of the nineteenth century were these defenses removed by statute law in England and in some parts of the United States. Because these defenses were available to the employer and because lawsuits were expensive, the courts were of little use to the injured man.

It gradually dawned upon thoughtful observers of the new industrial society that these accidents ought not to be considered as the fault of either employers or workmen but as a normal if regrettable part of the processes of industry. The burden of such accidents, the loss of earning power, and perhaps the support of dependents for some years, ought to fall neither on the injured workman and his family nor upon the general public. It ought to rest squarely on industry itself, to be met regularly and passed on to the consumer in the price of the product—indeed a new philosophy.

In Wisconsin the problem of compensation had been receiving attention for some years before the legislation of 1911. The state federation of labor had made proposals, and the judges of the state supreme court had been surprisingly critical of existing conditions. Finally a committee of the legislature was created in 1909. It made a very elaborate study, even sending one of its members to Europe to observe the working of compensation laws there. All this issued in an act which was to be administered by an Industrial Accident Board, but later in the same session, in June, 1911, this work was placed in the hands of the new industrial commission.

Maryland had passed a compensation law in 1902, but it was soon found unconstitutional. Several other states followed suit, but all of these either merely encouraged voluntary action or were declared unconstitutional. In 1911 ten states, including Wisconsin, enacted workmen's compensation laws. The Wisconsin law was the first to go into effect. In form it was optional with the employers, but in practice all were soon obliged to come under its provisions, and in 1931 it was definitely made compulsory. When there is an accident, compensation is paid in accordance with a scale established and published by the industrial commission. The old common law defenses were abolished: the assumption of the risk and the fault of a fellow servant in 1911, and contributory negligence two years later. Since some employers might be financially unable to pay the compensation in case of serious injury or death, insurance is compulsory except upon definite exemption by the commission. Several employers' mutual insurance companies were formed in Wisconsin to compete with the old line companies in this new field, and in 1937 they were carrying about 60 per cent of the business. What the act has meant to the working people of Wisconsin may be inferred from the fact that more than 20,000 compensation cases are now settled annually and payments in the decade 1928 to 1938 amounted to nearly $45,000,000. While the law has thus assured compensation to injured workmen or their families, there has also been a great movement for the prevention of accidents. Factory inspectors have required adequate safety appliances and the industrial commission has encouraged "Safety First" campaigns and the continuous education of employees.

During the past half century the hours of labor for men, women, and children have been shortened. The reduction in the hours for men has come in Wisconsin not by legislation, but largely as the fruit of trade union effort. There has been no comparable organization of women and children, and the state, as the guardian of the physical and moral well-being of mothers and of future citizens, has forbidden for them harmful occupations or hours of work so long as to be injurious. The industrial commission is the fact-finding body to determine just what is injurious. The essential legislation about women's work came in McGovern's time, the initial law in 1911 and great improvements two years later. During the World War the legislature stood firm against considerable pressure to relax existing rules. For women in industry today, the general rule is that they may not work more than nine hours a day or fifty hours a week, and night work is forbidden; though the commission provides for emergencies and for special types of work, as in sanatoriums, hotels, and telephone exchanges.

The state for the most part does not concern itself with children aiding their parents at home or on a farm. Children under twelve were excluded from certain harmful employments in 1877, but the law was ambiguous and there were no enforcement officials. The system of controlling the work of children by the issuance of permits began with the Bennett school law of 1889, and was retained when that law was repealed. Ten years later, in 1899, came "the first serious attempt to deal with the problem of child labor in the state." There were no restrictions on work during vacations, but, when schools were in session, children between fourteen and sixteen might not work more than ten hours a day or sixty hours a week. Normally children under fourteen might not work, but, if granted a permit, they might begin at twelve. Step by step standards were raised. In 1911, children between fourteen and sixteen years of age were limited to forty-eight hours of work a week. At present, all workers between the ages of fourteen and seventeen are required to have permits, which are issued only on condition that certain educational standards are met, and all workers up to the age of eighteen years are required to attend continuation schools.

Income measures the standard of living, and to those of the smallest earning power a higher or lower wage often means a real difference in health, efficiency, and general welfare. Why not by legislation simply forbid the payment of inadequate wages, wages below a certain minimum? There has been such legislation in certain foreign countries for a generation. Massachusetts established a board in 1912 to state what a minimum wage ought to be and recommended but did not require the payment of such a wage. In the following year eight states, among them Wisconsin, passed minimum wage laws. Until the era of the New Deal all such laws in the United States dealt with women and children, not with adult men.

A Wisconsin law of 1913 authorized the industrial commission to determine the minimum wages for women and minors, and its rulings have the force of law. For a good many years the rate for women was twenty-five cents an hour in cities and twenty-two cents in smaller places. In the spring of 1932 these rates were lowered by about 10 per cent. Special permission might be obtained to pay less than the scheduled rates to those not capable of doing a normal amount of work.

In setting these minimum rates the commission was guided by the words "living wage," in the law of 1913. In 1923 the Supreme Court of the United States declared unconstitutional a minimum wage law for the District of Columbia, and in the following year the Wisconsin law, in so far as it related to adult women, was similarly invalidated by the state supreme court. But in 1925 the Wisconsin legislature put the matter upon a different footing by enacting that employers of women must pay "a reasonable and adequate compensation for services rendered," declared that less than this was oppressive, and prohibited such "oppressive" wages under penalty. The industrial commission continued to declare its rates as before. In 1937 the Supreme Court of the United States reversed itself by upholding a minimum wage law for women in the state of Washington. The Wisconsin legislature thereupon repealed the clause about "oppressive" wages for women that had stood for twelve years and again required a "living wage." The National Fair Labor Standards Act, commonly called the federal wage-hour law, went into effect October 24, 1938. It prescribed minimum wages and maximum hours for men as well as women, but applied only to the production of goods for interstate commerce. A bill copying many of its provisions was introduced in the Wisconsin legislature of 1939, but failed to pass; Wisconsin is still without a minimum wage law for men.

The industrial commission also supervises apprenticeship contracts. The legislature of 1909 appointed a temporary commission to study "plans for the extension of industrial and agricultural training." Charles McCarthy of the Legislative Reference Library was secretary of the commission and went to Europe to study apprenticeship there. Resulting legislation in 1911 established the state control of apprenticeships, and the number of contracts in force climbed steadily until during the five years 1926 to 1930 it stood rather consistently at about three thousand. The depression caused a sharp decline in numbers. During 1934 and 1935 there were less than 1,200 indentures in force, but by the end of 1937 and throughout 1938 there were more than 2,500.

Wisconsin, first among the forty-eight states, passed an unemployment insurance act in January, 1932. Great Britain had had unemployment insurance since before the World War. Under the plan used there, a fund was built up by means of regular contributions from employers, employees, and the government, and the main purpose was to pay money to the unemployed. In contrast to this, the Wisconsin project was preventive in motive quite as much as remedial. After the compensation law of 1911 was passed, employers left no stone unturned to lessen the number of accidents. Could not a law be devised to make a discharged man a liability, and cause employers to make every effort to stabilize employment?

Bills with this central idea of prevention were introduced in every session of the legislature from 1921 onwards. Professor John R. Commons took a leading part in drawing up the bills and in advocating them, both before legislative committees and with the public at large. The Groves bill of the regular session of 1931 added a new feature, that of a separate accounting for each employer, and this bill, with many alterations, was the one finally passed in January, 1932. The depression caused delay, but in July, 1934, employers began building up reserves in the hands of the industrial commission. Two years later, in August, 1936, benefit payments began. The business recession that occurred in the latter part of 1937 was the first severe test of the system. Early in 1938 the number of insured persons was about 435,000, and in the whole of that year about 115,000 persons received payments which amounted altogether to more than $9,500,000. During 1939, payments amounted to about $3,663,000. Laws and regulations about payments into reserves have been changed several times since 1932. At the beginning of 1940, the standard rate was 2.7 per cent of the annual payroll; but after accumulated reserves reached 7.5 per cent of the payroll, the rate became one per cent. Whenever unemployment benefits depleted the reserve, the rate rose again. It was thus to the interest of the employer to avoid increasing his employees unwisely and to maintain steady employment. Early in 1940, employers of about half the insured persons were paying the reduced rate of one per cent.

LEGISLATION ABOUT TRADE UNIONS

On May 2, 1886, some three thousand men went on strike in Milwaukee in support of the eight-hour movement, then at its height, and within the next few days the number rose to seven thousand. It has already been told in the narrative of politics how Governor "Jerry" Rusk called out the militia and in the ensuing clashes nine men were killed. These "Bay View riots" were the occasion for the passing of laws in the next session of the legislature which in sum declared effective trade union activity to be conspiracy. The state federation of labor was formed in 1893, and soon thereafter the legislature began to deal more kindly with trade unions. There was an "anti-Pinkerton" law which forbade hired spies and imported strikebreakers, and a law against the employer's blacklist. In 1899 there was passed what we should today call a law against yellow-dog contracts: employers were forbidden to make a pledge not to join a trade union a condition of employment. This statute, however, was soon declared unconstitutional. Some years earlier in other parts of the United States it had been discovered that injunctions might be secured from courts of justice restraining trade unions from taking the steps necessary to make a strike effective. Apparently the first instance of such use in Wisconsin was in connection with a machinists' strike in Milwaukee in 1901. During the next decade injunctions against trade unions became frequent. In 1914 the federal Congress passed the Clayton Act, at the behest of the American Federation of Labor, to protect unions from the unfair use of the injunction. The act contained the notable sentence: "The labor of a human being is not a commodity or an article of commerce." In Wisconsin the state federation finally obtained in 1919 a law which stated that injunctions in labor disputes were to be issued only to prevent irreparable damage to property. This law also swept away the last shreds of the anti-union legislation of 1887 and declared what no one any longer doubted, that trade union activity was fully legal.

For many years after the World War every legislature improved the position of unions and of union members. In 1931 the advances were summed up in the "labor code," of which the three leading ideas were already familiar. The first was the outlawry of anti-union promises or conditions in agreements to hire, a repetition of an "anti-yellow-dog law" of 1929. The second was the legal recognition of normal strike methods, which were listed and stated to be rights. The third was a restriction in the use of injunctions and of contempt proceedings in support of injunctions.

Under Governors Schmedeman and Philip La Follette, Wisconsin lawmakers looked with favor on the activities of organized labor. In 1939, however, labor (according to its official leaders, at least) did not fare so well. In March the Catlin act defined a labor dispute as one in which a majority of the workers in a collective bargaining unit disagreed with the employer. This did not necessarily mean a majority of all employees in a plant; it might mean a majority of any group within a plant that bargained as a unit. Picketing was declared unlawful where no dispute existed as thus defined; that is, there was to be no picketing against the will of the majority of the employees. The Catlin act provided no penalty; those who broke it would not be liable to criminal action, but would be restrained, it was generally assumed, by injunction. Picketing had come to be used by organized groups and trade union leaders to accomplish a variety of objects in cases where there was no dispute between employers and employees; for example, to compel men to unionize or to affiliate with certain bodies of organized workers. All such uses of picketing now became illegal.

In May the Peterson bill was passed under the name of "the employment peace act." Its chief purpose was to set up a new board to settle labor disputes, but it was found necessary to repeat in it all the provisions of the Catlin act. Governor Heil and many prominent Republicans asserted that these acts were designed to benefit labor; but organized labor in the persons of its leaders took quite the opposite view, and A. F. of L. and C. I. O. officials appeared at legislative hearings and lobbied side by side in a vain attempt to prevent the passage of these laws.

The National Industrial Recovery Act (NIRA) of June 16, 1933, had a brief history, but in Wisconsin an aftermath of some length. According to the national act, industry was asked to end child labor, establish minimum wages, limit the hours of labor—in short, to assume a large social responsibility. As recompense for these burdens, industry was allowed to disregard anti-trust laws and to advance prices, which it did more rapidly than it raised wages. In each industry employers were authorized to prepare and issue a code which fixed wages and conditions of employment within the industry. These codes were minimum wage laws for men as well as women. The government tried by means of the Blue Eagle and an imposing array of national and local boards to keep in line the "chisellers" not disposed to abide by the codes. Before the end of 1933 it was clear that the purposes of the act were not being realized. Many codes were abandoned, and finally the whole system was overthrown by a unanimous decision of the United States Supreme Court, June 3, 1935, which declared that the act was an unconstitutional delegation of legislative powers to those who had written the codes.

Included in the NIRA was Section 7 (a), which put into every code that was issued the provisions that employees should have the right to organize and bargain collectively through representatives of their own choosing, that there should be no yellow-dog contracts, and that employers should observe code limitations as to maximum hours, minimum pay, and other conditions of employment set down in the codes. About six weeks after NIRA was passed, a Wisconsin law modeled upon it was enacted, and the details of 7 (a) were copied into the state law. The preponderant majority in an industry could promulgate a code and make rules and regulations regarding wages and hours. Three months before the United States Supreme Court invalidated NIRA, the Wisconsin Supreme Court, in March, 1935, declared the Wisconsin law unconstitutional, and by this decision twenty Wisconsin codes were ended. In June a new law took the place of the old, but now it was the governor who might issue codes and then only to eliminate unfair trade practices and unfair methods of competition. This law stood the test of the state supreme court, and appropriate officials and administrative bodies were created. It was allowed to expire in July, 1937, at a time when there were eleven codes in effect controlling the work of about 75,000 employed persons. Some trades desired regulation of this sort, and with slight changes the law was re-enacted in the special session of

October, 1937. There was to be no code save where a clear majority of the trade desired it, and this law, like its predecessors, was called an emergency law and had a time limit. By midsummer of 1938 some five groups, including, for example, barbers and the operators of beauty parlors, were again under codes. This law, and the codes drawn up under it, expired April 1, 1939. In October of the same year the legislators yielded to complaints of widespread price-cutting and again authorized codes, this time for four groups only, barbers, cosmeticians, cleaners, and shoe repairers.

In July, 1935, there was passed the Federal Labor Relations Act, often called the Wagner act. This law assured to working men the right to organize for collective bargaining and to be represented in such bargaining by negotiators of their own choice. The descent of this act from Section 7 (a) of NIRA is manifest. The board of three members which was set up as the National Labor Relations Board, when appealed to, would ascertain facts and give orders restraining employers who denied or impaired the rights assured by the statute. In the course of its first two years the board handled more than seven thousand cases.

A similar law was passed in Wisconsin in April, 1937, and was called by the newspapers, "Wisconsin's Little Wagner Act." Here, too, a board of three was to investigate and when necessary issue orders. Any form of company union was prohibited. These laws, both federal and state, were limited to one sort of labor dispute, that involving the kindred matters of organization and representation. The right to strike remained as before, and many matters such as hours, wages, and apprenticeship rules were not affected by these federal and state laws. The Wisconsin board was appointed late in April, 1937, and by November 30, 1938, it had settled by mediation 588 cases involving more than 110,000 workers, and had closed about 250 other cases.

The state labor relations board transacted very little business after the inauguration of Governor Heil, soon being reduced by the resignation of two of its members to less than a quorum. The "employment peace act" of May, 1939, besides defining labor disputes and placing a restraint on picketing as already indicated, repealed the "Little Wagner Act," and thus abolished the labor board created in 1937. At the same time it established a new board to handle labor disputes, and the governor at once (May 12, 1939) appointed its three members.

Selected Bibliography

Frederick Merk, *Economic History of Wisconsin During the Civil War Decade* (Madison, 1916), pp. 158-186, discusses trade union activity to about 1870. The work of John R. Commons and associates, *History of Labor in the United States* (2 vols., New York, 1918), gives both a necessary national background and many details of labor history in Wisconsin. John D. Hicks, *The Populist Revolt* (Minneapolis, 1931), is the standard work on the subject. The *Proceedings* of the Wisconsin State Federation of Labor (Milwaukee, annual since 1893) and *Wisconsin Labor* (Milwaukee, annual) together form a valuable record of the aims, methods, and activities of organized labor in the state. Election statistics are given in the biennial *Blue Books*.

Three B.A. theses contribute to our knowledge of the labor movement in Milwaukee: Selig Perlman, *History of Socialism in Milwaukee* (MS, Madison, 1910); Rosalind M. Drosen, *History of Socialism in Milwaukee, 1910-1930* (MS, Madison, 1931); and Mildred John, *History of Trade Unionism in Milwaukee* (MS, Madison, 1926). Valuable material is made accessible in *Voice and Pen of Victor Berger,* Congressional Speeches and Editorials (Milwaukee, 1929, published by the *Milwaukee Leader*). In testimony at the trial of the case of *United States vs. Berger et al.,* 66th Cong., 1st Sess., House Report, 413, Vol. B (Serial number 7595), Berger told much about his early life and his rise to leadership among American Socialists and in Milwaukee. Ora Almon Hilton, *Control of Public Opinion in the United States During the World War* (Ph.D. thesis, MS, Madison, 1929), discusses among other things federal control of newspapers and the Berger cases. Berger's influence on Eugene V. Debs is shown in the article on the latter in the *Dictionary of American Biography*. Daniel Hoan, *City Government—The Record of the Milwaukee Experiment* (New York, 1936), is valuable both as a contribution to the history of Milwaukee and as an authoritative exposition of socialism.

Arthur Joseph Altmeyer, *The Industrial Commission of Wisconsin,* University of Wisconsin Studies in the Social Sciences and History, No. 17 (Madison, 1932), is an important book written by one who was for many years secretary of the commission. Another excellent and lengthy study is Gertrude Schmidt's Ph.D. thesis, *History of Labor Legislation in Wis-*

consin (MS, Madison, 1933). The Legislative Reference Library compiled *Labor Laws of the State of Wisconsin and Orders of the Industrial Commission* (Madison, 1930), interspersing many useful historical notes. The industrial commission issues *Biennial Reports*.

William L. Crow is the author of two useful articles: "History of Legislative Control of Wages in Wisconsin," *Marquette Law Review,* Vol. XVI, pp. 188-198 (March, 1932); and "History of the Legislative Control of Workmen's Compensation in Wisconsin," *Illinois Law Review,* Vol. XXVII, pp. 137-153, (June, 1932).

The Rev. Francis J. Haas of the Wisconsin labor relations board wrote chiefly of Wisconsin experience in "State Labor Relations Boards," in *Labor Laws and Their Administration, 1937,* United States Bureau of Labor Statistics, Bulletin No. 653 (Washington, 1938), pp. 118-124. William Gorham Rice, Jr., "The Wisconsin Labor Relations Act in 1937," *Wisconsin Law Review,* Vol. XIII, pp. 229-280 (March, 1938), compares state and federal statutes and discusses judicial decisions. The history of the injunction is given in Edwin E. Witte, *The Government in Labor Disputes* (New York, 1932); this was a later version of a Ph.D. thesis, *The Role of the Courts in Labor Disputes* (MS, Madison, 1927). Joseph A. Padway, for many years chief legal adviser of the Wisconsin state federation of labor, wrote an "Analysis of Five Decisions" for *Wisconsin Labor, 1937,* pp. 51-63; there he summarized the cases in which the federal Wagner act was declared constitutional and compared that act with the Wisconsin labor relations act. The three members of the Wisconsin labor relations board, Voyta Wrabetz, Francis J. Haas, and Edwin E. Witte, submitted to Governor Philip La Follette a "Report Covering the Period from April 28, 1937, to November 30, 1938" (Madison, 1938, 28 pp. mimeographed), which is a valuable contribution to the labor history of the state.

CHAPTER XX

THE GROWING TASKS OF GOVERNMENT

Government in a New Age

THE demands made on government and the functions assumed by it constantly increase in number and importance. If Americans ever believed that the least government was the best government, they exemplify that belief no longer. This increase reflects both a change in the economic organization of society and the fact that, in a democracy, power is in the hands of the common man. Wisconsin in the beginning was almost entirely agricultural. Gradually industry grew to equal and in many parts of the state to overshadow agriculture. Concentration of wealth, particularly the concentration of the control of wealth by means of joint-stock companies, made giant strides. Life on isolated farms gave way to the more closely knit urban life. These developments were neither to be hindered nor to be condemned; they would not have come at all had they not brought with them great economic advantages. Because of them, however, unaided individuals found themselves confronted with difficulties and dangers which they were powerless to meet with their own strength. As the masters of the state through the ballot, they have called upon government to aid and protect them, and in so doing they have caused the government to enlarge its functions and multiply its agencies. The details of these changes are very numerous, but in them at least four purposes may be discerned.

The state, through its agent the government, should first of all afford protection where it is needed. It must protect workers from danger in industry and safeguard the health of all the population. It must protect consumers from false or adulterated products. Again, it must protect from fraud and incompetence those who entrust their savings to banks, insurance companies, and promoters or directors of enterprise. In these and in a multitude of other situations government has become a constant guardian of the people.

Another purpose inspiring the growth of government activities is the attainment and maintenance of equality in certain parts of the economic field. The evil of unequal railway rates for identical services was seized upon by the elder La Follette; now equal treatment is required not only of railroads but of all public utilities. The laws favoring labor unions and prescribing methods or machinery for settling labor disputes, mentioned in the preceding chapter, were intended to give employers and employees equal strength in bargaining, to end an inequality that was bound to work injustice. Taxes, too, should be equal; that is, the payment of them should involve equality of sacrifice. This principle, itself very old, has been applied in a world with new forms of wealth, with wealth in quantities unknown two generations ago, and it has led to new forms of taxation. Taxes laid upon great wealth have grown to be enormous. Behind these exactions are certain equalitarian ideas. One is that natural resources are the heritage of all the people, that the profits from their exploitations should be divided—if necessary, through taxation—to the equal advantage of all. Another is that a factory manager or owner who gains great profits does so only partially through his own skill, but to a considerable degree by the help of others, first of his employees, second of a wider circle that serves him and those whom he employs, and third of the state that educates his workmen, maintains public order, and renders possible the continuance of his enterprise.

The third purpose that appears increasingly in legislation is the elevation of the standard of living, which widely defined means the improvement of the whole population in health, material comforts, intelligence, wise use of leisure, and moral standards. This motive inspires legislation in favor of labor unions, which exist to protect the standard of living, as well as legislative efforts to provide better housing, to increase or maintain wages for certain groups, and to provide training which will increase earning power.

A fourth purpose that leads to increase in the functions of government is conservation. The present population is a trustee for future generations, and it should conserve and improve all natural resources such as mines, forests, wild life, water powers, scenic beauties, and human skills and abilities, lest later generations should be without these riches.

These purposes—the protection of the individual, the attainment of equality in certain relations of men with each other, the elevation of the standard of living, and conservation—have led to the greater part of the so-called progressive legislation of Wisconsin. This legislation has mirrored, of course, a changing conception of the very nature of the state. Even in the earliest days of Wisconsin's history the state acknowledged its responsibility in many matters, such as sound banking, the regulation and encouragement of means of travel, and education. Today the state government is a faithful servant and watchman in a much wider field. It is even planning for the future in ways probably unknown to the vast majority of its citizens. At every session of the legislature laws are passed that entail a further extension of the tasks of government. Some of these proposals come from pressure groups and are purely selfish; others are inspired by the sincerest altruism and genuine statesmanship. With every biennium, however, we are abandoning laissez faire and moving toward collectivism or community action in new areas.

The State and Health

Nothing would seem to be a matter more private and personal to each individual than his health; yet there is scarcely another phase of life in which the individual leans so heavily upon the safeguards erected and the help furnished by the government. A state board of health was established in Wisconsin in 1876, with an annual appropriation of $3,000. There was much for it to do. Over a fourth of those who contracted smallpox, then very prevalent, died of the disease, and in some years the percentage of fatalities from diphtheria was equally great. Typhoid fever was then one of the scourges of mankind, and in parts of Wisconsin it was of constant occurrence. The board pushed forward with a program of hygienic education, vaccination, isolation for communicable diseases, improvement of water supply, and the collection of statistics of disease. In 1883 a state law required the creation of local boards of health in every city, village, and town which should make reports of contagious disease. In 1894 the board issued an order making vaccination compulsory as a condition of attendance at school. Opposition developed, and the state supreme court decided that the board had exceeded the powers which the legislature had intended to delegate to it, but by the time the decision was handed down most of the school children had been vaccinated. Since 1897 the placarding of contagious diseases has been required.

After the turn of the century the work of the state board of health expanded steadily. In 1903 the system of state laboratories was begun in a small way, and now physicians have laboratory service at eight places in the state. Not long after this the board was given power to approve or disapprove plans for new water supply and sewage disposal plants throughout the state. This service grew until it called for the erection in 1919 of the bureau of sanitary engineering. The board of health also supplies serums, such as toxin-antitoxin, the safeguard against dipththeria. It has wide order-making powers and its codes have the force of law. It collects vital statistics. It licenses those whose employments touch public health, such as plumbers, embalmers, barbers, and those who operate beauty parlors. Hotels, restaurants, and lunch stands are likewise licensed and inspected.

One of the great accomplishments of Wisconsin has been its

progress in the struggle against tuberculosis. A generation ago this disease was responsible for more deaths in the state than any other. In 1905 the construction of a state sanatorium was authorized. This institution, which was located west of Wales in Waukesha County, was designed in the first place for cases in the early stages of the disease. A decade later it was supplemented by a camp for male convalescents at Lake Tomahawk in Oneida County. In 1910 those known to have tuberculosis were forbidden to attend school as teachers or students until after recovery, and other measures to prevent the spread of the disease followed. Wisconsin developed a plan of state-aided county sanatoriums, and between 1910 and 1930 eighteen county institutions of this kind were erected which now care for nearly 1,800 patients. The number of deaths from tuberculosis has fallen from 190.3 in each 100,000 of the population in 1908 to but 30 in 1938. The record of recent years is most encouraging. In 1928, deaths from tuberculosis numbered 1,698; the figure has been lower with each succeeding year, falling to 1,005 in 1937 and to 899 in 1938. Such an accomplishment in a period of depression is a triumph for medical science, and is also, some would contend, a justification of generous public assistance and relief.

While tuberculosis has thus been checked, smallpox and diphtheria have become much less dangerous than they used to be, and typhoid fever has almost disappeared in Wisconsin. The last great forward step in state medicine was the erection of the Wisconsin General Hospital at Madison. It was authorized by the legislature of 1920, and it furnishes hospital treatment first of all to those who lack the money to secure such services elsewhere.

THE CARE OF THE POOR, DEFECTIVE, AND DELINQUENT

Legislation for the relief of the poor in Wisconsin goes back to a law of territorial days which laid down the principle, never since departed from, that the town, village, or city in which the pauper had his legal residence was responsible for his support; by a law of 1849, however, it was provided that poor relief might be administered either by the separate towns or by the county as a unit. This distinction has persisted to the present. Where the town system is in force, as it now is in thirty-one counties, the supervisors of each town are ex officio overseers of the poor; under the county system the county board levies taxes and is otherwise responsible for the care of the poor. From the beginnings of the state some counties have had poorhouses, and the maintenance of these institutions is always a county enterprise, even in those counties where poor relief is handled by the separate towns.

If the poor are cared for in a poorhouse, they are said to receive "indoor relief"; if they get money and supplies while they continue to live in their own homes, they are receiving "outdoor relief." The two systems may, and in Wisconsin do, exist side by side. Of the seventy-one counties, forty-nine maintain poorhouses, now called "county homes," and there are two city homes. In nearly half of these counties the poorhouse and the asylum for the chronic insane are under the same management. In the poorhouses of Wisconsin a peak of 3,768 inmates was reached in 1933. During the next three years, because of the increased old age pensions, there was a considerable decline, but there is no prospect of the poorhouse becoming unnecessary. Since the great depression and the inauguration of the New Deal, there has been an immense increase in the amount of outdoor relief. For many years before that, however, some outdoor relief was dispensed by local officials, both in counties with poorhouses and in those without them. By 1931 this had come to amount to about a million dollars a year, and the recipients numbered about 35,000. These figures do not take account of the aid for dependent children nor of pensions to the blind and the aged.

State aid for the blind takes several forms. There is a school at Janesville, a workshop at Milwaukee, a field service, and, more recently, a pension. The school at Janesville is the oldest state institution. It was begun as a private philanthropy by citizens of Janesville and vicinity, and was transferred to the state in 1850. It provides for about 130 students during the regular academic year, and there is a summer session where seventy or eighty adult blind are given training. The workshop for the blind at Milwaukee was established in 1903 and in 1925 was put under the same management as the Janesville school. The field service maintains teachers who, besides teaching the blind in their homes, help them in many ways. They suggest means of earning, buy raw materials for home work, and help sell the finished products. They keep a record of all cases of blindness and attend to the getting of pensions. In 1907 the counties began to pay pensions to the adult blind. Over 1,200 received this pension in 1930, and by 1937, with federal help under the Social Security Act, about two thousand blind received pensions at a total cost of a little more than $500,000.

The state maintains a school for the deaf, established before the Civil War, at Delavan in Walworth County. It accommodates about two hundred students, teaching them, besides the ordinary school work, the art of lip reading and, if necessary, speech. In addition to this each one learns a trade whereby he may earn a living in later life. Students are admitted at all ages from four to twenty years. The school for the blind at Janesville and that for the deaf at Delavan were placed by Philip La Follette under the authority of the state superintendent of education. This transfer was first rescinded and then re-enacted by the legislature of 1939.

The care of the insane or feeble-minded individual is almost always beyond the resources of the unfortunate person's family. In Wisconsin, in the case of the insane, the state furnishes hospital treatment until the patient is cured or until it is demonstrated that he cannot recover, when he is transferred to the county of his legal residence. The two principal state hospitals for the insane are the Mendota State Hospital near Madison and the Winnebago State Hospital north of Oshkosh. At present the two together care for about 1,500 patients. In 1914 there was established at Waupun a special institution for the criminally insane known as the Central State Hospital. After the World War the Wisconsin

Memorial Hospital was located at Mendota, primarily to care for soldiers and sailors mentally impaired by their war experiences. Its first buildings were erected in 1921 and 1922, and until 1933 it was maintained largely at federal expense. After three years during which it was supported entirely by the state and the private means of its patients, it was taken over by the federal Veterans' Administration.

In the early days the counties kept their insane in the county poorhouses. Milwaukee County led the way in establishing a separate asylum for the insane in 1878; and other counties followed suit. Now there are, in all, thirty-six county asylums for the chronic insane and one for the tubercular insane; they contain about eight thousand chronic insane. Counties that do not have asylums pay other counties for the care of their insane. Besides its asylum Milwaukee County has a hospital with more than one thousand patients. There are two state institutions for the feeble-minded, one opened at Chippewa Falls in 1897, and the other at Union Grove in Racine County in 1919. These two together house more than 2,300 inmates who are receiving treatment or care at the expense of the state. All told, there are in the institutions of the state and the counties nearly fourteen thousand persons who are feeble-minded or insane.

Wisconsin has four penal institutions. The oldest, and for a long time the only one, the prison at Waupun, was opened in 1853. For a good many years, beginning in 1878, convict labor was sold to a Chicago shoe manufacturing firm at the rate of fifty cents for a ten-hour day. Since 1911 the largest number of prisoners at any one occupation has made binder twine, although this employs only about one-tenth of the men. The number of prisoners was just under a thousand in 1928 and about sixteen hundred in 1939, and it is difficult to provide work for all. In 1898 the second penal institution, the reformatory, was opened near Green Bay, and to it are regularly committed all male offenders between the ages of 16 and 30. It uses some of its man power on two farms and in a granite quarry, and altogether has charge of some five hundred men. The third institution is the Industrial Home for Women at Taycheedah, just east of Fond du Lac. It was opened in 1921 and in 1939 had something less than fifty inmates. On the same grounds is the state prison for women; since 1933, when this was opened, there have been no women in the prison at Waupun.

There are two educational institutions for delinquent young people. The Industrial School for Boys, long called the State Reform School, was placed at Waukesha in 1860 and of late years has housed about four hundred boys. The Industrial School for Girls began in Milwaukee in 1875 as a private institution known as the "House of Refuge" and came fully into the hands of the state in 1917. Following an appropriation in 1928, the board of control purchased a farm near Oregon in Dane County as a site for a new plant. By 1932 about half the projected buildings had been erected, but, because other buildings necessary to community life were still lacking, the new plant could not be occupied. Money to complete the establishment was appropriated by the legislature in 1939. During the past ten years the Industrial School for Girls in its old Milwaukee quarters has always sheltered between 118 and 200 girls.

As the earlier of these institutions were established each of them was given its own board of trustees, directors, or managers. By 1881 the state was maintaining six of these institutions, the two hospitals for the insane, the prison at Waupun, the reform school at Waukesha and the schools for the blind and the deaf. In that year the separate boards were abolished and all the institutions were placed under a board of supervisors composed of five salaried men. Ten years later the board of supervisors became the board of control, without much change in duties. In 1920 the board was reduced to three persons, two men and a woman.

Besides having seventeen or eighteen institutions directly in its charge (not all of them mentioned here), the board of control exercised general supervision over county institutions and county welfare work. The board also administered the laws regarding probation and parole. Many persons convicted of offenses against the law were not sent to a penal institution at all, but were placed on probation, and the board had a staff of probation officers to look after them. As to parole, the courts of Wisconsin often impose an indeterminate sentence, and those who behave well as prisoners are released on parole, but for a certain time must be controlled by parole officers.

In the spring of 1936 Governor Philip La Follette appointed a group of thirty-five citizens to make a study of the welfare problems of Wisconsin. In accordance with its recommendations a reorganization law was passed at the special session of 1937 which provided among other things for the eventual dissolution of the old board of control and the establishment in its place of two new departments. All institutions caring for the insane, feeble-minded, and epileptic, except the Central State Hospital, were to be placed under a department of mental hygiene; prisons and other correctional institutions were to be in charge of a department of corrections. Of the two, only the department of mental hygiene had progressed far in its organization when Heil became governor.

The legislature of 1939 repealed the whole La Follette reorganization plan, restored the board of control, and then, after some months, enacted its own plan. It created a state department of public welfare having a part-time policy-making board of seven members and a full-time executive director. The statute directed the establishment within the new department of five divisions: public assistance, child welfare, mental hygiene, corrections, and administration and research, and gave the board power to create other divisions at its discretion. To this great new public welfare department were assigned most of the duties and functions of the following: the board of control, the two departments authorized and partly organized under La Follette, the state pension department in the industrial commission, and the public welfare department. The last, which had borne the same name as the new department, was an agency, established within the industrial commission late in 1935 and soon made independent, whose function was to supervise and administer public relief.[1]

BANKING, INSURANCE, AND PUBLIC UTILITIES

Facing the mysteries of banking, insurance, and high finance, or confronted by the might of monopolies, the ordinary man stands bewildered and helpless. The government of Wisconsin has undertaken to supervise these financial institutions and to protect the individual as far as possible from losses due to mismanagement or fraud. Yet, despite the urgings of Socialists and other reformers, the state has not entered into competition with private enterprise or turned to public ownership to any significant extent.

It will be remembered that the fathers of Wisconsin were very suspicious of banks and provided in the constitution that banking laws should be submitted to popular referendum before they should take effect. This rather cumbersome provision was removed by amendment in 1902. Throughout the nineteenth century there was little real control of banks, and Governors Upham and Scofield both urged closer supervision of banking. In 1903, when La Follette was governor, a department of banking was established under a single commissioner, and in 1933 this was changed to a commission of three members. For many years under these authorities there has been supervision of state banks, building and loan associations, and loan and finance companies of various sorts. Since the depression the commission has urged on and guided the growth of credit unions. During 1932 and 1933 most banks were in difficulties, and some of those that were closed would never, if left to themselves, have opened again. It fell to the banking commission to take charge, and either arrange to reopen them or liquidate their assets for the benefit of the depositors. In this the commission coöperated with the agencies of the federal government.

The people of Wisconsin have come to pay more than one hun-

---

[1] The history of public relief and of this agency will be more fully discussed in Chapter XXIII.

dred million dollars a year in insurance premiums. This business is one that from its nature must be conducted on a large scale, and it takes highly expert and technical knowledge to determine the soundness of an insurance company. From 1850 onward Wisconsin required insurance companies to report regularly to the secretary of state on their financial condition. In 1870 a department of insurance was established in the office of the secretary of state and seven years later a separate department was set up. For thirty years beginning in 1881 there was an elected commissioner of insurance, but since 1911 he has been appointed by the governor for a four-year term. In Governor Davidson's time, 1906 to 1911, more complete regulation and supervision were required, and as a result twenty-four life insurance companies ceased doing business in Wisconsin rather than comply with these laws.

The chief work of the insurance commissioner is to enforce the laws relating to insurance and to make certain that companies are in a position to fulfil their contracts with policy holders. The department also collects more than two million dollars a year in taxes from companies operating in Wisconsin. In cities and villages where there are fire departments two per cent of fire insurance premiums are taken by the insurance department. This produces a sum of more than $250,000 a year which is applied to the support of the local fire departments.

The state of Wisconsin conducts what are really two insurance companies, the state insurance fund and the state life fund. The first of these, which was begun in 1903, provides fire and tornado insurance on the public buildings belonging to the state. The same protection may be secured by counties, cities, villages, towns, school districts, and library boards for public or semipublic buildings. The fund does not, however, insure private property. The state life fund has since 1913 offered life insurance to the people of Wisconsin, at present in amounts not to exceed $4,000 on a single life, but in spite of the very moderate cost to the insured, it has not proved popular.

Almost from the time when railroads began to operate in Wisconsin, farmers accused them of unfair practices and sought legislative control of rate making. By the famous Potter law of Governor Taylor's time, a railroad commission of three members was created with power to fix freight and passenger rates. The Potter law, however, was repealed in 1876, less than two years after its passage. The commission of three was replaced by one commissioner who had no power to determine rates and whose chief duty was to collect statistics. In 1881 this office became elective and so continued until 1905. In 1903 Governor La Follette secured the ad valorem taxation of railroads, but he knew that unless the state controlled rates, the railroads would pass the burden of increased taxation on to their patrons. Regulation of railway rate making was one of the chief issues in La Follette's last campaign for the governorship, and his victory was a mandate for such regulation. Consequently a new railroad commission was established in 1905 with power to control rates and the quality of the service, and to prevent discrimination. Two years later there was added the regulation of all utilities operating in the state, whether privately or municipally owned. In 1931 the railroad commission became the public service commission. According to a summary of its work written in 1937, it

. . . regulates about 1,250 public utilities supplying gas, water, electric, telephone, heating and toll bridge service; 23 steam railroad systems, 20 street and interurban railways and urban bus lines; about 142,000 trucks and busses operated by common carriers of passengers and freight, contract carriers of freight, and private carriers of freight; and matters involving water power and navigation, including operation of 1,200 dams.[2]

Before the commission was established many utility companies possessed franchises granted by city councils or other municipal authorities. Such franchises were almost always limited to a definite term of years, and this limitation was an inducement to extract all possible profit before the franchise expired. Indeterminate franchises were offered to these corporations in 1907, and in 1911

[2] *Wisconsin Blue Book, 1937*, p. 619.

all existing franchises were ended and the corporations received indeterminate permits. So long as these enterprises were carried on in a manner advantageous to the public, their monopoly was to continue. In contrast with the outcry against monopolies that marked the turn of the century, it is remarkable to find Wisconsin today protecting and perpetuating her well-behaved monopolies.

Since 1911 the railroad commission has had extensive authority over the water-power resources of the state. It must approve all plans and give permission for constructing dams on navigable waters. Under the so-called recapture clause of the water-power law, added in 1927, no permit is granted until the water power has been appraised. A corporation building a power dam agrees that "such dam may at any time after thirty years be taken over by the public at the value established by the railroad commission, plus actual investment in the dam." The state is making the path straight for the next generation if it decides to have state owner-ship and development of water power. This law was upheld by the United States Supreme Court in 1931.

A frequent cause of high public service charges is the necessity of paying interest on watered stock and other forms of overcapitali-zation. To forestall and avoid such burdens in Wisconsin the commission was given power, by the stock and bond law of 1907, to control the issues of securities of public service corporations. In 1913 by the first "Blue Sky Law," the commission was given authority to license stock brokers and after investigation to forbid the offering of any security for sale in Wisconsin. Later enact-ments of 1919 and 1933 have made Wisconsin security regulations very comprehensive and exacting. The securities division was transferred to the banking commission in 1938 and in 1939 it be-came an independent agency of the state government.

CONSERVATION

Throughout the last third of the nineteenth century some con-cern was felt, and some measures were taken, in the matter of conserving fish, game, and forests in Wisconsin. The care of fish began with the appointment of a fish inspector in 1866, and there was a commission to investigate forest conditions in the following year. Fish wardens were appointed in 1885 and game wardens two years later. The beginning of a state park system came with the purchase of lands along the St. Croix River in Polk County, and in the following year (1900) Minnesota and Wisconsin coöperated in establishing Interstate Park. Early in the twentieth century were set up the state board of forestry, a state park board, and the first conservation commission, this last in 1911. In his pre-election compaign in 1914 Governor Philipp promised consolidation of offices and departments for the sake of economy and efficiency. The creation of a new conservation commission was perhaps his most noteworthy accomplishment of this sort. Bringing together many existing bodies and services, too numerous to mention here, the new commission consisted of three men, one with a knowledge of forestry, another an expert on the propagation, care, and protection of fish and game, and a third experienced in business matters. After 1927 the commission was made up of six men who served without pay, except for expense incurred. The total personnel came by 1937 to include 247 permanent and almost as many seasonal employees.

Early warnings that some day the forests would be exhausted went largely unheeded. In 1878, to be sure, the state purchased 50,000 acres of virgin timber with the express provision that it should never be cut; but some twenty years later timber barons persuaded the legislature to reverse the action of its predecessor, and the reserve was sold. In 1897 Filibert Roth, an expert of the forest service of the United States Department of Agriculture, spent three months inspecting the woods of northern Wisconsin. He came to the conclusion that much of the land in that region was unfit for agriculture and urged reforestation.

In view of the importance of lumbering in the past history of Wisconsin and the fact that much of the cut-over land was valueless for agriculture, it was but natural that reforestation should find favor. A program for reforesting state-owned land was

under way when it was halted in 1915 by a decision of the state
supreme court to the effect that this use of state money was unconstitutional: the state might not be a party to works of internal improvement. This prohibition was removed by an amendment to
the constitution in 1924. Appropriate legislation authorized taxation for this purpose, the first money becoming available in 1930.

The forest crop law of 1927 was passed to encourage owners of
land other than the state to engage in reforestation. "It creates a
partnership between the state and the owner of land, whether it
is a private individual, company, or county, for the production of
forests." Contracts are entered into according to which the
owner pays annually to the state in taxes but ten cents an acre.
When the time comes to cut and sell the timber, 10 per cent of the
stumpage value will be paid into the state treasury. It took another
constitutional amendment to open the way for taxation at a rate
lower than was paid on other land.

As soon as the forest crop law was passed, some of the counties
inquired whether they might enter the lands that had become
county property through nonpayment of taxes. It was enacted
that counties might enter their lands, that they would not have to
pay the ten cents an acre, and that if the lands did not have a crop
of growing trees, the state would when necessary give financial
and other help to the counties to enable them to plant trees.
Where such help was given, however, the state's share of the proceeds from the timber would be 50 per cent.

Up to March, 1938, the county forest crop lands amounted to
about 1,746,000 acres and privately owned forest crop lands to
about 187,000 acres. Besides these there were state-owned forests
of about 170,000 acres, about four-fifths in one connected area in
Vilas County. In addition to all this, the federal government had
located two national forests in Wisconsin, Chequamegon Forest
with headquarters at Park Falls and Nicolet Forest with headquarters at Rhinelander. The federal authorities were planning
to build these up until together they covered about 1,800,000 acres.
By the summer of 1938 about two-thirds of this had already been

purchased.   Altogether, private, county, state, and federal lands
in Wisconsin ear-marked for reforestation amounted to about one-
tenth of the area of the state.   A group of six contiguous counties
in the west-central part of the state had established county forests;
those with the larger forests were Eau Claire, Clark, and Jackson

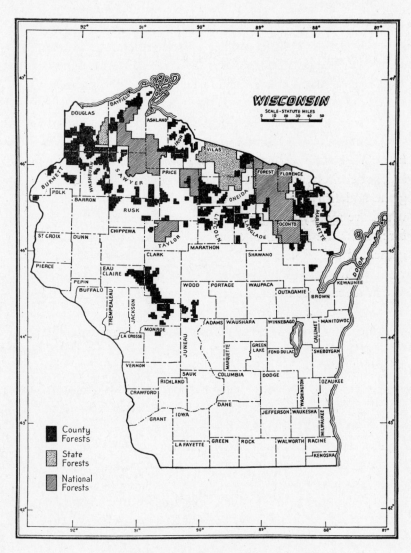

COUNTY, STATE, AND NATIONAL FORESTS

counties. Most of the other county reforestation projects lay in some twenty counties lying about three tiers deep along the northern boundary of the state.

The conservation commission has charge of eighteen state parks, several of them exceeding a thousand acres in area. Some of them are maintained because they have historic interest: one contains the first capitol building at Belmont, another the old shot tower at Helena. Most of them possess great scenic beauty. Rib Mountain near Wausau is the highest point in the state, Copper Falls is the highest waterfall, and Devils Lake is a fascinating exhibit in geology.

Up to about the time of the World War, the chief motive for reforestation was the production of timber, the raw material of so many Wisconsin industries. While this object has not been lost sight of entirely, it has come to be realized that forests filled with game and fish have great recreational value and attract tourists who have money to spend. The conservation commission therefore stocks the streams and lakes with fish and the forests with game. It established a recreational publicity division which advertised Wisconsin as the "Playground of the Middle West." When there is an open season for deer, 100,000 deer hunting licenses are sold, and licenses of all kinds produce over $600,000 a year, about a third of it from outside the state. It is estimated that the tourist trade spends over $200,000,000 a year,[3] and catering to it has become one of Wisconsin's leading industries. Beyond these commercial aspects of conservation, there is the benefit that accrues to Wisconsin's own people from their increasing use and enjoyment of the outdoors.

GETTING AND SPENDING: TAXES AND THE TAX COMMISSION

As the functions of the state multiplied, the expenditure of public money grew steadily until, in the fiscal year ending June

---

[3] Estimate of J. H. H. Alexander, superintendent of recreational publicity, conservation department.

30, 1931, Wisconsin and all its subdivisions including school districts spent $259,000,000. Thereafter, because of the depression, the total sank each year until in 1934 it amounted to a little more than $225,000,000. Some of the subdivisions of the state borrow, of late there have been large grants of federal money, and there are some other sources of income, but the greater part of public money spent in Wisconsin has always been derived from taxes. By 1930 the amounts collected in a year by the state and its subdivisions had reached $184,000,000. After that they sank year by year until 1935 when collections were about $136,000,000. Then for three years they rose steadily until in the year ending June 30, 1938, the people of Wisconsin paid in taxes (omitting those paid to the federal government) no less than $186,000,000. This increase of $50,000,000 within three years without doubt contributed to the defeat of Philip La Follette in the fall of 1938.

Several forms of taxation are used in Wisconsin, but among them the general property tax is the oldest and at present by far the most important. It yields about two-thirds of all the revenue from taxes, $122,000,000 in 1930 and $106,000,000 in 1938. Fundamental to the just incidence of this tax is the work of the assessors. These officials, now numbering more than 1,800 in Wisconsin, are elected for short terms of one or two years. It is necessary for fairness that the assessors proceed in a uniform manner in assigning values to property, and hence provision must be made not only to give them instructions but to hear appeals from their assessments and to revise their results. Locally this work is done by the equalization committee of the county board or in cities by a board of tax appeals. During the first half century of the life of the state there were in succession several boards of equalization for the whole state with varying memberships; these were the forerunners of the later tax commission. From 1873 to 1897 the board of equalization consisted of the secretary of state, the state treasurer, and the attorney general. Toward the close of the nineteenth century it was recognized that there were many inequalities in the Wisconsin system of taxation, and in 1897 a body of three unpaid tax commissioners was appointed by Governor Scofield to study the whole field. The legislature of 1899 authorized the governor to appoint a tax commissioner with two assistant commissioners and, though appointed for ten years, they were still not regarded as a permanent body. These three men were to investigate and make recommendations on matters of taxation, and also act as a board of assessment or of equalization. Before the ten years had run their course a permanent tax commission composed of three commissioners of equal rank was established. The commission had general supervision over the levying and collection of taxes by the state and its subdivisions. It gathered and published statistics about all taxes, often aided in drafting new tax legislation, and, with reference to the general property tax, instructed and advised county boards and all other taxing bodies. In 1939 the legislature abolished the tax commission and created in its stead a tax department with one man, called a director, at its head. Under the director was established a board of tax appeals of three members.

Besides the general property tax, there are special property taxes. The first of these was the famous ad valorem tax on railways, secured by the elder La Follette in 1903. Up to that time the railways had not paid a property tax at all, but a percentage of their gross earnings. Under the law of 1903, the tax commission each year added up the general property taxes imposed by the state and all its subdivisions and computed the ratio of the total to the assessed value of the properties taxed. In 1930, for example, this was a little over two per cent. The commission also estimated the physical value of the properties of railroad and other public utility corporations and applied to it the rate of the general property tax, but while the general tax rate may vary from county to county and from one school district to another, the rate applied to utilities is uniform throughout the state. These special property taxes produced about $14,000,000 in 1930, and $13,000,000 in 1938; of these sums street railways and light and power companies have come to pay about half, and steam railways about a third.

While property taxes are still the main support of Wisconsin and its subdivisions, the state has had an income tax since 1912. Congress imposed a federal income tax during the Civil War and again in the time of Grover Cleveland, but the law of 1894 was found to be unconstitutional and an amendment to the federal constitution was necessary before such a tax could be used. Similarly, Wisconsin had to have an amendment to her constitution, and this was obtained between 1905, when it first passed the legislature, and 1908, when the people voted favorably upon it. Legislation followed in McGovern's first year, and in 1912 the first collections were made. Income taxes are of two sorts, one laid on private incomes and the other on the earnings of corporations. The two together have come to produce about one-sixth as much as the general property tax, or about $20,000,000 a year. Down to 1926 the taxpayer was excused from a part of his income tax equal to the personal property tax he paid, but the last legislature under Governor Blaine (1925) repealed this "offset," and the income tax thereafter was twice as productive. In addition to the normal income tax, surtaxes have been placed upon incomes for certain special purposes. There was a surtax for a soldiers' bonus in 1919, another for a soldiers' educational bonus in 1920, and another to pay the state's share of a teachers' retirement fund from 1921 onward. The legislature of 1931 laid a surtax on income to provide funds for emergency unemployment relief.

The legislature of 1899 made the first attempt to establish an inheritance tax in Wisconsin, but its effort was declared unconstitutional. In 1903 a law with the same purpose was passed which stood the test of the courts, and the first collections under it were made in 1905. For many years the receipts were small, being still less than half a million dollars annually after ten years. By 1920, with the increasing wealth of the state, they had reached a million dollars. The legislature of 1925 so changed the rates and improved the methods of collection that the inheritance tax thereafter regularly yielded more than $2,000,000 a year, and in 1938 the amount exceeded $5,000,000.

Motor vehicles and gasoline are specially taxed. Since 1911 there has been a license fee; by 1930 this had come to produce about $12,000,000, and by 1938, about $13,300,000. A tax on gasoline was imposed in 1925. At two cents a gallon this produced about $8,000,000 a year. The legislature of 1931 raised the tax to four cents, and in 1937 and 1938 it was yielding nearly $20,000,000 a year. There are, in addition, special highway taxes for some trucks and busses.

The repeal of prohibition and the legalization of the manufacture and sale of alcoholic beverages has again opened up taxes in this field that yield about $7,000,000 annually. Some taxes have other purposes than revenue: since the tax on oleomargarine was made fifteen cents a pound it has produced almost nothing. It should be called a protective tariff. The chain store tax yielded nearly $50,000 in 1938, but was not designed to drive out the chain store, as some imagine. If the assessor visits two establishments that have approximately equal sales, one a chain store outlet and the other a locally owned independent business, he finds a far larger stock of goods on the shelves of the independent merchant, and this of course is followed by a heavier property tax. The chain store tax is intended to offset this inequality; to some it seems like a penalty on more efficient merchandizing. In the legislature of 1939 various forms of the general sales tax were seriously considered but none was imposed.

The main theme of this chapter has been the ever-expanding services undertaken and performed by the state and local governments. Leaders in humanitarian efforts and "social engineers" are constantly laying plans for more services and better care at the hands of the government. From some points of view these plans are to be commended; their realization is to be desired. The effective brake upon such progress is the cost. In 1901 the state and local taxes amounted to $21,000,000; in 1938 they were nine times as much. There was some change in the value of money in the interval, the population of the state increased by about a million or 50 per cent, and wealth also increased. At the beginning of the period two million people paid $21,000,000 annually in taxes; at the end three million paid $188,000,000. The voting public is torn between the desire for services and the wish to avoid increased taxes. Generally speaking, progressive Republicans and the later Progressive party have inclined to increase services and, inevitably, taxes. Regular or Stalwart Republicans have wished to pause in the spending and economize. As our survey of politics has shown us, it has not mattered much what the Democrats have thought: they have been in control of the state but two years in the twentieth century, and those were very unusual years when much that was normally the concern of the state was guided from Washington. Public assistance in the period of the New Deal belongs in a later chapter, essentially a continuation of the theme of this chapter into a different era.

SELECTED BIBLIOGRAPHY

There has been no recent book on the underlying ideas of social progress in Wisconsin comparable to those of Charles McCarthy and Frederick C. Howe issued in 1912 (see Selected Bibliography of Chapter XV). Reference may be made, as was done for Chapter XVIII, to the platforms of political parties and to the messages of governors to the legislature. Many acts printed in the *Session Laws* begin with statements of conditions to be remedied and aims to be achieved. The Joint Resolutions included in the volumes of the *Session Laws* are also frequently illuminating. Indispensable as a guide to the publications of all state departments is the monthly *Check List of Wisconsin Public Documents* prepared by the State Historical Society of Wisconsin.

There is a chapter, "The Work of the State Board of Health, 1876-1924," by C. A. Harper in Milo M. Quaife, *Wisconsin, Its History and Its People* (4 vols., Chicago, 1924), Vol. II, pp. 323-365. The state board of health issues a biennial *Report* which includes a "Report of the State Bureau of Vital Statistics."

The Twenty-third Biennial Report of the State Board of Control (Madison, 1936) was the last of a valuable series. Each report, often containing more than 500 pages, gave information about the care of the poor, defective, and delinquent, with statistics about state and county institutions. Beginning in February, 1937, the board of control issued a monthly periodical, *The Rebuilder,* containing statistics and relevant articles. The Children's code was Chapter 439, *Session Laws, 1929.* This was amended by Chapter 6 of the special session of 1937. The Wisconsin Conference of Social

Work published a study by Esther H. de Weerdt, *Five Years of Child Welfare under the Children's Code in Wisconsin, 1929-1934* (Madison, 1934).

Leonard B. Krueger, *History of Commercial Banking in Wisconsin,* University of Wisconsin Studies in the Social Sciences and History, No. 18 (Madison, 1933), pp. 141-230, shows the growth of state control of banking. Lewis E. Gettle wrote "The Work of the Railroad Commission," for Quaife, *op. cit.,* Vol. II, pp. 433-442. The railroad commission, and later the public service commission, have biennial *Reports.* An interesting account by Ernest Brown Skinner, "The Determination of the Value of the Right of Way of Wisconsin Railroads As Made in the Appraisal of 1903," is found in the *Transactions* of the Wisconsin Academy of Sciences, Arts, and Letters, Vol. XV, part 2 (1907), pp. 794-822. A thorough study of its subject is Frederick L. Holmes, *Regulation of Railroads and Public Utilities in Wisconsin* (New York, 1915).

The *Fifteenth Biennial Report* of the state conservation commission (Madison, 1938) is the most recent in a well written and well illustrated series. The commission also issues a monthly *Wisconsin Conservation Bulletin.* F. B. Trenk prepared a pamphlet published by the commission, *The County Forests of Wisconsin* (Madison, 1938), which summarizes the movement attractively. An older statement, "The Work of the Conservation Commission," by Wallis E. Barker, appeared in Quaife, *op. cit.,* Vol. II, pp. 381-409.

The tax commission issued biennial *Reports,* and bulletins at frequent intervals. Bulletin No. 82, January, 1938, gave statistics of receipts and disbursements, 1931-1936; Bulletin No. 85, October, 1938, reviewed grants in aid to municipalities over many years. There are articles on taxation in nearly every issue of the Wisconsin *Blue Book.* Attention may be called to those by J. Roy Blough, *Blue Book, 1931,* pp. 49-60; and Charles D. Rosa, *Blue Book, 1935,* pp. 29-44. Harley L. Lutz, *The State Tax Commission,* Harvard Economic Studies, No. 17 (Cambridge, 1918), pp. 237-288, deals with the Wisconsin Tax Commission at length, and the footnotes refer to a wide literature up to 1918. "The Genesis of Wisconsin's Income Tax Law," *Wisconsin Magazine of History,* Vol. XXI, pp. 3-15 (September, 1937), records the recollections of D. O. Kinsman, the principal author of the law of 1911. Nils P. Haugen, who was a member of the tax commission in its different forms from 1901 to 1921, in his *Pioneer and Political Reminiscences* (reprinted from *Wisconsin Magazine of History,* Vols. XI, XII, and XIII), reprint pp. 126-188, comments pithily on taxation problems in his time. Frederick K. Hardy discussed "Legal and Economic Aspects of Chain Store Taxation in Wisconsin," in *Wisconsin Law Review,* Vol. IX, pp. 382-387 (June, 1934); and "Wisconsin's New Chain Store Tax and Its Relation to Personal Property Taxation," *Bulletin of the National Tax Association,* Vol. XIX, pp. 66-72 (December, 1933).

CHAPTER XXI

EDUCATION

ELEMENTARY SCHOOLS

FOR nearly a century the support of education has been a part of the work of government in Wisconsin, both of the state itself and of its several subdivisions. When Wisconsin was receiving its first English-speaking settlers, the United States was about to begin in good earnest the transfer of the major part of education from private to public hands. The proponents of education at public expense won a great victory in the constitutional conventions, and from that time on there was a steady increase in the scope and expense of public education until about 1930, when the state and its subdivisions were spending for this purpose about $70,000,000 a year. Expenditure fell during the depression years and then regained most of its loss. Meanwhile student enrollment continued to rise steadily until 1934-1935, when there were almost 550,000 pupils in the public elementary and high schools. Since then each year has shown a small decrease, reflecting a decline in the number of those of school age in the state. No account of the development of Wisconsin should omit its greatest public enterprise, that of providing and maintaining the schools and institutions of higher learning in which, during most of the year, more than a fifth of its population is to be found. A detailed history of education, to be sure, is not here intended; education is treated chiefly as another illustration of the broadening services of the state to its citizens.

This limitation on the subject matter of the chapter excludes any discussion of the private and parochial schools affiliated with or conducted by churches. These schools are important in Wisconsin. In 1935-1936, Roman Catholic schools alone were instructing nearly 96,000 pupils in the elementary grades and more than 9,000 in high schools and academies. Schools connected with the various branches of the Lutheran church are also numerous and well attended.

While Wisconsin was still a part of Michigan Territory, a few elementary schools supported by fees were opened in the villages west of Lake Michigan. A series of enactments passed during Wisconsin's territorial years established the county, the town, and the school district as educational units, and gave to each of them authority to levy taxes for the support of schools. Counties and towns, however, did almost nothing in matters educational, while the districts did much. The "district as the local school unit virtually became supreme. It was to all intents and purposes a little independent school republic." [1] The district has held its pre-eminence down to the present time. A number of districts taxed themselves to erect school buildings, but while Wisconsin was a territory there were no free schools: part of the expense was always met by fees paid by parents.

The constitution of 1848, as we have seen in an earlier chapter, made provision for public schools "free and without charge for tuition." Generous federal land grants for education had been accepted, and proceeds from the sale of these lands were to go to the school fund or the university fund. In addition, the constitution allotted to the school fund all forfeitures, escheats, fines, and unassigned gifts to the state. Certain other lands were added to the school fund by the legislature of 1849, and thus there were assembled for this fund alone more than 1,705,000 acres. Foresight would have prescribed a policy of slow and careful sale; instead, the lands were rushed into the market, and within five or six years practically all of them had been sold at ridiculously low prices. The fund today, though exceeding ten million dollars, is

---

[1] Conrad E. Patzer, *Public Education in Wisconsin* (Madison, 1924), p. 9.

but a pathetic fragment of what it might have been if the federal land grants had been wisely handled.

There were many in territorial Wisconsin who believed that schools should be free and supported by the public. Chief among them was Michael Frank, a newspaper editor of Southport (Kenosha). As a member of the upper house of the territorial legislature he tried to secure a law providing schools of this sort throughout the territory, but his efforts were in vain. He did, however, gain permission to put his plan into operation in Kenosha, provided it was approved by referendum there. The necessary local approval was secured in 1845, a building was erected in 1847 and 1848, and on June 30, 1849, the first tax-supported and entirely free school in Wisconsin began its work. It was successful from the beginning, and was the object of pilgrimages on the part of schoolmen from far and near. Meanwhile the principle of free education had been written into the constitution, and by 1850 district schools throughout the settled part of the state were instructing nearly 60,000 pupils.

From 1849 to 1862 the key man in local school administration was the town superintendent. He was chosen by the voters of the town, usually from among their own number, to hold office for one year. Often entirely lacking in educational qualifications, since none was required by law, this official examined, licensed, and employed teachers, and advised and guided district boards. The teachers of the state, organized in the Wisconsin Teachers' Association, for some years carried on a concerted movement to get rid of him and finally succeeded. In January, 1862, 743 town superintendents gave up their powers to county superintendents, and these have held sway ever since. From time to time incorporated cities have detached themselves from the counties in which they lie, and have organized independently with their own superintendents. For many years there have been seventy-two county superintendents (Dane County boasts two), and in 1936 there were just a hundred city superintendents. There were, however, cities under the county superintendents of greater wealth and population than some of those that had chosen to organize separately.

The very size of city school systems gives them an advantage over the rural schools. Of the county schools about 6,500 are one-room country schools, and six hundred more are "graded schools wholly rural in their origin, development and attitude." In all fairness country children should have as good a training for life as city dwellers; such was apparently the intent of the framers of the constitution. But rural schools show many weaknesses. Their teachers have less training to begin with, and are not paid as well as city teachers, although minimum wage laws are improving conditions in this respect. Teachers of rural schools migrate to larger schools or desert the profession even more rapidly than do city teachers. Of 7,000 rural school teachers there are 1,200 or 1,300 every year who enter upon their work as new and inexperienced teachers. And into a teacher's day in a one-room school must sometimes be crowded twenty-five or thirty recitations. Not until 1937 did the state require a nine-month term in all schools. Apparently the "little red schoolhouse" can scarcely be counted an efficient educational instrument. These conclusions are drawn from the statistics of the situation, and the adverse criticisms may be stated without denying that there is devoted service and skilful teaching in hundreds of rural schools in the state.

The wiser educational leaders in Wisconsin have long been aware of certain unfortunate features in school organization and finance. In most districts there is a board of three persons, and thus there are more than 20,000 men and women charged with administering the rural schools. Since 1905 the clerk of each district has been required, and all board members have been invited, to attend an annual convention especially arranged in each county to train board members in their duties and show them their opportunities. Those who attend are paid for their time.

Many country schools are so small that they show a high per capita cost. In 1938 there were ninety-five schools operating with less than six pupils, and over 2,000, about one-third of all rural schools, with fifteen or less. Consolidation of districts has long been optional, but voluntary consolidation has been most infrequent, and apparently relief is not to be expected in that direction.

The school districts also differ greatly in financial strength, the assessed valuation of property within them varying from forty thousand to nearly a million dollars. The support of a school is a heavy and undeserved burden upon the poorer districts. In 1927 the legislature passed an equalization act, and now money is paid over by the state to the weaker districts as such. Besides this, there are other payments made partly by the state and partly by the county to all districts. Effectively, the wealthier parts of the state are helping to pay the expenses of education in the poorer districts.

The country school districts number on the average about a hundred to the county. Doubtless this was the best method of organization in the "horse and buggy era" during which most of them were established. But with modern means of transportation the continuance of these small districts seems wasteful and inefficient in the extreme. An interim legislative committee which reported in 1931 recommended the ending of the district system and a reorganization by counties, but the old system was strongly intrenched. Up to 1940 these recommendations had borne no fruit.

The kindergarten, educating children of preschool age largely through carefully planned and directed play, is now a recognized part of our public school system. The father of this method was Friedrich Froebel, who conducted experiments and expounded his doctrines in Germany for a generation before his death in 1852. He seems to have used the word "kindergarten" first in 1840. Wisconsin had a very early school of this kind. Margarethe Meyer, later Mrs. Carl Schurz, attended lectures and demonstrations by Froebel in Hamburg in 1849. An older sister of Mrs. Schurz started the first kindergarten in London and perhaps in England. Mrs. Schurz came to Watertown, Wisconsin, in 1856,

and there in November or December of that year she opened a
kindergarten, conducted in the German language, that is thought
to have been the first in the United States. This kindergarten
came to an end after two or three years, and did not lead on to the
present system in the state. The first kindergarten conducted in
English in the United States was started in Boston in 1860 by Miss
Elizabeth P. Peabody; by a strange coincidence it was largely a
chance meeting with Mrs. Carl Schurz that directed Miss Peabody's attention to this work in which she afterwards became a
national leader.

After the Civil War, kindergarten doctrine and practice took
hold of educators in the eastern part of the United States and,
spreading westward, ultimately reached Wisconsin. In the
Middle West the movements appealed strongly to German-Americans, and St. Louis and Milwaukee both became known as kindergarten centers. A private school known as the German-English
Academy had been established in Milwaukee in 1851 to train
children of German families in both languages. In 1874 a kindergarten department was added to this institution. Shortly afterwards German-Americans of several states looked about for a
place to locate a "seminary" or normal school for the preparation
of teachers to carry on the sort of bilingual education they desired
for their children. They decided to begin their institution in
Milwaukee in affiliation with, and under the same management as,
the long established German-English Academy. After 1878, this
seminary offered teacher-training in kindergarten methods and
was the first institution in the state to do so. In 1880 a kindergarten department was added to the state normal school at Oshkosh, and later to the normal schools at Milwaukee and Superior.

There were private kindergartens in the later eighteen seventies
at several points in the state, and during the decade of the eighties
the support of these kindergartens was gradually assumed by the
local school authorities. Kindergartens were made a part of the
city schools of Milwaukee in 1881, and a decade later there were
fifty-seven kindergarten teachers employed by the city. Kinder-

gartens have naturally developed more in urban centers than in the rural communities. In 1938 about 28,600 children were receiving kindergarten training in the public schools in Wisconsin, and there was similar training in various parochial and private schools. It appears that in this movement we have an instance of German influence upon the educational life of Wisconsin. Kindergartens would have come in any case, because they were eventually introduced in all parts of the United States; but the respect for Froebel felt by the citizens of Wisconsin of German birth gave kindergartens an early and vigorous development in this state.

High Schools and Junior High Schools

During the academic year 1937-1938 there were 152,000 students in grades nine to twelve in the high schools of Wisconsin. A large part of the population receives no education beyond what it gets in these schools, and in them character is definitely formed and fixed. Those graduating from the senior high schools have increased steadily in number: in 1928 there were more than 15,000; ten years later, more than 28,000.

Free high schools are of comparatively recent origin in America, but they had certain non-free forerunners in the colonial period. In New England in the seventeenth century colleges were founded especially to provide a ministry for the churches, and there were schools to be feeders to the colleges. Most of them were called grammar schools, and a law of 1647 provided that every town in Massachusetts of more than a hundred families should maintain such a school. The grammar schools insisted first of all upon a mastery of Greek and Latin; and while these particular subjects are not stressed in Wisconsin high schools today, the question is sometimes raised as to whether the present high school course of study is not too much loaded with traditional material not well adapted to modern needs.

What are the purposes of a public high school? Some answer that it should prepare for further training in colleges and universities. If this were the only goal, it would be logical for the high schools to teach what the colleges and universities prescribe. The high school curriculum is not determined in this way, however, because there are always other goals to be kept in mind and because high schools are autonomous and determined to keep their autonomy. Other educational leaders contend that the high school should concentrate on social and civic training, and thereby prepare its pupils to play their parts in American society. Still others demand that the high school should be frankly vocational, so that its graduates will function efficiently in their economic environment and more easily earn a living. There is much virtue in each answer. Since separate vocational schools are possible only in fairly populous and wealthy urban centers, the high schools are offering more and more vocational training, although, according to some opinions, not nearly enough. On the whole, however, it seems, at least to this observer, that the second purpose is at present the one most striven for by those with power to determine policy. There are no hard and fast lines between these various goals, but the pursuit of the second, which may be called social adjustment or adaptation, seems to lend itself in Wisconsin practice to more frequent combination with vocational training than with college preparatory work.

A little more than a century after the establishment of the first grammar schools appeared a new type of school called the academy, which offered a wider and more practical curriculum than did the grammar school. The first academy in America was founded, it is said, in 1751, by Benjamin Franklin, and ultimately became the University of Pennsylvania. Ten years later came the first academy in New England. By the end of the eighteenth century there were seventeen in the United States, and early in the following century they came to be the usual school throughout the United States for those of "high school age." By 1850 there were some six thousand in the whole country, and before the Civil War there were more than sixty in Wisconsin. In Massachusetts provision was made for the public support of high schools. At first such provision was local and temporary, but in 1857 it was made statewide and permanent, and when the Civil War broke out there were already sixty-three free high schools in Massachusetts. But in Wisconsin, free high schools were very few until after 1875, the academy being the typical school for those who went beyond the elementary school. The academy was supported by tuition, and those with a good reputation throve exceedingly. They trained most of the teachers of the district schools, and often their graduates went directly into professional schools. But their managers were not elected by the people, the schools were not supported by taxes, and, in comparison with the high schools of today, they educated but a small part of the population.

During the first quarter century after 1848 a number of plans for providing tax-supported high schools were advanced by educational leaders and discussed in the legislature, but no financial help was offered by the state. Meanwhile various cities provided for their own needs on their own initiative. Racine led the way by opening a free high school in December, 1853, and in due time had the first high school graduating class. At the close of the Civil War there were free high schools in about a dozen cities in the state. By 1873 perhaps thirty cities in Wisconsin were offering the equivalent of three years' work above the eighth grade. Persons with vested interests in academies opposed this development, but the laboring men of the towns, believing that academies were undemocratic, lent their support to the high school movement.

In 1875, while William R. Taylor was governor, a law was passed which authorized the formation of high school districts, and this new unit might be a town, or several towns, or a group of existing school districts. Subject to the limitation that the whole amount going to one school should not exceed $500, the state agreed to pay half the cost of instruction, provided the schooling was free. Within a little more than a year twenty high school districts organized or reorganized under the law and by 1880 there were more than a hundred. Increase in numbers and in attendance was especially rapid during the first two decades of the twentieth century and a slower increase has continued down to the present. In the year 1937-1938 there were in Wisconsin 459 high schools.

High school districts have come into existence as the result of local initiative during more than half a century, and certain bad results of their haphazard origin call for remedy today. These districts comprise less than one-fifth of the area of the state, and furthermore the distribution of the existing high schools is unsystematic in the extreme. Nearly 37,000 young people attend high schools as tuition pupils (1937-1938), and many others have no secondary school within reach. Many districts are too small, whether measured by the number of their pupils or by their financial resources, and small high schools in comparison with large ones mean poorer teaching and a higher cost per pupil. A strong argument can be made for scrapping the high school districts and transferring the responsibility for secondary education to the county as a whole or even to the state.

During the last quarter of the nineteenth century it was generally taken for granted that young America should spend eight years in the elementary grades and four years in the high school. Modifications of this plan were called for by some educators from about 1890 onward, and eventually the junior high school appeared. Under this plan the seventh, eighth and ninth grades are segregated in a building or a portion of a building, are put in charge of a separate staff of teachers, and have a definite curriculum of their own. Children at this age, it is maintained, are in process of finding themselves, and need a training and a testing suitable neither to the grades below nor to the grades above. A few cities, none of them in Wisconsin, acted as pathfinders in the new movement even before 1900; but it was not until about 1909 or 1910 that the so-called six-three-three arrangement was accepted as the standard form of organization. By 1916 there were fourteen junior high schools in Wisconsin, and four years later there were twenty-five. In 1938 there were some sixty junior high schools in Wisconsin caring for about 40,000 pupils.

Most of the public school teachers of Wisconsin are members of the Wisconsin Education Association, which, founded in 1853 as the Wisconsin Teachers' Association, is almost as old as the state. Within the present century it has successfully advocated, among many other projects, a pension system, a series of minimum wage laws, and a tenure law.

A plan to ensure pensions to teachers retiring after careers in the public schools of the state was launched by the legislature of 1911 and was greatly improved in 1921. From the salaries of teachers and school administrators five per cent is subtracted or withheld and placed in the Teachers' Retirement Fund. The state also makes contributions to the fund differing for different groups of teachers, but altogether equaling the compulsory contributions of the teachers. The state's share is provided by a special surtax on income; if the surtax fails to produce enough in any year, the amount lacking is taken from the general fund of the state treasury. There are now about 35,000 teachers and former teachers with a financial interest in the fund, and a separate account is kept for each member. In June, 1939, the accumulations of the fund had reached almost $47,000,000.

By the first Wisconsin law of its kind, passed in 1913, the minimum wage for teachers was set at $40 a month. If school boards paid less than this, they would not receive any state aids. By 1921 the amount had been raised to $75 and so remained until the depression. For two years beginning in 1933, the figure was reduced to $65; the importance of this law to the rural school teachers may be judged from the fact that in the school year 1934-1935 about two-thirds of the teachers in rural schools received less than $75 a month. The minimum wage was restored to $75 in the fall of 1935, and was subsequently raised first to $80 and then to $85.

The Wisconsin Education Association advocated for many years a law that would give to teachers and school administrators a security similar to that enjoyed by other public employees with civil service status. In 1937 a law was passed providing security of tenure for those who had taught more than five years in the same school system and who were doing satisfactory work; dismissal was possible only for cause duly shown. Teachers in their probationary period—that is, who had not yet taught for five years—were of course excluded, but the law gave security to about 15,000 teachers and executives. This enactment was displeasing to many rural school boards, and in 1939 an effort was made to repeal it. A compromise resulted by which the law of 1937 was continued, but was no longer to apply to one-room country schools, nor after July 1, 1940, to teachers who had reached the age of 65. School administrators over 65 still had security.

THE TRAINING OF TEACHERS

Part of the state's educational task is to provide for the training of recruits for its army of teachers, for the teaching staff must be constantly renewed. In the early days the only schools calling for teachers were the common schools of villages and rural areas; at that time almost any migrant from the East who had been educated in an academy or college might be pressed into service to teach for a winter or two. By an act of Congress of 1850 all swamp and overflowed land then in federal hands was granted to the states in which it lay. This and subsequent assignments brought the total of this grant to nearly four million acres, or about one-ninth of the area of the state. Much of the land turned out to be good farming and timber land. The legislature of 1857 set apart one-fourth of the proceeds of the swamp lands for a normal school fund, and provided a board of normal school regents to distribute the income from this fund to colleges and academies that offered normal school training. In 1865 half the proceeds from the sale of swamp lands was assigned to the normal school fund. By 1895 this contained almost two million dollars, and at present it exceeds three millions. At first it was hoped that the state university might train teachers, but this hope was not realized until 1863-1864, and then only for a short time. Finally the first state normal school was established at Platteville in 1866 in the buildings of a former academy. Others followed until with the opening of the normal school at Eau Claire in 1916 the number reached nine.

The normal schools of Wisconsin have served many purposes in the two generations since 1866. It might be said that they have adjusted themselves to the advancing needs of the state. At first most of their students came with but an elementary school education. Some of them were given a two-year course which qualified them to teach in a rural school. Others were given a four-year course which paralleled that of the now rapidly developing high schools and admitted them to the state university. A five-year course after the eighth grade qualified for teaching some subjects in high schools. Within the present century the function of preparing teachers of special subjects has been apportioned among the various schools. Whitewater, for example, trains teachers of commercial subjects; River Falls, agriculture; Stevens Point, home economics; Milwaukee trains teachers of music, art, and kindergarten, and so with several other schools and subjects. At the present time these schools still prepare more than one-fourth of the rural school teachers of the state, nearly all of the grade school teachers and perhaps 40 per cent of the high school teachers.

These institutions are also becoming colleges. Authorized by the legislature of 1911, several of them began to offer two years of college work. The legislature of 1925 permitted them to grant the degree of Bachelor of Education, and after July 1, 1927, they were to be known officially as State Teachers' Colleges. Increasing numbers of students study in them who have no intention of ever teaching; they desire instead to take the first two years of college work near their homes. Growth in this direction has been especially marked since the institutions have been able to grant degrees and have borne the name of colleges. The stronger among them are rapidly adding to their teaching staffs those with the now standard preparation for college teaching, the degree of Ph. D. They are thus coming to rival the privately endowed colleges, and, it might be added, are effecting a dispersal of some of the work of the state university throughout the state. The enrollment in the nine teachers' colleges reached 5,000 in the autumn of 1928, and ten years later it was 7,300. Each summer more than five thousand students are enrolled in the summer sessions of the teachers' colleges. The annual expenditure for the nine institutions has come to be about $1,750,000.

Besides the teachers' colleges, Wisconsin has Stout Institute, a nationally known training school for teachers of vocational subjects located at Menomonie, the county seat of Dunn County. The founding of this school was due to the public spirit of James H. Stout, a son of one of the original members of the great lumbering firm of Knapp, Stout and Company. For some twelve years the younger Stout made his home in St. Louis, where he became interested in the work of the Louis Soldan technical high school, one of the first in the United States for manual training and domestic science. Soon after taking up his residence at Menomonie in 1889, Stout began to introduce similar work into the public schools of Menomonie, all at his own expense. His first manual training building was destroyed by fire, whereupon he built and equipped another, completed in 1899, at a cost of more than $100,000. Around this nucleus were organized the Stout Manual Training Schools (1903); these became Stout Institute in 1908, by which time graduates were teaching in twenty-one states. Stout bore the expense of the enterprise until his death in 1910.

In 1911 the state took over the institute and placed it in charge of the board of vocational education set up in that year. In 1917, eight years before the regular normal schools, it received power to grant the degree of Bachelor of Education, and in 1929 it was authorized to bestow that of Master of Science in industrial education or in home economics. Under the reorganization law of 1937, Stout Institute was placed under the control of the board of regents of normal schools, along with the other teachers' colleges. The maintenance of the institute has in recent years cost about $300,000 a year. In the fall of 1938 it had 616 students, and these, added to the 7,300 in the other nine teachers' colleges, brought the total for the ten up to 7,916. A year later the total enrollment of the ten institutions had reached 8,681.

While the normal schools, now called teachers' colleges, have grown into something different from what they used to be, the call for teachers still comes from the rural schools. The teachers' colleges, to be sure, are still in this field, and have a two-year course of training for those wishing to teach in rural schools, in which over six hundred are found to be enrolled. In addition to this, two other sources for rural teachers have been developed, namely, special high school courses and the county rural normals. A law of 1913 authorized high schools to offer courses (now given in a fifth year) to prepare young people for rural teaching. Usually all the work of this sort in a high school was in the hands of one teacher. The state aids to these high schools for many years amounted to $25,000 annually, which paid about three-fourths of the salaries of those who gave the normal work. In 1929-1930 work of this character was given in eighteen high schools, and somewhat less than three hundred persons were each year prepared to teach in rural schools. When the depression came the state aid was at first reduced and then, in 1935, withdrawn entirely. Fifteen high schools were still carrying on this work in 1938.

Considerably more than half of Wisconsin's rural school teachers come from the county normal schools. The first institution of this kind was authorized by the legislature of 1899, and between that time and the end of 1924 no less than thirty-one had been established. By 1938 three of them had been discontinued. These schools, in any such numbers, seem to be peculiar to Wisconsin. The staff of each one consists of a principal and from two to five other teachers, and the student enrollment varies from twelve or fifteen to nearly a hundred. In the fall of 1939, 1,557 students were in training in the twenty-eight schools. They have for some years been turning out about a thousand graduates yearly. Recent regulation has made two years' training a requirement for rural school teachers, and the county normals are now offering a two-year course. For some years before 1933, about three-fourths of the cost of maintenance was borne by the state and the rest by the counties in which they are located. In that year the state's share was reduced to 60 per cent. Because of their rather small enrollments the per capita cost of teachers trained in them is comparatively high. It seems possible to obtain the same result in the teachers' colleges at less than half the outlay, and in the fifth year of high school at a still smaller expense.

Not all the teachers of Wisconsin, it should be added, are the products of the institutions just described. Persons from other states may, if they meet certain requirements, teach in Wisconsin. The private colleges within the state have trained large numbers of teachers, especially for high schools; and the University of Wisconsin, as we shall see, is giving professional training for teachers in increasing variety.

The University of Wisconsin

On August 18, 1848, three months after Wisconsin became a state, the first legislature, in obedience to the constitution, passed the act which established the University of Wisconsin. It was to be governed by a chancellor and a board of regents. In the autumn of 1848 the regents chose John W. Sterling as the first professor and John H. Lathrop as chancellor. The preparatory department was opened in rented quarters in February, 1849, the first college class was formed in the autumn of 1850, and the first B.A. degree was granted in July, 1854.

The legislature gave the university no direct financial help until after the Civil War. During 1849 the regents bought about 157 acres of land by making a small down payment with borrowed money. This purchase included the eastern part of the present campus, but little by little much of the tract was sold to provide money for current expenses. The first buildings were erected with money secured by loans to the university from the principal of the university fund and the school fund. The "Main Edifice," a part of what is now called Bascom Hall, was begun in 1850.

The first loan from the school funds became the precedent for other similar loans, until within a few years the university had borrowed more than $100,000, and interest charges made heavy inroads into the income from the university fund.

In July, 1859, Henry Barnard became the second chancellor. When he was inaugurated he was considered "the greatest educational scholar and reformer the United States had produced." It was he who, some thirteen years before, had addressed the first constitutional convention in behalf of a system of free public schools. His actual services as chancellor were limited to about a year, and during that time he gave almost all his attention to the improvement of the common schools and the problems of teacher training throughout the state.

Upon the departure of Barnard, in the summer of 1860, the administrative duties were distributed among the members of the faculty, with Professor Sterling carrying the chief burden. In the last full year before the Civil War the students numbered 228, but in the second year of the war there were, including those in the preparatory department, but sixty-three. Then a normal department was introduced, and during its first year, 1863-1864, it attracted 119 women and 43 men; three years later, when the first normal school was opened at Platteville, the department was discontinued.

The acceptance of the Morrill land grant entailed the establishment of an agricultural department and the teaching of military science, and these changes, authorized in 1866, were but part of a thoroughgoing reorganization. Of the land purchased in 1850 some forty acres still remained. Dane County was compelled to provide $40,000 and with that "gift" the university purchased 195 acres stretching along Lake Mendota to the west of the older campus. The last chancellor was replaced after an interregnum of seven years by the first president, Paul A. Chadbourne (1867-1870). Between 1867 and 1872 the state assumed the annual interest charges on the debts incurred by the university during its first decade, appropriated money to pay for Ladies' Hall (now

called Chadbourne), and provided by taxation a small annual
sum for maintenance. These contributions, not great in themselves, were an earnest for the future. A one-year law course was
instituted in 1868-1869, and at the beginning the justices of the
supreme court did some teaching without salary along with one or
two paid professors. Instruction in engineering began by utiliz-
ing the technical knowledge of the men trained at West Point who
were sent to Madison to have charge of the work in military
science. The first class of three engineers graduated in 1873.
Meanwhile in the central college the old classical studies were
yielding more and more to the newer scientific studies.

During the last quarter of the nineteenth century the University of Wisconsin had three presidents, Bascom, Chamberlin, and
Adams. John Bascom (1874-1887) came from a professorship
at Williams College, where the renowned teacher, Mark Hopkins,
had been his president. Bascom's chief desire was not to build a
university, but to improve the college and make it "the home of a
keen intellectual life." He wrote much on philosophy, psychol-
ogy, ethics, economics, and sociology; but long after his books are
forgotten the tradition of his broadening and elevating influence
in the classroom will live on. The university made great progress
in his time. Income rose from about $60,000 a year to nearly
twice that amount. The granting of a mill-tax for the support
of the institution meant that its income would increase with the
growing wealth of the state. Several new buildings were erected,
including the present Science Hall (1885-1888), and the observa-
tory, the gift of Cadwallader C. Washburn. All segregation of
men and women in separate classes and differences in their instruction were ended early in Bascom's time, and thus full coeducation was established. The preparatory department came to an
end in June, 1881: with the rise of high schools it was no longer
needed. In 1885 a chair of the Science and Art of Teaching was
established, and thus the university resumed normal work which
had been discontinued nearly twenty years before. In Bascom's

last year at Wisconsin the enrollment for the first time exceeded five hundred.

Bascom's successor was Thomas C. Chamberlin (1887-1892), previously state geologist and author of four large volumes on the *Geology of Wisconsin*. During his presidency students and faculty both doubled in numbers. Bascom had worked in the tradition of the New England college; Chamberlin had a vision of a university. There were to be four colleges, those of letters and science, agriculture, engineering, and law. Until past the turn of the century the college of letters and science continued larger than all the others combined, and its professors were the recognized leaders in the institution. In 1891 the law school moved from "downtown" to its present building on the campus, while about that time, under General E. E. Bryant as dean, it rapidly and markedly raised its standards. The school of engineering diversified its offerings in the early nineties, and by 1900 had over 400 students. The first and long the most eminent graduate school in the United States was that of Johns Hopkins, opened in Baltimore in 1876. Graduate study at Wisconsin was encouraged by the establishment in 1887 of eight graduate fellowships worth $400 a year. Principally to advance research and give graduate instruction, President Chamberlin added several Johns Hopkins men to his faculty. As the amount of undergraduate teaching increased, the number of assistants and instructors increased also, and their teaching supported their graduate work. In 1892 the first degree of Doctor of Philosophy was granted, the recipient being Charles R. Van Hise, later to become president of the university. In all these ways Chamberlin was building well for the future of Wisconsin; but he preferred scientific to administrative work, and in 1892 he accepted the headship of the department of geology in the new University of Chicago.

Chamberlin's successor was Charles Kendall Adams (1892-1902), a historian, who came to Wisconsin from the presidency of Cornell. Because of hard times, growth was slow during his first five years, but after 1897 increase was rapid, and in the fall of 1902, a few months after Adams' retirement, the enrollment passed two thousand.   One of the men whom Chamberlin brought from Johns Hopkins was Richard T. Ely, who was made head of the Graduate School of Political Science and History, a unit that existed for a few years.   In 1894, at the insistence of its ex officio member, the state superintendent, the board of regents tried Professor Ely on charges of radicalism.   He was exonerated, and in addition the board issued a statement of policy penned by President Adams which is the charter of freedom in research and in the expression of opinion at the University of Wisconsin.   Part of it is written in bronze at the entrance of Bascom Hall today. Adams had much to do with planning the State Historical Library building, which was well advanced when he retired.   Because of failing health he resigned in January, 1902.   For some time before this resignation and for a year after it, Professor Edward A. Birge, long dean of the college of letters and science, was acting president.

The next head of the university was Charles R. Van Hise (1903-1918).   A native of Wisconsin, he was graduated from the university in 1879, in the same class with Robert M. La Follette.   He immediately joined the staff of the university, and eventually became a leader in research in the allied fields of metallurgy, mineralogy, and geology.   Van Hise's presidency almost coincided with the first period of progressive rule in Wisconsin, and his ideas about the function of the university were akin to those of the progressives about the government.   He took "service to the state" to be the aim of the university.   He believed fervently in human progress, and in the university as promoting that progress.   He became a distinguished advocate of the conservation of natural resources, but believed equally in the development and conservation of human abilities.   "The greatest waste of this nation," he once asserted, "is the waste of talent."   He believed above all in democracy.   "I am not willing," he said in his inaugural address, "to admit that a state university under a democracy shall be of lower grade than a state university under a monarchy." [2]

These were some of Van Hise's ideals, and under his guidance the university expanded in fields old and new. Enrollment of full-term students rose from about 2,000 to more than 5,300, while the summer session grew from about 400 to more than 3,000 in his time. The faculty increased from less than 200 to about 750. The "central college" of letters and science continued the largest unit of the institution, and was always to be credited with about half of the long-term enrollment. The graduate school was organized in 1904 as a definite division with a dean of its own. The faculty was urged to do research and writing. The state was now ready for instruction in agriculture of college grade; and the long course in that college grew from less than forty students in 1902-1903 to more than 700. Two years of medical work were offered beginning in 1907. Home economics appeared a little later on, and extension work grew lustily. In all these ways the university strove to meet the needs of the people. The rapid growth in numbers was at once the result of the mounting wealth of the state and an evidence of popular approval of what the university was doing.

The World War could not fail to have a marked effect upon the university. Enrollment temporarily declined while faculty and students in large numbers served the nation elsewhere. President Van Hise died suddenly a few days after the armistice, and Dean Birge became acting president again. A few weeks later he was chosen president.

Edward A. Birge joined the university as an instructor in 1874, and a few years later became a professor of zoölogy. From 1891 onward he was dean of the college of letters and science. As president (1918-1925) he had to solve unusually difficult problems, chief among them the aftermath of war and a further great increase in attendance. Enrollment in 1919-1920 rose to

[2] J. F. A. Pyre, *Wisconsin* (New York, 1920), p. 342.

nearly 7,300 and exceeded by almost two thousand that of any previous year. The necessary readjustment was complicated by the prevailing price levels and the resulting need for increases in faculty salaries. Dr. Birge's leadership was marked by a capacity to see all sides of a situation and a rare tact. Perhaps the greatest addition to the physical plant of the university was the Wisconsin General Hospital. Its completion made possible a four-year medical course, and students who were ready for it began third year work in the autumn of 1924. When Dr. Birge retired from the presidency in September, 1925, he had been connected with the university for more than fifty years.

He was succeeded by Glenn Frank (1925-1937), a native of Missouri, who took his B.A. and M.A. degrees at Northwestern University. He had through several years been occupied with educational administration and research, and had attained eminence as a writer and speaker on public questions. He came to Wisconsin from the post of editor-in-chief of the *Century Magazine*. During the first five years of his presidency the flood of students continued to rise until in 1930-1931 it reached 10,000. Of these, 1,300 were graduate students, while the undergraduate members of the college of letters and science numbered about 5,700. At the summer session in 1930 more than 5,000 students were in attendance. During the next two years the depression and perhaps the growth of the teachers' colleges brought about a decline in enrollment in both long term and summer sessions.

It will be recalled that in 1885 a chair was established in the Science and Art of Teaching. From this beginning grew first a department of education and then a recognized course for teachers. In 1911 the Wisconsin High School was provided for observation, practice teaching, and experiments in education. In 1930 a School of Education, which had existed for a decade within the college of letters and science, was made a separate major unit, comparable with the colleges of law and engineering, with its own dean and separate faculty. It guides the professional training of teachers of many sorts, in some cases by arrangement with other parts of the university. "The school trains teachers in the following fields: music, physical training, agriculture, commercial subjects, home economics, art, playground and recreational supervision, teacher librarians, school administrators, high school and elementary grades." Here seems to be almost everything except manual training and kindergarten. Thus while the normal

AERIAL VIEW OF THE UNIVERSITY OF WISCONSIN*

In the foreground and left center are the engineering and agriculture buildings. In the upper right-hand section are the letters and science buildings. Near the shore of Lake Mendota is the carillon tower, to the right of which is Bascom Hall.

schools have become in part junior colleges and attendance at them often replaces two years or more at the university, the university has come to perform a large amount of the very work for which the normal schools were created.

In the spring of 1937, President Frank was dismissed by the

* By courtesy of the Bureau of Visual Instruction.

board of regents. This action provoked a storm of controversy within and without the state. Clarence A. Dykstra was chosen as his successor. For nine years he was a professor of political science at the University of Kansas. After various services in the field of municipal government at Cleveland, Chicago, and in California, he was for seven years (1930-1937) city manager of Cincinnati, whence he was brought to Wisconsin. His regime has begun auspiciously, but as yet scarcely belongs to history. Noteworthy, however, was the completion in 1939 of the Memorial Union Theater, beautiful and extraordinarily well equipped. This valuable addition to the university's physical plant was the last section of the Memorial Union project begun in 1924. Students in the fall of 1938 numbered 11,416, and if both semesters are included, enrollment in 1938-1939 exceeded 12,000. This was a peak for the time being; enrollment in the autumn of 1939 was 11,268.

Besides the institutions of higher learning supported by the state, there are several long-established private colleges in Wisconsin. Beloit, Carroll, and Lawrence were all begun in 1846 or 1847. Beloit was founded by a group of Presbyterians and Congregationalists, but in time the Congregational influence prevailed. Carroll was founded by the Presbyterians, and is the only one of this group still controlled by a church organization. Lawrence got its name from Amos A. Lawrence, a wealthy merchant and philanthropist of Boston, who made the initial gift and thus encouraged the Methodists to found the college. Ripon began as an academy in 1851 and undertook college work in 1863. All its presidents have been ministers of the Congregational Church. Milwaukee College was founded in 1851 by women who wished a women's college free from both denominationalism and state control. Downer College began under another name in 1855, and attendance was most of the time limited to women. The two were united as Milwaukee-Downer College in 1891. These five are the strongest private colleges in the state. There are a number of other colleges with denominational affiliations. Northland

College at Ashland is Congregational, Northwestern College at Watertown is Lutheran, and Milton College at Milton is Seventh Day Adventist.

Before the depression the five strongest colleges had not quite eight million dollars endowment, and their revenues, derived from endowment investments, gifts, and student fees, now amount to about one and one-half million dollars annually. At any time during the past decade the five have had in attendance about 2,700 students, and they seem somewhat overshadowed by the state institutions. At present more than 8,500 students are attending the teachers' colleges and Stout Institute, and of the 11,268 at the University of Wisconsin perhaps 6,000 are enrolled in the College of Letters and Science or are doing preliminary work roughly comparable to that done by the private colleges. Yet the growth of the state-supported institutions is not likely to overwhelm them as the public high schools forced the private academies out of existence after 1875. The endowments and physical plants of the private colleges make for permanence; they have enthusiastic faculties and devoted trustees; and each one is supported by the traditions of hundreds if not thousands of families. The endowments, to be sure, should be larger or the colleges in time may not be able to care for as many students as they do at present. These colleges offer a carefully supervised social life, teachers who give their best efforts to undergraduate teaching rather than to graduate work or writing, and most of them have a well-selected student body. Whatever the future holds in store, they will long continue to educate many sons and daughters of Wisconsin.

Marquette University, located at Milwaukee, is a Roman Catholic institution directed and to some extent staffed by the Society of Jesus (the Jesuits). The nucleus of the present university was Marquette College, which was opened to students in 1881. One of the parts of the university today is a college of liberal arts with more than nine hundred students. There are also a normal department with more than five hundred students and a graduate school with above three hundred. Besides these, there are several divisions with vocational or professional purposes, such as those of engineering, business administration, dentistry, medicine, law, and journalism. Counting in the summer session, the whole university comprises more than four thousand students. There are a number of other strong and growing Roman Catholic colleges. Among them are Mount Mary College at Milwaukee and St. Norbert College at De Pere. Mount Mary was founded as a secondary school for girls at Prairie du Chien in 1872, began to offer college work in 1913, and removed to Milwaukee in 1929. St. Norbert includes both a preparatory school and a college and is maintained by the Premonstratensian Order.

Other Educational Enterprises

We have sketched briefly the history of Wisconsin's elementary schools, high schools, means of training teachers, and state university. There are other lines of educational endeavor in which Wisconsin has been a leader. Three of them whose growth will be briefly recounted here are: university extension, training in agriculture, and vocational education.

As long ago as 1892 a professor at the University of Wisconsin wrote of it that it "now aims at nothing less than to carry the highest scholarship, the latest discoveries of art and science into every neighborhood in the state. . . . It has become the great discoverer and distributor of knowledge to the whole people." Even before that time individual members of the faculty had given lectures in many parts of the state, and study had been directed by correspondence. These activities continued through the succeeding years, but it was felt, especially by President Van Hise, that the people of Wisconsin were not getting all the benefit they might from their university. At his instance the regents in 1906 granted $7,500 for extension work, and Professor Louis E. Reber was brought from Pennsylvania State College to take charge. In 1907 the legislature granted $20,000 a year for two years, and by

1911 the annual appropriation had reached $100,000. In the following year a building was opened on the university campus to be used for extension work and home economics.

The extension division of the university renders services of many sorts. In recent years there have been about ten thousand registrants in correspondence work, most of it of college grade, but since some of the registrants take two courses concurrently, the number of those engaged in correspondence work at any one time is about nine thousand. Extension classes conducted in many parts of the state serve an even larger number.

The work of the Milwaukee center began with a few classes in 1908. After the World War the extension division made provision for the educational needs of returned soldiers living in Milwaukee and receiving the educational bonus. Other Milwaukee residents asked the privilege of attending the soldiers' classes, and beginning thus, day work has developed down to the present. In 1928 a seven-story building, erected by the state at a cost of $275,-000, was completed; there in recent years about fifty full-time instructors have taught about seven hundred full-time students. Many residents of Milwaukee and vicinity are thus enabled to take two years of college work without leaving home. The same classrooms are used for evening instruction, though but a small part of the evening work is for college credit. Fees are attached to all correspondence work and extension classes, so that the extension division pays about half its own expenses.

Other activities of this division are numerous and varied. There is lyceum service, whereby lecturers and entertainers are furnished on demand. A bureau of visual education furnishes slides and films, and even the speeches to be delivered with them. Seven or eight thousand packages of books are sent out every year, most of them going into communities that have no public libraries. One department conducts the Wisconsin High School Forensic Association to encourage debating and kindred work. Another department promotes amateur dramatic activity and furnishes books for the study of dramatic literature. There are short courses and institutes of many sorts.

The latest means of bringing the university to the people is known as the freshman-sophomore class program. It originated in the desire to aid high school graduates who had been deprived by the depression of their opportunity for college training. The plan was first tried out in 1934-1935. In 1938 it was thus described:

> The Extension Division provides the instructors, usually on the basis of four freshman instructors for a "circuit" of four cities or centers of instruction. The instructors then "ride the circuit," visiting each of the four centers in turn to teach their classes.[3]

In the fall of 1938, programs of freshman studies were going forward at sixteen centers, with sophomore subjects at some of them, and about six hundred students were participating. The expenses were usually divided between the community served and the students.[4]

In spite of some hard times and necessary readjustments, agriculture in Wisconsin has developed steadily. This advance has in no small part been due to the many efforts made to teach the farmers new methods and show them new opportunities. Both state and federal governments have made appropriations for research, have encouraged and subsidized instruction in agriculture in the schools, and have built up an elaborate system of extension work. By these means they have promoted scientific work in the interests of agriculture, have kept the farmers in touch with its results, and have not only increased the wealth but have elevated the standard of living among the rural population.

Instruction in agriculture is today a highly valued part of the course in the elementary schools and high schools of rural areas,

---

[3] John L. Bergstresser, "Classes Go to the Student," *Wisconsin Journal of Education*, Vol. 71, p. 48 (September, 1938).

[4] Statistics on the work of the extension division for the academic year 1938-1939 are as follows: 10,117 registrations of 9,024 students in correspondence courses; 6,963 registrations of 4,662 students in state classes outside Milwaukee (this includes the freshman-sophomore program); and 10,258 registrations of 5,939 students in Milwaukee classes. Altogether, there were 24,338 registrations and 19,620 students. *The Badger Quarterly*, Vol. 2, No. 2 (January, 1940), p. 6.

but it was rather late in gaining its present standing. Only since 1905 has agriculture been a required subject in the district schools. The teaching of agriculture in the high schools of Wisconsin awaited the stimulus of a federal subsidy, begun under the Smith-Hughes act of 1917 and still continuing. For this purpose money from the national treasury is at present distributed to about one-fifth of the high schools in Wisconsin and in them about three thousand boys are getting training in agriculture. To these same high schools come about a thousand farmers for evening classes. Under another federal law, the George-Reed act of 1929, the federal government contributes to the support of rural home economics schools.

The greatest single instrument in the promotion of agriculture in the state has been the University of Wisconsin College of Agriculture, which began as a small department. The federal Morrill act of 1862 provided an endowment for education in agriculture and the mechanic arts. In the reorganization of the state university in 1866 a department of agriculture was established; but for the next twenty years it was a department almost entirely without students, and the agricultural college funds in reality paid the salaries of professors of the sciences in the college proper. William Aaron Henry came to Wisconsin in 1881 as professor of botany and agriculture, and from the beginning he emphasized experimental work. After some years the federal government by the Hatch act (1887) provided $15,000 a year for agricultural research. A supplementary Morrill grant three years later provided further funds to be used in the teaching of applied sciences. With the money thus supplied by the federal government good men were rapidly added to the staff. The most renowned outcome of the experiments of these early years was the perfection of the Babcock milk test, which was announced in 1890.

In the meantime, in January, 1886, Professor Henry inaugurated the short course in agriculture, a most effective means of putting the knowledge of the scientist at the disposal of the practical farmer. The first year there was a twelve weeks' session in which four courses were offered, and it drew nineteen students to Madison. Later the number of weeks was increased, the list of subjects was lengthened, and a two-year course was mapped out. In the ninth year (1894-1895) the enrollment passed a hundred. The second director of the short course was Professor R. A. Moore, who brought immense enthusiasm to his work and made the agricultural college even more popular with the farmers. For several years before the World War the short course had more than four hundred students a year.

A winter course in dairying was organized similar to but more specialized than the short course. It was begun in a small way in January, 1890, and the college and, incidentally, the dairy course, were well advertised by the publicity given to the famous milk test. Enrollment reached a hundred in 1891-1892. Hiram Smith Hall was built that year for dairy work, and for the next quarter century enrollment in the winter dairy course was usually between 100 and 150.

About the time when the short course began to bring farmers to the agricultural college, institutes took the college to the farmer. For this purpose the sum of $5,000 was provided in 1885, and the next legislature increased the amount to $12,000. Farmers were gathered together near their homes to hear lectures and exchange their own experiences. The program usually lasted two or three days. The farmers welcomed the innovation, and by 1892 a hundred institutes a year were being held. The staff of the agricultural college led by Dean Henry, together with other Wisconsin farm leaders like Hiram Smith and William D. Hoard, and experts from outside the state, spoke at these institutes; and better farming followed in their wake.

Professor R. A. Moore, for a time director of the short course, also originated or introduced to Wisconsin many of the methods of present-day extension work. In 1898 he undertook to show groups of farmers how to combat oat smut by treating the seed grain, and many a mile he traveled on his bicycle in his campaign. In similar fashion he later took other messages to the farmers.

In 1906 he joined with the superintendent of schools of Richland County to organize what was probably the first club of farm boys in Wisconsin. Aided by the interest of bankers and professional men, the movement was going forward in fifty counties by 1912, and the county fairs were offering prizes amounting to $28,000 for boys' and girls' exhibits. After the World War the 4-H Club movement was inaugurated that still holds the field in juvenile extension work.

Since 1914 the federal government has helped the states in agricultural extension. In that year Congress passed the Smith-Lever Act, which authorized payments to the states to "diffuse . . . useful and practical information on subjects relating to agriculture and home economics." The Capper-Ketcham Act of 1928 provided further sums. Under these and minor acts about eight and one-half million dollars are annually distributed by the federal government for agricultural extension work. Wisconsin's share of this in 1929-1930 was $206,855. Contributions by the state and the counties bring the sum available in Wisconsin to considerably more than half a million dollars a year. This money is used to employ county agricultural agents, of whom Wisconsin had 66 in 1939. It is also used to support 4-H Club work among the boys and girls, and to further better farming and farm life through meetings, demonstrations, publications, and educational campaigns of many sorts.

Wisconsin has gained a nation-wide and even a world-wide renown by her system of vocational education. In the late eighteen eighties some vocational subjects such as manual training, domestic science, and bookkeeping were appearing here and there in the high schools. The legislature of 1909 established a commission of several of the state's leading educators, with Charles McCarthy of the Legislative Reference Library as secretary, to report on plans "for the extension of industrial and agricultural education." McCarthy was sent to Europe to gather information, and learned much from the practice of vocational education in the municipalities of Germany. The report of the commission was published in January, 1911, and called upon the legislature to take account of the change that was in process from agriculture to industry, and to make up for depletion of virgin soil and the exhaustion of natural resources by the creation and conservation of human skill and knowledge.

The legislation about vocational education dovetails into that dealing with compulsory school attendance and the apprenticeship system discussed in preceding chapters. Between 1911 and 1921 the amount of required part-time schooling was gradually increased and it became the rule that those between fourteen and sixteen must attend a vocational school half-time, and those from sixteen to eighteen at least eight hours a week. Employers of labor in this last age group pay wages for the time spent in school. Those who have entered into the apprenticeship contract under the supervision of the state must attend school four hours a week until they are eighteen.

Several vocational schools in the same vicinity often employ a master craftsman to teach his trade, and he goes from one city to another, usually spending one day a week in each of several schools. Girls are trained as they prefer, in general academic work or in skilful home-making or in industrial arts. Among both boys and girls there is a steady demand for commercial subjects such as bookkeeping and typewriting.

While the day classes are filled mostly by those between fourteen and eighteen, who are required by law to attend school, the evening sessions of the vocational schools are used by those of mature years. Classes are organized in almost any subject demanded by a considerable number of people. "The evening school is whatever the community wants to make it."

The original act of 1911 required all cities of five thousand population or better to establish daytime vocational schools. In 1930 there were thirty-seven such schools, and the attendance exceeded thirty-five thousand. All these cities and seven others also maintained evening classes in which about fifty thousand sought instruction.

LIBRARIES

As somewhat germane to education, a little may be said about libraries. The first legislature of the territory in 1836 authorized the purchase of books for the use of future law makers. From this nucleus grew the Wisconsin State Library of today, a law library of about 100,000 volumes. It is maintained in the capitol building primarily for the use of legislators, members of the supreme court, and other state officials, although it is also open to the public.

Historical workers the world over hold in high regard the library of the State Historical Society. The society was formed in January, 1849, by a few devoted citizens who held annual meetings at which they heard addresses on historical themes. The legislature granted a charter in 1853, and in the following year there was a change in character and purpose. The office of secretary was assumed by Lyman Copeland Draper, who was to guide the society for thirty-two years. It was Draper's unrealized ambition to write the biographies of men like Daniel Boone and George Rogers Clark, who led in the establishment of English communities west of the Alleghenies. He had been interviewing the descendants and collecting the papers of frontiersmen for years before he came to Wisconsin, and he continued this work from Madison, though travel largely gave way to a huge correspondence. His collection of manuscripts and newspapers in this field forms one of the priceless heritages of Wisconsin and the whole Middle West. All the while Draper was building up an historical library of printed books, and he began and carried to the tenth volume the series of the society's *Collections*.

The second director of the work of the society was Reuben Gold Thwaites. During his term of office (1886-1913), the building was constructed which has been occupied by the society and by the library of the University of Wisconsin since 1900. The fields of Dr. Thwaites' special interest were the French occupation of North America and the history of the fur trade. He edited the

Jesuit Relations and Allied Documents in seventy-three volumes, and he is said to have written or edited no less than 185 volumes. As the years pass the collections of the society, both of books and manuscripts, continue to grow. The society encourages work in local Wisconsin history; historians come from many states and from foreign countries to avail themselves of its treasures; and the staff of the society does invaluable service in writing and publishing Wisconsin and other American history. The library of the university supplements that of the historical society.

The movement to establish public libraries in Wisconsin was of slow growth. Legislation soon after the Civil War permitted towns (that is, rural areas) to raise by taxation small sums for free libraries, and during the seventies the same permission was given to all municipalities. Yet by 1895 there were only twenty-eight free libraries in Wisconsin, and six of these were supported chiefly by endowments from private sources. Among the latter was the library at La Crosse, for which Cadwallader C. Washburn had made provision in his will. A young men's association in Milwaukee assembled a considerable library. In 1877 this was transferred to the city, and was the beginning of the great Milwaukee Public Library.

The formation of the Wisconsin Library Association in 1891 led to the establishment of the Free Library Commission by an act of the legislature in 1895. The first secretary of the commission was Frank H. Hutchins, the man best entitled to rank as the founder of Wisconsin's library system. The first legislative appropriation was but $500, and the work of the first few years was financed by State Senator James H. Stout of Menomonie, the founder of Stout Institute. He paid a salary to Hutchins so that the latter could give all his time to the work of the commission. Communities were encouraged to establish local libraries, and during the nine years of Hutchins' secretaryship (1895-1904) the twenty-eight libraries had become 126, and separate library buildings had increased in number from six to fifty-five. During this period and later, Andrew Carnegie gave sixty-three library buildings to

Wisconsin.   Including some rather small club libraries there were 290 public libraries in the state in 1939.

To meet the needs of rural communities a county system of traveling libraries was developed under the leadership of Hutchins.   The innovation was first tried in Dunn County and Senator Stout paid the expenses.   Some of these county libraries were supported by taxes and others by private philanthropy, and as resources became available the commission at Madison also sent traveling libraries throughout the state.   Indeed, of late, the counties have pretty largely given this work over to the state.   The commission sends out on request either single books or collections of books.

The Legislative Reference Library was begun in 1901 as a part of the work of the library commission.   For the next twenty years it grew under the enthusiastic direction of Charles H. McCarthy. At first its chief duty was to gather information that might be of use to legislators.   It had scarcely begun its work when all its accumulations were destroyed in the capitol fire in February, 1904. It was directed by the legislature of 1907 to assume the task of bill-drafting, and since 1930 it has prepared the biennial *Wisconsin Blue Book*.   Its collection of books, pamphlets, magazine articles, and newspaper clippings makes it a most useful workshop for those interested in the social and economic history of recent times.

SELECTED BIBLIOGRAPHY

The master book on the greater part of this chapter is Conrad E. Patzer, *Public Education in Wisconsin* (Madison, 1924).   An older and somewhat encyclopedic book was that edited by J. W. Stearns, *The Columbian History of Education in Wisconsin* (Milwaukee, 1893).   Useful also is the *Educational History of Wisconsin,* edited by Charles McKenny (Chicago, 1912).   The *Memoirs* of Mary D. Bradford, who spent fifty years in a variety of educational posts in Wisconsin, appeared in the *Wisconsin Magazine of History*, Vols. XIV, XV, and XVI (1930-1932).   An offprint with some additional chapters was also published (Evansville, Wis., 1932). Two short sketches of the history of education in Wisconsin are: *Wisconsin in Three Centuries* (4 vols., New York, 1906), Vol. IV, pp. 159-180; and Edward W. Fitzpatrick, "The Educational System," in Milo M. Quaife,

Wisconsin, Its History and Its People (4 vols., Chicago, 1924), Vol. II, pp. 247-297.

Joseph Schafer contributed two articles of value: "Origins of Wisconsin's Free School System," *Wisconsin Magazine of History,* Vol. IX, pp. 27-46 (September, 1925); and "Genesis of Wisconsin's Free High School System," *ibid.,* Vol. X, pp. 123-149 (December, 1926). The Ph.D. thesis of Richard B. Thiel, *Fiscal Administration of the High School* (MS, Madison, 1926), while dealing with a wider area, is especially rich in details drawn from Wisconsin.

The early history of the kindergarten was written by Elizabeth Jenkins in "How the Kindergarten Found Its Way to America," *Wisconsin Magazine of History,* Vol. XIV, pp. 48-62 (September, 1930). The German-English Academy of Milwaukee appears in the *History of Milwaukee* (Chicago, 1881), pp. 550-578. An excellent history of the University of Wisconsin is that by J. F. A. Pyre, *Wisconsin* (New York, 1920). For the beginnings of vocational schools, the most important document is the *Report of the Commissioners Upon the Plans for the Extension of Industrial and Agricultural Training* (Madison, 1911). The Wisconsin State Board of Vocational Education issues a series of bulletins which includes biennial reports. There is a valuable chapter by C. B. Lester, "The Library Movement in Wisconsin," in Quaife, *op. cit.,* Vol. II, pp. 411-432. The same author wrote on "Public Libraries" in *Blue Book, 1925,* pp. 363-370. Louise P. Kellogg wrote of "The Services and Collections of Lyman Copeland Draper," *Wisconsin Magazine of History,* Vol. V, pp. 244-263 (March, 1922).

A Plan for Reorganizing Wisconsin's System of Education, report of the Wisconsin Interim Legislative Committee on Education submitted to the legislature of 1931, 208 pp., reveals conditions calling for remedy about 1930. James Sutherland wrote on the "Origin of our State Normal School System" in the *Proceedings* of the State Historical Society of Wisconsin, 1897, pp. 160-168. *Education in Wisconsin* is the title of the biennial reports of the state Department of Public Instruction. They contain short essays or chapters on educational topics and the essential statistics. Much historical material appears in the organ of the Wisconsin Education Association, the *Wisconsin Journal of Education* (Madison, monthly except in the summer).

CHAPTER XXII

LITERATURE AND THE FINE ARTS

The Growth of Newspapers

FOR more than a century incoming Americans and Europeans and their descendants have been building the state of Wisconsin. They have taken their part in the processes of self-government and have provided food and shelter for themselves and their families, but their life has been more than politics and they have not lived by bread alone. Most of them were literate and thinking persons who needed newspapers and books. Many of them also sought relaxation or inspiration in music and the other arts; and not a few have become creative writers and artists.

It would be something of a misnomer, however, to speak of Wisconsin literature or the Wisconsin fine arts as if the state had a language and a culture peculiarly its own. As we have seen earlier in this book, many events belonging to the history of Wisconsin actually occurred far from Wisconsin soil; state history could not be confined within any geographic boundaries. What was often the case with reference to economic life and the issues of politics is even more true in the realm of literature and the fine arts. Neither artists nor their patrons recognize state boundaries. Wisconsin authors present their offerings to the national audience and thus contribute their part to American thought as a whole. It is the whole and not the part that has the greatest significance. Many natives of Wisconsin, wishing to express themselves in literature or to make literature a profession, have sought the larger cities, the publishing centers of the nation, and a similar attraction

459

has drawn away many of the painters, sculptors, and musicians. As boundaries fail us on the side of artistic production, so are they lacking when we consider enjoyment and appreciation. From the beginning English-speaking Wisconsin has read English and American literature without much regard to its place of origin, and Germans and other non-English groups have read books and periodicals that can be understood only in the knowledge of a long literary past remote from Wisconsin. This chapter, then, deals with some manifestations of the American spirit that chanced to occur in Wisconsin, and to a lesser degree with the spirit of some natives of Europe already in the process of becoming Americans.

In the early days of farm making, life offered little leisure for reading. Most settlers brought some books from the East, but subsequent purchases were necessarily few, while public libraries, save in a few cities, were nonexistent until after 1890. These conditions gave the newspapers a unique importance; they provided virtually all there was to read. The early journals were much smaller than those of today, and they were often established as the vehicles of real estate promotion or to support a political party or candidate. Yet they frequently had considerable literary merit, and they seem to have been thoroughly read and much discussed. The capital investment in an early printing establishment was not large, and the newspaper printers were able to follow rapidly on the heels of settlement.

The earliest newspaper in Wisconsin was the *Green Bay Intelligencer*. Its first number was dated December 11, 1833, and its last known appearance was on June 1, 1836. The leading spirit in the enterprise was Albert G. Ellis, who had learned the printer's trade in New York state. He had come out to Green Bay to be a lay reader and teacher for the recently arrived Oneida Indians. He was later called General Ellis, not because he had any military competence, but because he was for a time surveyor-general for Iowa and Wisconsin. His newspaper was the second one west of Lake Michigan, John Calhoun's *Chicago Democrat* preceding it by about two weeks. Its avowed object was "the advancement of the country west of Lake Michigan" and, like many newspapers that were to follow it at Green Bay, it favored the canalization of the Fox-Wisconsin route. Its political complexion is indicated by the alteration of its title in 1835 to *Green Bay Intelligencer and Wisconsin Democrat*. After the paper under this title had expired, its equipment was sold to Henry O. and Charles C. Sholes. They started a newspaper called simply the *Wisconsin Democrat*, which lasted on at Green Bay until 1840.

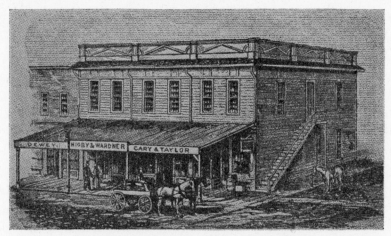

THE SENTINEL BUILDING, MILWAUKEE, 1843*

The building stood on the southwest corner of Wisconsin and Water streets, Milwaukee. It was erected by Charles C. Dewey in 1840 and was moved to another site in 1849. It was commonly known as the *Sentinel* building after the newspaper occupied a portion of the second story beginning in 1842.

Milwaukee's first newspaper was the *Milwaukee Advertiser,* which began publication July 14, 1836. It was founded to promote Byron Kilbourn's town on the west side of the Milwaukee River, and under its original title it lasted for about four and one-half years. Meanwhile the village on the east side of the river felt it must have its newspaper, and with the backing of Solomon Juneau the *Milwaukee Sentinel* made its first appearance in June,

---

* From J. S. Buck, *Milwaukee Under the Charter* (Milwaukee, 1884), Vol. III, p. 39. Engraving by Marr and Richards.

1837. Beginning as a weekly, the *Sentinel* in 1844 became the first daily newspaper in the territory.

A few more beginnings may be mentioned. The meeting of the first territorial legislature at Belmont in 1836 lured a printer there who published the *Belmont Gazette* for about six months. A newspaper appeared at Mineral Point in 1837, one of its proprietors being the well-known William S. Hamilton, son of Alexander Hamilton. A newspaper was begun at Racine in 1838, only to die within a short time. Madison's first newspaper came in November of the same year, the first of seven to be founded there before the end of 1850. In June, 1840, the *Southport Telegraph* was established in what is now Kenosha by Michael Frank and Christopher Latham Sholes. Michael Frank is best remembered as a leader in the cause of free public schools. Altogether about a hundred newspapers had been born in Wisconsin by the end of 1850, but infant mortality was very high. At the end of that year forty-two publications were being issued in twenty-three towns.

Among the early journalists were three Sholes brothers who had come from Pennsylvania. Each was a printer in several places in Wisconsin and all were active politically. Christopher Latham, the youngest (1819-1890), who was mentioned above, worked at his trade or edited newspapers successively in Green Bay, Madison, Kenosha, and Milwaukee. For two years during the Civil War he was editor of the *Milwaukee Daily Sentinel,* and at various times he was postmaster of Milwaukee, commissioner of public works, and a collector of customs. He deserves to be held in grateful remembrance by writers everywhere, for, more than any other one man, he was the inventor of the typewriter. There had been earlier attempts and patents, but the machines that meet modern needs are almost entirely descended from the models produced by Sholes and his partners. Their basic patent was taken out in June, 1868. Sholes continued to make improvements, doing his work in Kleinstueber's machine shop in Milwaukee.

Eventually he acquired the interests of his earlier associates, then found a new backer or partner, and finally in 1873 sold all his rights to the Remington Arms Company for $12,000. Shortly thereafter, the fruit of his labors was offered to the public as the Remington typewriter.

Newspapers in foreign languages appeared very early in Wisconsin. In 1844 Moritz Schoeffler began the publication in Milwaukee of the *Wiskonsin-Banner.* The *Volksfreund,* edited and later owned by Frederick Fratny, was begun there three years later, but when Fratny died in 1855, Schoeffler combined the two newspapers under the name *Banner und Volksfreund.* This, Schoeffler continued to manage until 1874, when he retired after thirty years of newspaper service. Both the *Banner* and the *Volksfreund* were displeasing to the Roman Catholic Church, and in 1851 the Catholic *Seebote* was established, first as a weekly and then as a daily.

A noteworthy if short-lived publishing venture was the *Deutsche Frauen-Zeitung,* a monthly publication devoted to the emancipation of women. It was edited by a remarkable woman, Mathilda Franziska Anneke, a poet and an editor of anthologies in Germany who had fought beside her husband in the German revolution of 1848. Her *Frauen-Zeitung* made its first appearance in Milwaukee in March, 1852; it was then issued in New York and finally from Newark, New Jersey. Altogether it lasted less than three years. Frau Anneke later returned to Milwaukee and conducted a girls' school there for many years.

At the village of Norway in Racine County, *Nordlyset,* the first Norwegian newspaper in the United States, was begun in 1847. In the fall of 1849, it was sold and removed to Racine, where, under the new name of *Democraten,* it lasted about six months longer. What is believed to be the first newspaper in the United States in the Dutch language was published at Sheboygan under the title *Nieuwsbode* from 1849 to 1861. In 1906, when the number of German-born residents was near its peak, ninety-six German newspapers were being published in Wisconsin. At the same time there were eleven newspapers in Scandinavian and an equal number in Slavic languages (Polish or Bohemian).

Including the foreign-language newspapers, all periodical publications in Wisconsin numbered in 1906 about 750. Of these, 64 were daily papers, 565 were weekly, and 19 semiweekly. The number has since been considerably reduced, partly by consolidation. In 1939 there were about forty daily papers issued in Wisconsin. The most important in the nineteenth century was the *Milwaukee Sentinel*. One of its editors, Horace Rublee (1829-1896), was perhaps the most significant figure in the whole history of Wisconsin journalism. His seven years (1869-1876) as United States minister to Switzerland divided his newspaper career into two parts. In the fifteen years before going to Europe he owned a half-interest in the *Wisconsin State Journal* of Madison and during that time achieved a leadership in the Republican party along with "Boss" Keyes. After his return from Switzerland he formed a company which bought the *Milwaukee Sentinel* and changed it from a Democratic to a Republican paper. At its head from 1883 until his death, Rublee spoke with an authority never exercised by any other Wisconsin editor, his opinions being quoted far beyond the limits of the state. George W. Peck, who owned the Milwaukee *Sun,* was widely known to the same generation, but more as a humorist than as a regular journalist. In the present century the *Milwaukee Journal* has come to have the largest circulation of any newspaper in Wisconsin, surpassing that of the *Sentinel* by more than 50 per cent. The *Journal* was begun in 1882 as an English-language edition of the German *Seebote*. In September, 1937, the *Sentinel* passed into the control of William Randolph Hearst.

BELLES-LETTRES

It is one of the conventions of Wisconsin history to regard James Gates Percival (1795-1857) as the state's earliest literary light. He was a New England poet born in Connecticut and he came to Wisconsin after all of his creative writing was done. In early manhood he wrote verse which was highly regarded by his contemporaries, who considered him the peer of William Cullen Bryant. Some of his shorter poems, such as "The Coral Grove" and "Evening," are still admired; but his longer pieces are largely forgotten. He was a man of vast and varied learning. As a philologist he assisted Noah Webster in the preparation of his famous dictionary. From 1851 to 1854, he surveyed the lead region of Illinois and Wisconsin for a mining company. In 1854 he was appointed state geologist of Wisconsin. In these last years he lived at Hazel Green in Grant County, alone with his ten thousand books, a solitary and pathetic figure; there he died and was buried.

At the beginning of the present century, Ella Wheeler Wilcox (1855-1919) was one of the favorite poets of the nation. Like the elder La Follette, she was born on a farm in Dane County, Wisconsin, in 1855; there and on another farm in the same county she lived until her marriage to Robert M. Wilcox in 1884. Long before that time she had won fame as a writer. Her *Poems of Passion* (1883) had, for a book of verse, a very unusual success. The poem for which she will be longest remembered is probably "Solitude," beginning, "Laugh and the world laughs with you," which first appeared in the New York *Sun* in 1883. After her marriage she did not reside in Wisconsin. She published many volumes of verse and also some novels, but her most interesting prose work was her autobiographical *The Worlds and I* (1918), the earlier part of which depicts life on a Wisconsin farm. Present critical opinion is that she expressed very well the mind of her own generation, but will probably not appeal strongly to posterity.

Bernard Isaac Durward (1817-1902) was a native of Scotland who has a notable place in the history of the fine arts in Wisconsin. He wrote an epic entitled *Cristofero Colombo* just before the World's Fair in 1893, and numerous shorter poems, many of them devotional in character. John Durward, one of his sons, was the

author of a long poem entitled "The Building of a Church."
Adelaide Crapsey (1878-1914) was educated at Kemper Hall,
Kenosha. She published a number of short poems, often on
rather macabre themes but marked by haunting beauty. The
most eminent living poet in Wisconsin is doubtless Professor William Ellery Leonard, who joined the staff of the English department at the University of Wisconsin in 1906. A man learned
in philology, he has a most unusual treasury of words from which
to draw, as well as a genuinely poetic elevation of thought. His
greatest work is a sonnet sequence entitled *Two Lives* (1925).
The Locomotive-God (1927) is a spiritual autobiography written
in prose.

Many of the early German settlers, especially the political exiles,
were familiar with the best in German literature and sought to
express their own thoughts in literary form. Consequently there
arose a considerable literature in German, and one especially rich
in poetry. The thought of the first-comers was really rooted in
Germany as long as they lived. Konrad Krez wrote "An mein
Vaterland," which was often acclaimed as the best German-
American lyric. The dear old homeland had cast him out, and
yet he loved it still. Another favorite subject was the scenic
beauties of the new world. Rudolph Puchner of Calumet County,
a prolific poet, shows again and again how his soul was stirred
as he contemplated Wisconsin's virgin forests. The *Banner und
Volksfreund* had a department called "Wisconsin's Deutsche
Dichterhalle" (Wisconsin's German poets' corner), filled year
after year with these outpourings from hundreds of German
hearts. In the next generation there were many who came as
small children from Germany or who were born in Wisconsin
whose main idea was to fuse the English and German cultural
traditions by adapting or translating the literature of each group
for the benefit of the other. Among a score or more of these
writers may be mentioned Henrik von Ende, who wrote for the
year 1876 a "Centennialphantasie" entitled, "Mississippi und
Rhein," and his widow, Amalie von Ende, who called herself the

discoverer of America for the Germans and wrote essays for German-language periodicals on such men as Whitman, Thoreau, and Stephen Crane. Frank Siller of Milwaukee turned Longfellow's *Evangeline* into German and Wilhelm Dilg did the same for *Hiawatha*. Otto Soubron translated much classical German literature into English, but also gathered Indian tales for translation into German. Milwaukee had an amateur German stage most of the time after 1850, and a professional stage from 1868.

John Muir (1838-1914) is best remembered as a champion of the conservation movement and as a naturalist who described the beauties of the Far West. He is often thought of along with John Burroughs, who was his contemporary (1837-1921) and a friend in later life. Muir came to Wisconsin with his parents from Scotland when he was eleven years old. During the next decade he helped his father clear and improve two farms in succession, both of them northeast of Portage in Columbia County. For four years (1860-1864), he attended somewhat irregularly the University of Wisconsin, where he took only such courses as pleased him and did not seek a degree. During this time he supported himself by farm work in the summer and by an occasional winter term as a teacher in a country school. He invented and constructed many curious mechanical devices, some of which may still be seen in the state historical museum at Madison. After leaving the university he embarked upon a long period of travel as a naturalist. Muir's first trip took him to Florida, but soon he turned to the Far West, where he made himself familiar with the Pacific Coast and adjacent mountains from Mexico to Alaska. After 1881 he had a permanent home in California. His writings came mostly after 1890, and called the attention of the nation to the beauties of Yosemite Valley and other parts of the West, and served well the cause of conservation and the movement for national parks. In one of his last books, *The Story of My Boyhood and Youth* (1912), he returned in thought to Wisconsin. These memoirs will always remain a precious document in the frontier history of the state.

It is difficult to call to mind any native of Wisconsin who has made a more significant contribution to American literature than has Hamlin Garland.   He was born in 1860 at West Salem in La Crosse County, of parents who had migrated from Maine.   A few years after the Civil War he accompanied his parents to Iowa, and later to South Dakota.   In 1884 he went to Boston, where during the next few years he made a beginning as a writer.   He wished to be the delineator of the West in fiction, and so he returned from the East to be in closer touch with the life he wished to describe.   About the time when Frederick J. Turner was first calling attention to the influence of the frontier in American history, Garland was asserting that those who had spent the prime of life following the lure of new land and had endured the hardships of a whole succession of frontiers had not found what they sought in the West, and that they and their children would do well to take the "back-trail," that is, return to the older part of the United States.   In 1893 he brought his parents back from the Dakota prairies to West Salem, and for many years he maintained two modest homes, one there and the other in Chicago.   Short stories and novels followed each other in rapid succession.   The earlier ones were for the most part laid in the Middle West; eventually he came to know the West beyond the Rocky Mountains and to write about it.   Gradually, too, he became less of a social crusader and more of an artist.   Between 1917 and 1928, he published the four volumes of the trail-maker series.   The second and third of these, *A Son of the Middle Border* and *A Daughter of the Middle Border,* have already become classics, the latter gaining a Pulitzer prize in 1921.   The four volumes are a history of Garland's family and an autobiography of the author. They acquaint later generations with that New England element which during the nineteenth century spread its manner of life and its ideals westward to the Pacific.   When this series was completed, he went on to write his literary reminiscences in four volumes (1930-1934).   Because of the multitude of his contacts and friendships with literary personages, these latest books almost constitute a history of American literature for the fifty years ending in 1934.

Zona Gale (1874-1938) was born at Portage, was graduated from the University of Wisconsin, and worked as a reporter, first in Milwaukee and then in New York City; but after 1905 she always lived at Portage. In 1928 she married William L. Breese, a manufacturer of that city. It was largely in this region that she found the scenes and the characters of her many short stories and novels. The dramatized version of *Miss Lulu Bett* received the Pulitzer prize as the best American play of 1921, and is probably in consequence her best-known work. Her earlier stories are sometimes called sentimental, but she came to depict with increasing realism and economy of words the tragedies and frustrations of ordinary, undistinguished human beings. She was interested in many public causes, worked actively as a supporter of the elder La Follette, and served for six years as a regent of the state university. She was an early and effective promoter of the Little Theater movement.

Edna Ferber is known as a writer of short stories, novels, and successful plays. She was born of Jewish parents at Kalamazoo, Michigan, in 1887. Ten years later the family began a residence in Wisconsin that was to last for thirteen years. Her autobiography, entitled *A Peculiar Treasure* (1938), tells of the happy years spent in Appleton, where she distinguished herself in declamatory contests, was graduated from high school, and did her first newspaper work. More reporting followed in Milwaukee, and then she began writing short stories. Her first novel, *Dawn O'Hara* (1911), was written in Appleton and mirrors her newspaper life in Milwaukee. After 1910 her home was no longer in Wisconsin; but in the novel *Fanny Herself* (1917), which is semiautobiographical, she again chose Wisconsin as a scene. In one of her latest novels, *Come and Get It* (1935), she portrays the life of the lumber barons as it used to be lived in upper Michigan and northern Wisconsin.

In recent years several natives of the state, most of them young men, have written novels of Wisconsin life. In all of them the authors are deeply conscious that institutions and social customs are changing. Several of them emphasize the conflict between the philosophy of the pioneers and that of their successors. The novel *Some We Loved* (1935) by Edward Harris Heth has as its central theme the transformation of Milwaukee from a city that had distinction, because it was German, to a very common-place American city. Sterling North, literary editor of the *Chicago Daily News,* in *Ploughing on Sunday* (1934), notes the changes in the habits and ideals of a southern Wisconsin farming community. Glenway Wescott was born in Kewaskum, Washington County, and has published both prose fiction and poetry. His novel, *The Grandmothers* (1927), which won him fame, was devoted chiefly to that pioneer generation which transformed Wisconsin wilderness into farmsteads. To him, as to Hamlin Garland, pioneering seemed but a life of hard work, with little to show for it in the end. "The West, that point of the compass which had glittered like a star, came to resemble the East—the light went out of it." His *Good-bye, Wisconsin* (1928) gives further realistic details about village and farming life. Westcott no longer resides in Wisconsin. August Derleth was born in Sauk City in 1909 and still makes his home there. He first saw his work in print at the age of fifteen and has been amazingly productive, writing poems, mystery novels, and short stories. He has begun a series of historical novels planned to narrate a century of life in what he calls Sac Prairie, that is, Sauk City. Three volumes in the series have appeared, *The Place of Hawks* (1935), *Wind over Wisconsin* (1938), and *Restless Is the River* (1939).

One of the most prolific storytellers Wisconsin ever had was General Charles King (1844-1933). A son of Rufus King of Civil War fame and a graduate of West Point, he was in the regular army from 1866 to 1880, campaigning against Indians in the western plains and mountains. After that he was in charge of the military courses at the University of Wisconsin, and at the same time was an instructor and inspector of the Wisconsin National Guard. He was adjutant-general under Governor Upham. Active service in the Spanish-American War gained him the rank of major-general. He began to write fiction about 1880 to eke out his income, using his western experiences as a background. His first book, *The Colonel's Daughter,* appeared in 1883. There was a steady demand for his stories of army life, and altogether he wrote more than fifty volumes.

In many northern lumber camps, from Maine to the Pacific Ocean, tales of Paul Bunyan used to be told. In recounting these tales, which constantly grew in the telling, Wisconsin helped to create a veritable cycle of native American folklore. Paul Bunyan, the hero, was a mythical lumber operator who, in the Wisconsin versions, had his camp about fifty miles west of Rhinelander. He was of great ingenuity and of gigantic stature; he was the possessor of Babe, the Blue Ox, who measured forty-seven axe handles and a tobacco box between the eyes; and much else in the camp was of equally heroic proportions. After his work in Wisconsin was done, Paul Bunyan logged in the Dakotas (witness their present treeless condition) and in the Pacific Northwest. The chief collections of these tales in book form appeared only in the 1920's, when logging by the old methods had taken on the golden glow of retrospect.

Some Great Scholars

Many learned men have lived and taught and written books in Wisconsin. Among hundreds of such persons a handful may be singled out here because they have become peculiarly a part of the Wisconsin tradition. Rasmus B. Anderson (1846-1936) was born of Norwegian parents in Albion, Dane County, Wisconsin, and was educated at Luther College, Decorah, Iowa. He served on the teaching staff of the University of Wisconsin for fourteen years (1869-1883), becoming in 1875 the first professor of Scandinavian. His books were not highly original, many of them being translations, but they did make educated people in the United States acquainted with Norse mythology and aware of the Scandinavian contribution to world literature and world culture.

A different strand in Wisconsin learning is the lifework of William Francis Allen (1830-1889). He was Massachusetts born, was graduated from Harvard, and studied for three years in Europe. For twenty-two years, beginning in 1867, he was a professor at the University of Wisconsin. Besides the ancient languages, he taught ancient, medieval, and modern history. He prepared helps for history students, edited classical texts, and wrote numerous reviews and notices, especially for the *Nation*. A bibliography of his writings compiled after his death contained over nine hundred items. He gave to his students a broad, philosophical view of history. One of his titles to fame is that he had a part in the training of Frederick Jackson Turner (1861-1932), who never ceased to acknowledge his debt to Allen.

Everyone at all familiar with American history knows the part played in that history by the lure of cheap or free land and the consequent westward-moving frontier. Always on the frontier itself existed conditions of comparative equality and a very real and characteristic democracy. Yet in any given locality the frontier period was short, and by 1900 there was little or no free land left unappropriated that was worth having: the frontier as an area had disappeared. Though impermanent, it had nevertheless left its mark upon the population of the West, had spread its influence eastward into the older parts of the nation, and had made an indelible imprint on American political and social thought. This "frontier hypothesis," as contained in Frederick Jackson Turner's essay, "The Significance of the Frontier in American History," has proved to be one of the most clarifying ever offered by an American historian. It was first presented in July, 1893, at a special meeting of the American Historical Association at the Chicago World's Fair, when Turner was but 32 years old. Born in Portage, where his father was a journalist, Turner was graduated from the University of Wisconsin, taught there for a few years, and then went to Johns Hopkins University, where he gained his Ph.D. degree under the guidance of Herbert B. Adams. From 1892 to 1910 he was professor of American history at the University of Wisconsin. From 1910 to 1924 he was a professor at Harvard, and he spent his declining years at Los Angeles.

Increase A. Lapham (1811-1875), Wisconsin's first scientist, was born in Palmyra, New York. Byron Kilbourn, well known as a promoter of real estate ventures, canals, and railroads, found him as the secretary of the Ohio State Board of Canal Commissioners, and persuaded him to come to Wisconsin. In the spring of 1836 he arrived in Milwaukee, where he was to spend the rest of his life. Before the end of that year, and almost as soon as there was a press in the village, he published Wisconsin's first imprint, a paper-covered booklet of twenty-three pages, entitled *A Catalogue of Plants and Shells found in the Vicinity of Milwaukee on the West Side of Lake Michigan.* The catalogue of plants was later enlarged and supplemented. Lapham's observations ended only with his death. In 1844 appeared his *Geographical and Topographical Description of Wisconsin* in 256 pages, a book which induced many families in the eastern states to choose Wisconsin for a home. Lapham sent a memorial to a Wisconsin congressman in which he pointed out the feasibility of weather forecasting and its value in preventing loss of life among navigators on the Great Lakes; this led to federal legislation setting up the weather bureau. Lapham also did invaluable service to archaeology by mapping and describing numerous prehistoric and Indian earthworks in Wisconsin before they were obliterated by the plow. His principal publication in this field was "The Antiquities of Wisconsin," which appeared in *Smithsonian Contributions to Knowledge,* Vol. VII (1855). From 1873 to 1875 Lapham was state geologist.

Thomas Chrowder Chamberlin (1843-1928) was born in Illinois, but when he was two or three years old his parents settled near Beloit, and thenceforth his home was in Wisconsin most of the time until 1892. He was graduated from Beloit College in

1866, and after some years of teaching elsewhere and a year of graduate training at the University of Michigan, he joined the staff at Beloit. Meanwhile he was giving much time to the state geological survey. In 1882 he resigned his teaching position in order to join the United States Geological Survey, in which he had a part for twenty-two years. For five years (1887-1892) he was president of the University of Wisconsin. Then in 1892 he became the head of the department of geology in the University of Chicago, a position he held until his retirement in 1919.

Rollin D. Salisbury (1858-1922) was born on a farm near the village of Spring Prairie in Walworth County. Three years at Whitewater Normal were followed by three years at Beloit College. There he became first the student, then the assistant, and finally the successor to Chamberlin. While Chamberlin was president of the University of Wisconsin, he brought Salisbury from Beloit to Madison. A year later he went with Chamberlin to Chicago, and he served that institution as teacher and administrator until his death forty years later.

There was a remarkable relationship between the careers of these two men. During most of the time when Chamberlin was teaching at Beloit, he was also engaged in the state geological survey. Between 1877 and 1883, a *Geology of Wisconsin* was published in four large volumes and an atlas. In this Chamberlin as editor-in-chief brought together the results of field work done by a score or more of workers; and of these contributors Salisbury was one. Since Wisconsin was to such an extent a glaciated area, both men became much interested in glaciation and pursued the subject further in many parts of the world. In 1904-1906 they published a textbook on geology in three volumes in the American Science series. During the latter part of his life Salisbury devoted himself chiefly to teaching and administration. At one time a third of the state geologists in the United States had been trained by him. By this devotion Salisbury largely relieved Chamberlin of administrative duties.

During the nineteenth century the accepted explanation of the origin of the solar system was the "nebular hypothesis" of the Frenchman, Laplace, first propounded at the close of the eighteenth century. According to this theory, the earth was at first hot, molten, and incandescent, and had gradually cooled. From the study of glaciers, Chamberlin went on to climate at the time of the glaciers, and an earth originally cold seemed to fit the facts better than one originally hot. Eventually Laplace's famous hypothesis was rejected, and an alternate explanation seemed called for. Chamberlin examined the evidence accumulated by physicists, mathematicians, and astronomers. Professor R. F. Moulton of the University of Chicago, an astronomer, was his leading collaborator. It came to be the idea of Chamberlin and Moulton that the earth and the other planets owed their birth to the approach of another sun or star so near our sun that an explosion or disruption of the sun occurred. The sun ejected a swarm of minute solid particles, called planetesimals, and these ultimately came together to form the earth and the planets. Thus the planetesimal theory came to replace the nebular hypothesis. Chamberlin published the results of these studies in two books, *The Origin of the Earth* (1916), and *The Two Solar Families* (1928). The theory is generally accepted by scientists today.

Painting, Sculpture, and Music

Before the days of photography the only pictorial record of events was that made by the painter or sketcher. Many of the armed expeditions sent against the Indians or into Indian country by the federal government were accompanied by artists. When Lewis Cass and William Clark negotiated treaties with the Indians at Prairie du Chien in 1825, a Philadelphia artist named James Otto Lewis (1799-1858) painted a general view of the assemblage and twenty individual portraits. He performed the same service at Fond du Lac two years later. Seth Eastman (1808-1875), later to teach drawing at West Point, was at Fort Crawford, Prairie du Chien, in 1829 and 1830. We have his sketch of the fort and an oil painting from the same period called "Squaws

Playing Ball." Last and greatest of these painter recorders in Wisconsin was George Catlin (1796-1872). He traveled up the Mississippi River from St. Louis to the Falls of St. Anthony (St. Paul) in 1835, stopping at Prairie du Chien, where he painted Wabasha's band of Sioux. In the following year he crossed from Green Bay to the Mississippi, and made a picture of Indians on the Fox River called "Spearing Fish by Torchlight." For seven years he worked among Indians in many parts of the West, painting altogether more than six hundred Indian portraits and many other pictures. He exhibited his works in the eastern United States and Europe with considerable public acclaim, and eventually published many of them in book form. It has often been said that he did for the Indian what Audubon did for the birds of North America.

The men who recorded the life of the Indians and the army posts stood a little apart from the history of art as it was developed by the permanent settlers of Wisconsin. Among the latter there appeared at an early date painters of panoramas, portraits, and landscapes. Some artists practiced more than one of these modes. For about two decades before the Civil War and for some time after it, "panoramas" had a large popular appeal, and some enterprising men made large profits from their production and exhibition. A series of pictures was painted on one long canvas, often of almost incredible size. To exhibit the work, two great spools were set up on the stage and the canvas was rolled creakingly from one to the other. One such artist was Henry Lewis (1819-1904), who painted scenes along the Mississippi River on a canvas twelve feet high and three quarters of a mile long. Other exhibitors showed the Garden of Eden or the Holy Land or famous scenes in history, including in the course of time some of the battles of the Civil War. Milwaukee was a great center for the production of these "moving pictures," and several young artists were brought from Germany expressly to paint them.

Photography appeared in Wisconsin about 1847. Portrait painting supported many artists before its appearance and for sometime afterwards, though photography was destined eventu-

ally almost to make an end of portrait painting. From England
to Milwaukee came Samuel Brookes and Henry Vane Thorne,
while from Scotland came Bernard Isaac Durward and Alexander
Marquis. Durward painted Bishop Henni in 1852, and at that
time he and his family became Roman Catholics. In 1862 he established himself in what is now called Durward's Glen in the
Baraboo Hills; many of his paintings may be seen there today.
His son, Charles, was also a gifted painter. Unfortunately he
died at the age of 31 from accidentally eating a root of water hemlock. Conrad Heyd, a German of a later generation, began portrait painting in Milwaukee in 1868. James R. Stuart (1834-
1915) painted portraits in Madison for many years beginning in
1872.

Heinrich Vianden (1814-1899) was, apart from the panorama
painters, Wisconsin's first landscape painter. He was trained in
Munich and represented a German enthusiasm for nature painting. Vianden's own forte was painting trees, but in early Milwaukee he had to support himself largely by giving lessons in
sketching and painting, including china painting. He trained
pupils that surpassed him, of whom the most famous was Carl
Marr, later Carl von Marr (1858-1936). He was born in Milwaukee, and Vianden, recognizing his talent, sent him to Germany. There he rose to be the head of the Royal Academy of
Munich, was ennobled, and became a leader in German art. He
frequently revisited the United States, and was in Milwaukee as
late as 1929. His gigantic painting, "The Flagellants," was shown
at the World's Fair in 1893 and is now in the Milwaukee Public
Museum. Richard Lorenz (1858-1915) was born in Germany,
but lived most of his life in Milwaukee. He traveled in the Far
West and painted pictures of Indians and cowboys, thus resuming
in a way the work of George Catlin. His "Winter Afternoon"
and "Coming Spring," both in Milwaukee, show him in his most
attractive manner.

Wisconsin's best-known sculptors in the nineteenth century
were two women. Vinnie Ream (1847-1914) was born in Madi-

son and spent her earliest years there, but had little other connection with the state. At the age of eighteen she was in Washington working on a statue of Abraham Lincoln. She had half-hour sittings with him daily for five months just before he was assassinated. Her parents took her abroad, and her work represents French and Italian tradition rather than anything American. She married Richard L. Hoxie, an officer of the United States army, and was for many years a popular hostess in Washington, D.C. Helen Farnsworth Mears [1876(?)-1916] came of a talented family of Oshkosh. Her mother had some success as a writer under the nom de plume of Nellie Wildwood. Helen, the daughter, began to model clay at a very early age. With some assistance from Lorado Taft in Chicago, she executed for the Chicago World's Fair a nine-foot statue called "The Genius of Wisconsin," now in the capitol at Madison. She became an assistant to Augustus St. Gaudens, studied in Paris, and established herself in New York City. Her most ambitious work was a three-paneled wall fountain in bas-relief called "The Fountain of Life." She is also remembered for her bust of Frances E. Willard in the Hall of Fame at Washington, D.C., a bas-relief of Edward MacDowell, and some medallion portraits.

The growth of widespread popular interest in art is perhaps of more significance in cultural history than the accomplishments of a few gifted artists. One measure of this growth is the establishment of galleries and museums to preserve art and make it accessible to the public. In this development Madison and Milwaukee are far ahead of the rest of the state. In the preceding chapter mention was made of the great services of Dr. Lyman C. Draper in collecting manuscript material for the State Historical Society. In 1854 Dr. Draper established a museum in connection with the society, and began the collection of portraits and other paintings. Draper's efforts and later acquisitions by the society have provided excellent material for the study of early Wisconsin art. Since the erection of the new Union building (1927) on the university campus, Madison has had a second art center, where exhibitions are frequent. In 1888 the Layton Art Gallery, the gift of Frederick Layton, was opened in Milwaukee. Besides the building and an endowment of $100,000, Layton gave many original paintings, especially much nineteenth century French work. In 1901 the Society of Milwaukee Artists was organized, and this was followed by the formation of the Milwaukee Art Institute in 1910. Now maintained by a society of more than eight thousand members, the institute gives its attention especially to contemporary art. The organization known as the Wisconsin Painters and Sculptors has an annual exhibition at the art institute in April and other exhibits are numerous throughout the year. There are museums at Beloit, Fond du Lac, Oshkosh, Green Bay, and other cities in the state.

Another evidence of artistic advance, almost all of it occurring within the present century, is the increasing attention given to art in general education. Six of the teachers colleges, including Stout Institute, give instruction in art for future teachers. Among the private colleges, Beloit, Lawrence, and Milwaukee-Downer give much attention to the fine arts. The University of Wisconsin has an art department with nine instructors and about 550 class enrollments (1938). From the teachers trained in these institutions knowledge of art and some competence in simple art practice are spreading through the whole population. In Milwaukee the Layton School of Art was organized in 1920 as a professional school for training in "painting, sculpture, commercial art, teacher training, industrial design and interior decorations."

If the musical abilities of Yankee and German immigrants in early Wisconsin could be compared, the balance would undoubtedly tip heavily in favor of the Germans. Puritanism and several generations of life on the frontier had, in the matter of music, rather impoverished the Americans of New England stock. The Germans, and especially the Forty-eighters, had come out of a background where music of high quality was a necessary part of a cultured existence. In Milwaukee the first steps were taken in November, 1849, which led to the definite organization in May,

1850, of the Milwaukee Musical Society, better known by its German name of *Musikverein*. There were, however, a few English-speaking members from the beginning, and Rufus King was the first vice-president. By 1865 two-thirds of the supporting members were Anglo-Americans. The first musical director of the Verein was a Bohemian German named Hans Balatka. Not a very learned musician, he was possessed of the ambition, which he realized, of making his chorus the best in the Middle West. He performed Haydn's "Creation" in his second season and subsequently went on to light opera. He had a genius for getting people to work together harmoniously and continued as director until 1869, when he was called to do similar work in Chicago. Another founder of Milwaukee's musical greatness was Christoph Bach, who began his long career there in 1855. It was his purpose to build an orchestra of professional musicians. As late as 1902 his Sunday afternoon concerts in the west-side Turnhalle were one of the city's greatest attractions. Bach's own compositions numbered between three and four hundred, and in his lifetime some of them were played in St. Petersburg, Vienna, Berlin, and London.

The language of the Musikverein was for the most part German. By 1880 other choral societies had appeared in which English was used, but again many of the members and leaders were of German stock. As other German communities developed, they, too, had their singing societies; statewide and even more inclusive *Sängerfeste* followed as a matter of course. These great gatherings did much to develop an understanding and appreciation of music among the English-speaking population and to raise the status of the Germans in their eyes.

As one views the united musical world of Europe and her offspring and considers the work of its greatest artists and composers, it must be confessed that Wisconsin's part in the advance of music has not been large. Naturally Wisconsin could not have any contemporaries of the great composers of the eighteenth century or the first part of the nineteenth. And since 1850 the state has not produced the peers of the world-renowned Europeans, of Wagner or Brahms or Verdi. The greatest musician to have any connection with Wisconsin has doubtless been Edgar Stillman Kelley, who was born at Sparta in 1857. Most of his musical education was obtained in Chicago and in Germany, and he has never since his youth made his home in Wisconsin. He has to his credit numerous compositions in many forms. Among them may be mentioned incidental music to *Macbeth* and to the play *Ben Hur,* which is said to have been performed more than five thousand times; and a symphony, entitled *Gulliver, His Voyage to Lilliput,* which was presented in Cincinnati when the composer lacked but a few days of being 80 years old.

Hundreds of songs have been written by persons living in Wisconsin, and a few of them have become known throughout the English-speaking world. In 1857 Dr. William S. Pitts of Rock County, Wisconsin, visited Bradford, a little community in Chickisaw County, Iowa, where at that time there was no church edifice. Upon his return to his home in Wisconsin, with the future church at Bradford in mind, he wrote both the words and the music of "The Little Brown Church in the Vale." Today young couples come long distances to be married in the church made famous by Dr. Pitts' song. Eben E. Rexford (1848-1916) came with his parents from New York state to Wisconsin in 1855. While he was a student at Lawrence College in 1866, he wrote the words of the song, "Silver Threads Among the Gold." Most of his subsequent life was spent very quietly in the village of Shiocton in Outagamie County, where he continued to write poetry and devote himself to his flowers. Out of the same decade (1868) came "In the Sweet Bye and Bye"; the words were written by Sanford Fillmore Bennett and the music was composed by Joseph P. Webster, both of them at that time residents of Elkhorn, the county seat of Walworth County. The Rev. W. D. Cornell, pastor of a church in Fond du Lac, wrote the hymn, "Wonderful Peace," in 1892. Carrie Jacobs Bond was born in Janesville in 1862. She has composed the music of more than three hundred songs, and for some she has written the words.   Among the latter is her most popular song, "A Perfect Day."

Charles Kassell Harris (1865-1930), a very successful commercial song writer and music publisher, came to Milwaukee with his parents at the age of fourteen and lived there until he was a nationally known figure.   His most successful hit, and one of his earliest, was "After the Ball is Over" (1892), the music of which was played day after day by Sousa's band at the Chicago World's Fair.   It was still selling at the rate of five thousand copies annually as late as 1912 and altogether netted the author more than $100,000.   His "Break the News to Mother" (1897) was popular during the Spanish-American War.   In 1901 came "Hello Central, Give Me Heaven."   Harris gradually developed business connections outside of Wisconsin and in 1893 he moved to New York City.   In all he wrote about 125 songs.

The well-known football song, "On Wisconsin," was written in Chicago in the fall of 1909 and was launched just before a Wisconsin-Minnesota game.   William T. Purdy, who composed the music, was not a Wisconsin man.   The words were written by Carl Beck, who was graduated from the University of Wisconsin in 1910.   The first words differed a little from those sung today.

The world of music is indebted to Wisconsin for many other famous composers and artists.   Alexander MacFadyen, who was born in Milwaukee in 1879, has composed piano pieces and songs that have had wide popularity on the concert stage.   Dr. Charles H. Mills, an Englishman for many years director of the University of Wisconsin School of Music and an organist of repute, is famous for a cantata, "The Wreck of the Hesperus," with orchestra accompaniment.   Cecil Burleigh of the same school is a composer for both violin and piano.   To the number of great concert singers Wisconsin has given Luella Chilson Melius, the daughter of an Appleton dentist, and May Peterson, who was born in Oshkosh and spent her youth there.   Arthur Shattuck, of a Neenah paper-manufacturing family, is internationally known as a concert pianist.   It is even more true of musicians than of painters and sculptors that those who seek the highest places in their art go almost without exception to Europe for their training, and the majority afterwards make their headquarters in the large eastern cities.

Turning from the famous artists to the enjoyment of music by the masses, we observe that the number of musical organizations in Wisconsin today is legion. They are especially frequent among the various immigrant groups. Music as a part of good living is held in high and universal esteem. Musical training is not equally accessible in all parts of the state, but music in the schools is steadily growing in the number of participants and in the quality of their performance. The coming of the automobile has made easier the assembling of choruses, bands, and orchestras. And if the radio has cut into the patronage of concerts it has given good music to many more persons than were formerly able to have it; and it exhibits standards of artistic work toward which young performers may aspire. On the whole we live in a more musical world than we did a quarter of a century ago.

ARCHITECTURE—FRANK LLOYD WRIGHT

Man's type of shelter is an important expression of his life and is an index of his advancement. The early Wisconsin farmer, using the materials at hand, usually began with a substantial log house. There was a widespread ambition, however, to progress to a house of sawed lumber, and in southern and eastern Wisconsin this ambition was realized sooner than one might expect. Public or semipublic buildings such as hotels, churches, and courthouses appeared in the new villages and self-styled cities. As a project to give work to unemployed architects and draftsmen, a survey was recently made of a score of early buildings still standing in the state, all of them built between 1838 and the Civil War. Some features of the buildings were due to the availability of local material. There is an inn located in Waukesha County whose three-story walls are constructed of small field stones, veritable cobblestones. But as is only natural, these early builders had brought their ideas about architecture with them: their styles are strongly reminiscent of the East.   In several buildings all the mill-work was manufactured in New York state and brought to Wisconsin by boat.   In other instances the builders showed great fa-

FRANK LLOYD WRIGHT*

miliarity with the traditional styles then current in the eastern states.   Those making the survey repeatedly used the words colonial, post-colonial, and Greek revival to describe what they found. The entrance of the Iowa County courthouse at Dodgeville, built

---

* By courtesy of the Bureau of Visual Instruction, University of Wisconsin.

in 1859, "in its entirety was cribbed" from Edward Shaw's *The Modern Architect,* published in 1855. The First Presbyterian Church at Racine (1851) was planned by an architect of excellent training, and reminds the connoisseur of the churches of Sir Christopher Wren.

There is not much to distinguish the architecture of Wisconsin from that of neighboring states. It has for the most part followed the fashions and kept pace with the progress of the nation. In so far, however, as Wisconsin produced Frank Lloyd Wright, it has given to the world something that marked an epoch. Of no other resident of Wisconsin is the word genius used so often as of this man; and, as is usual with geniuses, he has aroused the greatest enthusiasm and the most violent hostility. His grandfather, Richard Jones, was married in Wales to Mary Lloyd, and the family name became Lloyd-Jones. When Richard Lloyd-Jones was 50 years old he crossed the Atlantic with his already numerous family and eventually established his home north of the Wisconsin River in Sauk County. Anna, one of his daughters, married William Russell Cary Wright, a music teacher of New England ancestry and breeding, and from time to time a Unitarian minister. Their first child, Frank Lloyd Wright, was born at Richland Center in June, 1869, and spent much of his boyhood with his maternal relatives in Wisconsin. The family lived for a time in Madison, and Frank almost finished an engineering course in the University of Wisconsin.

Architecture in America in the nineteenth century was dominated by the past. Its practitioners used details which they consciously borrowed from Greece or Rome, Byzantium or the Gothic of the Middle Ages. Some few men towards the end of the century were urging that America should cease to copy Europe. The arrival of the skyscraper, too, inevitably worked great changes. A skyscraper, as the word is used by architects, is a building with a steel frame which takes the weight of the building from the masonry walls that have carried it from time immemorial; the outer walls become merely a screen to protect from the elements.

Two Views of Modern Office Building,* at Racine, Wisconsin, Designed by Frank Lloyd Wright

* By courtesy of S. C. Johnson & Son, Inc.

As steel construction became more general, much of the older architectural stock-in-trade, such as buttresses, arches, and columns became merely decorative. Some contended that the use of these details as trimming in a building with a steel frame was downright dishonesty. One of the pioneers of a newer architecture in America was Louis Sullivan of Chicago. He kept urging that "form follows function." Wright was employed by Sullivan's firm as a draftsman for six years, learned much from him, and years later wrote about him as the *Lieber Meister* (dear master).

Wright believed that a building should have a relation to its surroundings, to the purpose for which it is intended, and to the materials readily available for its construction. During his first few years as an independent architect, he developed a new style in residences, sometimes called the "prairie style." His houses were distinguished on the outside by low roofs, emphasis on horizontal lines, and the grouping of windows. Inside, ceilings were lowered, traditional ornamentation almost disappeared, and division into separate rooms gave way as far as possible to an open treatment that made for spaciousness. Wright planned the Larkin administration building at Buffalo (1903), which marked a great advance in simplification with a view to utility. He again exemplified simplicity and a careful study of purpose in the Unity Temple at Oak Park, Illinois (1904), in which he broke with old traditions in church architecture.

When Wright wrote his autobiography in 1932, he had 179 constructed buildings to his credit. He changed his style as he went from one material to another. The residences designed in his first period were largely of wood or stucco. In the vicinity of Los Angeles he made epoch-making experiments with houses of poured concrete. Another group of his buildings explored the possibilities of artistic concrete blocks and slabs. From 1914 to 1917 he was directing the construction of the Imperial Hotel in Tokio. The building had to be able to withstand earthquake shocks, and Wright carefully analyzed the factors involved in this problem. In 1923 Tokio had its worst earthquake in half a century, and the Imperial Hotel emerged unscathed. About two miles from Spring Green, in the valley where he had spent much of his boyhood, Wright built himself a home, "low, wide and snug." It was given the name of Taliesin, a Welsh bard who had sung the glories of fine art. The first Taliesin was destroyed by fire in 1914. Rebuilt, it was again burned in 1924, and then built a third time. Wright conducts there the Taliesin Fellowship, a school with about twenty-five apprentices in training.

Students of art and architecture today give Wright a very high rank, higher doubtless than would a convention of middle-aged architects. Several books presenting designs and photographs of his buildings have been published in Germany and Holland, the first in 1910; and his influence in Europe has been enormous. During the past ten or fifteen years the newer architecture, stripped of useless inherited detail and reduced to essentials, has been growing in public esteem in the United States. In bringing about this change of mind, Wright's books, exhibits, and lectures and the buildings he has designed have had no small part. His words are sometimes devastatingly direct, as when he told Milwaukeeans that their new courthouse, costing nine million dollars, had set Milwaukee back fifty years from every cultural standpoint. A building that was steel within and stone without, he said, was an anachronism. He has written much about the buildings of the future. Some day skyscrapers will be supported by a central core of steel and concrete, the floors will be carried by cantilever arms, and the exterior will be all glass and sheet metal. At the age of seventy, having lived through many personal tragedies, he has come to be regarded as something of a seer and a prophet. Since the death of the elder La Follette, he is probably the most famous living son of Wisconsin.

Selected Bibliography

The history of Wisconsin newspapers down to the end of 1850 is best presented in Douglas C. McMurtrie, *Early Printing in Wisconsin* (Seattle, 1931). It includes short sketches of about 150 printers and editors. William J. Anderson wrote "The Press of Wisconsin" for Milo M. Quaife,

Wisconsin, Its History and Its People (4 vols., New York, 1924), Vol. II, pp. 569-583. Articles on Christopher L. Sholes, Horace Rublee, and George W. Peck are included in the *Dictionary of American Biography*. There is a list of "Principal Wisconsin Publications" in *Blue Book, 1937,* pp. 484-491. Ayer's *Directory of Newspapers and Periodicals* (Philadelphia, annual) gives the dates when newspapers were established and circulation figures. Lillian Krueger contributed "Madame Mathilda Franziska Anneke, An Early Wisconsin Journalist" to the *Wisconsin Magazine of History,* Vol. XXI, pp. 160-167 (December, 1937).

A great help in studying Wisconsin authors is *One Hundred Years of Wisconsin Authorship* (Madison, 1937), compiled by Mary Emogene Hazeltine. About seven hundred Wisconsin authors are listed with the titles of their principal works, and there are some brief biographical notes. An earlier work prepared by the staff of the State Historical Society, entitled *Bibliography of Wisconsin Authors,* is a list of books and other publications written by Wisconsin authors in the library of the State Historical Society of Wisconsin (Madison, 1893, 263 pp.). William A. Titus, *Wisconsin Writers* (Chicago, 1930), gives sketches of about seventy authors with extracts from the works of most of them. Edgar G. Doudna, "Wisconsin Writers," *Blue Book, 1927,* pp. 69-75, is brief but well-written. A chapter called "In the World of Letters, Science and Art," *Wisconsin in Three Centuries* (4 vols., New York, 1906), Vol. IV, pp. 181-203, contains much information. For those who read German a most valuable work is Wilhelm Hense-Jensen and Ernest Bruncken, *Wisconsin's Deutsch-Amerikaner* (2 vols., Milwaukee, 1900, 1902). There is information in both volumes on the German-language press. Chapters I-III of Vol. II are devoted to literature and the fine arts. The whole work is a valuable account of the *Geistesleben* of the Germans of the state. The chapter written by J. H. A. Lacher, "The German Element in Wisconsin," in Quaife, *Wisconsin, Its History and Its People,* Vol. II, pp. 152-206, contains sections on the press, literature, and the fine arts. Mr. Lacher also published a booklet, *The German Element in Wisconsin* (Milwaukee, 1925). Francis Magyar wrote "The History of the Early Milwaukee German Theatre, 1850-1868," *Wisconsin Magazine of History,* Vol. XIII, pp. 375-386 (June, 1930).

The anthology, *Poetry Out of Wisconsin,* compiled by August Derleth and R. E. F. Larsson (New York, 1937), contains brief biographical notes. Interesting is Oscar Wegelin, "Wisconsin's First Versifiers," *Wisconsin Magazine of History,* Vol. I, pp. 64-67 (September, 1917). In the same magazine, Vol. II, pp. 340-342 (March, 1919), is an account of the writing of the song "The Little Brown Church in the Vale." The history of "On Wisconsin" was given by Louise Phelps Kellogg, *ibid.,* Vol. XXI, pp. 35-38 (September, 1937). In the text of this chapter attention was called to autobiographical writings of Ella Wheeler Wilcox, John Muir, Hamlin Garland, and Edna Ferber. An obituary notice on Zona Gale Breese appeared in *The New York Times,* December 28, 1938, p. 21. There is an excellent thesis by Gretchen Schmidt, *Contemporary Novels About Wisconsin* (B. Sc., Madison, 1936). General Charles King wrote an autobiographical sketch entitled "Memories of a Busy Life," which appeared in the *Wisconsin Magazine of History,* Vols. V and VI (1922).

Fred L. Holmes, in *Alluring Wisconsin* (Milwaukee, 1937), described his pilgrimages to the homes of several persons mentioned in this chapter. His *Badger Saints and Sinners* (Milwaukee, 1939) included brief essays on Percival, C. Latham Sholes, Lapham, and Garland. The chapter, "Eugene Shepard, Raconteur of the Bunk Houses," is a good introduction to the Paul Bunyan stories. These tales may be read in: Esther Shephard, *Paul Bunyan* (New York, 1924); James Stevens, *Paul Bunyan* (New York, 1925); and Charles E. Brown, *Paul Bunyan Tales* (Madison, 1927).

A bibliography of the writings of Rasmus B. Anderson with a brief evaluation by Einar I. Haugen appeared in the *Wisconsin Magazine of History,* Vol. XX, pp. 255-259 (March, 1937). There is an autobiography, *Life Story of Rasmus B. Anderson* (Madison, 1915). There are articles on Allen, Turner, Lapham, Chamberlin, and Salisbury in the *Dictionary of American Biography,* with references to further reading. The University of Wisconsin Press has published *The Early Writings of Frederick Jackson Turner: With a List of All His Works,* compiled by Everett E. Edwards, with an introduction by Fulmer Mood (Madison, 1938). Turner's famous essay appears in this book in its first form. In its latest form it gave its title to a collection of essays (New York, 1920). The differences are not important. E. F. Bean, state geologist, wrote "Increase A. Lapham, Geologist," and added a list of Lapham's geological publications, in *Wisconsin Archaeologist,* Vol. XVI, pp. 79-84 (July, 1937). This was followed by a selection of Lapham letters edited by Charles E. Brown. George L. Collie wrote of Chamberlin in "A Distinguished Son of Wisconsin," *Wisconsin Magazine of History,* Vol. XV, pp. 263-281, and pp. 412-445 (1932). Hiram D. Densmore similarly wrote of "Rollin D. Salisbury," in the same volume, pp. 22-46, and pp. 119-147 (1931, 1932). H. L. Fairchild contributed an article on "Thomas Chrowder Chamberlin" to *Science,* Vol. LXVIII, pp. 610-612 (December 21, 1928).

Porter Butts, *Art in Wisconsin* (Madison, 1936), is the best introduction to its subject. It is a cultural study of art in relation to the frontier and tells little of the present century. George Catlin, *North American Indians,* a collection of letters, has been many times printed since the first edition in 1842. There is a good modern reprint with 320 illustrations (2 vols., Edinburgh, 1926). *The Dictionary of American Biography* has articles on George Catlin, Vinnie Ream Hoxie, and Helen F. Mears.

Charlotte Russell Partridge prepared "Wisconsin in the Field of Art," for the *Blue Book, 1929,* pp. 103-110, in which she gave the names of many contemporary artists. *The American Art Annual,* Vol. 34 (Washington,

1938), has information about galleries, museums, and art education in each state. *Who's Who in American Art* (Washington, 1938, Vol II, for 1937-1938) lists seventy-two painters and ten sculptors residing in Wisconsin. The *Bulletin of the Milwaukee Art Institute,* now in its fourteenth year, keeps one in touch with current activity, especially exhibitions. Winifred V. Miller wrote an excellent little article, "Wisconsin's Place in the Field of Music," *Blue Book, 1929,* pp. 97-102.

Alexander C. Guth wrote "Early Day Architects in Wisconsin," *Wisconsin Magazine of History,* Vol. XVIII, pp. 141-145 (December, 1934). In the same, Vol. XXII, pp. 15-38 (September, 1938), he described the work of the "Historic American Buildings Survey," in Wisconsin.

Frank Lloyd Wright has told his own story well in *An Autobiography* (New York, 1932). Other writings by him are *Modern Architecture* (Princeton, N. J., 1931) and *The Disappearing City* (New York, 1932). The regard in which he is held by younger critics may be seen in Sheldon Cheney, *The New World Architecture* (New York, 1930), or in Thomas Craven, *Modern Art* (New York, 1934), pp. 273-289.

CHAPTER XXIII

DEPRESSION AND A NEW SOCIETY

INTRODUCTION TO THE LAST CHAPTER

A NOVEL or a play is usually planned to lead to some natural or reasonable conclusion, but a historical narrative that comes down to the present cannot be logically complete: the outcome, whatever it is to be, lies in the future. In spite of the well-worn saying that one historical period fades imperceptibly into its successor, it appears to be true that a new era began either in 1929 with the famous depression, or in 1933 with the inauguration of the New Deal. One of those years might have served better than 1939 as the end of an epoch and a point at which to conclude, but the years since 1929 have been marked by such great and significant changes that some attempt, however inadequate, must be made to record them. In previous chapters several strands in the web of Wisconsin's life were followed down to 1938 or 1939. In the treatment of politics, labor, the tasks of the state, and several other matters, it was not possible or desirable to omit all reference to the depression, but the main discussion of that subject was reserved for this final chapter.

The depression itself is so recent and so familiar that its main features scarcely need to be mentioned. It came upon Wisconsin, as upon the rest of the United States, in the latter part of 1929, and grew steadily worse until the early months of 1933. In one way or another it affected all groups of the population. To the farmer it meant low prices for what he had to sell, and consequent inability to meet the demands of his creditors. Factory employment in forty-four months fell to about 58 per cent of what it was in the summer of 1929, and, because of wage cuts, what the workers were receiving fell even farther. There were unprecedented demands on public relief. Construction work almost ceased. The salaries of teachers and other public employees were lowered. Doctors and lawyers could not collect their bills. In the general lack of confidence banks felt that it was unwise to lend, and a paralysis crept over normal business operations. Young

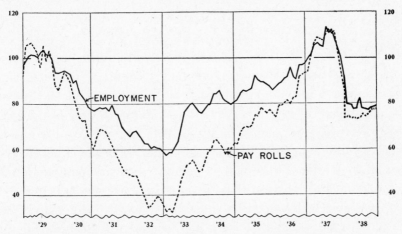

Index Numbers of Employment and of Weekly Pay Rolls in Manufacturing Industries in Wisconsin, 1929-1938 (Average 1925-1927 = 100)*

people looked out upon a world that did not need their services. And all with one accord began to besiege the government—local or state or federal—for help in their distress.

In answer to this call many important measures were taken. Some were intended to alleviate existing distresses; others, to prevent the recurrence of a depression. In sum, the measures were so numerous, they involved such vast expenditures, and some of them were so at variance with American tradition that the hackneyed words, a rapidly changing society, took on a new and

* From the *Wisconsin Labor Market* (February, 1938, and February, 1939). By courtesy of A. O. Fried, Chief Statistician of the Industrial Commission of Wisconsin.

vivid meaning.   Among all the changes, the two most arresting
were: first, the large number of individuals in our society no longer
able to live without assistance from the government; and second,
the assumption of enormous responsibility by the federal government in fields up to that time for the most part reserved to the
state and local governments.

THE BURDEN OF RELIEF

Unemployment and public relief are twin shadows that wax
and wane together.   Organized labor and a few students have
long been aware of unemployment as a menace to health and
morals; and since 1929 we have all been unemployment-conscious.
No one should be permitted for lack of the necessities of life to
sink into a subnormal or unemployable condition.   From the beginning of Wisconsin's history as a state, the care of the needy
poor has rested with the local governments, and back in 1928 they
were helping perhaps 15,000 outdoor relief cases at an annual
cost of about a million dollars.   Beginning in October of 1929
employment dropped steadily for forty-four months.   As families
exhausted their resources they were forced to turn in large numbers to their local governments, and by 1931 demands were pain-
fully taxing municipal resources.

Meanwhile Wisconsin was addressing herself to the problems of
means and methods of assistance.   The calling of a citizens' committee on unemployment in July, 1930, was followed in September
by the establishment of a bureau of unemployment research within
the industrial commission.   This new body continued for two
years to make studies and formulate standards relating to relief.
In March, 1931, the legislature authorized a program of grade
crossing elimination which provided work for about 7,500 men
for several months at a cost of about $6,500,000.   This action was
epoch-making as an acknowledgment that responsibility rested
with the state as well as with the local governments.   In the following February (1932), the emergency relief act imposed special
taxes for general relief purposes which produced more than $5,-

000,000 for distribution among the counties and other local units. At the same time there was set up within the industrial commission the unemployment relief department, the principal state relief agency for more than two years.

At first the federal government, later to play such a great part in relief, was hesitant in assuming new responsibilities. In 1931 there was a federal emergency advance of more than a million dollars for highway construction in Wisconsin, and in the following year there was a similar grant of nearly two millions, both made to create employment. In February, 1932, the federal Reconstruction Finance Corporation (RFC) was established to lend to banks and to "aid in financing agriculture, commerce and industry." In July the RFC was authorized to make loans to states and their subdivisions to finance the construction of public works; by May, 1933, under this act, Wisconsin had borrowed $12,395,000. Congress later transformed these loans into outright gifts.

For the year 1932 the cost of relief in Wisconsin, not counting part of the grade crossing elimination which fell within this year, was about $20,500,000. Of this the local governments furnished about half, and the state and federal governments about 25 per cent each. In January, 1933, Philip La Follette was succeeded as governor by Albert C. Schmedeman, and soon Herbert Hoover gave place to Franklin D. Roosevelt.

From the beginning of the Roosevelt administration, the federal government, in order to create employment and relieve the distress of the needy, aided the states without stint and in a manner quite without precedent in the United States. The first important step in this outpouring of assistance was the act of May 12, 1933, which created the Federal Emergency Relief Administration (FERA). The chief duty of this body was to distribute money to the states. The term, general relief, was used to include both direct and work relief as handled by the local governments, and the cost of this in Wisconsin was $19,000,000 in 1933, $30,000,-000 in 1934, and $39,000,000 in 1935. Of these sums about four-fifths were from the federal government and most of the rest from the counties and other subdivisions of the state. Until April 1, 1934, the unemployment relief department set up in 1932 continued to be the central relief agency of Wisconsin, receiving federal money and distributing it to the local governments. Through the summer of 1933 work projects were carried on by county and other local units, the cost of which was included in the figures just given above. These local units were at the same time distributing outdoor relief. In the following winter the short-lived Civil Works Administration (CWA), presently to be described, was built up alongside of FERA and temporarily over-shadowed it. In the spring of 1934 the legislature, copying FERA, set up the Wisconsin Emergency Relief Administration (WERA). This took on rather more functions than its predecessor, the relief department, and lasted for about twenty months (April 1, 1934 to December 6, 1935), in fact, as long as there was FERA money to distribute.

The Civil Works Administration (CWA) was an effort on the part of the federal government to provide work for four million unemployed persons and thus tide them over the winter of 1933-1934. It began with an executive order issued by President Roosevelt under the National Recovery Act on November 8, 1933, and was practically ended on March 31, not quite five months later. Most of the projects undertaken were sponsored by local governments and were for the construction or repair of highways or school buildings. Relief need was not a prerequisite for employment. The federal government paid all wages and up to 25 per cent of the cost of material. It was reported in the newspapers at the time that two Wisconsin men, Arthur J. Altmeyer and Aubrey Williams, "sold" the idea to President Roosevelt. Wisconsin's assigned quota of jobs was gradually increased from 68,000 to 100,000, but the first Wisconsin civil works administrator by the end of the year had 166,550 persons at work, and was seriously overdrawing Wisconsin's allotment of funds. On January 31, 1934, this official gave up his post at the request of federal authorities, and thereafter the Wisconsin CWA lists were smaller. The total cost of CWA in the nation was $877,000,000, and in Wisconsin, $36,000,000. Among all the states Wisconsin stood fourth in the amount of money received. While CWA was in operation all local government work projects were absorbed or suspended, and general relief shrank in January, 1934, to 59,000 cases. There had always been a certain stigma attached to "going on relief," and it was contrary to American tradition to bare the details of household management to the eye of a social worker, as had been required when relief was given before CWA. But CWA work was paid for in cash, and no questions were asked about the spending of the money; it was at this time that many families took the plunge and for the first time applied for work relief.

Just as CWA came to an end, WERA began in Wisconsin, and the one turned over to the other many unfinished projects together with relief clients to work at them. Among a great variety of WERA projects, the most numerous were for building roads, small bridges, sidewalks, culverts, and the like. Drainage and flood control improvements were undertaken in Juneau, Portage, and neighboring counties. At the peak in November, 1934, WERA had 49,000 persons at work, most of them men. Earnings, though paid in cash, were limited by the budgetary deficiency of the family. Throughout the WERA period of twenty months, outdoor relief had to be given to from 80,000 to 120,000 cases. The number of individuals in these families varied between about 250,000 and 400,000. Since transients have no established residence, they cannot qualify for relief on the usual terms. Early in 1933 the state was maintaining eight transient depots. In 1934 and 1935, when the federal government paid the whole cost, more than a million dollars was spent in Wisconsin each year for transients, the case load varying from 8,000 to 11,000.

In the spring of 1935 the federal government announced that it would no longer assist in general or outdoor relief. WERA work projects were greatly reduced in August, and Wisconsin received its last money from FERA in November. But at the same time the federal government was inaugurating its works program, and was therefore assuming primary responsibility for providing employment for several million unemployed persons. The phrase "works program" was used to cover the operations of at least forty federal agencies. Some were regular departments whose activities were expanded to give employment relief; others were special agencies, some of them dating from 1933, like PWA and CCC; and others were freshly created or else reorganized in 1935.

The greatest of the new agencies, which accounted for perhaps three-fourths of the employment provided under the works program was the Works Progress Administration (WPA). Projects assumed by WPA originated with local and state agencies known as sponsors. The "detailed planning involved in each project, including the engineering, architectural, legal, financial and employment aspects, is the basic responsibility of the local sponsoring body." By October, 1935, actual work was beginning under the new setup, and from this time until the end of 1937, WPA spent about $94,000,000 of federal money in Wisconsin and about $35,-000,000 furnished by the sponsoring bodies. The number of men employed on these projects varied from about 35,000 to about 75,000, being less in 1937 than in 1936, but rising again with the business "recession" that began late in 1937. By June, 1938, when WPA was about three years old, the amount of federal money spent in Wisconsin on WPA projects was about $120,000,000.

While the federal government, through WPA and some lesser agencies, was giving work relief from October, 1935, onward, Wisconsin and its subdivisions had still to meet the heavy demands of outdoor relief. WERA, established in April, 1934, was abolished by an executive order of Governor La Follette, and at the same time there was established as its successor, with considerably wider functions, the public welfare department. Early in 1936 it was made an independent department outside the industrial commission, and so continued for about three and one-half years. In October, 1939, it became the division of public assistance in the new and larger public welfare department. At the close of 1935

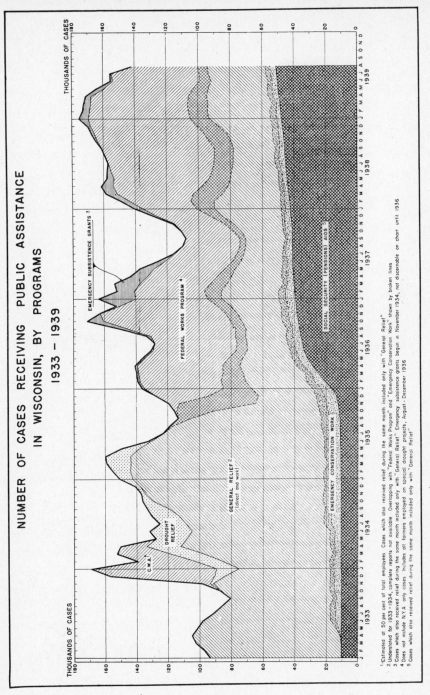

NUMBER OF CASES RECEIVING PUBLIC ASSISTANCE
IN WISCONSIN, BY PROGRAMS
1933 - 1939

THOUSANDS OF CASES

EMERGENCY SUBSISTENCE GRANTS [3]

FEDERAL WORKS PROGRAM [4]

GENERAL RELIEF [2]
(direct and work)

DROUGHT RELIEF

C.W.A.

EMERGENCY CONSERVATION WORK

SOCIAL SECURITY (PENSIONS) AIDS [5]

1933 1934 1935 1936 1937 1938 1939

[1] Estimated at 50 per cent of total employees. Cases which also received relief during the same month included only with "General Relief."
[2] Understated for 1933-1934, complete reports not available. Overlapping with "Federal Works Program" and "Emergency Conservation Work" shown by broken lines
[3] Cases which also received relief during the same month included only with "General Relief." Emergency subsistence grants begun in November 1934, not discernable on chart until 1936
[4] Does not include N.Y.A. only cases. Includes all farmers employed on special drought projects, August-December 1936
[5] Cases which also received relief during the same month included only with "General Relief."

499

there were about 70,000 outdoor or general relief cases and during the next four years the number varied between 70,000 and 30,000. The average for the first nine months of 1939 was about 50,000 a month. The cost of this general relief from 1936 to 1939 was about $13,000,000 a year. As the federal government had withdrawn from this field, most of the load had to be borne by the local governments, with the help of subsidies from the state treasury. These subsidies varied according to need, the richer areas thus contributing to those with inadequate resources. It will be recalled that before the depression outdoor relief was costing the local governments about a million dollars a year.

Federal aid in combating the depression was given throughout the United States in another form by the Federal Emergency Administration of Public Works or the public works administration (PWA), which was authorized by Title II of the NIRA in June, 1933. Its two chief purposes were to give employment when employment was sorely needed and to provide the public with new equipment, chiefly, though by no means exclusively, in the form of public buildings. First of all, many federal buildings were erected throughout the country. PWA also encouraged the states and their subdivisions to move their building programs "out of the future into the present" by offering them help on very generous terms. It gave 30 per cent of the needed money and lent the rest. Later these figures were changed to 45 per cent for the grant and 55 for the loan.

The PWA examined carefully the financial standing of municipalities, and some requests for money were refused because the credit of the petitioner was not sound. As it paid over the money lent, it became the owner of the bonds of cities, counties, and other subdivisions of the state; then, as opportunity offered, these securities were sold to the investing public. Throughout the nation the grants during the first five years, that is, up to June 30, 1938, totaled $663,752,000. Of this Wisconsin's share was $12,-317,000, or about one fifty-fourth of the whole. During the slightly longer period ending December 31, 1938, the PWA authorities had loaned almost $700,000,000.[1]   The state government of Wisconsin, because of the constitutional prohibition on borrowing, made almost no use of this means of financing.   The most interesting project within the state was perhaps Parklawn, a housing enterprise of the city of Milwaukee, designed to provide modern, sanitary housing at moderate rentals for 518 families.

FARMERS IN DISTRESS

Wisconsin farmers tasted real prosperity during the World War. Since then, by comparison, they have always been in distress. Their principal griefs are three: prices received for produce are too low, they must pay too much for what they buy, and their burden of debt is too heavy.   To these are added occasional catastrophes such as drought and flood.   Most of these troubles have called forth government action.

There were 193,000 farms in Wisconsin in 1925 and just under 200,000 in 1935, but some of the farms enumerated by the census takers were the homes of some who had a principal occupation other than farming, such as mining or lumbering.   In 1938 there were probably not many more than 185,000 who were full-time or nearly full-time farmers.   The gross income of Wisconsin farmers was above $400,000,000 a year for the five years 1925-1929, the average being about $422,000,000.   Then year by year it fell until in 1932 it was only $188,000,000, or 45 per cent of what it had been. For the nation as a whole it was estimated that the farmer had in 1929 18 per cent of the national income; in 1932, but seven per cent.

It has long been the opinion of many economists that prices paid to farmers are too low.   If their purchasing power were increased, this in turn would start the wheels of industry and all would enjoy prosperity.   The most famous among many plans to accomplish this end was the McNary-Haugen bill, which was be-

---

[1] The total amount loaned was about $697,000,000. How much of this was borrowed by governmental units in Wisconsin is not known. Using the same ratio as obtained for the grants and dividing by fifty-four, we have as a quotient almost $13,000,000.

fore Congress from 1924 to 1928.   The idea was to subsidize the
export of farm products, thus by exportation to decrease the home
supply and automatically raise prices, and to recoup the treasury
by a tax on the share of the commodity sold in the domestic market.   Four years of ardent debate ended when President Coolidge
vetoed the bill.

The first New Deal Congress set out to raise the farmers' purchasing power to a parity with that of the industrial classes.   It
sought to raise prices by producing an artificial scarcity.   In May,
1933, an Agricultural Adjustment Administration (AAA) was set
up within the Department of Agriculture.   Farmers were invited
to enter into voluntary contracts to decrease and limit production,
and if they accepted the invitation they were to be paid for what
they abstained from producing.   Products raised and marketed
paid a processing tax, and the proceeds from this paid the farmers
who by agreement produced less than usual.   In January, 1936,
the United States Supreme Court declared the act unconstitutional,
saying, "Congress has no power to enforce its commands on the
farmer to the ends sought by the AAA.   It must follow that it may
not indirectly accomplish these ends by taxing and spending to
purchase compliance."   The government had signed contracts
with the farmers covering the year 1936 and those contracts had to
be carried out.   By the time the last checks were distributed,
Wisconsin farmers had received a little less than $14,000,000.
Four-fifths of this sum was for not raising corn and hogs.   Tobacco payments came to more than $2,000,000 and there were
smaller amounts allotted to producers of wheat and sugar beets.
In 1935, the year of largest disbursements, AAA payments made
up less than three per cent of the gross income of Wisconsin
farmers, about a third of whom participated.

As soon as the Supreme Court declared the act of 1933 to be unconstitutional, Congress passed the Soil Conservation and Domestic Allotment Act (SCDA).   Farmers under this act were paid
for planting certain soil-building and soil-conserving crops, while
the Department of Agriculture still sought to stabilize prices by

limiting production and storing surpluses in accordance with the idea of the ever-normal granary.   To this end the department fostered associations of farmers willing to submit to crop restriction. While all this was ostensibly but the voluntary action of the participating farmers, those who complied were paid for their compliance, in that they had more land on which to plant soil conserving crops for which they were paid.   Disbursements in Wisconsin under SCDA for the year 1936 were more than $10,000,000, or about three per cent of the gross farm income.   Since about two-thirds of the Wisconsin farmers participated, this made the average receipts per farmer considerably less than in 1935 under AAA. Disbursements for 1937 were a little less than in 1936.   The Agricultural Adjustment Administration still exists as a division of the Department of Agriculture.   It stands ready to lend money on stored grain in order to encourage farmers to keep it out of the market in years of overproduction.

The AAA and SCDA represent what has been done by the government thus far to gain better prices for the farmers.   There is no doubt that farm prices did rise during the last three-quarters of 1933 and throughout the following year.   They were also rising during the second half of 1936.   But it is impossible to say how much of this was due to government action and how much to the droughts of 1934 and 1936.   One suspects that man is not quite in control of the situation.   What may be accomplished is limited by three factors.   First, to be effective, quota systems should include the whole world.   Secondly, in the United States these should be universally applied: at present only a part of the American farmers are coöperating.   And finally, to increase the effectiveness of such plans, it would be necessary to regiment much more strictly the American farmer who is already saying that he does not like to be told what to do.   In the political campaigning of the fall of 1938 in Wisconsin, several candidates thought it expedient to declare in favor of ending the control of agriculture.

The second major grief of the farmers is that they must pay too much for what they buy.   The farmers used to blame the trusts and money magnates for high prices. While this idea still persists, there has latterly been a feeling among farmers that on the whole the labor organizations which keep wages high in the cities keep up also the prices which farmers have to pay for all kinds of manufactured articles. About all that has been done for and by the farmers to remedy this particular distress is the movement for consumer coöperation.

We come now to the farmers' burden of debt, which has so often been a factor in American political life. Of the nearly 200,000 farmers in Wisconsin in 1935, one-fifth were tenants and four-fifths were owners. Of farms operated by owners more than half have been found to be mortgaged at every census since 1910. This group of owner-operated farms carried a mortgage indebtedness in 1930 of $355,000,000 and in 1935 of just under $400,000,000; and if we count in the tenant farms, the mortgages in 1935 added up to about half a billion dollars. Before the readjustments which began in 1933, there was an annual interest charge of from twenty-five to thirty million dollars.

This problem was an old one. Woodrow Wilson was exercised in mind by the plight of debt-burdened farmers, and in his time an act was passed which set up twelve federal land banks, and also inaugurated the system of coöperative national farm loan associations organized by the borrowers. In all the United States, the federal land banks lent about $1,700,000,000 of which about $1,100,000,000 was outstanding at the beginning of 1933. Of the latter amount a little more than $23,000,000 was owed by Wisconsin farmers.

Excellent as were the services rendered by these banks, they could not cope with the crisis approaching in 1932 and 1933. A joint resolution of the Wisconsin legislature in January, 1932, protested that the federal land bank system was unfair to farmers in holding them to the full amount of their mortgages. The amounts ought to be reduced, so it was asserted, "to figures for which these same farms were later sold."

The tremendous drop in farm income from 1929 to 1932 has

been mentioned.   Farmers with mortgaged farms, nearly 110,000 of them in Wisconsin, were in a desperate situation.   If they could borrow, they went deeper into debt merely to carry on. Their constricted budgets had no place for interest payments. Frequently the lender, himself in sore straits, insisted harshly on his legal rights.   In 1932 and 1933 foreclosures in Wisconsin were five times as frequent as in 1926.   There were occasions when enraged farmers forced postponement of sheriff's sales.   Help for the farmers took three forms.   They were given more time in which to pay, credit was made available, and, extra-legally perhaps one should say, the amount of the debt was scaled down.

On January 13, 1933, Governor Schmedeman asked the circuit judges of the state to hold in abeyance all mortgage foreclosure proceedings until the legislature, then just beginning its session, should enact relief legislation.   The legislature promptly authorized judges to delay proceedings and give more time in which to redeem the property.   With slight variations this law was repeated in 1935, 1937, and 1939.   These laws were emergency measures with time limits, and were known as the mortgage moratorium laws.   Provision was also made for a mediation board in each county.   These boards, of three members, attempted to show the creditors that they would do better to accept a lower figure as the principal of the debt than to take the farm away from the debtor. In Wisconsin these boards never had power to compel reduction of debt.   The federal Frazier-Lemke Act of June 28, 1934, provided that a federal district judge should arrange for an appraisal of a mortgaged farm.   The owner then had to pay the principal of the new valuation within six years, meanwhile paying taxes and at least one per cent on the principal annually.   If the creditor did not agree to these terms, the debtor was to pay a fair annual rental on the appraised valuation.   At the end of five years there would be a new appraisal and the debtor would pay this valuation.   This procedure really was a compulsory reduction of the debt.   A number of farmers in Wisconsin took advantage of this law, but in May, 1935, it was declared unconstitutional by the

United States Supreme Court. It was, of course, possible for a farmer to declare himself bankrupt, but the number of those who chose this way out of their difficulties was very small, never exceeding two hundred in any one year.

In 1933 the new federal Farm Credit Administration (FCA) was established. Wisconsin lay in the district of the federal land bank of St. Paul. The FCA was established not to lend government money to farmers, but to tap the credit resources of the nation on their behalf. Investors bought the bonds of FCA, and the FCA lent the money to the farmers, not as individuals, but as "national farm loan associations." Through these organizations, in the next two and one-half years, the FCA took over about 25,000 farm mortgages in Wisconsin, that is, nearly one-fourth of all of them. As time passed the interest rates were lowered, eventually to four per cent. The lowering of the federal rate was followed by some reduction on the part of ordinary commercial lenders. This lessening of interest has been of great benefit to farmers. By the end of 1937 the average rate for all farm mortgages was slightly above five per cent.

The FCA did not lend money unless it believed that the loan was safe. It sent an appraiser to view the farm, and did not lend more than 70 (later 75) per cent of the appraised value. In many cases FCA would not lend enough to clear the existing liens against the property. Unless the former mortgage holders could be induced to compromise, that is, to accept less than the face value of the debt and thus clear the farm of its encumbrance, there could be no FCA loan. Governor Schmedeman in 1933 created a state farm credit administration, and its agents went about to aid in scaling down debts of farmers to the point where they would be eligible for federal farm loans. Later this service became the Wisconsin Farm and Home Credit Administration. By the spring of 1939, this agency claimed that it had helped prevent the foreclosure of 6,700 mortgages, most of them on farms. The existence of this agency was terminated by Governor Heil in September, 1939. The county mediation boards were still in existence to continue work of this kind. The estimated farm mortgage debt, which had exceeded half a billion dollars in 1930, amounted to only about $390,097,000 by January 1, 1939.

Two other forms of help were provided for Wisconsin farmers, drought relief and rural rehabilitation. Rainfall comes in cycles, and it is to be expected that several years of abundant moisture will be followed by a series of years marked by scant precipitation. Unfortunately the depression coincided with a period of relatively sparse rainfall in the Middle West. In September, 1933, the federal executive authorized the FERA to grant funds for relief to drought-stricken states. To administer this aid in Wisconsin a drought relief department was set up within the industrial commission. Money was advanced to farmers for the purchase of seed grain and feed for livestock. The farmers either gave their notes or agreed to work out their loans on WPA projects, which were started in forty-five counties under the direction of the highway commission. There was one peak for such work in May, 1934, when 26,000 farmers were employed, and there was another peak in March and April of the following year. Altogether, before June, 1935, some 40,000 farmers received $8,400,000. Drought conditions again called for relief in 1936. During the four months from August to December of that year, nearly 32,000 farmers, duly certified as being in need of assistance, were given work on WPA projects, and their earnings totalled more than $3,000,000.

The WERA, which began in April, 1934, had a rural division which had much to do with directing drought relief. In the fall of 1934 federal government funds were made available for loans to Wisconsin farmers who could not borrow anywhere else. This putting of down-and-out farmers on their feet was called rehabilitation. This service has continued under a series of agencies to the present. On July 1, 1935, all rural assistance, both drought relief and rehabilitation, was put in charge of the Federal Resettlement Administration; and on September 1, 1937, a little more than two years later, this gave way to the Farm Security Administration. Besides making loans the resettlement administration and its successor also gave subsistence grants to needy farmers for the purchase of food, shelter, clothing, and indispensable medical service. The resettlement administration also assisted several hundred farm families to remove from submarginal land to better farms. Wisconsin is not one of the states where the evils of tenancy are most pronounced, but something has been done, under the federal Bankhead-Jones Farm Tenant Act of 1937, to advance money to tenant farmers to enable them to buy farms.

Rural electrification has long been the desire of forward-looking farmers. In 1935 about 35,000 Wisconsin farms had electric power. The federal Rural Electrification Administration (REA) was established by executive order of President Roosevelt, May 11, 1935. As in the case of WPA, its parent law was the appropriation for relief purposes of April 8 of that year. A sum of $100,-000,000 was made available for loans. In October, 1935, Governor La Follette established the rural electrification coördination office, headed by a coördinator who should serve as a liaison officer between Wisconsin groups and the federal government. The farmers who wanted electrification grouped themselves in coöperative associations, varying in size from 150 to 1,500 customers, and in 1936 united in a group or corporation, popularly known as "Statewide," to secure accounting and engineering services for the local associations. In the spring of 1938, three years after the initiative was taken by the federal government, nineteen local associations with 16,000 members had built over 5,000 miles of power lines. They had borrowed more than six million dollars of federal funds, which they were to repay within twenty years with interest at three per cent. This development of the coöperatives had also stimulated the already existing private power companies to be more active in extending their lines, and extensions by them in the same three years had brought electricity to 12,000 farms. In the special session of 1937, the legislature gave power to the Wisconsin Development Authority (WDA) to make use of certain state funds for promotional ends. There was delay because the constitutionality of this procedure was challenged; but during the last five

months of 1938 much of the work formerly done by the REA was
carried on by the WDA.   In 1939, however, WDA ceased to be
an agent of the state.   The work of dispensing information and

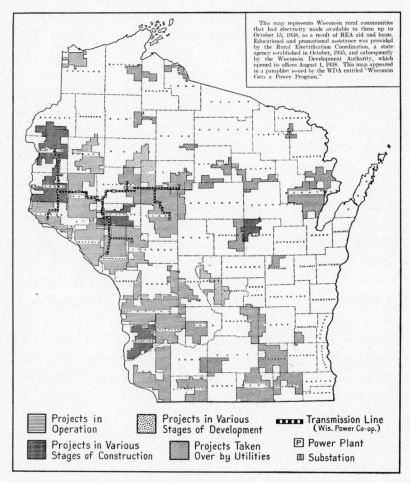

ELECTRIC SERVICE PENETRATES RURAL WISCONSIN

advice on the organization and management of rural electric co-
operatives was given to the state department of agriculture.   By
June 30, 1939, the number of coöperatives in Wisconsin borrowing
from REA had risen to 28, the amount allotted to them was

$12,566,000, and the money already advanced to them (comparable to the six million dollars mentioned above) had reached $7,408,000.

OTHER FORMS OF FEDERAL ASSISTANCE

A period of depression may have especially serious consequences for certain groups of young people. There are those who have finished their school attendance, but can find no employment. Faced with months and perhaps years of involuntary idleness at the very time when they should be establishing habits of regularity and industry, they run the risk of sinking into a condition either of despair or of chronic unemployability. And there are others who would normally continue in school, but are unable to do so because of diminished family resources. Most of the assistance to these two groups has come from the federal government, though the state of Wisconsin did something for a time to enable needy students to continue in schools and colleges.

A very early project of the New Deal was designed to put needy young men into useful outdoor work. Authorized by a law of March 31, it began work April 5, 1933. Its official name was Emergency Conservation Work (ECW) until July 1, 1937, when it received by law the label already in common use of Civilian Conservation Corps (CCC). Young men between the ages of 17 and 24, upon recommendation of public welfare or relief officials, were gathered into camps, and along with them came a much smaller number of veterans of the World War. They earned $30 a month, but usually assigned $22 or $25 to their needy families. Enrollment was for six months at a time but it was possible to re-enlist, although by a regulation of 1937 no one might spend more than two years in the organization. The camps, which usually numbered between fifty and eighty in Wisconsin, were managed by the War Department and staffed from the regular army. The daily work was directed either by the Department of the Interior or the Department of Agriculture, and was done in national forests, state forests, state parks, or at soil conservation projects. At any one time there were between 5,000 and 8,000 men in these camps, and altogether during the first five years, 1933 to 1938, 38,500 young men were enrolled in Wisconsin. The cost to the federal government of what was done in Wisconsin ran to about $14,000,000 a year, and of this sum the young men sent home perhaps $2,000,000. Some voluntary educational work was carried on, for a large part of the enrollees had had but a common school education or less. Good food and outdoor work benefited the men physically: on the average they gained nine pounds in camp. There are no statistics to show what became of them after their service was ended. There is probably a relation between the existence of these camps and the fact that during these years there was a marked decrease in the number of young men committed to the state reformatory.

From 1933 onward both state and federal governments gave financial help to needy young people so that they could continue their education. The Wisconsin legislature in July, 1933, provided $30,000 to pay tuition fees in university extension correspondence courses, and later made another grant for the same purpose. In 1933 to 1935, three appropriations were made which, taken together, placed $510,000 in an unemployment relief student loan fund, to be administered by the industrial commission. In the five years beginning in September, 1933, loans were made from the fund to 11,883 students. By July 1, 1938, nearly 1,900 of these loans had already been repaid in full. Thus the enterprise can go on indefinitely without the appropriation of further funds.

Under FERA, federal money was made available to students. In the academic year 1933-1934, about two thousand in Wisconsin were aided each semester, and the number was about the same the following year. On June 26, 1935, the National Youth Administration (NYA) was established within WPA. Aubrey Williams, former director of the Wisconsin Conference for Social Work, was made executive director. Through this agency needy students were enabled to work and partially support themselves, not only in colleges and universities, but in most of the high schools in the state. During the academic year 1936-1937, those assisted in this way in Wisconsin numbered in the high schools about 7,500; those of college grade numbered between 3,500 and 4,000; and those in graduate schools, something over 200. High school students in need of help received on the average a little less than $5.00 a month; the college students, about $12 a month. Students worked for these payments, and the total earned by them in Wisconsin that year was about $750,000. In the following year the number assisted was reduced by about one-fifth, and the monthly payments were made a little less per person, so that in 1937-1938 the amount expended in Wisconsin was reduced to about $475,000.

The NYA also undertook work projects of educational value, several of them in conjunction with existing vocational schools or normal colleges. Some of these enterprises involved living in camps, and for this purpose a number of abandoned CCC buildings were used, along with others. These projects got well under way in February, 1936, and those aided thereby varied in number during the next two years from three to nearly five thousand, and the cost in 1936 and 1937 was each year just under a million dollars.

The federal Social Security Act speeded up and carried further several types of social assistance that had already begun in Wisconsin. In 1913 the Wisconsin legislature passed a mothers' pension law, afterwards several times amended. At first counties might, and later they were obliged to, give aid to mothers or other custodians of children under fourteen or in certain circumstances under sixteen years of age. Until 1936 almost all the money for this purpose was provided by the counties. Disbursements by the seventy-one counties had risen by 1924 to a million dollars annually, and in 1931 they passed two millions. The annual figure remained at about two and a quarter millions for the five years 1931-1935, and with that sum between eight and nine thousand families with about 20,000 children were regularly assisted. Thereafter the picture was altered by the operation of the federal Social Security Act of 1935. The contributions of the local units of government were diminished by a third, those of the state were greatly increased, and the federal government came to put in nearly a million dollars a year. At the end of 1938 more than 25,000 children in about 10,700 families were being assisted at a cost of about $4,000,000 for the year.

In 1907 some Wisconsin counties began to pay pensions to the blind, and over 1,200 received the pension in 1930. The cost was then $352,000, of which the state paid $50,000 and the counties the rest. By 1935 the state was paying $80,000 and the counties more than $400,000, and the number receiving the pension had passed 2,000. With the advent of federal money under the Social Security Act, the number of pensioners remained about the same, but the annual cost passed $500,000 with the federal government bearing about half the expense.

A Wisconsin law of 1925 permitted counties, upon a two-thirds vote of the county board, to pay a pension to needy persons over 70 years of age, the state to furnish one-third of the money. Later a majority of the board was sufficient, while the share of the state was made smaller. The number of counties pensioning their aged stood at six in 1929 and at twenty-one at the end of 1935. A referendum of November, 1934, gave a mandate for a state-wide system. The addition of federal money, the reduction of the age to 65, and the payment of the pension in every county in the state raised the cost from $733,000 in 1935 to nearly $6,000,000 in 1936 and to more than $8,500,000 in the following year. Of these latter sums the federal government paid about half. In December, 1938, the number of those receiving the old age pension was approaching 43,700, and was nearly one-fifth of all those in the state over the age of sixty-five.

It thus appears, in summing up, that by the end of 1938 about 43,700 needy aged, 2,000 needy blind, and 25,000 dependent children, a total of over 70,000 persons, were pensioners of the state. A state pension department was set up in 1935, and the counties, which actually disbursed the money, were supervised by the new department. State and county practice in pension matters had to meet the requirements of the federal Social Security Act "to enable Wisconsin to secure the full benefits under the act." The cost of these three aids, known in relief circles as the "categorical aids," in 1937 was $12,689,000, of which the federal government paid about 43 per cent, the state 31 per cent, and the local units 26 per cent. In comparing the costs in 1937 with those in 1935, the last year without federal aid and control, we find that pensions to the blind had increased six per cent; to dependent children, 60 per cent; and that the cost of old age pensions had been multiplied by twelve.

One final illustration of federal assistance, in no way related to what has just preceded, may be added. Home owners in cities and villages are as much troubled by mortgages and fear of foreclosure as are their farm cousins, and when the depression came many of them were soon in sore straits. For the relief of this group the federal government established, by the act of June 12, 1933, the Home Owners' Loan Corporation (HOLC). Through this agency the federal government took over the mortgage of the distressed home owner, even if it was in default by as much as two years, and gave to the mortgagor the bonds of HOLC, which were easily marketed. Banks were able to exchange defaulted mortgages for bonds which could be converted into cash, and some closed banks were by this means enabled to resume business. Another happy issue was the payment to local governments of large sums due in delinquent taxes. As for the home owner, the HOLC took a new first mortgage on his property, and principal and interest were amortized on a fifteen year basis. For three years the rescue work continued, and after that no new contracts were made. During that time the HOLC saved more than 33,000 homes in Wisconsin for their owners, and came to hold mortgages in the state totaling about $115,000,000.

It was still a moot question in 1939 whether we had emerged from the depression; but there could be no doubt that the people of the United States were in the process of forging a new society. The state of affairs in Wisconsin, as described in the last few pages, may in most respects be taken as typical of the whole United States. The most obvious point is the increase in the cost of public relief. In the pre-depression year, 1928, about $1,000,000 was spent on outdoor relief in Wisconsin, and if the upkeep of poorhouses and the cost of the hospitalization and burial of the indigent were included, it was possible to reach a total of $2,500,000 for all poor relief. Ten years later public assistance in Wisconsin was costing about $100,000,000 a year (nearly $114,000,000 in 1936, $90,000,000 in 1937 and $108,000,000 in 1938).[2]

Another outstanding feature of recent years, the inverse of the expenditure on public assistance, is the number of persons on relief. Adding the recipients of general outdoor relief to those employed on federal work projects of which WPA is the chief, and in both cases including their dependents, we have a total at any time during the past five years of more than a tenth of the population of the state. To these should be added about 6,000 young men in CCC camps, many in transient depots, and 70,000 receiving the categorical aids. Some of these groups overlap a little, but, eliminating duplications, there were in December, 1938, about 503,000 persons, a sixth of the population of the state, receiving aid from public funds. Both on outdoor relief lists and on the work projects there is a considerable movement on and off. Instead of thinking of a sixth of the people on relief all the time, we should think of 20 per cent or more who have come to rely on relief for part of their income, and who receive it intermittently. This is

[2] The following explanation, appropriate at this point, is taken from the Wisconsin *Public Welfare Review* (quarterly), December, 1938, p. 3.

"During the calendar year 1938 over $108,000,000 was spent for public assistance in Wisconsin." [The words, 'public assistance,' were intended to include: General Relief, Federal Works (WPA and some other federal agencies, but not PWA grants and loans), Civilian Conservation Corps, Social Security Aids (the categorical aids), Emergency Subsistence Grants (by the Rural Rehabilitation Division of the Farm Security Administration), and food supplied by the Surplus Commodities Corporation.]

"This definition [of public assistance] is partially one of convenience excluding soldiers' and sailors' relief, and hospitalization and burials not authorized by relief agencies, because these data are not regularly available on a comparative basis. Other programs intended for needy persons, such as the student NYA and child welfare services are not included because a means test is not employed in the same sense as for the other public assistance programs. Unemployment compensation and old age insurance are excluded because no means test is in effect, and the primary purpose of these programs is not relief. However, if all these types of aid were added to the public assistance total cited above we would arrive at a total exceeding $130,640,000 for 1938."

not the place to argue the question, nonhistorical because it deals with the future, as to whether Wisconsin, along with the rest of the United States, will continue to support such vast numbers wholly or partially on relief. For the moment, at any rate, the older America, where any man with a willingness to work could support himself, has passed away.

While the great and rapid increase in public assistance shows that many Americans are no longer masters of their own destiny, the numerous extensions of government activity in recent years have been accompanied in many instances by significant limitations on the freedom of all individuals. Much of the doctrine of laissez faire as understood and practiced in the nineteenth century has been abandoned. Wisconsin's history, especially since about 1900, illustrates this change at many points. During the World War Americans submitted to strange new controls, and, when the depression came, to others yet more strange and more numerous. Most of the time since 1933, the price of a haircut has been part of a code of fair practice with a legal sanction to uphold it. The milkman may not sell milk at nine cents a quart in a city where the established price is ten. These regulations, taken separately, each contribute to the public good; but the thoughtful observer may wonder how soon he will buy a standard suit of clothes at a price fixed or maintained by the state; or how soon the state will provide housing and regulate the medical profession in a thoroughgoing way. In other words, he wonders what the end is to be. Perhaps there will be no end. Eventually the generation that wonders will pass from the stage and younger men will carry on in an atmosphere congenial to them because they have never known any other.

One last development made obvious by a review of the recent past is the great extension of the activities, financial and otherwise, of the federal government. An enumeration of the loans and gifts made by this government to the states and municipalities, especially since 1933, raises the question of the source of the money. Much of it has been borrowed: in the eight-year period ending

June 30, 1938, the indebtedness of the federal government increased by twenty-one billion dollars. But taxes, both direct and indirect, have also greatly increased. Before the World War the federal government sometimes derived half its income from the customs duties. Customs collections, however, were actually less in 1933 to 1938 than they had been in 1923 to 1928, and though producing in these last five years about a third of a billion dollars annually, they were quite dwarfed by the income from internal revenue. In the fiscal year 1938, internal revenue amounted to fifteen times as much as the customs, reaching a total of more than $5,658,000,000. Of this sum $96,000,000 was collected in Wisconsin. Some of the sub-heads under internal revenue, with the amounts collected in Wisconsin, were: federal income taxes, both corporation and individual, nearly $37,000,000; estate or inheritance taxes, $6,600,000; liquor taxes, chiefly on beer, $30,000,000; manufacturers' excise taxes, $5,700,000; payroll taxes under the federal Social Security Act, $11,000,000. A tax of nearly half a million dollars was paid on messages sent by telephone, telegraph, cable, and radio, and more than six hundred thousand dollars came from stamp taxes on documents.

Some of these taxes are really borne by the ultimate consumer as part of the price of commodities. In this way residents of other states pay taxes on articles manufactured in Wisconsin. Similarly, Wisconsin consumes commodities on which the federal government collects taxes in other states; for example, cigarettes. Many large corporations furnishing goods or services to Wisconsin are taxed at their central offices in New York or in other eastern states. Thus to the question of how much Wisconsin pays in taxes to the federal government, only an approximate answer can be given. It has been estimated that Wisconsin has one-fortieth of the taxpaying capacity of the nation. This would mean that in the fiscal year 1938 its share of the internal revenue was in reality about $140,000,000. And while in this particular year the people of Wisconsin paid something between $96,000,000 and $140,000,000 in federal taxes, they also paid taxes of $185,000,000 to the state and its subdivisions. Altogether, in the last year for which figures are available, the people of Wisconsin paid more than $300,000,000 in taxes. State and local taxes after the lean years of the depression had in 1938 climbed back to about what they were in 1930; but the federal taxes had grown to be about twice what they had been between 1923 and 1929. Federal demands, in thus doubling within a decade, had come to compete seriously with state and local taxes; for both of necessity drew from the same reservoir.

The federal government gives as well as takes, and in giving, it exercises control. Long ago we saw it granting public lands to finance canals and railroads and to endow education. Later it gave money for a host of beneficent enterprises. It supported agricultural and other special types of education, fought plant and animal diseases, and gave money for highway construction. It lent money to farmers before we entered the World War. Now it holds or guarantees the mortgages on 13 per cent of all Wisconsin farms and on perhaps 30,000 ordinary dwellings. There were forerunners of many New Deal activities; what is without precedent is the scale of its operations, which is best exemplified, of course, in public relief. Almost always when the federal government has given money it has asserted the right to supervise expenditure. The state, in handling so much money given for relief purposes and for social security, has become at least in these fields merely an agent of the federal government. In matters of relief, state legislation has followed federal models very closely. Some Wisconsin laws have been almost verbatim copies of federal statutes, and others have merely authorized or commanded state officials to conform to regulations sent from Washington. So long as the outpouring of federal funds continues, there is no reason to expect that federal leadership and control will diminish.

SELECTED BIBLIOGRAPHY

No attempt can be made here to give a bibliography for the depression, the New Deal, and the recent relations between state and federal governments. Charles A. Beard and Mary Beard, *America in Midpassage* (New

York, 1939), is a vigorous and valuable narrative of the years 1928 to 1938. The latter part of Dwight L. Dumond's *Roosevelt to Roosevelt: the United States in the Twentieth Century* (New York, 1937) was an early summary. With it may be used Louis M. Hacker, *American Problems of Today* (New York, 1938). Much may be learned from V. O. Kay, Jr., *The Administration of Federal Grants to States* (Chicago, 1937). Maria D. Lane and Francis Steegemuller, in *America on Relief* (New York, 1938), evaluated some of the principles underlying relief activity. Marietta Stevenson, *Public Welfare Administration* (New York, 1938), is a valuable condensation of a great amount of material. There is an excellent short bibliography, pp. 333-342. Under the general title, "Financial Relief and Recovery," several writers of the highest authority discussed the alphabetical agencies, RFC, FERA, CWA, WPA, and PWA in the *Municipal Year Book, 1937* (Chicago, 1937), edited by C. E. Ridley and O. F. Nolting. All these books deal with the whole United States.

A Review of Work Relief Activities, April, 1934 to August, 1935 (Madison, 1935, 97 pp.) recounted relief history in Wisconsin from 1930 onward. After its establishment in December, 1935, the Public Welfare Department issued valuable historical and statistical material on relief in Wisconsin. *Public Relief, Emergency Employment and Welfare Expenditure in Wisconsin, 1933-1936,* a book of charts illustrating three and one-half years of relief activity (January, 1937), was followed and partly superseded by *A Half Billion Dollars for Public Welfare in Wisconsin, 1931-1936* (February, 1938). An *Annual Report* was prepared covering the period December 7, 1935, to December 31, 1936 (July, 1937). The department also issued a history, *General Relief in Wisconsin, 1848-1935* and *The Public Welfare Department Report, Jan. 1, 1937-June 30, 1939* (both in October, 1939). The *Wisconsin Relief Review* was begun in October, 1934, under WERA. From December, 1935, it was continued as the organ of the public welfare department with the title, *Wisconsin Public Welfare Review*. At first a monthly, it has been issued quarterly since July, 1937, and it is invaluable. George W. Hill and Ronald A. Smith made an excellent study, *Rural Relief Trends in Wisconsin from 1934 to 1937* (Madison, 1939). A summary of one federal activity is *Report on Progress of the W.P.A. Program, June 30, 1938*. This has statistics of WPA and NYA by states. The work in NYA resident centers is described in a pamphlet or prospectus entitled *Youth Training: The National Youth Administration in Wisconsin* (Madison, 1938).

A convenient source of information on recent borrowing by farmers is the *Agricultural Finance Review*, issued by the United States Department of Agriculture semiannually beginning in May, 1938. Volume 2, No. 2 (November, 1939), pp. 90-97, has statistics for many types of farm borrowing by states and by years from 1910 onward. Debts and interest rates are also to be found in *Wisconsin Agriculture*, Bulletin No. 188 (1938), pp. 13-15. The history of the work of the federal government in helping farmers carry their debt burden is given by William L. Myers in *Co-operative Farm Mortgage Credit, 1916-1936* (Washington, 1936, 24 pp.). T. S. Stone discussed "Mortgage Moratoria in Wisconsin," in the *Wisconsin Law Review,* Vol. XI, pp. 203-237 (February, 1936).

On rural electrification there is a pamphlet, *The First Year of the REA Program in Wisconsin,* covering the period from October, 1935, to October, 1936. Of kindred interest is the pamphlet, *Wisconsin Gets a Power Program, a Story of the WDA* (Madison, 1938, 24 pp.).

One of the earliest competent discussions of the federal social security program under the act of August 14, 1935, was that by fifteen authors in *Law and Contemporary Problems,* Vol. III, No. 1 (January, 1936). The state pension department has issued a *Statistical Summary of the Development of the Social Security Aids in Wisconsin to June 30, 1938* (Madison, 1938). This shows the annual payments made to or on behalf of blind and aged persons and dependent children from 1911 through 1937. The last ten pages (pages not numbered) summarize Wisconsin legislation dealing with these aids and give references to *Session Laws* from 1907 onward.

APPENDIXES

APPENDIX I

THE GOVERNORS OF WISCONSIN

Name and Party	City or Village	County	Assumed Office
TERRITORY OF WISCONSIN			
Henry Dodge, *Dem.*	Dodgeville	Iowa	July 4, 1836
James Duane Doty, *Whig*	Neenah	Winnebago	Oct. 5, 1841
Nathaniel P. Tallmadge, *Dem.*	Fond du Lac	Fond du Lac	Sept. 16, 1844
Henry Dodge, *Dem.*	Dodgeville	Iowa	May 13, 1845
STATE OF WISCONSIN			
Nelson Dewey, *Dem.*	Lancaster	Grant	June 7, 1848
Leonard J. Farwell, *Whig*	Madison	Dane	Jan. 5, 1852
William A. Barstow, *Dem.*	Waukesha	Waukesha	Jan. 2, 1854
Arthur McArthur, *Dem.*	Milwaukee	Milwaukee	March 21, 1856
Coles Bashford, *Rep.*	Oshkosh	Winnebago	March 25, 1856
Alexander W. Randall, *Rep.*	Waukesha	Waukesha	Jan. 4, 1858
Louis P. Harvey, *Rep.*	Shopiere	Rock	Jan. 6, 1862
Edward Salomon, *Rep.*	Milwaukee	Milwaukee	April 19, 1862
James T. Lewis, *Rep.*	Columbus	Columbia	Jan. 4, 1864
Lucius Fairchild, *Rep.*	Madison	Dane	Jan. 1, 1866
C. C. Washburn, *Rep.*	La Crosse	La Crosse	Jan. 1, 1872
William R. Taylor, *Dem.*	Cottage Grove	Dane	Jan. 5, 1874
Harrison Ludington, *Rep.*	Milwaukee	Milwaukee	Jan. 3, 1876
William E. Smith, *Rep.*	Milwaukee	Milwaukee	Jan. 7, 1878
Jeremiah M. Rusk, *Rep.*	Viroqua	Vernon	Jan. 2, 1882
William D. Hoard, *Rep.*	Fort Atkinson	Jefferson	Jan. 7, 1889
George W. Peck, *Dem.*	Milwaukee	Milwaukee	Jan. 5, 1891
William H. Upham, *Rep.*	Marshfield	Wood	Jan. 7, 1895
Edward Scofield, *Rep.*	Oconto	Oconto	Jan. 4, 1897
Robert M. La Follette, *Rep.*	Madison	Dane	Jan. 7, 1901

Name and Party	City or Village	County	Assumed Office
James O. Davidson, *Rep.*	Soldiers Grove	Crawford	Jan. 1, 1906
Francis E. McGovern, *Rep.*	Milwaukee	Milwaukee	Jan. 2, 1911
Emanuel L. Philipp, *Rep.*	Milwaukee	Milwaukee	Jan. 4, 1915
John J. Blaine, *Rep.*	Boscobel	Grant	Jan. 3, 1921
Fred R. Zimmerman, *Rep.*	Milwaukee	Milwaukee	Jan. 3, 1927
Walter J. Kohler, *Rep.*	Kohler	Sheboygan	Jan. 7, 1929
Philip F. La Follette, *Rep.*	Madison	Dane	Jan. 5, 1931
Albert G. Schmedeman, *Dem.*	Madison	Dane	Jan. 2, 1933
Philip F. La Follette, *Prog.*	Madison	Dane	Jan. 7, 1935
Julius P. Heil, *Rep.*	Milwaukee	Milwaukee	Jan. 2, 1939

WISCONSIN VOTES IN PRESIDENTIAL ELECTIONS

Year	Candidates	Popular vote	Per cent	Electoral
1848	Lewis Cass, *Whig*	15,001	38.3	4
	Zachary Taylor, *Dem.*	13,747	35.1	
	Martin Van Buren, *Free Soil*	10,418	26.6	
	Total	39,166		
1852	Franklin Pierce, *Dem.*	33,658	52.0	5
	Winfield Scott, *Whig*	22,210	34.4	
	John P. Hale, *Free Dem.*	8,814	13.6	
	Total	64,682		
1856	John C. Fremont, *Rep.*	66,090	55.3	5
	James Buchanan, *Dem.*	52,843	44.2	
	Millard Fillmore, *American* or *Know-Nothing*	579	.5	
	Total	119,512		
1860	Abraham Lincoln, *Rep.*	86,113	56.6	5
	Stephen A. Douglas, *Dem.*	65,021	42.7	
	John C. Breckenridge, *South. Dem.*	888	.6	
	John Bell, *Const. Union*	161	.1	
	Total	152,180		
1864	Abraham Lincoln, *Rep.*	83,458	55.9	8
	George B. McClellan, *Dem.*	65,884	44.1	
	Total	149,342		
1868	Ulysses S. Grant, *Rep.*	108,857	56.2	8
	Horatio Seymour, *Dem.*	84,707	43.3	
	Total	193,564		

Year	Candidates	Popular vote	Per cent	Electoral
1872	Ulysses S. Grant, *Rep*............	104,994	54.6	10
	Horace Greeley, *Dem. & Lib. Rep.*	86,477	45.0	
	Charles O'Conor, *Dem*..........	834	.4	
	Total.................	192,308		
1876	Rutherford B. Hayes, *Rep*.......	130,668	51.0	10
	Samuel J. Tilden, *Dem*...........	123,927	48.4	
	Peter Cooper, *Greenback*..........	1,509	.6	
	Green Clay Smith, *Proh*..........	27	—	
	Total..................	256,131		
1880	James A. Garfield, *Rep*..........	144,398	54.1	10
	Winfield S. Hancock, *Dem*.......	114,644	42.9	
	James B. Weaver, *Greenback*.......	7,986	3.0	
	J. B. Phelps, *American*...........	91	—	
	Neal Dow, *Proh*................	68	—	
	Total..................	267,182		
1884	James G. Blaine, *Rep*...........	161,157	50.4	11
	Grover Cleveland, *Dem*..........	146,477	45.8	
	John P. St. John, *Proh*..........	7,656	2.4	
	Benj. F. Butler, *Greenback*........	4,598	1.4	
	Total..................	319,888		
1888	Benjamin Harrison, *Rep*.........	176,553	49.7	11
	Grover Cleveland, *Dem*..........	155,232	43.7	
	Clinton B. Fisk, *Proh*...........	14,277	4.2	
	A. J. Streeter, *Union Labor*.......	8,552	2.4	
	Total..................	354,614		
1892	Grover Cleveland, *Dem*..........	177,325	47.7	12
	Benjamin Harrison, *Rep*.........	171,101	46.0	
	John Bidwell, *Proh*..............	13,136	3.6	
	James B. Weaver, *Populist*........	10,019	2.7	
	Total..................	371,581		

Year	Candidates	Popular vote	Per cent	Electoral
1896	William McKinley, *Rep*.........	268,135	59.93	12
	William J. Bryan, *Dem*..........	165,523	36.99	
	Joshua Levering, *Proh*...........	7,507	1.68	
	John M. Palmer, *National Dem*....	4,584	1.02	
	Charles H. Matchett, *Soc. Labor*...	1,314	.29	
	Charles E. Bentley, *National*......	346	.08	
	Total....................	447,409		
1900	William McKinley, *Rep*.........	265,760	60.06	12
	William J. Bryan, *Dem*..........	159,163	35.97	
	John G. Wooley, *Proh*...........	10,027	2.26	
	Eugene V. Debs, *Soc. Dem*........	7,048	1.59	
	Joseph Malloney, *Soc. Labor*......	503	.11	
	Total....................	442,501		
1904	Theodore Roosevelt, *Rep*........	280,164	63.23	13
	Alton B. Parker, *Dem*...........	124,107	28.01	
	Eugene V. Debs, *Soc. Dem*........	28,220	6.37	
	Silas C. Swallow, *Proh*..........	9,770	2.2	
	Thomas E. Watson, *Populist*......	530	.12	
	Charles H. Corrigan, *Soc. Labor*...	223	.05	
	Total....................	443,014		
1908	William H. Taft, *Rep*...........	247,747	54.51	13
	William J. Bryan, *Dem*..........	166,632	36.67	
	Eugene V. Debs, *Soc. Dem*........	28,164	6.11	
	Eugene W. Chafin, *Proh*.........	11,564	2.55	
	August Gillhaus, *Soc. Labor*......	314	.06	
	Total....................	454,421		
1912	Woodrow Wilson, *Dem*..........	164,230	41.07	13
	William H. Taft, *Rep*...........	130,596	32.65	
	Theodore Roosevelt, *Prog*........	62,448	15.61	
	Eugene V. Debs, *Soc. Dem*........	33,476	8.37	
	Eugene W. Chafin, *Proh*.........	8,584	2.1	
	A. E. Reimer, *Soc. Labor*.........	632	.16	
	Total....................	399,966		

Year	Candidates	Popular vote	Per cent	Electoral
1916	Charles E. Hughes, *Rep*.........	220,822	49.38	13
	Woodrow Wilson, *Dem*...........	191,363	42.79	
	Allan Benson, *Soc*..............	27,631	6.11	
	J. Frank Hanly, *Proh*...........	7,318	1.63	
	Total...................	447,134		
1920	Warren G. Harding, *Rep*........	498,576	71.09	13
	James M. Cox, *Dem*............	113,422	16.18	
	Eugene V. Debs, *Soc*...........	80,635	11.5	
	Aaron S. Watkins, *Proh*.........	8,647	1.23	
	Total...................	701,280		
1924	Robert M. LaFollette, *Prog*......	453,678	54.44	13
	Calvin Coolidge, *Rep*...........	311,614	37.39	
	John W. Davis, *Dem*...........	68,096	8.17	
	Total...................	833,388		
1928	Herbert Hoover, *Rep*...........	544,205	53.51	13
	Alfred E. Smith, *Dem*..........	450,259	44.23	
	Norman Thomas, *Soc*...........	18,213	1.79	
	William F. Varney, *Proh*........	2,245	.22	
	William Z. Foster, *Workers*......	1,528	.15	
	Verne L. Reynolds, *Soc. Labor*....	383	.04	
	Total...................	1,016,831		
1932	Franklin D. Roosevelt, *Dem*.....	707,410	63.5	12
	Herbert Hoover, *Rep*..........	347,741	31.1	
	Norman Thomas, *Soc*...........	53,379	4.8	
	William Z. Foster, *Communist*....	3,112	.29	
	William D. Upshaw, *Proh*.......	2,672	.24	
	Verne L. Reynolds, *Soc. Labor*....	494	.05	
	Total...................	1,114,808		
1936	Franklin D. Roosevelt, *Dem*.....	802,984	63.8	12
	Alfred M. Landon, *Rep*.........	380,828	30.3	
	William Lemke, *Union*..........	60,297	4.77	
	Norman Thomas, *Soc*...........	10,626	.84	
	Earl Browder, *Communist*........	2,197	.17	
	David L. Colvin, *Proh*..........	1,071	.08	
	John W. Aiken, *Soc. Labor*.......	557	.04	
	Total...................	1,258,560		

APPENDIX III

THE POPULATION OF WISCONSIN

1830.	3,245
1836.	11,683
1840.	30,945
1850.	305,391
1860.	775,881
1870.	1,054,670
1880.	1,315,497
1890.	1,693,330
1900.	2,069,042
1910.	2,333,860
1920.	2,632,067
1930.	2,939,006

The Wisconsin *Blue Book, 1937,* page 492, gives the annual estimates of the population of Wisconsin from 1930 to 1937 made by the United States Bureau of the Census. That for July 1, 1937, the last to be issued before the federal census of 1940, was 2,926,000, indicating an estimated decrease since April 1, 1930, of 13,006. In *Wisconsin Vital Statistics for 1936 and 1937,* Tables 1 and 2, however, the estimated population given for both years was 3,032,174, an increase since April 1, 1930, of 93,168.

INDEX

531